SOUTHEAST ASIA'S MODERN ARCHITECTURE

SOUTHEAST ASIA'S MODERN ARCHITECTURE

Questions of Translation, Epistemology and Power

Editors Jiat-Hwee Chang and
Imran bin Tajudeen

NUS PRESS
SINGAPORE

Published by:

NUS Press
National University of Singapore
AS3-01-02, 3 Arts Link
Singapore 117569

Fax: (65) 6774-0652
E-mail: nusbooks@nus.edu.sg
Website: http://nuspress.nus.edu.sg

ISBN 978-981-4722-78-0 (paper)

First Edition 2019
Reprint 2020

National Library Board, Singapore Cataloguing in Publication Data
A catalogue record for the book is available from the National Library, Singapore

Cover image: The Singapore Conference Hall and Trade Union House under construction, c.1964. Courtesy of Datuk Seri Lim Chong Keat.
Printed by: Markono Print Media Pte Ltd

Contents

Section Three: POWER

List of Illustrations

Acknowledgements

The idea for this book came out of the inaugural SEAARC (Southeast Asia Architectural Research Collaborative) symposium held in January 2015. We would like to thank the contributors to this book for their trust in us during the three-year journey leading to this publication. Although Lee Kah Wee, the third member of SEAARC, did not participate directly in this book project, he co-convened the inaugural symposium and led the second symposium in 2017, from which selected papers will be published in a special issue of *South East Asia Research* journal. We would like to thank Kah Wee for running SEAARC with us and for his intellectual companionship.

Besides the contributors to this volume, many other scholars participated in the symposium and contributed to its stimulating discussions. They are: Lilian Chee, Francis Chia-Hui Lin, Cecilia Chu, Chomchon Fusinpaiboon, Hilde Heynen, Mark Hinchman, Xiao Jing, Kemas Ridwan Kurniawan, William Logan, Pirasri Povatong, Anooradha Iyer Siddiqi, Iwan Sudradjat, Tan Yuk Hong Ian, Gunawan Tjahjono, Lorelei D.C. de Viana, and Indah Widiastuti. We would like to thank them for their spirited engagement.

The symposium was supported by funding from the Department of Architecture, HCF and Associates, and Lee Foundation. We would like to thank these organisations for their support, in particular Wong Yunn Chii, then head of Department, and Fong Hoo Cheong, principal of HCF and Associates, for believing in our project of promoting research in Southeast Asian architecture. Part of the research for this book is supported by AcRF Tier 1 Projects "Agents of Modernity: Pioneer Builders, Architecture and Independence in Singapore, 1890s-1970s" (WBS No. R-295-000-127-112) and "Architectural Encounters and Disciplinary Categories in Maritime Southeast Asia" (WBS No. R-295-000-150-114) that we gratefully acknowledge.

This publication is also supported by a wonderful team at NUS Press, particularly Peter Schoppert, Pallavi Narayan, and our copy editor Lindsay Davis.

Jiat-Hwee Chang and Imran bin Tajudeen

INTRODUCTION

Historiographical Questions in Southeast Asia's Modern Architecture

JIAT-HWEE CHANG AND IMRAN BIN TAJUDEEN

In a widely cited essay on the field, "'Southeast Asia': What's in a Name?", Donald K. Emmerson provocatively raises questions about the validity and utility of the fundamental geographic designation – that of Southeast Asia – that the field of modern Southeast Asian studies rests upon. Citing J.R.E. Wadell's caution against reifying Southeast Asia, Emmerson writes, "Words like 'Southeast Asia' and 'unicorn' enable us to discuss topics about which we would not otherwise be able to hold a conversation, but we should be wary of attributing any more solidity to these concepts than the facts will allow." Alongside Wadell's caution, Emmerson also cites Shakespeare's *Romeo and Juliet*: "What's in a name? That which we call a rose by any other word would smell as sweet." He then argues:

> Some names like "rose" acknowledge what exists. Others, like "unicorn," create what otherwise would not exist. In between lie names that *simultaneously describe and invent reality*. "Southeast Asia" is one of these (authors' emphasis).[1]

Emmerson's is one of the seminal essays in the recurring debates within Southeast Asian studies that try to make sense of and come to terms with the social, cultural, political, religious and linguistic diversities of Southeast Asia. Furthermore, as a geographic unit that was first invented by outsiders as a part of their World War II military strategies and only institutionalised as a region worthy of political-economic study on its own rather than as an appendage of larger geographic and civilisational entities in the immediate post-war years, Southeast Asia leads an unstable and uncertain epistemic existence that has to contend with incessant questioning.[2] Southeast Asia's precarious position as a valid field of enquiry in the social sciences has been further exacerbated by the crisis experienced by area studies in general.[3]

As this book explores the histories of Southeast Asia's architecture and built environment in the twentieth century as well as its architectural historiography in general, we share similar anxieties about the validity and utility of Southeast Asia as a geographic unit and taxonomic device for framing and understanding the built environment. However, like Emmerson, we believe that Southeast Asia serves the dual function of concurrently describing and revealing architectural commonalities otherwise invisible or occluded by the use of other frameworks. In other words, Southeast Asia approximates what Heather Sutherland calls a "contingent device", a heuristic aid or "conceptual apparatus with all its artifice [that] remains an essential first step towards [meaningful] analysis".[4] Furthermore, as a contingent and unstable geographic construct, Southeast Asia as a region offers analytical advantages. Being an entity that hovers somewhere between the universal and the local, the global and the national, the regional concept occupies an in-between scale and an interstitial position between two powerful – even hegemonic – and oft-taken-for-granted scales of architectural and spatial analyses. Being a rather indeterminate in-between, the regional concept of Southeast Asia spurs contributors to this volume to question the self-certainties of both national and global architectural histories. Thus, this volume is unlike existing regional architectural histories of Southeast Asia that are either compilations of discrete architectural histories of individual nations or component parts in larger global architectural histories.[5] Instead, as Anoma Pieris and Mark Crinson suggest in their contributions to this volume, the open-ended interstitialities of the regional concept allow contributors in this volume to question national and global historiographies as well as their attendant epistemologies through architecture. Or, as the contributions by Hazel Hahn and Lawrence Chua demonstrate, travelling selves and the ideas they embody, imbibe or propagate, traverse assumptions of neatly bounded entities in analysing a world on the move.

We are in agreement with the recent interrogation of metageographical constructs, and attempt to shift the scope of investigation from rigid, bounded and essentialist continental imaginaries to fluid, open and relational oceanic or nautical imaginaries through a comparative framework based on methodological challenges rather than received notions of boundaries, although the latter frame remains inevitable when authors engage current scholarship.[6] The very idea of "Southeast Asia" is conceived from a continental point of view – as a portion of "Asia" lying between East and South Asia with an inherent bias towards comparisons with these two regions, while oceanic links that breach these divisions and also extend beyond "Asia" are ignored.[7] Meanwhile "Asia" as a unit of historical inquiry has also been contested, both from a more general historical perspective and from a specifically architectural one.[8] Conversely, nautical imaginaries inform the non-Western geographic-linguistic constructions of portions of the region of Southeast Asia historically, as can be observed through such terms as Nusantara, the hybrid Javanese-Sanskrit for archipelago; Suvarnadvipa and Suvarnabhumi, Sanskrit for golden islands/lands often used to designate island and mainland Southeast Asia respectively; and Nanyang, Chinese for south seas.

It would, however, be a mistake to assume any neat correlation between geographical nomenclature and architectural culture. To a limited extent, the geographic constructions just mentioned share some resonance with architectural knowledge. A typological study of Southeast Asia's vernacular architecture, for instance, reveals transoceanic connections pointing to the agency of the Austronesian-speaking world – a domain of study that disturbs received continent-centrism in current categories of Asian architecture surveys and discourse.[9] As Brian Bernards notes, the instability of Southeast Asia as a regional concept could be productive as it is conducive to what he calls "archipelagic imagination" that prioritises "contact, exchange, heterogeneity, and creolization instead of [ethnic, cultural and social] uniformity and singularity".[10] However, the dominance of received traditions of scholarship and its prevailing taxonomies may impose their own biases in discerning such connections, as seen, for instance, in how presumptions of Indian influence in the case of Java's Hindu–Buddhist monuments have obscured an understanding of the shared bases with the architecture of the Austronesian world, which may only be appreciated through typological analysis.[11] We believe that such geographically and culturally open constructions and reconstructions, coupled with rigorous analysis and an active questioning of received epistemologies, when applied to the study of architecture in the modern period, will similarly reveal the commonalities and connections between different entities in various parts of Southeast Asia and beyond.

Indic Classical and Vernacular Architecture in Southeast Asia

Indeed, Southeast Asia as contingent device has been made to work productively in the study of the Hindu–Buddhist or Indic religious monuments of the classical period and the vernacular architecture of the region. The former includes monuments such as the Angkor temples, the Bagan temples, Borobudur and Prambanan that have been closely studied in the established scholarship in Southeast Asian archaeology and art history.[12] The latter comprises of the various house-types of the region.[13]

These two fields of scholarship focus primarily on architecture as built artefacts, studying their spatial configuration, typology and symbolism, among other aspects. The study of the region's Indic monuments, initiated by colonial officials and the archaeological service, was gradually systematised as the preserve of Indology, Hindu or Buddhist studies, archaeology, and art history, although colonial-era scholars questioned the received biases of India-centrism quite early on, using terms such as indigenisation, local genius, and, more recently, convergence to emphasise the agency of Southeast Asians and the contemporaneity of developments in southern India and Southeast Asia.[14] The study of the region's vernacular architecture has largely focused on examples that were seemingly frozen in time, isolated in space, and characterised by inertia but also threatened by the encroachment of capitalist modernisation today. Elsewhere, Greig Crysler characterises such approaches of seeing the pre-modern built environment as the "other" to be idealised or romanticised as narratives of the "ethnographic pastoral".[15]

Since the 1990s, however, scholarship on Southeast Asia's vernacular architecture has moved beyond static contexts and timeless frames, to talk about model transformations and cultural rivalry expressed in new forms and modern materials.[16] Recent scholarship on Southeast Asia's Indic and vernacular architecture has also taken a critical turn, acknowledging the utility of these domains of knowledge in justifying and legitimising colonial rule and, more generally, how historical monuments and vernacular architecture have been appropriated and transformed by political and socio-economic developments in the nineteenth and twentieth centuries, particularly by diverse forces connected to colonialism, nationalism and globalism, thereby unmasking the underlying relations of power.[17] This emerging body of work points to attempts to move away from the lingering influence of Orientalist and colonialist constructs of the so-called "non-West".[18]

In spite of this encouraging development, Southeast Asian indigeneity and its Hindu–Buddhist syncretic civilisation is still inherently equated with the timeless – there is a neglect of, first, the urban vernacular architectural traditions of coastal indigenous groups and their interactions with colonial models and adaptations to modernity in colonial cities,[19] and second, the continuities of the architecture of the classical period into the early modern era of the fifteenth century onwards.[20] The temporal and geographic frames of reference for studies of Southeast Asia's vernacular and Indic architecture emphasise the rural, the geographically remote, and the distant past – such predilections are inherited from the Orientalist and colonialist constructs of the region, which followed on from the nineteenth-century European fascination with antiquities and the tendency to privilege Indic historical monuments as representing the "golden age" from the distant past that they sought to revive or preserve as ways to legitimise colonial rule, or that emphasise vernacular dwellings as representing the "noble savage" tribal other, or the bucolic peasantry that was idealised and stereotyped by the colonisers as untainted by the corrupting influences of modern civilisation and the colonial city.[21]

Modern Architecture in Southeast Asia

In a similar vein, the emerging, though comparatively neglected body of scholarship on modern architecture in Southeast Asia encompasses both the uncritical narration of stereotypes, and more sophisticated studies into the imbrication of colonialism and nationalism in the production of architecture, but have retained certain frames of reference that have restricted scholarship from breaking new ground. At the risk of overgeneralisation, we divide this scholarship into at least three different groups.

The first group is the Eurocentric history of colonial architecture. It consists of a number of recent books that focus primarily on monumental or iconic colonial architecture in Southeast Asia conceived and built primarily by the Europeans, and often solely for either the use of Europeans and/or for fulfilling certain expediencies of colonial economy and politics.[22] Written by expatriates, members of the former metropole and/or advocates of heritage conservation, these books tend to reminisce about the "good old days" that the colonial architecture evokes and lament the demise of these mnemonic devices as they were either demolished or threatened with demolition. In celebrating these colonial buildings in a nostalgic and sentimental manner, these writers gloss over what the colonised populations might have perceived as exploitative political economic conditions and asymmetrical power-relations behind the production of these works,[23] or they overlook the involvement of indigenous agency and overstate the supposed European antecedents in the formation of new, hybrid colonial building models.[24]

The second refers to the critical history of modern architecture published since 2000.[25] Given that modern architecture in Southeast Asia is a construct that needs explanation (as we shall elaborate upon later), this group of scholars do not necessarily share a common framework of modern architecture, especially since they each focus on a different Southeast Asian nation with its own particularities of modernisation and modernity. However, they all deal with architecture around the mid twentieth century – though two of them see the mid twentieth century in a longer historical framework – and engage with the issues of architecture and nation-building. Unlike the previous body of scholarship that tends to romanticise the past and depoliticise architecture, this group of scholars sees politics as an inextricable part of architecture, especially in shaping the planning and design of public buildings. Based on a combination of exhaustive archival research and theoretically sophisticated frameworks of analysis, these scholars provide refreshing insights into how modern architecture was deployed under different politics of nation-building in Southeast Asia in the service of diverse political regimes, from military and civilian dictatorships to royalist and democratic governments. Furthermore, instead of privileging a colonialist or Eurocentric view of architecture in Southeast Asia, these scholars show that the indigenous populations – at least the sociopolitical elites and the professional classes within them – have agency and actively participate in shaping their built environment, often subverting, appropriating or resisting the spatial order of the (post)colonial built environment in the process. They demonstrate that the internationalisation or globalisation of modern architecture did not lead merely to the one-way diffusion of a standard set of architectural knowledge and practices from the purported cultural centres in Western Europe and North America to the rest of the world and the supposed convergence and homogenisation of the world's built environment. Rather, they argue there are a plethora of forms of modern architecture in Southeast Asia produced by the two-way exchanges and translations of Western ideas and norms by indigenous agents for local social, cultural and political conditions.[26]

Closely related to the second group is a third body of scholarship on the urban histories of various Southeast Asian cities.[27] Like its immediate predecessor, this scholarship focuses on the modern era – broadly speaking the colonial and postcolonial periods in the nineteenth and twentieth centuries – and it attends to the politics, architectural legacies and culture of the built environment in theoretically sophisticated ways or sheds light upon hitherto undocumented processes of architectural production or transformation. Whereas the second body focuses primarily on notable or representative architecture, the third group adopts a broader scope and examines the everyday landscape and the ordinary built environment. It also takes a more interdisciplinary approach to the understanding of the built environment. In its discussion of the spatial production of the cities, this group of scholars adopts a more inclusive approach, encompassing the views, contributions and involvements of broader segments of not just the sociopolitical elites but also the lower strata and peripheral groups of societies, such as marginalised ethnic communities, convict labourers and migrant workers. Focusing on individual cities, this body of scholarship looks primarily at the capital cities, but newer studies have also begun to look at the built environment in the secondary cities of Southeast Asia.[28]

The body of scholarship just reviewed has restricted its scope to individual nations or discrete cities within Southeast Asia. Meanwhile, two edited volumes that seek to provide an overview of modern architecture in Southeast Asia treat the modern nation state as discrete components and have refrained from constructing any overarching regional framework or connective narrative.[29] The only body of scholarship on the built environment in Southeast Asia that attempts to provide a regional framework is in the domain of urban studies.[30] Informed by the seminal work of T.G. McGee, these urban studies scholars seek to understand and explain the recent social, cultural, political and economic processes behind urbanisation and the formation of cities, metropolises and mega-urban regions in Southeast Asia – but the endeavour to construct a regional model is not without problems. The legacy of McGee's perspective on abstract political economic forces, centred on the Chicago school developmentalist paradigm and large-scale spatial patterns of urbanisation, neglects sociocultural practices and the materiality and attendant material culture of the built environment of the Southeast Asian city. As a result, a more concrete understanding of the built environment that stems from a close examination of the ways the material built environment – in terms of space, form and construction – interacts with the larger abstract political economic forces and everyday sociocultural practices is missing from this scholarship.

Moreover, McGee's regional framework rests upon gross generalisations that have been specifically criticised – the urban geography model of the "Southeast Asian city", that besides being based only upon Bangkok, Singapore and Kuala Lumpur, also stems from a perspective and model that has now been deemed limited in scope and outmoded in its assumptions. Crucially, it carries the reductive glosses expected of the developmentalist, Chicago school of urban studies – namely that it privileges a typification of cities based on an economic world system and accordingly emphasises the instrumentalist view of urban space and neglects the multiple aspects of urban life, including the agency of the citizenry.[31]

Three Methodological Challenges Across Chronological Themes

Given the problems just highlighted, what then would a regional comparative framework for Southeast Asian modern architecture look like if it were to resist the seduction of grand theorising schemas yet avoid retreating into the atomised particular? This book proffers that such a framework should emerge from a careful consideration of contexts and a grounded study of particular situations. This framework would benefit from cross-comparisons that are based not on theoretical assumptions, but rather on three key methodological challenges in the architectural historiography of Southeast Asia: translation, epistemology and power. The chapters in this volume are organised around these three methodological critiques of historiography. Simultaneously, each chapter foregrounds one of three time periods that are each characterised by different configurations of political governance, sociocultural formation and conditions of architectural production. These three overarching chronological themes of governance and desired outcomes in Southeast Asia are identified as a basis for elaborating on the common social, cultural, political and economic issues that undergirded architectural production in the region. They are colonialism and the emergence of modern state; nationalism and the construction of sovereign state; and globalisation and its transnational connections. While these three periods varied in their spatial and temporal manifestations across the region, they nonetheless provide bases for contextualising the discourses and examples discussed for each of the methodological challenges. The chronological themes appear in the different chapters as the chronological/period-specific or "historicised" expressions of the methodological challenges.

Based on this comparative framework, this edited volume attempts to fill in the gaps between, firstly, the prevalence of discrete approaches and the absence of a regional framework in the many grounded and rich architectural and urban histories; and secondly, the insufficient concrete understanding of the material built environment in the abstract interdisciplinary theories in urban studies of Southeast Asian cities. Consisting of contributions from scholars of architecture and other disciplines, this book combines the material understanding of the built environment through the architectural analyses of form, space and construction with interdisciplinary insights on space, society and history. Moreover, this book broadens the concerns of traditional architectural historiography with architects and buildings by engaging with social, cultural and political dimensions of the built environment upon which scholars in Southeast Asian studies and urban studies have shed much light. But this book also examines the significant but oft-ignored roles that architecture performs in projecting political ambitions, facilitating economic programmes, disciplining the population, constructing new social norms and creating new cultures, bringing these matters to bear on the interdisciplinary debates.

Translation

In discussing modern architecture in Southeast Asia, we encounter the movement of ideas and their translation – themes that must be engaged with and foregrounded in order to develop perspectives that break away from simplistic narratives of transfer or transplantation from the West. The universal application of ready-made modernist precepts in the region will have to engage with and foreground the movement of ideas and their translation. Such movements are embodied or imbibed by individuals moving through different networks and across domains, and involve their agency and responses through the mediation of translation. This concern with agency echoes the long debate about externalist and autonomous history in Southeast Asia – which witnessed a shift in emphasis from the assumption of Southeast Asia's passive acceptance of external influences to the study of the circumstances, dynamics and mechanisms behind active borrowing, strategic appropriation, and selective reinterpretation.[32] The book therefore begins by looking at the translations that took place in Southeast Asia's modern architecture in the colonial, nationalist and globalised periods of connections and movement.

Chronologically, the introduction and appearance of modern architecture in Southeast Asia coincided with the era of late colonial rule and the hegemony of Western ideas of modernity in the region. Indeed, the modern colonial state of the early twentieth century concerned itself with the management of indigenous "traditions" and other cultural initiatives as a part of the colonial civilising mission.[33] Such cultural initiatives have at least two types of architectural implications. Firstly, grand cultural edifices such as theatres and museums were erected by colonial states in European historicist styles which, in the case of French Indochina, avowedly replicated such structures as those found in Paris. As Hazel Hahn's chapter shows, many such cultural edifices were included in the itinerary of Rabindranath Tagore's visit to French colonial Saigon to showcase the achievements of the colonial state. Secondly, these initiatives might be manifested in the creation of syncretic architectural style through the incorporation of vernacular architectural elements into European architectural forms. Many of the buildings planned and designed by Ernest Hébrard in French Indochina and Henri Maclaine Pont in the Netherlands East Indies are exemplars of such syncretic architectural style in colonial Southeast Asia.[34]

Hahn's chapter on the reception of Tagore and his syncretic ideas in Saigon highlights some of the tensions and divisions within colonial plural society, the multicultural context of colonial Southeast Asia which J.S. Furnivall has defined as one in which different ethnic groups "mix but do not combine [...] living side by side, but separately, within the same political unit".[35] Plural society, a product of colonial economy, was characterised by hierarchical economic specialisation along ethnic lines with limited social intermingling, thus creating particular forms of social tension and antagonism. These came to the fore through competing claims for relevance and legitimacy manifested by the Indian community of Saigon and the Vietnamese in their differing emphases in conducting an architectural itinerary for Tagore and their divergent interpretations of Tagore's pan-Asianism.

Translation as a methodological approach takes on a different dimension in the nationalist mode of governance and its concern with defining and managing the contours of citizenship and belonging. New nation states, formed in Southeast Asia around the mid twentieth century, by their very definition begin with the need to "produce" citizens and consolidate imagined communities.[36] Different means were mobilised in this endeavour, including space and architecture,[37] especially public buildings such as stadia, museums, universities and memorials.

Lawrence Chua's chapter examines the translation of fascist ideas and European architectural forms by the People's Party and its appointed architects in post-absolutist Thailand. He does this by looking at how the dome was creatively mistranslated in the Central Building of Thammasat University, Bangkok, by its architect Miw Aphaiwong and other local actors around him. Drawing on other related episodes in Thailand's architectural history, Chua shows that the conscious misreading of meanings and modifications of forms by Thai politicians and architects were central to their appropriation of modern European ideas and forms that were in circulation. Indeed, he argues that the mistranslation or "misunderstanding of forms and ideas is actually an important step in the universalisation of these ideas".

Just as the driving forces behind and the nature of architectural translation changed with the transition from colonialist to nationalist mode of governance, they were also altered when the nationalist mode of governance had to reckon with radical territorial reconfiguration of different scales, from architecture to urban and even the planetary, brought about by the forces of globalisation in the past few decades.[38] While there has been much debate about the nature of globalisation and the relationships between the global and the local, there is no doubt that globalisation necessitates a broadening of our understanding of architectural production beyond the nationalist framework and directs greater attention to transnational connections.[39] Some of the most innovative and nuanced works on globalisation show that this process is not about homogenisation, Westernisation and the accentuation of previous centre-periphery or metropole-colony relations. Instead, these works argue that globalisation is about new networks of connections that defy such geographic binaries and diffusionist narratives.

In their chapter on the invention of the Bali Style, Peter Scriver and Amit Srivastava examine one such network of transnational connections, centred primarily on Australian architects and artists whose personal and career trajectories crossed in Bali. They show that the creation of a local or regional style is not always tied to the creation of a subset of the nationalist aesthetic that is controlled by actors or agencies linked to the state. They also argue against reading this development as an imperialist or neocolonialist imposition from the West. Instead Scriver and Srivastava show that transnational connections strategically converged with forces of global tourism, especially the travel circuits of privileged individuals, to create a particular brand of resort architecture. Also known as Bali Style, this brand of resort architecture was based on the translation of traditional Balinese architectural forms, mediated through the refined sensibilities of a group of cosmopolitan aesthetes.

The three chapters on architectural translations in Southeast Asia have each dealt with the reception and reworking of sources and ideas about architecture, whether "Western" or Southeast Asian traditional. To varying degrees their investigations foreground the agency of individuals in appropriating or reconfiguring these sources. While Chua looks at a form of localisation to suit a particular ideological regime, Hahn as well as Scriver and Srivastava show how multiple perceptions and interpretations of architecture and built environments by different groups or individuals resulted in variant outcomes and consequences. Together these chapters caution against simplistic narratives on the transfer of ideas or forms, particularly in contexts of cultural diversity.

Epistemology

Implicit in all three chapters that deal with architectural translation is their challenge to colonial/Eurocentric epistemic structure, especially the hierarchy it assumed between certain binaries, such as centre and periphery, metropole and colony, and universal and local. Continuing from the last section, the chapters in this section confront these epistemological issues directly, beginning with insights from postcolonial studies.

As the path-breaking works in postcolonial studies from the 1980s show, colonial dominance could be attributed as much to European cultural hegemony as to its military might and industrial strength.[40] Among other things, the foundational knowledge in many disciplines – such as anthropology, geography, urban planning and architecture – were produced during the colonial era as handmaidens of the colonial project in order to know and govern colonised populations.[41] Architectural history was also an inextricable part of such colonial power-knowledge. Knowledge of architectural history was mobilised by colonial architects for various purposes under different colonial contexts. One of those was to create the aforementioned syncretic architectural styles that represented the colonisers' familiarity and affinity with local architectural traditions and thus legitimised their rule.[42]

A more lasting and influential legacy of colonialism, one which lingers on after the end of formal colonialism, is the Eurocentric epistemic structure – in terms of architectural historiography and nomenclature – that was laid down by the colonial scholars and continued to undergird the ways architectural history in and of Southeast Asia is written. Various scholars on the built environment in Southeast Asia have written against such Eurocentric epistemic structures.[43] Drawing on postcolonial theories, these scholars seek to liberate the histories of modern architecture of Indonesia and Thailand respectively from the clutches of colonial epistemology, which has had particular longevity, in reincarnated forms, in nationalist scholarship. Given how the modern nation states in Southeast Asia are "defined by accidents of colonial rule rather than natural ethnic, linguistic or cultural entities",[44] and have been constituted from the "ruins of Empire", there is little wonder that inherited categories, which had held such ex-colonial entities together, continue to maintain their hold. Besides the nationalist framework, the epistemological challenge to architectural historiography in Southeast Asia also arises from the transnational networks and movements that are associated with globalisation. The chapters in this section by Tim Winter and Anoma Pieris, like the chapter by Peter Scriver and Amit Srivastava discussed above, also reveal to us new epistemologies forged through these new transnational connections and alliances in architectural production.

Tim Winter's chapter on heritage conservation in Myanmar shows that heritage diplomacy and aid programmes in the past decade or so sponsored by new economic powers in Asia – such as China, India, Japan and Korea – are challenging the old Western hegemony on the theories and practices of heritage conservation. The established post-war international norms of heritage conservation and historical authenticity – premised on "scientific knowledge" developed from colonial knowledge of understanding and recovering the ancient past – have been recently challenged by the "Asian" approach, i.e. that taken by conservation institutions funded by Asian countries just mentioned. His discussion points to the impact of globalisation on contemporary inter-Asian heritage diplomacy and the emergence of new hierarchies that have already begun to reconfigure the construction of architectural historical knowledge in its utility for heritage narratives and conservation.

Anoma Pieris' chapter likewise urges us to move beyond nationalist frameworks and attend to inter-Asia and southern connections, and offers a number of new approaches that are intended to shift the focus of study away from the uncritical continuation of inherited categorical predilections. She reviews recent theoretical challenges to both Eurocentric and nationalist discourses on architecture and cities in Southeast Asia, focusing on southern theory, inter-Asia cultural studies, and how these could lead to new spatial conceptions and alternative subjectivities.

Although not strictly on modern architecture per se, the two chapters on the epistemological challenge in writing Southeast Asian architectural history problematise many of the modern epistemic categories they have selected for discussion. The chapters by Winter and Pieris work with postcolonial theories as part of their larger engagement with other interdisciplinary theories and the attendant issues. Winter suggests that the cracks and gaps in the colonial epistemic edifice of antiquity and classical architecture, partially created by postcolonial critique, have allowed new counterheritage practices to emerge. Winter also argues that these new practices should be understood in relation to the political economy of their knowledge production, or what he calls intra-Asia heritage diplomacy. Unlike Winter, Pieris seeks intellectual autonomy from the prevailing political economy of scholarship and advocates for an alternative episteme that counters the hegemonic discourses established by nation states and globalisation.

Power

One of the reasons the two chapters in the second section focuses on epistemology is because, as Michel Foucault famously suggested, "power and knowledge directly imply one another, that there is no power relation without the correlative constitution of a field of knowledge, nor any knowledge that does not presuppose and constitute at the same time power relations."[45] The chapters on power in the third section move away from Foucauldian power-knowledge to address directly the analytics of power in the built environment. It is well established that architecture and the built environment are not just isolated material artefacts and autonomous aesthetic objects; they shape and are shaped by the sociocultural and political economic conditions of their production, consumption and circulation. In the recent scholarship of architectural history, power has emerged as a key analytical theme in the discussion of architecture's entanglements with society, culture, politics and economy. However, some of this scholarship is rooted in traditional art historical approaches and relies mainly on formal analysis – the effect of power is at times too easily correlated with formal qualities. The consequent focus on buildings as "visible politics" or on the "aestheticisation of politics" might not be adequate in understanding the nuances of space and power-relations.

A way to expand from the conventional analytics of power in the built environment is to attend to the planning and building activities of the modern state in the nineteenth and the early twentieth centuries. Various scholars have traced the emergence of the modern state in Southeast Asia to the decades around the turn of the twentieth century, when the various colonial powers ruling different parts of Southeast Asia embarked on the expansion, functionalisation and rationalisation of their presence and their institutions of governance.[46] The modern colonial state not only reformed and strengthened the old functions of the state but took on the new rationality of governance and engaged in new activities – such as education, public health and social welfare – to improve the biopolitical lives of the population. This new political order had a direct impact on the built environment, particularly on the planning and design of public works and public buildings. New typologies of hospitals, schools and housing were first built in many colonial cities in the early twentieth century.[47] Sanitation and town planning improvements were also undertaken in many of Southeast Asia's colonial cities at around the same time.[48] Gerard Lico's chapter in this book examines one such instance – the sanitary improvement and "beautification" of Manila undertaken by the American colonial government at the turn of the twentieth century. Lico argues that these improvements were part of a Foucauldian disciplinary regime that combined systematic surveillance and spatial regulation to control the social conduct of the indigenous population.

Similar disciplinary power was also at play in the urban improvement and public housing schemes carried out by the colonial and postcolonial state in Singapore. Through the planning and design of the People's Park Complex in the 1960s and 1970s, Eunice Seng's chapter examines the planning and design of an urban complex in a space that the colonial government tried but failed to regulate previously. However, instead of disciplinary power, Seng explores a form of developmental power deployed by the post-independence state through its urban renewal programme. Through co-financing, planning and managing the urban complex, the post-independence state was able to ensure that the developer was aligned with its vision of remaking the city and the identity of its Chinese middle-class inhabitants. In the process, the architects' resistance to the state's vision proved to be inconsequential.

Continuing the discussion of power and the built environment in the nation state, Koompong Noobanjong's contribution looks at Thailand's semi-colonial nation-building project – specifically two monuments erected by the People's Party following the overthrow of the absolute monarchy in 1932 as statements of power, namely the Democracy and the Constitutional Defense monuments. Noobanjong also discusses how power circulated through their changing meaning from about 1947 and especially their semantic reappropriation by successive regimes after 1957, in which royalist military dictators emphasised Thai ethno-nationalism over exogenous abstract values such as democracy or constitutionalism, leading to the era of "Hyper Royalism" beginning in the 1970s and culminating in the erasure and effacement of the structures of the previous era. However, the citizenry's capacity to reappropriate and revive the significance of the Constitutional Defense Monument in a 2010 demonstration is also foregrounded.

A different form of response to the power of the colonial and nationalist regimes can be found in the modernising and reformist Islamic organisations working on such issues as education, provision of health, and women's emancipation. These movements were founded and articulated explicitly as a response to the challenge of colonial modernity. Tutin Aryanti looks at one such influential movement, Muhammadiyah in Yogyakarta, Indonesia, and its influence on the provision of women's prayer spaces in mosques, and the building of women's mosques, which form an aspect of Islamic architecture that has been neglected in the scholarship. The creation of a progressive Islamic ecumene that included women in the public congregation in mosques or that empowered women in hitherto non-existent domains is discussed from a gender perspective on power-relations in the negotiation of space and leadership over bodies in space.

One of the analytical tools that Aryanti mobilises in her chapter is visual theory. Indeed visibility and invisibility are critical to any discussion of power in architecture, especially its place in empowering or disempowering any group of people in society. By challenging Indonesian society's patriarchal outlook, Aryanti is also questioning social and cultural norms. Likewise, the other chapters in this section highlight both visible and invisible spatial articulations of power to interrogate the conventional – i.e. depoliticised – understanding of the built environment in Southeast Asia.

Concluding Notes

As one of the few works to explore the twentieth-century architectural histories of Southeast Asia and probably the only one to take a transnational perspective and focus on historiographical issues, this book has not attempted to be geographically exhaustive, preferring instead to strategically deploy Southeast Asia as a contingent device and, in place of metatheory, to selectively foreground a number of pertinent historiographical questions through the themes of translation, epistemology and power, in order to point to at least two possible pathways of broadening the writing of architectural histories of Southeast Asia.

The first pathway goes beyond the current discrete and aggregative approach to the task of conducting a regional survey. Instead of writing architectural histories that are bounded within contemporary nation states in Southeast Asia, we suggest attending to intra- and inter-regional connections to discern commonalities and provide bases for comparative histories in the future. In order to attend to broader historical connections and linkages beyond the nation state, contributors to this book have shown us that we need to be sensitive to how ideas and concepts were translated as they circulated. Similarly, received architectural nomenclature and its underlying epistemic constructions have to be critically examined.

The second pathway critiques the prevailing tendency to see modern architectural history in Southeast Asia primarily as a professional and/or aesthetic discourse. Rather than see architecture as aesthetic objects and architectural history as an evolution of spatial and typological configuration or style, contributors to this book situate architecture and architectural production in larger social, cultural and political contexts. Nevertheless, while we see architecture as inextricably linked to the contexts and conditions of its production, architecture is irreducible to these contexts and conditions, for design has the agency to reshape or transform its very contexts and conditions of production. However, design is not automatically or exclusively linked to professional designers. The agency of non-architects in shaping both the production of architecture and its reproduction as texts or as popular images that feed into further creation and reiteration is often neglected, and in this volume we hear of social and religious reformers, cultural doyens, hoteliers, privileged aesthetes, political demagogues and nationalist scribes. In this sense, this volume on modern architecture and architectural knowledge has taken on what Dell Upton has called the vernacular approach to architectural historiography, "an approach to architectural studies that complements more traditional architectural historical inquiries".[49]

In speaking of historiographical questions in modern architecture in Southeast Asia, this volume has attempted a conscious search for connections and commonalities through discussions of agency in architectural translations, the problems of epistemological bases for its histories, and of the spatialisation of power. Such a prospective, expanded outlook necessarily involves a dialogue between architectural history and other disciplines in the social sciences and humanities in a quest to explore the mutual grounds for raising broader social, cultural and political questions in Southeast Asia and beyond. It is hoped that the chapters in this volume point to the need for more such engagements and that a methodological emphasis on regional historiographical comparisons provides a useful frame for conceiving such exchanges.

Notes

1. Donald K. Emmerson, "'Southeast Asia': What's in a Name?" *Journal of Southeast Asian Studies* 15, no. 1 (1984): 1–2.
2. Paul H. Kratoska, Remco Raben, and Henk Schulte Nordholt, *Locating Southeast Asia: Geographies of Knowledge and Politics of Space* (Singapore: Singapore University Press, 2005); J.D. Legge, "The Writing of Southeast Asian History," in *The Cambridge History of Southeast Asia. Vol. 1, Part 1: From Early Times to c.1500*, ed. Nicholas Tarling (Cambridge: Cambridge University Press, 1999).
3. A rather different set of questions concerns historians of Southeast Asia's *longue durée*, which is not covered by the essays on the modern in this volume. See for instance Craig J. Reynolds, "A New Look at Old Southeast Asia," *The Journal of Asian Studies* 54.2 (1995): 419–446.
4. Heather Sutherland, "Contingent Devices, " in *Locating Southeast Asia: Geographies of Knowledge and Politics of Space*, ed. Paul H. Kratoska, Remco Raben, and Henk Schulte Nordholt (Singapore: Singapore University Press, 2005), 21.
5. For the former approach, see Jon Lim, ed. *Transforming Traditions: Architecture in the Asean Countries; Brunei, Malaysia, Indonesia, Phillippines, Singapore, Thailand* (Singapore: ASEAN Committee on Culture and Information, 2001); for the latter, see Kelly Shannon, "Beyond Tropical Regionalism: The Architecture of Southeast Asia," in *A Critical History of Contemporary Architecture: 1960–2010*, ed. Elie G. Haddad and David Rifkind (Burlington, VT: Ashgate, 2014). Some histories are a combination of both approaches. See for example, Kenneth Frampton, William S.W. Lim, and Jennifer Taylor, ed., *World Architecture 1900–2000: A Critical Mosaic, Volume 10, Southeast Asia and Oceania* (Vienna and New York: Springer, 1999).
6. For a critique of metageography, see Martin W. Lewis and Karen Wigen, *The Myth of Continents: A Critique of Metageography* (Berkeley: University of California Press, 1997). For recent scholarship based on oceanic or nautical imaginaries, see Paul Gilroy, *The Black Atlantic: Modernity and Double Consciousness* (Cambridge, MA: Harvard University Press, 1993); Sugata Bose, *A Hundred Horizons: The Indian Ocean in the Age of Global Empire* (Cambridge, MA: Harvard University Press, 2006); Sunil S. Amrith, *Crossing the Bay of Bengal: The Furies of Nature and the Fortunes of Migrants* (Cambridge, MA: Harvard University Press, 2013).
7. Imran bin Tajudeen, "Java's Architectural Enigma: The Austronesian World and the Limits of 'Asia'," in *Architecturalized Asia: Mapping a Continent through History*, ed. Vimalin Rujivacharakul et al. (Honolulu and Hong Kong: University of Hawai'i Press and Hong Kong University Press, 2013), 121–138.
8. Victor Lieberman, *Beyond Binary Histories: Re-imagining Eurasia to c.1830* (Ann Arbor: University of Michigan Press, 1999); Vimalin Rujivacharakul, et, al., eds, *Architecturalized Asia: Mapping a Continent through History* (Honolulu and Hong Kong: University of Hawai'i Press and Hong Kong University Press, 2013).

9. Roxana Waterson, "Origins," in *The Living House: An Anthropology of Architecture in South-East Asia* (Singapore; New York: Oxford University Press, 1990), and Imran bin Tajudeen, "Java's Architectural Enigma".
10. Brian Bernards, *Writing the South Seas: Imagining the Nanyang in Chinese and Southeast Asian Postcolonial Literature* (Seattle: University of Washington Press, 2015).
11. On the relative merits of categories of Asian architecture (Hindu–Buddhist and mainland–island Southeast Asia) as comparative frames, taking Java as illustrative case and the Austronesian world as a counterpoint, see Imran bin Tajudeen, "Java's Architectural Enigma."
12. Daigoro Chihara, *Hindu–Buddhist Architecture in Southeast Asia* (Leiden: E.J. Brill, 1996); George Michell, "Southeast Asia," in *The Hindu Temple: An Introduction to its Meanings and Forms* (Chicago, University of Chicago Press, 1977).
13. Roxana Waterson, *The Living House: An Anthropology of Architecture in South-East Asia* (Singapore; New York: Oxford University Press, 1990).
14. H.G. Quaritch Wales, *The Making of Greater India: A Study in South-East Asian Culture Change* (London: Quaritch, 1951); Hermann Kulke, "The Concept of Cultural Convergence Revisited: Reflections on India's Early Influence in Southeast Asia," in *Asian Encounters: Exploring Connected Histories*, ed. Upinder Singh and Parul Pandhya Dhar (New Delhi: Oxford University Press, 2014).
15. C. Greig Crysler, *Writing Spaces: Discourses of Architecture, Urbanism, and the Built Environment, 1960–2000* (New York: Routledge, 2003), 95–98.
16. Roxana Waterson, "Migrations," in *The Living House: An Anthropology of Architecture in South-East Asia* (New York: Oxford University Press, 1990); Reimar Schefold, Gaudenz Domenig, and Peter J.M. Nas, ed., *Indonesian Houses Vol 1: Tradition and Transformation in Vernacular Architecture* (Singapore: Singapore University Press, 2004); Reimar Schefold, Peter J.M. Nas, Gaudenz Domenig, and Robert Wessing, ed. *Indonesian Houses Vol 2: Survey of Vernacular Architecture in Western Indonesia* (Leiden: KITLV Press, 2008); Marcel Vellinga, *Constituting Unity and Difference: Vernacular Architecture in a Minangkabau Village* (Leiden: KITLV Press, 2004).
17. Philip Goad, *Architecture Bali: Architectures of Welcome* (Sydney: Pesaro Publishing, 2000); Penny Edwards, *Cambodge: The Cultivation of a Nation, 1860–1945* (Honolulu: Hawai'i University Press, 2007); Tim Winter, *Post-Conflict Heritage, Postcolonial Tourism: Culture, Politics and Development at Angkor* (Abingdon, Oxon: Routledge, 2007); Maurizio Peleggi, *The Politics of Ruins and the Business of Nostalgia* (Bangkok: White Lotus, 2002).
18. Gülsüm Baydar Nalbantoğlu, "Toward Postcolonial Openings: Rereading Sir Banister Fletcher's 'History of Architecture'," *Assemblage*, no. 35 (1998); Abidin Kusno, *Behind the Postcolonial: Architecture, Urban Space, and Political Cultures in Indonesia* (New York: Routledge, 2000); Jiat-Hwee Chang and William S.W. Lim, "Non West Modernist Past: Rethinking Modernisms and Modernities Beyond the West," in

Non West Modernist Past: On Architecture and Modernities, ed. William S.W. Lim and Jiat-Hwee Chang (Singapore: World Scientific, 2011).

19. Imran bin Tajudeen, "Beyond Racialized Representation: Architectural Linguæ Francæ and Urban Histories in the Kampung Houses and Shophouses of Melaka and Singapore," in *Colonial Frames, Nationalist Histories: Imperial Legacies, Architecture and Modernity*, ed. Mrinalini Rajagopalan and Madhuri Desai (Burlington: Ashgate Publishing Company, 2012), 213–252.
20. Imran bin Tajudeen, "Java's Architectural Enigma".
21. Ibid.; Sarah Tiffin, "Java's Ruined *Candi*s and the British Picturesque Ideal," *Bulletin of the School of Oriental and African Studies* 72.3 (2009): 525–558; Sarah Tiffin, *Southeast Asia in Ruins: Art and Empire in the Early 19th Century* (Singapore: NUS Press, 2016).
22. Peter Jenkins and Waveney Jenkins, *The Planter's Bungalow: A Journey Down the Malay Peninsula* (Singapore: Editions Didier Millet, 2007); Jon Sun Hock Lim, *The Penang House and the Straits Architect 1887–1941* (Penang: Areca Books, 2015); C.J. van Dullemen, *Tropical Modernity: Life and Work of C.P. Wolff Schoemaker* (Amsterdam: SUN, 2010); Wim Ravesteijn and Jan Kop, ed., *For Profit and Prosperity: the Contribution Made by Dutch Engineers to Public Works in Indonesia: 1800–2000* (Leiden: KITLV Press, c.2008).
23. For a critique of such scholarship, see Jiat-Hwee Chang, *A Genealogy of Tropical Architecture: Colonial Networks, Nature and Technoscience* (London: Routledge, 2016); Freek Colombijn and Joost Cote, ed., *Cars, Conduits, and Kampongs: The Modernization of the Indonesian City, 1920–1960* (Leiden; Boston: Brill, 2014); Rudolf Mrázek, *Engineers of Happy Land: Technology and Nationalism in a Colony* (Princeton, N.J.: Princeton University Press, 2002); and Gwendolyn Wright, *The Politics of Design in French Colonial Urbanism* (Chicago: University of Chicago Press, c.1991).
24. Imran bin Tajudeen, "Clients, Architects, and the Persistence of Type: A Review of *The Penang House and the Straits Architect 1878–1941* by Jon Lim Sun Hock," *The Singapore Architect* 01 (2015): 96i–96iv.
25. Mark Crinson, "The View from Penang Hill: Modernism and Nationalism in Malaysia," in *Modern Architecture and the End of Empire* (Burlington, VT: Ashgate, c.2003); Noobanjong Koompong, *The Aesthetics of Power: Architecture, Modernity, and Identity from Siam to Thailand* (Bangkok: White Lotus Press, 2013); Chee Kien Lai, *Building Merdeka: Independence Architecture in Kuala Lumpur, 1957–1966* (Kuala Lumpur: Gelari Petronas 2007); Gerard Lico, *Edifice Complex: Power, Myth, and Marcos State Architecture* (Quezon City: Ateneo de Manila University Press, 2003); Helen Grant Ross and Darryl Leon Collins, *Building Cambodia: New Khmer Architecture 1953–1970* (Bangkok: The Key Publisher, 2006); Kusno, *Behind the Postcolonial.*
26. See also William S.W. Lim and Jiat-Hwee Chang, ed., *Non West Modernist Past: On Architecture and Modernities* (Singapore: World Scientific, 2011).

27. Brenda S.A. Yeoh, *Contesting Space: Power Relations and the Urban Built Environment in Colonial Singapore* (Kuala Lumpur: Oxford University Press, 1996); Christopher Silver, *Planning the Megacity: Jakarta in the Twentieth Century* (London: Routledge, 2008); Anoma Pieris, *Hidden Hands and Divided Landscapes: A Penal History of Singapore's Plural Society* (Honolulu: University of Hawai'i Press, 2009); Abidin Kusno, *After the New Order: Space, Politics and Jakarta* (Honolulu: University of Hawai'i Press, 2013); Yat Ming Loo, *Architecture and Urban Form in Kuala Lumpur: Race and Chinese Spaces in a Postcolonial City* (Burlington: Ashgate, 2013); Hans-Dieter Evers and Rüdiger Korff, *Southeast Asian Urbanism: The Meaning and Power of Social Space* (Münster: Lit Verlage, 2000).
28. Handinoto. *Komunitas Cina dan Perkembangan Kota Surabaya: Abad XVIII Sampai Pertengahan Abad XX* (Yogyakarta: Penerbit Ombak, 2015); Andrew Alan Johnson. *Ghosts of the New City: Spirits, Urbanity, and the Ruins of Progress in Chiang Mai* (Honolulu: University of Hawai'i Press, 2014); William S. Logan, ed. *The Disappearing Asian City: Protecting Asia's Urban Heritage in a Globalization World* (Oxford: Oxford University Press, 2002).
29. Frampton, Lim, and Taylor, ed., *World Architecture 1900–2000*; Lim, ed. *Transforming Traditions*.
30. T.G. McGee, *The Southeast Asian City: A Social Geography of the Primate Cities of Southeast Asia* (New York: Praeger, 1967); Peter J. Rimmer and Howard Dick, *The City in Southeast Asia: Patterns, Processes, and Policy* (Singapore: NUS Press, 2009); Tim Bunnell, Kong-Chong Ho, and Lisa B. W. Drummond, *Critical Reflections on Cities in Southeast Asia* (Singapore: Times Academic Press, 2002); Evers and Korff, *Southeast Asian Urbanism*.
31. Yeoh, *Contesting Space*, 5; Robbie Goh and Brenda Yeoh, *Theorizing the Southeast Asian City as Text: Urban Landscapes, Cultural Documents, and Interpretative Experiences* (Singapore: World Scientific, 2003), 3.
32. John R.W. Smail, "On the Possibility of an Autonomous History of Modern Southeast Asia", *Journal of Southeast Asian History* 2.2, 1961: 72–102; Jacob Cornelis van Leur, *Indonesian Trade and Society: Essays in Asian Social and Economic History* (The Hague: W. Van Hoeve Publishers, 1967); Legge, "The Writing of Southeast Asian History," 9.
33. Gwendolyn Wright, *The Politics of Design in French Colonial Urbanism* (Chicago: University of Chicago Press, 1991); Paul Rabinow, *French Modern: Norms and Forms of the Social Environment* (Chicago: University of Chicago Press, 1989).
34. Helen Jessup, "Four Dutch Buildings in Indonesia I: Henri Maclaine Pont's Institute of Technology of Bandung," *Orientation* 13 (1982); "Four Dutch Buildings in Indonesia IV: Henri Maclaine Pont's Pohsarang," *Orientation* 13 (1982).
35. J.S. Furnivall, *Colonial Policy and Practice* (New York: New York University Press, 1956), 304–305.

36. Benedict R. Anderson, *Imagined Communities: Reflections on the Origin and Spread of Nationalism*, Revised ed. (London: Verso, 1991 (1983)).
37. Thongchai Winichakul, *Siam Mapped: A History of the Geo-Body of a Nation* (Honolulu: University of Hawai'i Press, 1994).
38. Neil Brenner and Christian Schmid, "Towards a New Epistemology of the Urban?," *City* 19, no. 2–3 (2015); Donald McNeill, *The Global Architect: Firms, Fame and Urban Form* (London: Routledge, 2009).
39. For a critique of globalisation theory, see Anna Lowenhaupt Tsing, "The Global Situation," *Cultural Anthropology* 15, no. 3 (2000); Frederick Cooper, *Colonialism in Question: Theory, Knowledge, History* (Berkeley: University of California Press, 2005).
40. See, among others, Edward W. Said, *Culture and Imperialism*, 1st Vintage Books ed. (New York: Vintage Books, 1994); *Orientalism* (New York: Vintage Books, 1994 [1978]); Partha Chatterjee, *Nationalist Thought and the Colonial World: A Derivative Discourse* (Minneapolis: University of Minnesota Press, 2001 [1986]).
41. Anne Godlewska and Neil Smith, ed., *Geography and Empire* (Cambridge, MA: Blackwell, 1994); James Ferguson, "Anthropology and Its Evil Twin: 'Development' in the Constitution of a Discipline, " in *International Development and the Social Sciences: Essays on the History and Politics of Knowledge*, ed. Frederick Cooper and Randall M. Packard (Berkeley: University of California Press, 1997); Robert K. Home, *Of Planting and Planning: The Making of British Colonial Cities* (London: Spon, 1997).
42. See, for example, the case of Indo-Saracenic architecture in British India in Thomas R. Metcalf, *An Imperial Vision: Indian Architecture and Britain's Raj* (New Delhi: Oxford University Press, 2002 [1989]).
43. See for example, Iwan Sudradjat, *A Study of Indonesian Architectural History* (Unpublished dissertation, University of Sydney, 1991).
44. Legge, "The Writing of Southeast Asian History," 5.
45. Foucault, *Discipline and Punish*, 27
46. See for example, Carl A. Trocki, "Political Structures in the Nineteenth and Early Twentieth Centuries," in *The Cambridge History of Southeast Asia Volume 2: The Nineteenth and Twentieth Centuries*, ed. Nicholas Tarling (Cambridge: Cambridge University Press, 1993); Robert E. Elson, "International Commerce, the State and Society: Economic and Social Change," in *The Cambridge History of Southeast Asia. Vol. 3 : From c.1800 to the 1930s*, ed. Nicholas Tarling (Cambridge: Cambridge University Press, 1999).
47. Chang, *A Genealogy of Tropical Architecture.*
48. Warwick Anderson, *Colonial Pathologies: American Tropical Medicine, Race, and Hygiene in the Philippines* (Durham: Duke University Press, 2006); Yeoh, *Contesting Space.*
49. Dell Upton, "The Power of Things: Recent Studies in American Vernacular Architecture", *American Quarterly* 35, no. 3 (1983): 262–279, 263.

Section One

TRANSLATION

CHAPTER 1

Tagore as a Celebrity Tourist?: Urban Planning, Tourism and Architecture in Colonial Saigon[1]

H. HAZEL HAHN

In 1929 the Bengali poet Rabindranath Tagore (1861–1941) visited Saigon for three days, where he encountered a reception ranging from enthusiastic welcome to hostility. Tagore was partly turned into a tourist by the very itinerary of his visit to Indochina. How the officials and civilians of French Indochina prepared for Tagore's visit, interacted with him, and debated his ideas reveals much about the state of local society and politics. I place this little-known visit onto intertwined developments in urban planning and tourism.[2] Much of Tagore's time was to be filled with visits of numerous carefully selected sites such as the botanical garden, museums, schools, administrative buildings, theatres, temples and pagodas, the kinds of sites highlighted in guidebooks for tourists as well as publications glorifying the French empire. A close look at both Tagore's itinerary and the impact of his visit highlights both competing narratives and spatial, architectural and cultural practices around the sites. We can glimpse not only how the public experienced the city, but also the varied perspectives and wishes of various components of the society. Seeking to understand the reception of Tagore by groups of the Vietnamese, French, Indians and Chinese helps us understand the stakes at hand. I explore the tensions and divisions within the complex and diverse colonial society regarding both Tagore's ideas and the state of French Indochina that the various components wanted Tagore to see and comprehend. In the process, I examine examples of architectural, cultural and religious syncretism, and also argue that both urban planning and tourism were fraught, contested topics.

Tagore, who became the first Asian Nobel Laureate in 1913, was a literary celebrity. Tagore travelled not only throughout India but also in much of

Europe, Asia and North America for lecture tours, invited by governments, institutions and individuals. He spent about three and a half years between 1919 and 1929, a decade marked by internationalism, travelling abroad.[3] Yet, his travels have never been placed in the history of travel, or studied from the angle of the development of tourism. This essay delves into both, by exploring the idea of Tagore as a figure of famous and influential worldly traveller and even a celebrity tourist. Tagore's own reasons for travel have been well documented by Sabyasachi Bhattacharya and others: he travelled to spread his ideas, make contacts, raise funds for the Visva-Bharati University he founded in 1921, to see the world, and to renew himself from the ceaseless conflict between his aspirations as a poet and a visionary missionary of sorts.[4] Clearly, there is no sign that Tagore saw himself as a tourist in the sense of a traveller primarily seeking leisure. However, distinctions between traveller and tourist were (and continue to be) often nuanced. Tagore can be placed, I suggest, in long worldwide traditions of literary, philosophising or teaching travellers. His elite status as a celebrated intellectual and a Brahman placed him in the tradition, common in many parts of Asia, of male aristocratic travellers and travelling holy men. And in Europe, North America and elsewhere, he could be placed in a long line of celebrity travellers for whom a performative aspect was important. Indeed, Tagore had misgivings about himself being seen as a "show lion in a circus", a celebrity performer.[5] And everywhere, he could be seen at least partly as a cultural diplomat or dignitary. In colonies, the ceremonious welcoming of aristocrats and officials from metropoles was a significant part of the spectacle of empire.[6] In this last regard, Tagore had a rather ambiguous status as a visitor of Indochina. As an officially invited guest of the city of Saigon, he was a subject of a colony visiting another colony. He was a highly unique and unusual traveller whose reception everywhere mobilised and tested existing modes of perception and interaction. His very popularity was based in large measure on his uniqueness as a traveller. And in Asia, he was an inspiring, provocative and at times even an infuriating traveller.

The idea of Tagore as a celebrity tourist highlights the fact that his travels were enabled by rapidly developing transportation networks and other forms of tourism infrastructure, and that many of the places he visited were popular with tourists. The identity of tourist could be a largely unintended aspect of most travellers especially in this period, when the capacity and time for leisure expanded for broad sectors of society, and tourist activities began to form a significant, organised part of leisure in many parts of the world.[7] Two of Tagore's aims of travel correspond to two of the most popular aims of modern tourism: seeing the world – and subsequently being acquainted with different cultures – and renewing himself by taking a break from his inner conflicts, through *dépaysement* – getting away from familiar surroundings.

Tagore's Travels and Universalism

Tagore was not only a prolific poet, novelist, dramatist and painter, he was also an essayist and lecturer deeply interested in the state of world civilisations. One of his most profound convictions was universalism, a belief in the unity of the world drawn from his deep religious sense of a harmony interconnecting all things.[8] This syncretism led to his unwavering wish to bring the various religions of the world together, and an abiding effort at a dialogue between the "East" and the "West".[9] He envisioned the Visva-Bharati University, which was expanded from the Santiniketan school in Bengal, as a unique cultural institution, an international, "Universal Indian" university.[10] In Santiniketan, varied architectural styles were employed, true to his syncretism.[11] This universalism and aversion to aggressive nationalism can be seen in a talk he gave in Tokyo in 1916. He declared that "in the hidden heart of Europe runs the purest stream of human love" but criticised Western racial exclusionism and its "political civilisation" with "carnivorous and cannibalistic ... tendencies" that fed "upon the resources of other peoples". He criticised the hypocrisy of the West which, "in spite of its boasted love of freedom ... produced worse forms of slavery than ever were current in earlier societies".[12] Tagore thus professed his love of Europe and its cultural accomplishments while criticising Western nationalism and imperialism. He praised Japan's modernisation but appealed to Japan to apply its "Eastern mind" and its "spiritual strength", not to be a "mere reproduction of the West".[13] Initial Japanese enthusiasm for Tagore waned after this talk.[14]

In 1924, seeking to renew the links that had unified India with other Asian countries in the past, he visited British Malaya, China and Japan.[15] However, his effort to spread pan-Asianism through a renewal of Eastern spirituality was not welcomed in a China torn asunder by civil war and rampant warlords who aimed to destabilise the new republic. Chinese radicals rejected Tagore's appeal for ancient Chinese spirituality, including Buddhism and Confucianism, and branded Tagore a man from "a lost country".[16] Tagore's ideas produced much more contention there than in Europe or North America precisely because the issues he raised hit home. In China in particular, the path for the future was being intensively contested. A new nation had to be built, and the issues of history, culture and identity, in respect to "Eastern" and "Western" civilisations, could be profoundly divisive. In 1927 Tagore visited British Malaya, Java, Bali and Siam.[17] This travel inspired his poem "Sagarika" ("The Sea Maiden"), about the influence of ancient Indian civilisation in this region, an influence seen as peaceful, full of humanistic ideals and devoid of imperialism. The poem emphasised the necessity of the renewal of this bond through mutually respectful syncretism; the poem marked, according to Sagarika Chakraborty, the "epitome" of Tagore's "ideas on diplomacy and foreign relations".[18] This kind of literary musing while travelling had the potential to influence tourist sensibilities in addition to literature and study of the history of the region.[19]

Tagore was welcomed enthusiastically in much of Europe, although not always without controversy. When he visited Italy in 1926, he was welcomed by Sanskritists Guiseppe Tucci and Carlo Fromichi, who were Mussolinian fascists; this stirred criticism from the French surrealist René Daumal and others.[20] Tagore faced a muted reception in England, following his public renunciation of his knighthood in 1919 to protest against the Jallianwala Bagh massacre.[21] He was under secret police surveillance.[22]

In India, Tagore's discomfort with some of Gandhi's strategies for his nationalist movement, his refusal to unconditionally support Gandhi's movement – although he and Gandhi continued to have deep regard and respect for each other – and his abiding belief in the East–West synthesis, caused him to be severely criticised by Gandhi's followers and other nationalists during the 1920s.[23] It was in Asia, and his homeland most of all, that Tagore's ideas could be the most provocative.

Tagore in Colonial Vietnam

Tagore was greatly admired by many Vietnamese intellectuals of Cochinchina, who keenly followed events in India with an interest in comparing the paths of India and Vietnam under colonial powers. He was one of the thinkers, along with Gandhi and various European authors, introduced to the Vietnamese public by Nguyễn An Ninh's paper *La Cloche fêlée*. Ninh believed that, in order to reassert Vietnamese culture for national survival, it was necessary to integrate Western analytical and comparative methods.[24] Tagore's visit was instigated by Vietnamese intellectuals. In January 1929, Bùi Quang Chiêu and Dương Văn Giao, the leaders of the Indochinese Constitutionalist Party, paid their respects to Tagore at the Visva-Bharati University, and persuaded him to visit Saigon.[25] The Constitutionalist Party had a reformist (rather than anti-colonialist) agenda and held some sway among the Vietnamese, but did not have a broad appeal especially among the young generation. When formally invited by the French Embassy of Japan to tour French Indochina, Tagore accepted, hoping to visit Angkor, although this plan would not pan out due to his frail health.[26]

Tagore's impending visit caused greater interest in his work in Saigon. Bùi Quang Chiêu's newspaper *La Tribune indochinoise* published numerous excerpts of Tagore's work and articles written by the Vietnamese on Tagore. The Vietnamese wished Tagore to visit certain sites that would help him accurately understand the state of their society and in turn enable him to advise them on a viable path for the future. During and after the visit, the Vietnamese gravely engaged with and debated his ideas the way the public did in China, Japan and other Asian countries. They carefully avoided any overt anti-French or anti-colonialist expressions in public speeches, but they could debate their ideas more openly through the Francophone press of Saigon. The intensity of such debates occasioned by Tagore's visit reveals deep divisions and tensions among the Vietnamese, as Chi Pham also suggests.[27]

On the French side, initially the news of the planned visit produced a much more muted reaction in the French papers published in Saigon and almost none in French papers in Tonkin. However, one French paper, *Le Merle mandarin*, called Tagore "the greatest poet of our time".[28] In France, Tagore's reputation had been spreading through the influence of his friends Romain Rolland, André Gide, and Sylvain Lévi.[29] These figures were widely read by Saigon's Vietnamese intellectuals.[30] Lévi, a famed Orientalist and Indologist who was the first foreign scholar to teach at Santiniketan,[31] was a specialist of Vietnamese religion and culture. His meeting with the Governor General of French Indochina Paul Doumer (g.1897–1902) in Saigon in 1899 resulted in the creation of the Permanent Archeological Mission in Indochina.[32] In 1922 Lévi visited Phnom Penh and Angkor, and travelled from Saigon to Hanoi by land, visiting Hue and the Cham monuments in Annam.[33] He would direct the official volume on Indochina for the 1931 Colonial Exposition in Paris.[34]

And finally, Indians of Saigon and Cholon, the group perhaps most enthusiastic about Tagore's visit, sought a unity among themselves to welcome Tagore with dignity, and use the occasion to publicise the contribution of Indian civilisation in the region, something that – as we shall see – both the Vietnamese receptive to Tagore's ideas and Tagore himself highlighted. However, the reconstructed narrative of the influence of Indian civilisation in the region would also expose tensions within the stratified colonial society.

Tagore visited Saigon on his way back to India from a tour of Canada, the United States and Japan.[35] In Saigon, a welcome committee was formed, representing the French, Vietnamese and Indian populations of Saigon. Béziat, the mayor of Saigon, was the honorary president of the committee while Bùi Quang Chiêu was the president. Monribot, a Frenchman, and Xavier, an Indian, were both vice presidents. Nguyễn Văn Của and Lê Trung Nghĩa served as the treasurer and secretary respectively.[36] The committee met at the office of the Constitutionalist Party to plan the programme for Tagore's visit.[37] In addition, a large delegation of the reception was composed of the six members of the welcome committee, Vietnamese dignitaries, municipal council members of Saigon and Cholon, Vietnamese members of the Chamber of Commerce and the Chamber of Agriculture, two French journalists, all the newspaper directors or their delegates of Saigon, and five "Hindus". A lecture organisation committee, likewise, was composed of French, Vietnamese and "Hindu" members. In sum, *L'Écho annamite* (a newspaper run by members of the Constitutionalist Party) declared, these committees were "composed of all the elected members and all the French, Annamite [Vietnamese] and Hindu journalists and intellectuals".[38] As Chi Pham notes, the elaborate organisation of the committees was meant to reflect the efficiency and hierarchy of the colonial regime as well as set clear limits on possible activities.[39] While the ethnic Chinese were represented in the reception delegation although not in the welcome committee, the Khmer or the Chams (whose monuments Tagore might also have been interested in) were absent from both. At the same time, the organisation indicates the significance of Tagore's visit for both colonial authorities and Cochinchinese society as a whole.

Tagore's Itinerary

Tagore arrived in Saigon on 21 June 1929. Bùi Quang Chiêu, Béziat, and members of the public greeted him on the ship. In the evening he was welcomed at City Hall.[40] At a later public reception at the Municipal Theatre for which tickets were sold, Bùi Quang Chiêu presented Tagore who gave a speech, and others spoke as well.[41] On the second day, according to the publicised planned itinerary, Tagore was to visit the Botanical and Zoological Garden, museums, several schools, a Chinese temple and a Vietnamese temple in Cholon, and also make an excursion outside the city to visit two art schools that opened in 1905 in Biên Hòa and Thủ Dầu Một. This was an unrealistically full itinerary for a single day, and the actual itinerary was shorter. Tagore met with the Governor of Cochinchina Jean-Félix Krautheimer (g.1929–1934) early in the morning for half an hour, and during this meeting Tagore reiterated his wish to visit Angkor. Then he went to an art school in Biên Hòa, and then visited the tomb of Lê Văn Duyệt (1763–1832). In the evening, he went to a party hosted by the publisher Nguyễn Văn Của, and then attended the screening of documentaries on Indochina at Eden Cinema.[42] On the third day, Tagore visited Catinat Street, went to a reception in Cholon organised by the Chinese Chamber at the "Cantonese Pagoda", visited a Tamil temple, and also met with the Governor General Pierre Pasquier (g.1928–1934).[43]

The carefully organised itinerary of Tagore's tour of Saigon and nearby areas clearly reflected the colonial hierarchy, but also nonetheless indicated a compromise drawn from the wishes of the French, Vietnamese and, to a lesser extent, Indian and Chinese perspectives. The sites visited on the first day highlighted the power and achievement of the colonial state as well as a sense of official welcome. Those of the second day were meant to further demonstrate the achievement of the state and the superiority of French civilisation. However, rather than primarily symbolising the power of the colonial state, the botanical garden, schools and museums were sites that were heavily publicised by the colonial regime as particularly benefiting the colonised. They were frequented by the broader public, and some of the schools were built specifically for indigenous pupils. Only in the later part of the tour (mostly on the last day) Tagore was taken to Vietnamese, Chinese, and Indian temples and pagodas, sites of indigenous and local spirituality, religions and customs, and thus seen as furthest removed from French civilisational influence.

Le Merle mandarin captured the French perspective precisely when it reported that the "itinerary of [Tagore's] promenades", subject to approval by the authorities, was to be put together so that it would "allow [him] to appreciate the work jointly done [by the French and the indigenous people] in the intellectual field: visit of schools, museums etc".[44] This was the perspective propagated through publications including photographs and postcards, as well as displays at exhibitions in Europe and Indochina. Temples and pagodas, on the other hand, were publicised as picturesque tourist destinations providing alterity. In other words, French officials sought to turn Tagore into a tourist and cultural diplomat of sorts, appreciating the fruits of French colonisation and, to a lesser extent, picturesque local sites. While Tagore saw himself foremost as a

Figure 1.1: People's Committee Building, Ho Chi Minh City (formerly Saigon City Hall). Source: the author.

Figure 1.2: Municipal Theatre, Ho Chi Minh City (also known as the Opera House). Source: the author.

Figure 1.3: Hotel Continental. Source: the author.

cultural missionary, for the French appreciating or engaging with Tagore's ideas was only of secondary importance and done only very selectively.

The first two buildings that Tagore was taken to, City Hall (Figure 1.1) and the Municipal Theatre, were grandiose French-style buildings (although they harboured local influences), representing an official welcome from the colonial authorities, civic spirit and culture. City Hall, completed in 1908, was modelled on the Renaissance-style Hôtel de Ville of Paris, which itself is a copy of the original building that burned down in 1871 during the suppression of the Paris Commune. The Municipal Theatre (Figure 1.2), completed around 1900, was near City Hall and the famous Hotel Continental (Figure 1.3) (built from 1878) located on Catinat Street, the most fashionable street.[45] Thus the welcome of Tagore began in the administrative, civic and tourist heart of Saigon and the mayor's greeting and a reception at City Hall showed that Tagore was to be an honoured guest of the city. Since he was invited by a French embassy, he was an official guest. That he met with the Governor of Cochinchina signalled that he was to be considered a high-level guest. However, this was a brief meeting without the presence of the public, rather than a reception. And when Tagore met with the governor general, who resided in Hanoi – the capital of the Indochinese Union – it was for "tea" with the welcome committee, an informal event that made it seem like it was an honour for Tagore to meet with the highest official of the colony and not the other way around. They discussed East–West relations, a topic of interest to Pasquier, who worried that traditional Vietnamese culture was being effaced.[46] Thus Pasquier selectively engaged with a topic that also appealed to other Europeans. As this meeting was in the afternoon of the third and last day of the tour, it functioned as a wrap-up session meant to provide Tagore with a final positive impression of a French-run colony. The itinerary reveals that the reception of Tagore was carefully orchestrated from the French perspective (likely coordinated with the government of France) to strike the right tone: he was to be a guest of the city of Saigon, rather than a guest of the state. Tagore's standing as a visitor to Indochina was higher than that given to him in France. In 1920 in Paris he was given a reception at the Musée Guimet,[47] the premier museum of Asian art in France, but not at a government building.

The sites on both the planned and the actual itineraries on the second day were meant to show off the highlights of Saigon and varied aspects of the achievements of the colonial civilising mission, but also emphasised Vietnamese perspectives and contributions. The Saigon Botanical and Zoological Garden (Figure 1.4) was considered the topmost tourist attraction of Saigon. In 1864, two years after French conquest of Saigon, the establishment of a botanical and zoological garden was decreed, and was dramatically developed under the directorship of J.B. Louis Pierre until his return to France in 1877.[48] This early establishment of the garden shows the significant place of the botanical garden in French plans

Figure 1.4: Botanical and Zoological Garden, Ho Chi Minh City. Source: the author.

for colonisation. The garden was to participate in an intercontinental system of applied botanical gardens and experimental stations, as part of the French network of gardens, with the Jardin des Plantes in Paris as the centre, to cooperate but also compete with other imperial networks. The garden was also envisioned as part of the system of regional exchange and competition for research of crops and other plants in Asia.[49] The design of the garden followed European trends which included fascination with chinoiserie and "Anglo-Chinese" styles, as well as Alphonse Alphand's parks created in Paris under the Second Empire.[50] Saigon was admired for its European architecture and wide boulevards with tall trees. Vegetation was one of the most striking traits of Saigon as observed by European visitors.[51] At dusk, Europeans, and increasingly middle-class Vietnamese, took their favourite daily drive in carriages, and later in automobiles, called the "tour de l'inspection", which went by the garden.[52]

The Botanical Garden was dramatically expanded and embellished between 1925 and 1929, under the directorship of André-René Neveu, applying plans overseen by the governors of Cochinchina Maurice Cognacq (g.1921–1926) and Paul Blanchard de la Brosse (g.1926–1929).[53] An "Annamite Temple of

Figure 1.5: Museum of Vietnamese History (formerly Musée Blanchard de la Brosse). Source: the author.

Remembrance" was built primarily for honouring fallen Vietnamese soldiers who fought in World War I. It was designed by Auguste Delaval, head of the Service Central du Bâtiments Civils. The temple was surrounded by a new French-style garden with allées of greenery and flowers.[54] A new archaeology museum (Figure 1.5), the Musée Blanchard de la Brosse, was inaugurated on 1 January 1929. Facing the temple across a wide avenue, this museum was also designed by Delaval. As with the temple, a large new garden surrounded the museum.[55] Adding to the existing nursery and arboretum of fruit trees, vast new cages for monkeys, panthers, tigers and other animals were built, as well as an ornithological museum, which was the Pavilion of Tonkin purchased at the Fair of Saigon that was turned into an aviary containing stuffed animals and birds.[56] A 500-metre-long deer park was established, and a new bridge connected across a canal to a 10-hectare English garden.[57] A new monumental metal gate (Figure 1.6) was placed at the entrance, created by students of L'École professionnelle and L'École pratique des mécaniciens asiatiques (Vocational School for Asian Mechanics).[58] Thus five months before Tagore's visit a major expansion and embellishment project of the botanical garden had been completed.

Figure 1.6: Metal gate, Botanical and Zoological Garden, Ho Chi Minh City. Source: the author.

In 1937, Louis Malleret, the conservator of the Blanchard de la Brosse Museum, would praise its syncretic design for its "balanced composition, harmonious ordering of façades" and a "calming perspective of interior courtyards" that achieved "a most flexible adaptation of an Asian-inspired architecture for modern ends".[59] The museum's octagonal rotunda with a double roof resembles the rotunda of the Louis Finot Museum (built 1925–1932) in Hanoi that was designed by Ernest Hébrard, who had been invited in 1921 by Governor General Maurice Long to create plans for the main cities of Indochina and design model architecture in Indochina.[60] Hébrard was the first architect to theorise a genuinely syncretic style inspired by vernacular architecture in Indochina. Caroline Herbelin shows that in practice it was functional aspects rather than techniques and aesthetics that Hébrard integrated from vernacular architecture.[61] Hébrard's works were appreciated in the press, but not so much by colonial officials.[62] In a 1933 obituary of Hébrard, *L'Opinion* (a Saigon-based French paper) noted that it was in Indochina that Hébrard's major projects were implemented, and that "unfortunately few people understood this great town planner or that Indochina [briefly] possessed ... one of the truly rare creative minds".[63]

Also on the second day, Tagore was to visit several schools, including the aforementioned L'École pratique des mécaniciens asiatiques (1906);[64] Collège de Jeunes Filles Indigènes (1915), the second secondary school to be established in the colonial era; and the Collège des Jeunes Filles Françaises (Lycée Marie-Curie) (1916–1918) for French girls.[65] The Lycée Pétrus Ky (Figure 1.7) (built from 1928), a secondary-school complex for the Vietnamese built on 13 hectares, was Hébrard's largest-scale building project to be realised. Hébrard drew inspiration from the Temple of Literature in Hanoi.[66] Yet, the project was his most modernist work, with three distinct areas for learning, dormitory and sport, and buildings that were evenly spaced apart that recalled in part Le Corbusier's urban-planning precepts. At the 1931 Colonial Exposition in Paris a model of the school was exhibited, and the project praised as a masterpiece remarkable for its originality, grandiose scale of conception, and adaptation to its surroundings that future schools would emulate.[67] The school was named after Pétrus (Truong Vinh) Ky (1837–1898), a Catholic linguist who worked in the colonial administration. His books helped explain Vietnamese culture to the French, and he also translated *nôm* literature into *quoc ngu* (romanised Vietnamese).[68] In the end, Tagore seems to have visited just one school, the art school in Biên Hòa, which specialised in ceramic and bronze. The school was one of those being widely publicised by the colonial regime as an example of the fruits of the civilising mission, and would be featured at the 1931 Colonial Exposition.[69]

Figure 1.7: Lê Hồng Phong High School (formerly Lycée Pétrus Ky). Source: the author.

Also on the second day, Tagore visited the tomb of Lê Văn Duyệt (1763–1832) with the society of the cult of Lê Văn Duyệt. Lê Văn Duyệt was a counsellor of Prince Nguyễn Ánh whose naval strategy enabled the defeat of other contenders for the throne in 1810. After Nguyễn Ánh became Emperor Gia Long, he acted as a diplomatic intermediary between the emperor and the Europeans visiting Vietnam, and defended Christian missionaries.[70] His grave was declared a national monument during the reign of Thiệu Trị (r.1841–1847).

Tagore was to also see the private boarding school run by Huỳnh Khương Ninh, and the house of Nguyễn Văn Của, the president of the Pétrus Ky Monument committee.[71] The latter, who was also a district chief, hosted a large party at his publishing house, which his employees – including two Bengali workers with whom Tagore talked – and the members of the welcome committee also attended.[72]

Thus, much of the second day's programme was about the activities of the Vietnamese in culture, education and spirituality, and the sites were carefully chosen to reflect a pro-French orientation. The diverse array of spiritual and religious sites on the planned and actual itineraries included sites affiliated with Christianity, although no churches were visited.

The art deco-style Eden Cinema was one of the two most elegant cinemas in the city. Centrally located off Catinat Street near City Hall and the Hotel Continental, it was divided into first- and second-class sections. Eden Cinema was a prominent urban site of leisure, culture and information, and the majority of its audience was Vietnamese by this period.[73] At the cinema, in Tagore's presence, the film company Indochine Films et Cinémas presented documentaries on Indochina, including ones for tourism publicity.[74] This company, founded in 1924, was contracted by the General Government of Indochina to exclusively produce, distribute and project films in Indochina, and it established a number of cinemas.[75] The projection of promotional films about Indochinese tourism was part of the broader efforts by the colonial government to establish the infrastructure for tourism and publicise Indochina as a tourist destination. The Economic Agency of Indochina (created in 1918 after inheriting the Agence de l'Indochine which was established in 1903), located in Paris and in charge of publicising Indochina and its economic opportunities including by participating in exhibitions, accumulated a great number of photographs as well as some films.[76] In 1928 the government created the Office Indochinois du Tourisme et le Bureau de la Propagande, and the same year Thomas Cook, American Express, and the Messageries Maritimes together founded a travel agency, the Tourism Bureau of Indochina, in Saigon.[77]

In the morning of the third day, Tagore went to Catinat Street and nearby streets, visiting several Indian shops and a Vietnamese fabric store where he watched the weaving and dying of silk textile and also purchased some silk.[78] He also had a Vietnamese tunic made for himself by a tailor.[79] He stopped by the editorial bureau of *Phụ Nữ Tân Văn*, a nascent Vietnamese-language women's weekly that had been launched a month earlier.[80] Later in the day, he attended a reception organised by the Chinese Chamber at the "Cantonese Pagoda" (Chùa Bà Thiên Hậu) in Cholon, where he conversed about the significance of Chinese culture in Asia.[81]

Some of Tagore's activities on this last day, such as visiting shops on Catinat Street and visiting the "Cantonese Pagoda", could be potentially considered as typically touristic, in that these were sites popular with tourists. However, the Tamil temple that Tagore also visited that day had a local significance that was not all positive. Tagore, along with Bùi Quang Chiêu and Lefebvre, participated in a religious ceremony at the Sri Thenday Yuttapani Temple, built by Tamil Chettiars around 1880.[82] A girl chanted a song by the Indian poet Passecarane, and the Indians presented to Tagore money they had raised from the Indian community.[83] The oldest of the three main Tamil temples located in central Saigon, this temple was known locally as "the Chetty Temple", although the temple was frequented not only by Chettiars but a diverse group of Tamils including Christians who were French citizens and functionaries.[84] The complex interconnections among Tamils is also indicated by the fact that one administrative council oversaw both the Sri Thenday Yutthapani Temple and the Tamil mosque located at Amiral Dupré Street (now 66 Đông Du Street).[85] Indians had been awaiting Tagore's visit for a while. Five years earlier, in July 1924, anticipating a visit by Tagore, a group of Indians of Saigon and Cholon gathered at the Sri Thenday Yutthapani Temple and elected members of a welcome committee, including a renounced Indian, "four Chettiars, two Muslims, four Indian French subjects, four Bombay merchants, four Hindus and three Parsis".[86] The committee sent a welcome programme, that featured a procession with elephants and music, to Saigon newspapers; a visit of Angkor was planned as well.[87]

Tagore's visit to the temple was not widely reported in French- or Vietnamese-language papers. The situation of Tamil Chettiars in Saigon was fraught with controversy. Chetty moneylenders were, although only a small part of the diverse Indian population in Indochina, highly visible and despised by both the Vietnamese and French due to their exploitation of poor peasants and perceived lack of financial contribution to the local economy, as they repatriated much of their profits to India.[88] *L'Écho annamite* reported on the popular annual festival organised by the temple, famous for a parade featuring a silver float and fireworks, with an ambivalent tone. In 1926 the paper reported that "our Chettiars know how to liven up the public [with their festival] and calculate the interest of their loans at 36% with equal skill".[89]

Tensions in Tourism and Urban Development

The "Chetty Temple" was far from the only site that Tagore visited that was fraught with tension. Underneath the glamour and glitter of monumental buildings, and the signs of progress shown by museums and schools, there were pervasive tensions that stirred controversies. In French Indochina tourism was mostly planned and managed by or through contracts with the colonial government, from the creation of an overall plan to the infrastructure, including roads and grand hotels.[90] The centralised plan for tourism, of which Angkor was the most significant attraction, was one of the aspects of colonialism that provided volition for a unified sense of Indochina increasingly shared in particular by the Vietnamese but not by Cambodians or Laotians.

However, many aspects of this programme for tourism were intensely criticised by the Vietnamese, some French civilians, and even functionaries. Bockor Palace, built by the Resident Superior of Cambodia François Baudoin (r.1914–1927) at the top of the Elephant Massif in Kampot, Cambodia and which opened in 1925, was infamous for the fact that hundreds of people lost their lives building the road to the site. In 1920, the interim Resident Superior of Cambodia Georges Maspéro temporarily halted the road construction as a "humanitarian measure", noting that 331 prisoners out of the 800 to 900 working on the road died in less than two and a half years.[91] While Maspéro's report was not known to the public, it was well known that R.A. Lortat-Jacob, during his defence of Cambodian villagers accused of murdering the Resident of Kompong Chhnang Felix Louis Bardez, linked this murder to the construction of Bockor Palace. He called the route to Bockor "the Appian way bordered by tombs", which an inspector of colonies described as "the model of what not to do".[92] Many Cambodians and Vietnamese regarded Bockor Palace as the unwise and wasteful fancy of a single man, not only due to the human toll but also given the 6 metres of annual rainfall and frequent heavy fog.[93] The isolated location was hard to reach and therefore upkeep of the hotel was difficult, and it was not in any way helpful for visiting Angkor.

While Bockor Palace was a singularly notorious grand hotel, the whole programme of having luxury, grand hotels built by the Société des Grands Hôtels (SGH) financed through heavy government subsidies was often criticised by Vietnamese papers as a costly project that added to the heavy burden placed on indigenous taxpayers. *L'Écho annamite* lambasted the contract signed in 1924 between SGH and the government as a scandalous ruse on the part of SGH. The firm's initial capital was only 25,000 piastres (250,000 francs). Building five grand hotels – including the Hotel Le Royal in Phnom Penh that opened in 1929 and the Raffles Grand Hotel d'Angkor (Figure 1.8) which would open in 1932 – for a total of 1.2 million piastres (12 million francs) required heavy government subsidies.[94] Such a venture seemed to fit all too well into a pattern

Figure 1.8: Raffles Grand Hotel d'Angkor, Siem Reap. Source: the author.

of French entrepreneurs coming to Indochina with little funds of their own but, thanks to connections with highly placed officials, starting and running extremely lucrative projects with large amounts of capital. *L'Éveil économique de l'Indochine*, a French paper published in Hanoi, also regularly criticised the authorities' vision of what it called "haute tourisme", tourism for the rich, seemingly aimed at a tiny minority of wealthy Americans. The paper argued that instead of building grand hotels at great cost to the state and taxpayers, the government should encourage private entrepreneurs to build and maintain much more modest-scale hotels that could actually make a profit.[95] The paper praised the Morin family who built hotels in Hue with their own funds, and accused SGH, in consort with the government, of attempting to ruin the Morins' enterprise.[96]

It is notable that Tagore was not taken to or put up in any of the grand hotels. In Saigon he stayed in a private residence.[97] This highlights the distinction between him and the wealthy tourists the grand hotels were aimed at. Although much of his itinerary resembled that of a foreign tourist, grand hotels were a point of divergence, since, particularly given the controversy, they were not widely viewed as sites showcasing the benefits of colonisation. French authorities who planned the tourism infrastructure conceived tourism as potentially contributing greatly to the colony's economy and, eventually, to the overall well-being of society, as Aline Demay argues.[98] Yet, the lack of consensus even among the French on the benefits of centralised, top-down, publicly funded tourism development was not something the authorities would have liked Tagore to observe. It was especially unlikely for Tagore to be taken to Bockor Palace, around which swirled intense controversies in the order of ethics and economic impact.

Another site Tagore visited that was subject to controversy was the Municipal Theatre. The theatre season was a point of contention, because French theatre troupes visiting Saigon for performances during the season were given significant subsidies, which many Vietnamese thought could be much better used to help the poorer sectors of the society. In 1924 the nascent Indochine Films et Cinémas agreed to run the theatre season in addition to the film industry and received 80,000 piastres (800,000 francs), double the amount of the subsidy given in the previous season.[99] The justification was that in 1922–1923 the quality of the performances was so low that hardly anyone attended – subsequently leading to the cancellation of the 1923–1924 theatre season – and that more funding was needed in order to attract a better troupe.[100] The Municipal Theatre, then, was another example of how monumental buildings were built and managed, as well as what they symbolised, and that they provided fodder for continually contentious debates. Because the audience at the theatre was largely French, it was not seen as benefiting the indigenous populace the way the botanical garden, schools or museums did. Further, that Indochine Films et Cinémas ran the Municipal Theatre showcases the dominance of this company in both theatre and film, and also its connections to the colonial government.

The gap between what the French officials hoped Tagore to appreciate through visits to colonial buildings, and the controversies swirling around many such buildings within the colonial society, reveals the limits of the symbolic and disciplinary power of monumental architecture and points to the need to resituate such architecture as shared and lived in spaces with fluctuating and evolving meanings and uses.

Tagore's Ideas and Vietnamese Debates

Tagore's visit created a festive atmosphere but also highlighted political divisions among the Vietnamese. In this period, anti-colonialist leaders such as Phan Bội Châu, Phan Châu Trinh (who died in 1926), Nguyễn An Ninh, and numerous others were persecuted by the colonial regime for their political activities. There was street violence and numerous strikes, and both anti-colonial and reformist movements galvanised large sectors of the Vietnamese public.[101] Tagore's visit occasioned reflections on the shared cultural heritage of India and Vietnam, and also inevitable comparisons between the two colonised regions. In presenting Tagore to the public at the Municipal Theatre, Bùi Quang Chiêu recalled the atmosphere of spirituality and serenity in Santiniketan, where Tagore officiated a

Hindu ceremony at which students recited songs and Tagore chanted. Bùi Quang Chiêu noted that Tagore envisioned the "Asian ideal" coming to rescue a Europe "threatened by unbridled materialism".

> Tagore does not cultivate a narrow nationalism: he would like to unite Hinduism, Islam, Buddhism and Christianity in the harmony of an active cooperation … towards the cult of the beautiful, good and true. … [He seeks] a coordination of the civilizations of the East and the West in order to give to the world their full generating value of beauty and goodness. … The French, Indians, Chinese and Annamites are united in the same spirit of universal fraternity.[102]

The socialist mayor, Béziat, then paid tribute to the "magnificent privilege of a marvellous life" led by Tagore, "wholly dedicated to the cult of the beautiful and the pursuit of the most noble human ideal: the universal fraternity".[103] Thus both Bùi Quang Chiêu and Béziat highlighted Tagore's pursuit of East–West syncretism and universalism as well as poetic beauty, and the former also expressed his vision of a harmonious colonial society and aversion to "narrow nationalism".

Then Dương Văn Giao, in the name of the Vietnamese, spoke. He paid tribute to the profound influence of the civilisation of India, "alma mater of all the nations," on the "Indo-Chinese peninsula". Although "ancient India was dismembered, looted, ravaged, conquered successively":

> thanks to her religious faith, her secular moral incentives, and her customs and manners against which time has had no influence, India still emerges amidst dispersed empires in the dust, following the course of her own destiny.
>
> And you have come here today … to give us the proof of her extraordinary vitality. Thanks to you, our traditions and our relationships are going to be renewed usefully from now on.[104]

Dương Văn Giao emphasised cultural flow from India towards the Indochinese region. He then went on to conclude his speech in a potentially provocative way:

> You avoid, you disdain politics, and you are right.
>
> A spirit such as yours should not stop at such limited horizons but take a flight and move well above human passions. The primary duty of a Brahman, a priest that you are, is to open … the temple's door to anxious souls.

> You dispense the secret of peace. You are, Teacher, a pacifist.
> It takes much more courage and heroism to dare to be a pacifist when one is a citizen of a conquered country!
>
> Please believe that your lesson is heard. … the Annamite people aren't motivated by hate at all. Their labour is also aimed at a friendship with the whole world; they also struggle for the life of the soul.[105]

Dương Văn Giao's speech can be read as – albeit discreetly – anti-colonialist, in its references to the history and contemporary reality of India being conquered and subjugated. And the phrase "It takes much more courage and heroism to dare to be a pacifist when one is a citizen of a conquered country" could be seen as an ironic one expressing a criticism that could not be directly pronounced for fear of provoking the colonial authorities. The reference to Tagore being a Brahman could potentially be read as part of a discreet reproach as well, reminding the audience that he holds a very privileged status in society, one that makes it easier for him to sidestep the ideological and political struggles of those of lower stations in life. We see tensions between Bùi Quang Chiêu's Francophilia and praise of universalism, on the one hand, and Dương Văn Giao's view of Tagore's ideals as separated from political realities.

Then Tagore spoke. He said he brings "the memory of an encounter … that awoke the soul of this country, to thread it into a new path of accomplishment, with all the wealth in Art and Ideas". He said he sensed that this "distant India came" in him "to visit once again her abandoned home".[106] He concluded:

> Please know that before human joys and human miseries, my heart always beats with the same rhythm as that of those of my predecessors who in the most distant past lived among you. My voice always expresses man's aspiration towards Light, Love and Liberty. It is always for the triumph of the divine martyr over all that is basely cruel and meanly selfish. I bring you the greetings of that radiant India, who lavished her light on this land, as well as the message of sympathy and brotherhood of present India who lives separated from you by geographic distance and by the dead solitude of her own darkness.[107]

Thus, Tagore invoked India's cultural contribution in the region in the creation of the rich and vital shared past as well as his ideals, the themes harking back to the poem "Sagarika". In the last sentence, he also discreetly referred to the shared fate of India and Indochina as colonies. The speech did not really elaborate on his key ideas that were interesting to the Vietnamese, thus leaving considerable space for interpretation and potentially frustrating attempts at gleaning precise implications and advice. The universal ideals and the historical contribution of the Indian Hindu civilisation in Indochina that Tagore invoked left ambiguity as to how the past could reinspire and renew the current society, or how the "Asian ideal" Bùi Quang Chiêu mentioned could help in forging ahead in the colonial situation.

It was well known that Tagore considered Hinduism to have provided India, marked by a great diversity of races, with a unity in the realm of ideas.[108] He accepted the invitation to tour Indochina because he hoped to visit Angkor, which he likely saw as a centre of the flowering of Indian Hindu civilisation. This view was precisely what many of the Indians of Saigon wished to publicise on the occasion of Tagore's visit; they were already eagerly anticipating his visit to Angkor in 1924.[109] *Réveil Saigonnais*, a paper for Indian French subjects, saw Tagore's visit as an occasion not only for unifying the Indians of Vietnam, but also for asserting the notion of Greater India – Indian influence in Asia in ancient times.[110] However, such a view could be potentially provocative – in Vietnam and Cambodia in different ways – in its implications of pan-Asianism with Indian Hindu civilisation as the centre. The view that Angkor and Southeast Asia had been largely influenced by India (as well as China) had also been propagated by Europeans as the name "Indochina" indicates.[111]

Tagore's hope that Asian civilisation could come to the rescue of a West threatened by materialism was shared by many Indian intellectuals who emphasised Indian spirituality. They agreed with the European perception of India's civilisation as highly spiritual, and also the view, widespread since the mid nineteenth century, of "Asia" as the cradle of world's civilisations.[112] Europeans saw Indian civilisation (including in Angkor) as having subsequently fallen into stasis while European civilisation continued to evolve.[113] Tagore noted that Europeans saw the ideals of the East as "static", without "impetus ... to open out new vistas of knowledge and power".[114] Tagore was getting at a core Western imperialist rhetoric. Indeed, Malleret believed that many of the 200,000 annual visitors of the Blanchard de la Brosse Museum "see, in the development of the Museum, the promise of a fruitful alliance of the active thought of the West and the meditative wisdom of old Asia".[115] In Tagore's vision, however, Europe's own evolution was unbalanced and ultimately self-destructive due to its heavily materialist orientation.

The speeches by the Vietnamese allow us to glean why many Vietnamese were enthusiastic about Tagore's visit, but also how they tried to get at the questions and paradoxes his ideas raised, and assess their applicability. Tagore was a colonised subject from Asia who rose to a unique standing in the world and, as such, many Vietnamese hoped that he could inspire them to create a plan for the future. Yet many found it difficult to wholly adhere to Tagore's vision of universal fraternity, deeming it a poet's ideal impossible to aspire to under the condition of colonisation. Dương Văn Lời wrote in *L'Écho annamite* that during World War I India made great sacrifices to aid England, but that after the war, England, instead of providing promised reforms, suppressed existing liberties. India revolted, and since Gandhi declared non-cooperation in 1920, India was living "a life of hell". Tagore, a "victim of imperialism and suffocating material civilization", Lời asserted, who sings "his serene indifference", choosing to ignore that "European and American civilisation is imperialist and utilitarian and increasingly tends to turn the universe into a 'generalised West'." Tagore's appeal for a universal university and East–West cooperation would be in vain, "so long as one half of men subject the other half to dependence".[116] Lời's view of Tagore was unfair, given Tagore's criticism of Western imperialism and nationalism which he saw as causing World War I.[117] In 1930 in the US he would say in a lecture that "a great portion of the world suffers from your civilisation".[118] Lời also overlooked Tagore's subtle reference to India's state of subjugation in his phrase. Lời's view was akin to how many Chinese intellectuals saw Tagore as a man from "a lost country". For those who saw political action and a rebuilding of the very foundation of society as the most urgent task, a regeneration of Eastern spirituality could be seen as a reactionary and dangerous ideal.

Tagore and many of the Vietnamese seemed to agree on one major point: India was continuing to chart its course in the face of dominance and dismemberment. In this period "India" and "Indochina" were increasingly redefined as "countries" or "nations".[119] The very conception of cultural flow from one region to another as two wholly separate and distinct entities, yet both within "Asia" as distinct from the "West", was a modern one. Tagore was seen as an emissary for proving the vitality of an India seen as timeless. What Tagore himself described as "the looseness of [India's] diversity and the feebleness of its unity"[120] could provide a model for the emerging idea of the Vietnamese nation. This new nation could be redefined as possessing a continuous history with deep-rooted connections to the broader surrounding region, with the influence of European civilisation having much more recent origins. Even if the latter were considered crucial for the future, it could be seen as subordinate to the destiny of the nation, similar to the way in which India's destiny was seen as being based on its ancient past. However, for those who considered modernisation to be the primary force of progress, some of Tagore's key ideas proved problematic.

Some tensions among the Vietnamese erupted into open hostility towards Tagore. Just before his departure (several hours after his visit to the "Chetty Temple"), some members of the Vietnamese Labor Party showed up and criticised him for failing to give a talk to the peasants as he had promised, or showing gratitude to the labourers.[121] Lê Thành Lư told Tagore to "take a look at the people who had come to this land to suck the blood [of the Vietnamese]".[122] The interpreter did not translate this. By "the people" he clearly meant Chetty moneylenders whom he was referring to as Tagore's fellow compatriots. Such linking of Tagore, however implicit, to Chetty moneylenders was only one part of a wide spectrum of Vietnamese reactions and ideas brought forth by Tagore's visit. However, such a reference also highlights the prevailing negative perception of Tamil moneylenders as materialistic exploiters, in stark contrast with the spiritual and peaceful influence of Hindu civilisation that Tagore invoked. Tagore's visit to the "Chetty Temple" thus exposed an instance of the mutual misunderstanding of the hopes of Tagore, the Indians of Saigon who sought to emphasise the same type of history in order to elevate their own status in Saigon, and the Vietnamese who had a different, and far-from-uniform, set of hopes.

It was in southern Vietnam much more than in East Asia that Tagore's universalism, syncretism and pan-Asianism had striking resonances, in particular with Cao Dai, a syncretic religion with a nationalist political character formally established in 1926. Founded on the belief in the essential unity of all humanity, Cao Dai's revered figures include Jesus, Kuan Yin, Li Bo, Sun Yat-sen, Buddha Gautama, Confucius, Victor Hugo and Joan of Arc.[123] Many Vietnamese admirers of Tagore had strong ties to Cao Dai. Nguyễn An Ninh was fascinated with Cao Dai,[124] Bùi Quang Chiêu was a Freemason who collaborated with Caodaists, many of whom were in the Constitutionalist Party, and Nguyễn Phan Long, the founder of *L'Écho annamite* (and a future prime minister), would become a Caodaist by 1937.[125] Lê Văn Duyệt's spirit appeared at Cao Dai seances.[126] Cao Dai's nationalist orientation went against what many saw as Tagore's pacifism, but Tagore, along with Gandhi – whose impact is much better documented – clearly influenced Cao Dai to develop ideas of Asian spirituality, a pan-Asian liberation movement, and respect for Asian arts and literature.[127] Here, the dream of a renewed pan-Asian spiritual civilisation was not wholly rejected among many non-communist nationalists and reformists.[128] However, the nationalistic tone of Cao Dai reveals that this was a case of the "mistranslation" of Tagore's ideas.[129] The syncretic architecture of the Cao Dai Temple, built from 1933 in Tay Ninh, blended styles of Baroque churches with their twin towers and elongated layout (although the temple narrows towards the alter, symbolising the soul's journey towards enlightenment), Vietnamese and Chinese temples, and even Peranankan villas. In the interior, pink columns encircled by dragons reach up to a domed ceiling that represents heaven. In this way, the renewed spiritual civilisation could also be seen as bringing syncretic modernity.

Conclusion

In Saigon of 1929 Tagore was received as a guest of higher standing than he had been in France or England. As not only a worldly traveller and celebrity, but also a citizen of a colony visiting another colony, he hardly fit the figure of an ideal tourist targeted by the French authorities, since he was not a wealthy, leisure-seeking American or European staying at luxury hotels. Yet, there were inevitable overlaps between Tagore's itinerary and that of an ideal tourist, as the French sought to impress Tagore with the beauty of Saigon, and the architectural and cultural signs of the positive effects of colonisation by mobilising the power of space and architecture.

However, far from being just nodes of power, grand architectural structures such as luxury hotels and the Municipal Theatre were the subject of controversies that undermined the credibility of the colonial government and colonialism itself. Bockor Palace was widely seen as a symbol of colonial oppression and waste. While schools and museums were certainly more appreciated by the Vietnamese public, the French rationale for building them also supplied justification for colonialism. Yet the schools, museums and temples Tagore visited were far from simply being signs of a well-functioning colonial society; they could be experienced and interpreted in a multitude of ways. The construction of architecturally impressive schools did little to improve the big picture of education: only a tiny fraction of the population received any secondary education.[130] Even the botanical garden, a site genuinely enjoyed by the broader public, could be a potentially tense site, given that one of its initial, instrumental purposes of plant research linked it to exploitative plantations. Also, having the new Temple of Annamite Memory be designed by a French architect could be perceived as an arrogant gesture on the part of the colonial regime. The tomb of Lê Văn Duyệt also had a variety of meanings; Lê Văn Duyệt was seen not only as a defender of Christians but also a patriotic national hero and a source of inspiration for Cao Dai. Tagore spoke at the "Cantonese Pagoda" about Chinese cultural influence in Asia, but for the locals, the Chinese in Cholon were the drivers of the modern economy. Even the Sri Thenday Yuttapani Temple, identified reductively as a "Chetty Temple", was a centre of a diverse Indian population with complex ties to the broader society. Rather than sites of fixed symbolic meanings of power dynamics, all of these spaces and structures were shared spaces with layers of meaning and experience.

The welcome committee and the itinerary put together for Tagore were officially vetted to reflect a pro-French orientation and a strict hierarchy. Yet, it was the Constitutionalists who overall organised Tagore's visit. The Vietnamese saw Tagore not only as a great Hindu poet but as a representative of the cultural and spiritual heritage of the Indian subcontinent and also the emerging Indian nation. The visit stirred pride in the richness and strength of shared Indian and

Vietnamese cultural heritage, but also revealed the diversity of opinions among the Vietnamese as well as their anguish in seeking a clear path to follow.[131] Many of the Vietnamese saw Tagore's message of universal fraternity as idealistic, preferring Gandhi's overtly political movement, and were frustrated by the lack of clarity regarding the meanings and implications of universal fraternity and pan-Asian syncretism. Further, Tagore's emphasis on the Indian Hindu civilisation brought out tensions surrounding Chetty moneylenders. Other Vietnamese, as Chi Pham highlights, fixated on Tagore's striking appearance with piercing eyes,[132] falling back not only on the long-standing trope of the wandering holy man (with mysterious powers), but also on the modern stereotype of the celebrity performer. At the same time, Tagore's poetic musings on the influence of India on Southeast Asia as expressed in "Sagarika" continued to have a powerful afterlife not only on history and literature but also tourism – a topic that needs further investigation.

Tagore's visit instigated a spectrum of aspirations, and in the process underscored the hierarchical and stratified nature of colonial society into which Tagore landed awkwardly as a celebrated guest. The notion of the historical Greater India marked by harmony, peace and pan-Hinduism that Tagore was implicitly propagating did not correspond neatly to the reality of the role of the Chetty moneylenders in Saigon. And that the latter sought to emphasise the same Greater India only served to highlight ethnic stratification and irk some of the Vietnamese. Paradoxically, what was at the heart of Tagore's visit was something absent: it was Angkor, which Tagore actually wished to visit as tangible evidence of the influence of ancient India. It was also Angkor that the French were heavily promoting as the centre of their efforts at developing tourism in Indochina and thus they would have been glad to see Tagore visit, but for the different reason of showcasing French contribution in "discovering", "restoring", protecting, and turning it into a destination for modern tourism. In this regard, the aims of Tagore and the French were mutually mistranslated.

Tagore's syncretism clearly influenced southern Vietnam, with marked tendencies of religious syncretism and flexible, creative interpretation. It was the definition of the "East" and "West" as entirely distinct entities from the early nineteenth century that eventually gave birth to the notion of syncretism or hybridity, which presupposes two wholly separate cultures. While Tagore fought the notion that the East was stagnant, he accepted the idea that it was essentially different from the West. Regardless, the architectural syncretism of new museums and some of the schools of the Saigon region were far from isolated or unique manifestations but rather an integral part of a rapidly evolving culture in which customs and trends from diverse sources were continuously integrated into daily life.[133] Syncretism, thus redefined, was much closer to the norm rather than being the exception.

Notes

1. I would like to thank the editors, Vimalin Rujivacharakul, Samuel K. Parker, Judith Henchy, Philippe Peycam, Janet Hoskins, Sonora Jha, and the anonymous reviewers for their comments and suggestions on this essay.
2. The main reason why this visit is little known seems to be that Tagore did not write anything about it. Chi Pham is the first to extensively analyse the visit particularly from the Vietnamese perspective; Pham, "The Rise and the Fall of Rabindranath Tagore in Vietnam," Unpublished master's thesis, U.C. Riverside (2012).
3. Sabyasachi Bhattacharya, *Rabindranath Tagore: An Interpretation* (New Delhi: Penguin Books, 2011), 140.
4. Ibid., 133, 140–42; Marie-Roberte Guignard, Bernard Pauly and Jean Bruno ed., *Rabindranath Tagore: 1861–1941*, exhibition catalogue (Paris: Bibliothèque nationale, 1961), 24.
5. Tagore's letter to Harriet Monroe, cited in Bhattacharya, *Rabindranath Tagore*, 142. The influence of literature and tourism has been best studied in the case of Britain and the US; see for example George G. Dekker, *The Fictions of Romantic Tourism: Radcliffe, Scott, and Mary Shelley* (Stanford, CA: Stanford University Press, 2005); N. Watson and Richard H. Gassan ed., *Literary Tourism and Nineteenth-Century Culture* (New York: Palgrave Macmillan, 2009). The connections between celebrity and tourism, especially outside of Britain and the US, are under-studied.
6. On this topic see H. Hazel Hahn, "Indian Princes, Tigers and Dancing Girls: The Tour of the Prince of Wales through India and Ceylon, 1875–1876," *Postcolonial Studies* 12/2 (June 2009), 173–192.
7. The history of tourism in the US in particular has been expanding. See, for example, *The Birth of American Tourism: New York, the Hudson Valley, and American Culture, 1790–1835* (Amherst: University of Massachusetts Press, 2008). On colonial tourism in Indochina see Aline Demay, *Tourism and Colonization in Indochina 1898–1939* (Cambridge: Cambridge Scholars Publishing, 2014); Eric Jennings, *Imperial Heights: Dalat and the Making and Undoing of French Indochina* (Berkeley: University of California Press, 2012).
8. William Radice, "Introduction," *Rabindranath Tagore, Selected Poems* (London: Penguin, 1994), 23.
9. Radice, "Introduction," 23. In my essay the terms "East" and "West" should be considered as always being in quotes.
10. Bhattacharya, *Rabindranath Tagore*, 133.
11. See Samit Das, *Architecture of Santiniketan: Tagore's Concept of Space* (New Delhi: Niyogi Books, 2012).
12. Rabindranath Tagore, *The Message of India to Japan: A Lecture* (New York: The Macmillan Company, 1916), 15.
13. Ibid., 16–21, 29.

14. Guignard, Pauly and Bruno ed., *Rabindranath Tagore*, 22; Bhattacharya, *Rabindranath Tagore*, 23.
15. Guignard, Pauly and Bruno ed., *Rabindranath Tagore*, 24.
16. Pankaj Mishra, *From the Ruins of Empire: The Intellectuals who Remade Asia* (New York: Farrar, Straus and Giroux, 2012), 219, 235–240.
17. Guignard, Pauly and Bruno ed., *Rabindranath Tagore*, 26.
18. Sagarika Chakraborty, "Tagore the Diplomat," *Muse India* 68 (July–Aug. 2016), http://www.museindia.com/focuscontent.asp?issid=33&id=2134.
19. See note No. 4.
20. Roland Lardinois, *Scholars and Prophets: Sociology of India from France in the 19th–20th Centuries*, trans. Renuka George (New York and Abingdon: Routledge, 2018), 251.
21. Bhattacharya, *Rabindranath Tagore*, 134.
22. Ibid., 137–139.
23. Ibid., 135–137; Mishra, *From the Ruins of Empire*, 225–226.
24. Philippe Peycam, *The Birth of Vietnamese Political Journalism: Saigon, 1916–1930* (New York: Columbia University Press, 2011), 127–218.
25. "Rabindranath Tagore à Saigon," *L'Écho annamite*, 22 June 1929, 1; Ralph Smith, *Vietnam and the West* (Ithaca: Cornell University Press, 1971), 96–97.
26. Supryia Roy, "Rabindranath Tagore: Stopover at Saigon" (Unpublished Papers of the Conference of R. Tagore in Hanoi, November 2011), cited in Pham, "The Rise and the Fall of Rabindranath Tagore in Vietnam," 10.
27. Pham, "The Rise and the Fall."
28. "Rabindranath Tagore à Saigon," *Le Merle mandarin: Satirique hebdomadaire*, 28 June 1929, 2.
29. Rolland was Tagore's most steadfast foreign friend, and Gide translated several of Tagore's works beginning in 1913. Guignard, Pauly and Bruno ed., *Rabindranath Tagore*, 121.
30. *L'Écho annamite*, *La Tribine indochinoise* and *La Clôche felée* all cited them.
31. Guignard, Pauly and Bruno ed., *Rabindranath Tagore*, 25.
32. Goloubew Victor, "Sylvain Lévi et l'Indochine," *Bulletin de l'École française d'Extrême-Orient* 35 (1935), 553–554.
33. Ibid., 555–557. At a talk at AFIMA (Association pour la Formation Intellectuelle et Morale des Annamites) Lévi criticised the English education system for Indians which, in his view, through English disdain of Hindi and Bengali, resulted in deeply wounded Hindu sentiment. Victor, "Sylvain Lévi et l'Indochine," 558. Lévi, who leaned towards socialism, also criticised Tagore for poorly understanding world politics. Lardinois, *Scholars and Prophets*, 260.
34. Sylvain Lévi, *Indochine* (Paris: Société d'éditions géographiques, maritimes et coloniales, 1931).
35. Guignard, Pauly and Bruno ed., *Rabindranath Tagore*, 27.

36. "Réception de Rabindranath Tagore et Programme de reception," *L'Écho annamite*, 20 June 1929, 1.
37. "Chronique de Saigon: Reception de Rabindranath Tagore," *L'Écho annamite*, 17 June 1929, 2. "Réception de Rabindranath Tagore," *L'Écho annamite*, 20 June 1929, 1.
38. "Réception de Rabindranath Tagore," *L'Écho annamite*, 20 June 1929, 1.
39. Pham, "The Rise and the Fall," 10.
40. "Rabindra Nath Tagore est arrivé," *La Tribune indochinoise*, 21 June 1929, 1.
41. "Rabindranath Tagore à Saigon," *Le Merle mandarin*, 28 June 1929, 2.
42. "Rabindranath Tagore à Saigon," *L'Écho annamite*, 18 June 1929, 1.
43. "Un thé en l'honneur de Tagore," *L'Écho annamite*, 24 June 1929, 2.
44. "Réception à Saigon de Rabindranath Tagore," *Le Merle mandarin*, 21 June 1929, 3. That this article was published on p. 3 shows that the French did not consider Tagore's visit to be as important as the Indians or the Vietnamese did. The first column of this edition was "Nouvelles de Paris. Revue de la presse."
45. The Municipal Theatre was designed by Félix Ollivier, Ernest Guichard and Eugène Ferret.
46. "Un thé en l'honneur de Tagore," *L'Écho annamite*, 24 June 1929, 2. On Pasquier see David G. Marr, *Vietnamese Tradition on Trial, 1920–1945* (Berkeley: University of California Press, 1981), 293.
47. *The Collegian and Progress of India: A Fortnightly Journal of Indian Educational Progress in All Its Branches*, 14–16 (1920), 259; catalogue, 24.
48. Govindsamy Agoramoorthy and Minna J. Hsu, "Saigon Zoo and Botanical Gardens," *Encyclopedia of the World's Zoos* vol. 3, ed. Catharine E. Bell, 1105. The size of the garden remained 12 hectares until 1875. Corroy, *Annales du Jardin botanique et de la Ferme expérimentale des Mare (Cochinchine française)* (Saigon: Imprimerie du gouvernement, 1878), 575; Nguyễn Nghĩa Thìn, "Saigon Botanic Garden – The First Botanic Garden in Vietnam," BGCI.org Botanic Gardens Conservation International 2:4 (Dec. 1994). http://www.bgci.org/resources/article/0183/.
49. James E. McClellan III, *Colonialism and Science: Saint Domingue and the Old Regime* (Chicago: The University of Chicago Press, 2010), 149.
50. Gwendolyn Wright, *The Politics of Design in French Colonial Urbanism* (Chicago and London: University of Chicago. Press, 1991), 174.
51. Pierre Barrelon, "Saïgon," *Le Tour du monde* vol. 65–66 (1893), 238.
52. Ibid., 232.
53. "Les travaux d'embellissement du Jardin Botanique de Saïgon," *L'Impartial*, excerpted in *L'Éveil économique de l'Indochine*, 18 March 1928, 19.
54. "Les travaux d'embellissement," 19; "Le jardin botanique de Saïgon," *L'Impartial*, excerpted in *L'Éveil économique de l'Indochine*, 11 January 1925, 19.
55. "Les travaux d'embellissement," 19.
56. "Le jardin botanique de Saïgon," 19.

57. Ibid., 19.
58. "Les travaux d'embellissement," 19.
59. Musée Blanchard de la Brosse, *Catalogue général de collections par Louis Malleret* vol. 1 (Hanoi: Imprimerie d'Extrême-Orient 1937–1938), 22.
60. Arnauld Le Brusq, *Le Vietnam à travers l'architecture coloniale* (Paris: Editions de l'Amateur, 1999), 5–6. On Hébard's "Indochinese style" see Caroline Herbelin, "*Construire le style indochinois*: Identity Formation through Geopolitical Territory and Architecture," in *Architecturalized Asia: Mapping a Continent through History*, ed. Vimalin Rujivacharakul et al. (Hong Kong University Press and University of Hawai'i Press, 2013).
61. Herbelin, "*Construire le style indochinois*," 179.
62. William Logan, *Hanoi: Biography of a City* (Seattle: University of Washington Press, 2000), 107; Herbelin, "*Construire le style indochinois*," 180.
63. "Décès de M. Ernest-Michel-Hébrard," *L'Opinion*, excerpted in *L'Eveil écnomique de l'Indochine*, 9 April 1933, 18.
64. Xavier Guillaume and Marie-Christine Guillaume, *La Terre du Dragon: Voyage à travers le Viet-Nam* vol. 1 (Paris: Éditions Publibook, 2004), 38.
65. Guillaume and Guillaume, *La Terre du Dragon*, 36.
66. Ibid., 37.
67. Indochine. Direction de l'instruction publique, *La Cochinchine scolaire: l'enseignement dans le pays le plus évolué de l'Union indochinoise* (Hanoi: Imprimerie d'Extrême-Orient, 1931), 25–26.
68. Guillaume and Guillaume, *La Terre du Dragon*, 63–65, Justin J. Corfield, *Historical Dictionary of Ho Chi Minh City* (London & New York: Anthem Press, 2013), 146.
69. Indochine française, Section des services d'intérêt social, Direction générale de l'instruction publique, *Trois écoles d'art de l'Indochine: Hanoï, Phnom-Penh, Bien-Hoa. Exposition coloniale internationale, Paris 1931* (Hanoi: Imprimerie d'Extrême-Orient, 1931), 34.
70. "Le Van Duyet," Britannica http://www.britannica.com/EBchecked/topic/333453/Le-Van-Duyet. Accessed 15 October 2014.
71. "Société Annamite de Crédit," *L'Écho annamite* 20 July 1928, 4. Nguyen Van Cua was listed as a publisher; *L'Echo annamite*, 17 March 1928, 2. His house was at 13 Rue Lucien Mossard, Saigon. "Réception â Saigon de Rabindranath Tagore," *Le Merle mandarin*, 21 June 1929, 3.
72. "Ba ngày thi sĩ R. Tagore ở Saigon," *Đuốc Nhà Nam*, 27 June 27, 1929, cited in Chi Pham, "Rabindranath Tagore in Colonial Vietnam and Anti-colonial Nationalisms," unpublished essay. Thanks to Chi Pham for sharing this essay.
73. Dang Bui, "The Cinemas of Old Saigon," *The Saigoneer*, 4 September 2014. http://saigoneer.com/saigon-buildings/2630-the-cinemas-of-old-saigon. Accessed 15 October 2014. The cinema was located at the rear of the Eden Arcade, inside an art deco building built around 1947. The building and the cinema

were demolished in 2010. Marguerite Duras wrote a play titled *L'Eden Cinéma* (1977). Her mother worked as a pianist at the cinema. Matt Gross, "The Saigon of Marguerite Duras," *The New York Times*, 30 April 2006. http://www.nytimes.com/2006/04/30/travel/30footstep.html?pagewanted=print. Accessed 28 October 2014.

74. "Rabindranath Tagore à Saigon," *L'Écho annamite*, 18 June 1929, 1.
75. Anon., *Marché de Gré à Gré entre le Gouvernement Général de l'Indochine et la Société "l'Indochine Films et Cinéma,"* Hanoi: Imprimerie d'Extrême Orient, 1924; Panivong Norindr, "Vietnam," in *Encyclopedia of Early Cinema*, ed. Richard Abel (London: Routledge, 2005), 678.
76. On the publicity of Indochina see Thomas Geoffrey August, *The Selling of the Empire: British and French Imperialist Propoganda, 1890–1940* (Westport, CT: Greenwood Press, 1985).
77. Aline Demay, "Saigon: une métropole touristique?" *French Colonial History*, 12 (2011), 128.
78. *Phụ nữ tân văn*, 4 July 1929, cited in Pham, "Rabindranath Tagore in Colonial Vietnam."
79. Ibid.
80. "Rabindranth Tagore ghé viếng tòa báo Phụ nữ tân văn," *Phụ Nữ Tân Văn*, 4 July 1929, cited in Pham, "Rabindranath Tagore in Colonial Vietnam."
81. Pham, "Rabindranath Tagore in Colonial Vietnam."
82. Pham, "The Rise and the Fall," 15; "Seminar on Chettiars and Hinduism in South-East Asia," in *Bulletin of the Institute of Traditional Cultures* (University of Madras) (July–December 1972), 109. On the history of this temple see H. Hazel Hahn, "Absent Narratives and Missing Jewels: Cultural Heritage of a Tamil Temple in Ho Chi Minh City," forthcoming in 2019.
83. Pham, "The Rise and the Fall," 15.
84. For a classification of Indians donating money for Tagore's planned visit in 1924 see "En l'honneur de Tagore," *L'Écho annamite*, 2 July 1924, 1.
85. Trung Tâm Lưu Trữ Quốc Gia (National Archives of Vietnam, from here on TTLTQG) 2, file Goucoch D9–15 "L'organisation, statuts des pagodes Mariammane et Sri-Soubramniassmy des indiens bouddhistes de Saigon 1918–1942," letter to the Head of the Service or Immigration and Identity, 14 May 1928.
86. "Pour Recevoir Tagore," *Réveil Saigonnais*, 1 July 1924, cited in Natasha Pairaudeau, *Mobile Citizens: French Indians in Indochina, 1858–1954* (Copenhagen: NIAS-Nordic Institute of Asian Studies, 2016), 250.
87. "En l'honneur de Tagore," *L'Écho annamite*, July 2 1924, 1.
88. Geoffrey C. Gunn, *Rice Wars in Colonial Vietnam: The Great Famine and the Viet Minh Road to Power* (Lanham, MD: Rowman & Littlefield, 2014), 37; Michael G. Vann,

"The Good, the Bad, and the Ugly: Variation and Difference in French Racism in Colonial *Indochine*," in *The Color of Liberty: Histories of Race in France*, ed. Sue Peabody and Tyler Stovall (Durham: Duke University Press Books, 2003), 198.

89. "La fête des chettys," *L'Écho annamite*, 29 January 1926, 2.
90. On the planning of tourism by the colonial government see Demay, *Tourism and Colonization in Indochina.*
91. National Archives of Cambodia file 1440, "Reconnaissance de Popokvil, Bokor, massif des éléphants 1917–20," Maspéro's report to the Governor General, 31 July 1920; National Archives of Cambodia file 5596, "Inauguration à Bokor 1925-25."
92. "L'Affaire Bardez aux assises de Pnom-Penh," *L'Écho annamite*, 29 December 1925, 4.
93. *Courrier à Haïphong*, excerpted in "À travers la presse d'Indochine," *L'Écho annamite*, 20 July 1925, 4.
94. "Le scandale de la Société des Grands Hôtels Indochinois," *L'Écho annamite*, 15 October 1930, 1.
95. "La Haute Fumisterie du Grand Tourisme," *L'Éveil économique de l'Indochine*, 21 June 1925, 18–19.
96. Barbisier, "Un grand Hôtel a Huê," *L'Éveil économique de l'Indochine*, 5 April 1925, 5–6.
97. Tagore and his companions stayed at the villa of Diệp Văn Giáp, the colonial counselor. Pham, "The Rise and the Fall," 10–11.
98. See Demay, *Tourism and Colonization in Indochina*, especially Chapter 1.
99. "L'utile et l'agréable," *L'Écho annamite*, 20 November 1924, 1.
100. TTLTQG 2, file IA.18/236 (1–2) "Ville de Saigon. Extraits des procès verbale des délibérations de la commission municipale de Saigon. 1924–25. 4e bureau," Report to the Municipal Commission, 14 February 1924.
101. There is an extensive bibliography on this topic. See for example Peycam, *The Birth of Vietnamese Political Journalism*; David G. Marr, *Vietnamese Tradition on Trial, 1920–1945* (Berkeley: University of California Press, 1984); Hue-Tam Ho Tai, *Radicalism and the Origins of the Vietnamese Revolution* (Cambridge, Mass: Harvard University Press, 1992); and Peter Zinoman, *The Colonial Bastille: A History of Imprisonment in Vietnam, 1862–1940* (Berkeley: University of California Press, 2001).
102. "Rabindranath Tagore à Saigon," *L'Écho annamite*, 22 June 1929, 1.
103. Ibid.
104. Ibid.
105. *La Tribune indochinoise*, 21 June 1929, excerpted in *L'Écho annamite*, 22 June 1929, 4.
106. "Rabindranath Tagore à Saigon," *Le Merle mandarin*, 28 June 1929, 2. This part of Tagore's speech is my translation from the French text published in *Le Merle mandarin*, rather than Tagore's original English text which I have not located.

107. *La Tribune indochinoise*, 21 June 1929; Nguyen-Dang-Thuc, "Tagore and Vietnam," *Rabindranath Tagore: A Centenary Volume 1861–1961* ed. S. Radhakrishnan (New Delhi: Sahitya Akademi, 1961), 362.
108. Tagore, *The Message of India to Japan*, 20.
109. "En l'honneur de Tagore," *L'Écho annamite*, 2 July1924, 1.
110. Un Hindou, "Un appel aux Hindous!," *Réveil Saigonnais*, 2 June 1924, cited in Pairaudeau, *Mobile Citizens*, 250.
111. On the evolution of the term "Indochina" see H. Hazel Hahn, "Abstract Spaces of Asia, Indochina, and Empire in the French *Imaginaire*," in *Architecturalized Asia.*
112. On Indian nationalism see Partha Chatterjee, *The Nation and Its Fragments: Colonial and Postcolonial Histories* (Princeton: Princeton University Press, 1994).
113. Hahn, "Abstract Spaces of Asia, Indochina, and Empire," 91–93.
114. Tagore, *The Message of India to Japan*, 23.
115. Musée Blanchard de la Brosse, *Catalogue général des collections*, 25, 26.
116. Duong Van Loi, "L'Inde et Tagore," *L'Écho annamite*, 29 June 1929, 1. Loi saw, in Dương Văn Giao's phrase "It takes much more courage and heroism to dare to be a pacifist when one is a citizen of a conquered country" a discreet reproach that dampened the praise.
117. Bhattacharya, *Rabindranath Tagore*, 142–143.
118. Ibid., 143.
119. On historical notions of "India", "Vietnam" and "Asia" see Rujivacharakul et al. ed., *Architecturalized Asia*, in particular chapters by Zoltán Biedermann and H. Hazel Hahn.
120. Tagore, *The Message of India to Japan*, 18.
121. "Ngoài cuộc tiếp rước thi si Tagore vừ a rồi" [Anecdotes marginal to the ceremony to welcome Tagore], *Đuốc Nhà Nam*, July 2, 1929. Cited in Pham, "The Rise and the Fall," 16.
122. "Ngoài cuộc tiếp rước thi si Tagore vừ a rồi." Cited in Pham, "The Rise and the Fall," 16.
123. See Gabriel Gobron, *History and Philosophy of Caodaism* (Rockville, MD: Wildside Press, 2008).
124. Hue-Tam Ho Tai, *Radicalism and the Origins*, 189.
125. Jacques Dalloz, "Les Vietnamiens dans la franc-maçonnerie coloniale," *Revue française d'histoire d'outre-mer* 85:320 (1998), 103; Gabriel Gobron, *History and Philosophy of Caodaism* (Saigon: Tu-hài, 1950), 150; R.B. Smith, "Bui Quang Chiêu and the Constitutionalist Party in French Cochinchina, 1917–30," *Modern Asian Studies*, 3:2 (1969), 147.
126. Victor L. Oliver, *Caodai Spiritism: A Study of Religion in Vietnamese Society* (Leiden: Brill, 1976), 10.

127. Janet Hoskins notes the influences of Tagore and Gandhi on Cao Dai in *The Divine Eye and the Diaspora: Vietnamese Syncretism Becomes Transpacific Caodaism* (Honolulu: University of Hawai'i Press, 2015).
128. Mishra argues that this dream died, as seen in the responses of the Chinese and Japanese. *From the Ruins of Empire*, 240.
129. "Mistranslation," Philippa Levine notes, is "less about confusion than about incommensurability, the nonequivalence of ideas or customs in different parts of the world." Levine, "Preface," in *Gender and Empire*, ed. Philippa Levine (Oxford: Oxford University Press, 2004), ix.
130. In 1937 only 4,611 students received secondary education in French Indochina. Corfield, *Historical Dictionary of Ho Chi Minh City*, 93.
131. Chi Pham argues that the visit did not produce a clear direction for Vietnamese nationalists to follow. See Pham, "The Rise and the Fall," 4.
132. Ibid.
133. On this topic see, for example, Erica J. Peters's *Appetites and Aspirations in Vietnam: Food and Drink in the Long Nineteenth Century* (2012), which shows how Vietnamese cuisine evolved over a long period of time.

CHAPTER 2

The Aesthetic Citizen: Translating Modernism and Fascism in Mid Twentieth-Century Thailand

LAWRENCE CHUA

Remarks made by English-language commentators in early twenty-first-century press and social media indicated considerable confusion over the proliferation of fascist images in contemporary Thailand. In May 2013, a political blogger tweeted an image of the Hitler Fried Chicken restaurant in Ubon Rachathani,[1] calling it "very bizarre".[2] A few months later, newspapers around the world expressed their shock at a mural painted to commemorate the graduating class of 2013 at Chulalongkorn University. The mural featured an image of Adolf Hitler nestled between those of Superman, Captain America and the Hulk.[3] Other commentators noted the availability of Hitler-themed T-shirts and souvenirs throughout Bangkok suggesting that most Thais didn't know what such images meant, lacked empathy, or could not distinguish between the appearances of different white people.[4] What these responses failed to grasp is that these images are vestiges of Thailand's unresolved historical relationship with fascism in the middle of the twentieth century. By 1932, the year that the absolute monarchy was overthrown by the People's Party, a group of military and civilian leaders who sought to institute a constitutionalist form of government, Thailand's rulers saw European fascism as a panacea for the evils of both colonialism and communism that threatened their sovereignty in the early twentieth century.

Some of the paradoxes of the period can be discerned from the story of twenty-two-year-old Vicha Dhitavadha, who travelled from Bangkok to Berlin for military training in 1939. Vicha allegedly succeeded in rising to the rank of captain in a Wehrmacht unit. In his memoir, *Khon thai nai kong thap nasi* (*A Thai in the Nazi Army*), he noted that Germany was a country that had produced first-rate philosophers like Nietzsche, Hegel and Kant, as well as musicians like

Strauss, Haydn, Schubert and Brahms, but that it had declined after its defeat in World War I. He described Hitler as a painter and former soldier who couldn't bear to see this decline and had devised a solution to Germany's problems that appealed to people of "all classes": "Rich people wouldn't be vexed by the communist system and poor people would have a better position."[5] Vicha's observations about the cross-class appeal of fascist rhetoric, the association of fascism with modernity, and his very journey suggest that aesthetics, politics and bodies circulated in the middle of the twentieth century in a way that was not purely mimetic. What appears to be a misunderstanding of forms and ideas is actually an important step in the universalisation of these ideas. Such concepts became universal not because there was something inherently universal about "modernity" and its architectural forms but because they were used, and misused, in diverse situations. Freed from their context in central and southern Europe, ideas like fascism and historicist forms like the dome found fertile ground in Siam where they produced an aesthetic conception of architectural space and the bodies within it that transcended class-based affiliations.

In the mid twentieth century, the post-absolutist Thai state sought to create an aesthetic *prachachon* or citizen, by engaging the human body in a historical dialogue with an imagined national past through the public spaces of the capital, Bangkok. The term "aesthetics" here refers to a diverse set of artefacts and abilities through which human beings experience and understand the world around them. Describing the citizen of mid twentieth-century Bangkok as "aesthetic" does not suggest that what makes this citizen aesthetic is that they are an imitation or an ersatz participant in the imagined community of the nation, but demonstrates instead how design, media and state policies sought to instill ideas about national community, racial belonging and, ultimately, patriotic sacrifice that could transcend class, regional and linguistic affiliations through sensuous impulse and shared feeling, as well as by the coercive force of law. The formulation of legal and extra-legal aesthetic codes in mid twentieth-century Thailand produced an embodied politics in which architects and other political actors sought to regulate the appearance of not only the nation and its capital but also its citizens.

In his initial conception of the nation as an "imagined community", Benedict Anderson believed that the models of official nationalism in the colonised worlds of Asia and Africa were the dynastic states of nineteenth-century Europe. In subsequent editions of his influential study, he came to understand that it was the colonial state that provided the real model of the imagined community by examining how three institutions that shaped the way in which the colonial state imagined its dominion – the census, map and museum – were transformed in nineteenth-century colonial zones. I am interested in the ways, that in spite of the transformation, the colonial state's "grammar" – to use Anderson's term – was redeployed allows us to see the lineage of the nation state more clearly.[6] Although Thailand was never directly colonised by a European power, the Bangkok-based monarchy deployed colonial methods in the nineteenth and twentieth centuries to create a nation state. By the time the absolute monarchy was overthrown, such methods were used to persuade the diverse peoples of the Thai nation state of their membership not only in a bounded territorial grid but in an unbounded series of modern subjects.[7] This chapter builds on Anderson's understanding of the ways the technical, material and ideological dimensions of institutions shaped the domain of the nation – the nature of its citizens, the geography of its territory, the legitimacy of its ancestry – by pointing out the ways that the transformation of the techniques, forms and aesthetics used to produce modern architecture across different regions and periods was an important stage in the production of not only a national architectural vocabulary but a universal grammar of modern architecture. I do so by looking at the translation of ideas that produced sometimes radical transformations of the physical geometries and intellectual aspects of the built environment and its users as they moved between locations that have been deemed peripheral to a conventional history of modernism: fascist Europe and twentieth-century Southeast Asia.

While a growing body of scholarship addresses the importance of architecture built with the patronage of European fascist regimes, less research has been done on the same period in Southeast Asian architectural history and even less has explored the relationship between the two.[8] This is surprising, given that this is one of the few moments in which the relationship between the two regions was not defined by the unequal power-relations of European colonialism. In Thailand, the period gave rise to a paradoxical form of aesthetic-based politics that continues to inform current events. Due to the complex relationships between civilian politicians and military leaders in the People's Party, the 1932 change in government in Siam marked not only the birth of constitutional democracy but also set the precedent for military dictatorship. One of the terms that Thai historians have used to describe the political system that was produced by this fractious alliance is *prachatipthai* or **ประชาธิปไตย**.[9] Thai speakers will understand the play on the words for "democracy" and "Thai" here, but an English approximation of this term is suggested by the mash-up: "paradoxocracy". The term also suggests the paradoxes inherent in the translation of words and concepts that circulate globally.

Numerous studies on translation have noted the impossibility of fully transmitting a text, while others have noted that translation is the fundamental way in which we understand and create across the multiple languages that form part of a universal society.[10] The translatability of an idea confirms the universality of that idea. On the other hand, Jacques Derrida has famously pointed out no translation can be complete, and the assumption of perfect translation assumed a violence that erased the histories of the language that produced the idea.[11] Japanese literature scholar Christopher Hill has persuasively argued that as concepts moved around the world in the nineteenth and twentieth centuries, they experienced multiple mediations, including translation into other languages and mass reproduction in the form of textbooks and mass publications. Mediation and abstraction allowed the "universalisation" of concepts like "modernity" and "society" as if they were valid in all places at all times. Hill uses the paradigm of "intercrossing" from the work of Michael Werner and Bénédicte Zimmermann to understand the ways that two or more concepts or bodies of thought are modified through mutual contact. In contrast to linear trajectories of influence and diffusion that studies of conceptual transfer suggest, contact affects all parties in an exchange even if the resulting transformations may be asymmetrical.[12] This insight should be of particular relevance to scholars of modern architecture who have found conventional histories of modernism to be a story of diffusion from central Europe to the peripheries of the world capitalist economy increasingly unable to address the heterogeneity and complex transformations of modern architecture in diverse locations. Examining a similar period in Turkish architectural history, Esra Akçan has noted that architectural translation, unlike literary translation, is not burdened by "fidelity" and aims at precisely this "distance, distortion, or transmutation".[13] In this chapter, I explore such distortions in the translation of concepts and forms as they travelled along routes more complex than the binaries of "West" and "Non-West" might suggest, as well as the importance of mutated translations in the communicative or creative aspects of architectural production.

The Dome and the "Dome"

The dome of Rachadamnoen Boxing Stadium is an excellent example of how architectural materials, forms and aesthetics mutated in their circulation (Figure 2.1). The stadium was built by order of Prime Minister Phibul Songkhram in 1941, the same year that Thailand signed a Pact of Alliance with Japan.[14] An Italian company, Imprese Italiane All'Estere Oriente, won the contract for the stadium's construction, but building halted due to a shortage of materials. It was not until August 1945 that work began again. The preparation was rapid, but incomplete. The first bout was held in the roofless stadium on 23 December of that year. The stadium operated without a roof until 1951, when the Crown Property Bureau, the stadium's owners, appointed the Danish-Thai engineering company, Cristiani & Nielsen, to build a dome. In early images of the stadium, the square boxing ring is at the centre of the circular dome.

Figure 2.1: Imprese Italiane All'Estere Oriente/Cristiani and Nielsen, engineers, Rachadamnoen Boxing Stadium, Bangkok, 1941–1951. Source: C&N, Thailand.

The friezes on the façade of the stadium suggest the dome's two trans-regional trajectories that converge in mid twentieth-century Bangkok (Figure 2.2). Depicting Thai martial sports on the left side of the entrance and European martial sports on the right, the friezes suggest the invented histories that Thai architects during the period sought to reconcile. The first comes

Figure 2.2: Friezes on Rachadamnoen Boxing Stadium. Source: the author.

through fifteenth- and sixteenth-century architects of the Italian Renaissance like Alberti and Cesarino, who placed the figure of man at the centre of this ideal form, suggesting the place of a universal figure of man at the centre of the cosmos.[15] However, the dome's first significant appearance in modern Siamese architecture appears in a revival form on the Ananta Samakhom throne hall, which was commissioned by King Chulalongkorn, but completed under the reign of his successor King Vajiravudh (architects: Mario Tamagno and Annibale Rigotti, 1907–1915, Bangkok) (Figure 2.3). Here, the dome signified the absolute monarchy's positioning of itself as a civilised or *siwilai* institution, equivalent to modern European political institutions.[16]

Here, the dome encountered its second trans-regional trajectory from Buddhist architecture. The Mahastupa at Sanchi is an example of how the construction of a semi-spherical mass connected the three planes of cosmological existence. The main mass of the classical stupa consisted of a solid hemisphere known as the *grbḥa* or womb.[17] The curve of this volume contained the symbolic cosmic mountain, Mount Meru, and referred to the innermost centre of the universe, conceived either macrocosmically or microcosmically, as well as to the outermost confines of the universe.[18] The stupa formed around a longitudinal axis that punctured the surface of the earth and was organised according to the movement of the earth around the sun. Both container and centre, macrocosm

Figure 2.3: Mario Tamagno and Annibale Rigotti, Ananta Samakhom Throne Hall, Bangkok, 1907–1915. Source: National Archives of Thailand.

and microcosm, the stupa was "the simultaneous and punctural coincidence of the cosmic circumference and the cosmic centre": of phenomenal existences and their principle.[19] The multi-tiered parasol was the visible extension of the longitudinal axis or *yasti* that ran through the centre of the stupa. Both the dome and the stupa unified this longitudinal extended axis and a celestial cupola into a meaningful whole, joining the cosmic order and lived experience. The *harmika* is the tip of the mountain peak emerging from the mound. The *chatri*, or three-tiered umbrella that crowns the Mahastupa's *harmika*, was appropriated and multiplied into a nine-tiered parasol by the Thai monarchy as a symbol of its place in the cosmos. Sited in accordance with the cardinal directions, the hemispherical form of early Buddhist stupas came to place royalty at the apex of a cosmological body, kin with celestial beings.

The relationship between these two trans-regional trajectories and their implicit philosophical meanings was a subject of inquiry among architects working in Bangkok during the middle of the twentieth century. In particular, the dome as a form based on the measurements of the universal human figure influenced the work of architects after the overthrow of the absolute monarchy. The idea of universal suffrage that the People's Party sought to introduce throughout the country was a radical idea. Architects sought to translate this idea into built forms and purge Thai architecture of its hieratic royal symbolism.

Figure 2.4: Jitrasen (Miw) Aphaiwong, Thammasat dome, Bangkok, 1936. Source: the author.

The architecture of common humanity that they sought to create appealed both to a universal concept of modernity while seeking to assert the cultural and political sovereignty of Thailand. This attempt to create a new architectural vocabulary can be seen in the dome of the central building at Thammasat University (Figure 2.4), the first school open to commoners that was founded by Pridi Banomyong, one of the first civilian leaders of the People's Party. Pridi charged the architect, Miw Aphaiwong, with designing a building for the open university that was "beautiful, economical and modern" as well as a symbol for universal education.[20]

Miw Aphaiwong was born in Battambang in present-day Cambodia into the family of the governor of the then-Siamese province in 1905. His siblings included several important figures in the history of modern Thailand, most notably former Prime Minister Khuang Aphaiwong. He and his brother were among a group of young Siamese who travelled to France to study before World War II. While his brother studied politics in Tours, Miw went on to study at the École des Beaux-Arts.[21] As one of a small but influential group of Thai students in France during the time, Miw mixed with future leaders of the People's Party, both militarists like Phibun Songkhram and civilians like Pridi. These connections would later serve Miw well as he designed nearly all of the constitutionalist government's architectural works between 1932 and 1947. Between 1935 and 1936 he designed the dome and several other buildings at Thammasat University, but only the dome was built.[22]

Thammasat's first secretary general, Duan Bunnag, was tasked with finding someone to come up with an ordinary plan for the renovation of the buildings that the university had inherited when they purchased land belonging to the Ministry of Defense. He requested a working plan from the Architecture Office of the Department of Fine Art. At the same time, Duan was familiar with Miw's plan for the Bangkok Central Post Office (discussed later in this chapter), and asked him to submit a plan for that as well. "When I compared the plan of the Architecture Office with Miw's, I believed the latter plan was a much more beautiful form. I therefore asked Miw to continue and draw up a more detailed plan and requested directly that the *dôme* be placed between building 2 and 3 first."[23] It is notable that Duan wrote the word "dome" in his own hand in a memo typewritten in Thai to Pridi Banomyong, suggesting that the Thai word for the dome did not exist yet and that Pridi, having been educated in France, would immediately recognise the term. Duan requested a bonus for Miw for his drawings and also asked that he be appointed to take charge of the construction of the dome. Miw was delighted, according to Duan, and requested 350 baht plus a salary of 150 baht a month from 1 June until the construction was finished, which they estimated would take another six months.[24]

Why Miw chose this particular form has never been clearly stated. Phunsuk Phanomyong, the wife of founding rector Pridi Phanomyong, said that Pridi wanted the dome to reflect the sixth principle of the People's Party, to give a full education to the masses. The two stories of the structure reflected this principle for Phunsuk. Pridi had compared the university to a well that could quench the thirst of the masses. Phunsuk commented in an interview, "The dome was not French or Russian, but we might say that it has a particular identity due to its circumstances, but I don't remember why it's called a dome, because the word '*dôme*' in French is from the Greek word '*doma*', meaning a roof with a spherical shape."[25] The dome came to symbolise the utopian strivings of the university after the 1932 change in government, as captured in a poem by Pluang Wannasri.

> These things at the dome have inspired me
> To keep my strength, courage, and dignity
> Without the dome, the Chao Phraya River at Phra Chan pier
> Would also lack the symbol of defending justice.[26]

The dome of Thammasat resists a simple reading in either purely symbolic or formal art historical modes. Some Thai historians have interpreted Miw Aphaiwong's Thammasat dome as a symbolic work.[27] In the form of a sharpened pencil, its sides could represent the six principles of the People's Party (the supreme power of the Thai race, national security, the economic welfare of the Thai race, equality, human rights, and public education). However, a careful observation of the "dome" reveals that it is, in fact, octagonal and not hexagonal. Another reading of the Thammasat dome might situate it using the precedents of an art history based on stylistic physiognomies and consider the debt that its central form owes to northern Gothic architecture. This is plausible, given Miw Aphaiwong's education in L'École des Beaux-Arts and the revival of the northern Gothic as a distinctly national style for British and French architects in the nineteenth century.[28] However, it does not account for the curious division of the Thammasat "dome" into two parts. Here, it might be useful to examine several examples of early twentieth-century Thai palaces. Several throne halls on the grounds of Phya Thai palace reflect an ongoing conversation during the height of the absolutist period with the forms of the dome and steeple (Figure 2.5).[29] Designed by members of a group of Italian architects and engineers from Turin who were active in Bangkok during this period, the steeples of the Phiman Cakri and Suthiniwat throne halls approach minarets in their execution. Construction of the two throne halls was part of a building programme undertaken during the reign of King Vajiravudh (r.1910–1925) and under the administration of Phra Yawisukkamsilpprasit (Noi Silpi), the chief official of public works in the Department of Fine Arts.[30] Several Italian engineers and architects were employed by the Department during this period, but Emilio Forno was directed to oversee the completion of the project and direct the non-structural aspects of the work. Thai architects have considered the architecture of the throne halls built under Forno's supervision as an example of *romaentik* or "Romantic" architecture.[31] Under the category of the *romaentik*, the architect Watsu Potsayanan includes diverse forms that respond to the feelings and moods similar to those produced reading novels. This included the use of historicist forms associated with the Gothic, the Romanesque, and rococo. The *romaentik* became the preferred architectural tendency for works patronised by King Vajiravudh and can be seen in the diverse forms of the miniature city, Dusit Thani, which was installed first in Dusit Palace and later at Phaya Thai Palace. The resemblance of the various cupola and steeples in the profile of both Phaya Thai Palace and Dusit Thani to Islamic architecture might better be understood by looking at the circulation of Turinese architects and engineers between the Ottoman Empire and Siam during the early twentieth century. Rigotti, for instance, worked in Constantinople between 1868 and 1896 before arriving in Bangkok.[32] The Ottoman court was overthrown some ten years before the change in government in Siam but this early exchange of architectural expertise between the two locations suggests that the *romaentik* emerged as a conscious misreading of historicist tropes that were integrated into a trans-regional history of collapsing royalty.

Yet Miw Aphaiwong's dome is not simply an emulation of royal styles appropriated as a monument to commoners. The dome was meant to tie together two buildings and to serve as a clock tower for the university. A page of photographic studies of other clock towers found in the archives of Thammasat University depicts clocks embedded in the façades of a Catholic

Figure 2.5: Emilio Forno, Phiman Cakri Throne Hall, Phaya Thai Palace, Bangkok, 1909. Source: the author.

Church, a Chinese godown, the clock tower at Lumphini park, in a Khmer-style *rakhang*, and on a parapet (Figure 2.6). Except for the clock tower at Lumphini Park, none of these have been decisively identified but they appear to all be approaches that were undertaken in Bangkok during the absolutist era. All of these might have served as studies for Miw and one can see the development of the various forms: Gothic, Classical Revival, Khmer, and Chinese all being redrawn and reformulated by Miw into the dome at Thammasat with the same creative misreadings that an earlier generation of Turinese architects had brought to the absolute monarchy's public works.[33] By placing the work within the global circulation of ideas about nation, democracy and the rights of universal humankind, we can better understand Miw Aphaiwong's insistence that this was to be called a "dome" in the Thai language. The architect, like the university's founding rector, struggled to reconcile the meanings of democracy and modernity in a place that lacked both an autonomous bourgeoisie and the industrial base that gave rise to modernity in European and American contexts.

Figure 2.6: Miw Aphaiwong, Photographic studies for Thammasat dome. Source: Thammasat University Archives.

The terms of what modernity meant and what modernism looked like in a Thai context were never fully settled. In the middle of the twentieth century, older hierarchies and newer spatial orders informed one another in the chedi of Wat Phra Sri Mahathat (Figure 2.7). During the absolutist period in which he began to work for the Department of Fine Arts, Phraphrom Bhichitr was one of the first Thai architects to try to reproduce the forms of timber and plaster architecture in ferroconcrete. After the overthrow of the absolute monarchy, he used the same characteristics of ferroconcrete to purge Thai architecture of its royalist symbolism to create an architecture of commonness. His stupa or chedi houses Buddha relics. While the form of the chedi has historically been a solid mass that functions as a reliquary, Phra phrom Bhichitr opened up the chedi to both worshippers and light. A smaller reliquary nestles within a larger twin form. The substructure is punctuated with four entrances, which are topped by gable windows. The gable windows are repeated around the base four more times. On top of this are stacked three discs, radial protrusions that are often curved, but

Figure 2.7: Phraphrom Bhichitr, Phra chedi, Wat Phra Sri Mahathat, Bang Khen, 1940. Aerial photograph by Peter Williams Hunt. Source: National Archives of Thailand.

in this instance are flattened. The diameter of each disc diminishes progressively upwards. Eight clerestory windows punctuate the grooves beneath the third protrusion. The bell sits on top of this superstructure. On top of the bell sits the spire, which is crowned by a multiple sunshades or *chatri*.

The design of the chedi was based on the Panthéon and intended as both a site of worship and as a monument to the leaders of the People's Party, whose remains would be interred in the outer walls of the chedi. Historically, the relics of members of the royal family would be interred in separate chedi, which were positioned around the main Buddha reliquary. It was unheard of for commoners, even powerful ones, to be enshrined next to such potent religious objects. In between the state leaders and the bones of the Buddha knelt the common masses. A plaque in front of the altar to the Buddha reliquary instructs worshippers to pay homage not only to the Buddha, his doctrine, and the community of monks that supports it, but also to the nation. The bodies of the citizens at the centre of these ideal forms were subjected to the hierarchy of a cosmological order in which the state provided the ideal proportions.

Bodies and Space

In the post-absolutist period that followed the 1932 change in government, architects and their state patrons sought to create built structures in which audiences could not only observe leisure displays as passive spectators but participate in athletic events and experience the visceral thrill of being part of an imagined national community. Sport was a part of the urban consumer culture and was used to reconfigure the time and space of Siam's changing labour force in the twentieth century. The first use of sport as a method of inculcating values associated with *siwilai* or "civilisation" occurred, albeit in a qualified fashion, during the absolutist period under King Vajiravudh. Displays of public expression like the crowd jeering King Vajiravudh's favourite Royal Pages team in August 1919 were indications that the new spectacle of sport provided an opportunity for public demonstrations of opinion.[34] This power, like other forms of energy expounded by new forms of labour in early twentieth-century Bangkok, needed to be disciplined.

Architecture was key to harnessing this chaos. The architect Ithithepsan Kridakon noted that only architecture could give the masses the "faith and reverence" to "sacrifice their life" for the nation, religion and king.[35] He distinguished between *sanam kila* or stadia that served the higher purpose of uplifting the spiritual condition of the masses and stadia that were purely about spectatorship. The Greeks, he wrote, saw the objective of sport to be the strengthening of the body politic, while, under the Roman Empire, the objective of sport had changed to an assembly for "seeing". Sport had become more of an entertainment for the visual pleasure (**ขวัญตา**) of audiences than the "blood and bodies" of the young men and women of the nation. It had changed into an activity that lacked "innocence, taste, and beautiful moral standards". Ithithepsan compared the "lazy" citizens of the Roman Empire with modern day citizens who "only like to watch football but not play it, who like watching horse racing, dog racing, and boxing". He fretted that Bangkok, like Rome, would become a "capital of entertainments".[36]

Ithithepsan's comments suggest that sport was no longer seen by Siamese society as simply games, but was related to industry and city building. While the industry of "seeing" sporting spectacles was interested in turning a profit, sport was also a means of shaping public spirit. Ithithepsan went on to note that over the past fifty years, the construction of sports architecture was part of a larger desire to expand the capital's geographic boundaries, develop the nation and solve problems of hygiene that were a result of industrialised life.

> All things that can have a positive impact on individuals can have the same result for groups and companies. Protection is better than amending something. Likewise, it's better to build sports stadia than to build hospitals. In the future, when machinery replaces human labour in doing business, it will give humans a lot more free time, but they won't know how to use it well. Construction of stadia and fun, healthy, comfortable places to exercise can then appropriately be said to be more valuable than suppression with machine guns. Moreover, construction of stadia and support for more sports clubs, which can be run inexpensively, is surely not a wrong thing to do. It will also surely be a better improvement for the blood and body of the race than the construction of beer halls.[37]

Ithithepsan's pointed use of the terms "blood and body" and "race" (*luad nua chua chat*) might be translated simply as "nation", but during this period, this compounded term bore an uncanny resemblance to the German term *Blut und Boden* in Nazi propaganda and suggested the widespread influence of fascist concepts through the nation and its citizens. Combined with the modern invention of leisure, sports architecture offered an opportunity to rethink the body and its uses in nation-building from medical, social and aesthetic viewpoints. Its modern potential was not only in turning a profit as the locus of a growing industry, but of disciplining the labour force into a productive citizenry.

The leaders of the People's Party took a growing interest in the discipline of the labour force through sports architecture and established a Department of Physical Education in 1934. The Department's first major building project was the construction of the country's first national stadium. Headed by Navy Colonel

Figure 2.8: Jitrasen (Miw) Aphaiwong, National Stadium, Bangkok, 1938. Source: the author.

Supachalasai (né Bung Supachalasai), the Department of Physical Education moved the annual athletic competitions that were held in the field of Suan Kulap School, the first secondary school in Siam founded in 1892 for Royal Page Lieutenants, to the public field at Sanam Luang in 1934. The same year, he jointly leased land in the area of Tambon Wang Mai with Chulalongkorn University from the Crown Property Bureau and appointed Miw Aphaiwong to design an international standard stadium, the National Stadium (Figure 2.8). The land was the site of Wang Winsor or Windsor Palace, a small palace built by order of King Vajiravudh in 1881 to house the young prince Chao Fa Mahawachiranohit and which vaguely resembled the English monarch's royal palace. The young prince died only thirteen years later at the age of sixteen. The wooden palace was razed in 1936 and construction of the stadium began on 10 February 1937. It was finished four years later at a cost of 170,000 baht. The opening ceremony of the stadium on 4 May 1941 was officiated by the young King Ananda Mahidol. The stadium could reportedly accommodate 10,000 people, an unprecedented capacity for any public structure in Thailand and, if the figures are correct, one of the largest stadia in the world at the time of its construction.[38]

New policies focused on incorporating the bodies of citizens into the stadium's spectacles. Supchalasai moved athletic competitions out of the rarefied grounds of the Suan Kulap school to the National Stadium where they would be more readily accessible to commoners. The razing of a royal palace, albeit an abandoned one, to make way for the new stadium also suggested a certain shift in priorities. Sport and the spaces in which it was performed were no longer the exclusive preserve of the aristocracy. This is reinforced by an examination of the stadium's façade, where the symbolism of the absolute monarchy has been streamlined to emphasise the functional aspects of the structure.

This turn towards austerity both exploited the material characteristics of concrete and was part of rhetorical shifts at global and national levels. The National Stadium was the first modern stadium in Thailand and was built during the same period as the Nürnberg Stadium (Otto Ernst Schweizer, Nürnberg, 1927–1928), the Florence Municipal Stadium (Pier Luigi Nervi, Florence, 1930–1932), and the Olympic stadia of Amsterdam (Jan Wils, Amsterdam, 1928) and Berlin (Werner March, Berlin, 1933–1936). These stadia referred to antiquity in a non-literal manner and privileged the building structure over ornament. In Siam, the movement to streamline architectural forms also lent itself to a new aesthetic of "commonness" or *samanchon*, and simplicity or *khwam riap ngai* that was consistent with the political tendency away from absolutism and its symbols. The stadium's pilasters conjured Wang Winsor's crenellated façade, but were presented as abstracted forms rather than literal quotations, the effect is more spectral than a triumphal glorification of the monarchy. The only real concessions to literal ornamentation are the two identical sculptured capitals of the deity Indra riding the three-headed elephant Erawan on the engaged columns flanking the central bay. The clock above the entrance is a later addition to the façade. The procession of Indra mounted on Erawan was the symbol of the Physical Education Department and was rendered in strong, physical lines that were characteristic of sculpture during the constitutionalist period. Even when viewed from the ground, the figures of Indra appear physically powerful. Their strongly defined musculature mirrored the dynamic gesture of the two pillars at the stadium's entrance. Similar in form to the "wings" that orbit the central turret of the Democracy Monument, these pillars animate the stadium façade and suggest a forward moving vehicle. Indeed, for many years, the façade itself stood as a fender attached to the playing field and stands. The powerful, orderly projection of the stadia heralded the arrival of a new physicality in Siam that was reinforced through architecture, urban planning and government policies that regulated not only the appearance of the city but its economy and the physical practices of its citizens.

Cultural Mandates

On 24 June 1939, the Office of Prime Minister Phibun Songkhram issued an announcement changing the name of the country from Siam to Thailand. This state policy, or *rathaniyom,* was the first in a series of twelve proclamations that sought to discipline the nation and its citizens into a modern political entity by purging Thai society of its "flaws".[39] These "flaws" were the unsightly appearance and undisciplined social behavior of the capital and its residents. They made Thailand seem unprogressive to foreigners and therefore unworthy of its sovereignty. This was a thinly veiled critique of the labouring and anti-Japanese nationalist sections of the Chinese community as well as the peasantry and non-Buddhist members of the population. As extra-juridical pronouncements engineered by a special committee headed by Luang Wichit Wathakan, the *rathaniyom*'s real value was in creating opinion and comportment around the city's appearance and its citizens' attire, manners and speech.[40] Subsequent *rathaniyom* pronounced the language, architectural standards, dress code, daily activities, and consumer habits of citizens that had now been defined as "Thai". The racialised quality of the *rathaniyom* was made explicit in the third proclamation of the Office of the Prime Minister on 2 August 1940, which decreed usage of the word "Thai" for all "Thai" ethnic groups regardless of whether they were from the historically and linguistically distinct regions of Lan Na (the north), Isaan (the northeast), or Pak Tai (the south), or whether they were Islamic Thais.[41]

While rooted in autarchy, the *rathaniyom* were also concerned with appearance. To the state, both the population and the built environment were not only a source of labour and income that needed to be disciplined into consuming domestically produced materials, they were images that needed to reflect the values of the modern era. The importance of the *rathaniyom* to architecture and urban development in World War II-era Bangkok is made explicit in a 1942 memo from the Ministry of Education.

> Out of concern for the deterioration of the country's reputation and the loss of value of the nation, the Ministry of the Interior therefore tries to be strict: those who dress in violation of the Royal Decree of 2484 establishing the cultural practice of Thai citizens ... must not appear in communal or public places. If anyone defies this order, the police will arrest them. Furthermore, we recommend to people who build along the streets that foreigners travel on, to build orderly and systematically and to try to maintain the utmost cleanliness. If anyone defies this order or cannot practice it, they will be compelled to move and build behind the parts of the road where travellers might be able to see disorderly buildings.[42]

The drive to render Bangkok and Thailand into a modern nation state could be seen in the building projects undertaken by the Thai state along Rachadamnoen Klang Avenue the following year. The government issued an expropriation order to land owners along the avenue to surrender their properties so that the government could build new commercial buildings. Phibun Songkhram appointed

Miw Aphaiwong to build ten four-storey commercial buildings along both sides of Rachadamnoen Klang Avenue that led from Sanam Luang to the edge of the royal precincts and the oldest part of the city, Rattanakosin. Part of this project included the Democracy Monument and the Sala Chaloem Thai cinema. The buildings' concrete façades were a part of the *rathaniyom*'s insistence on not only the appearance of national order but the development of a national economy that was based on industries like the production of ferroconcrete.[43] At the opening ceremony of the renovated avenue on 24 March 1943, people were reported to be startled by the strong appearance of the unembellished steel-reinforced concrete buildings and wondered how buildings that were square with flat roofs could stand.[44] This anecdote suggests that contrary to European modernism's drive to render the building's structural properties visible, the new architecture of Rachadamnoen Klang Avenue appeared as a sleight of hand. This is further supported by the look of the buildings' façades, which were designed to read as masonry from the street. Rather than transform the old order of the city, the uniform façades of the avenue were intended to mask the messier urban reality in the *soi* or alleys that run behind it.

Virility and Monumentality

The construction of the buildings and monuments along Rachadamnoen Klang Avenue signalled a turn towards a new kind of embodied monumentality in Thai architecture. While nineteenth- and early twentieth-century monuments had used the figure of the king's body as the focal point of monuments, these new monuments of the People's Party like the Victory Monument and Democracy Monument (Pum Malakun, Bangkok, 1939) used abstract symbolic forms like the soldier's bayonet or the enshrined constitution, along with an idealised form of the commoner's body. Although state ideologues extolled these new forms as the representation of a new ideal of equality and democracy, they lent themselves easily to the celebration of virility and imperialism. Sports and architecture saw the idealisation of war and the identification of the human family with the nation.

In "Human Revolution", a lecture delivered at the Ministry of Defense Club on 15 November 1939, Luang Wichit argued that the history of Thai culture was rooted in the lionisation of the weak, slender bodies of aristocrats like Rama who had never worked. The historian Scot Barmé has noted that this provided a conceptual framework for participating in the growing market economy by developing a fusion of a bourgeois-type work ethic, religion and national identity.[45] Luang Wichit went on to argue that a revolution in the very image of the human body was necessary.

> The literary story of the Ramakian that we have critically admired is a thing that has influenced and determined our characteristics incorrectly since ancient times. The hero of the Ramakian is Rama, who is the most delicate person. He has never worked hard for anything. Going off to battle, when the character Phiphek tells him, "Today the destiny of the commander-in-chief of the enemy to die will be difficult, so send someone else to battle; until the time when it's easy, you don't have to do anything except raise your Brahma-arrow." Rama does everything like this. The author gives the reader the impression that Rama is a person from a high class. He is a meritorious and superb person. The Ramakian is an example of our epic poetry that has influenced many other stories. Our heroes in almost every story are greedy because they do not want to do anything. These stories often praise people who sleep well as people who have merit and speak of people who must work until they are tired as people who have sin. Our poems often sculpt an image of the hero as a person who is thin and delicate. Even if he has to work at something for a little bit, he is described as suspicious … The bodies of our heroes (in these old stories) are supposed to be slender, so that they aren't quite able to even walk. This is contrary to foreign and Chinese epics in which the hero must be someone big, sturdy and strong who can fight things and kill dragons or can shoulder logs … I would like to use this lecture to call on all of our writer friends to help us for a while. Those who write stories, entertaining stories, plays, or any stories at all, please draw a picture of the protagonist in your stories as a strong, sturdy person who is diligent and hard working, who loves work, who works hard through difficulties. Please don't give us stories of "laziness-but-got-lucky" anymore. Fairy tale books, magic stories, or any fanciful stories where striking a gong once will get you three castles, or stories about just lying around and then the royal chariot comes and transforms you into a king: I want to burn all of those stories.[46]

This call to train the nation to become a disciplined labour force through literature can also be discerned in the sculpture and architectural detail of the period. Artists working in the Fine Arts Department, like Silpa Bhirasri (né Corrado Feroci) and Bunchuea (né Sitthidet) Saenghiran, sought to glorify the bodies of labouring Thai citizens (Figure 2.9). The musculature of the two garuda that nest in the top corners of the main entrance (Silpa Bhirasri, 1930) to the Central Post Office (Miw Aphaiwong, Bangkok, 1930) on Charoen Krung Road in Bangkok attest to the depth that Luang Wichit's sentiments had permeated the imagination of artists and architects (Figure 2.10).[47] The garuda, a mythological bird with human aspects that had become a state symbol through the absolute monarchy, became a hyper-masculine emblem of the new constitutionalist state. Far from

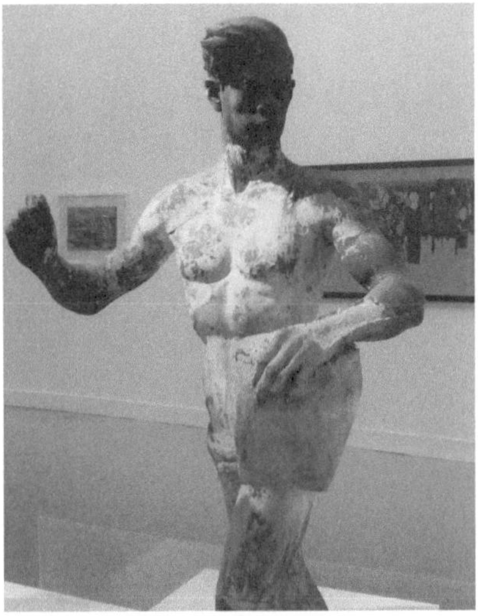

Figure 2.9: Bunchua Saenghiran, *Lak setthikit* (*Foundations of the Economy*), c.1937, wood. Source: the author.

Figure 2.10: Jitrasen (Miw) Aphaiwong, General Post Office, Bangkok, 1939. Source: the author.

Figure 2.11: Bunchuea Sithidet Saenghiran, sculpture of the ideal Thai family, 1940. Source: the author.

heroising the working man or extolling the labour process, the idealised body in sculpture, architecture and mass media of this period became a symbol of the state's virility. Implicit in these exaggerated bodies was a critique of materialism, a call to a form of spiritualism that demanded living sacrifices to the nation, and the heroisation of war. The nuclear family, as the ideal primary unit of the new economy, came to figure prominently in the iconography of the period (Figure 2.11). The father of the ideal family was now a soldier in the service of the state and his wife, a woman who dressed following the conventions of the *rathaniyom*. Their infant child attested to their success in reproducing the labour force and contributing to the war economy.

Conclusion

How successful was the campaign to create an aesthetic citizen? A 1957 publication of the Department of Public Relations aimed at fostering an image of Thailand as a democratic tourist destination, suggested the continued importance of the new physical culture after World War II. The publication featured an image of then Prime Minister Phibun Songkhram and First Lady La-iad Songkhram in its pages.[48] Phibun's picture is accompanied by a quote comparing sport to democracy. In his estimation, both require rules in order to be played. The back page of the tourist brochure gives an indication of the stakes of this sporting form of politics. A photograph of one of the soldiers on the Victory Monument bears a headline that exhorts the public to sacrifice their lives willingly for the nation.

The presence of this call in the pages of a magazine promoting tourism after World War II speaks to the continued importance of the previous era's militarised aesthetics in seeking to cultivate politically obedient and pleasure-seeking citizens. The rhetorical deployment of materials like concrete and the development of autarchic economic policies sought to destabilise the influence of non-Thai merchants and create a culture of self-consciously Thai architecture, cuisine and fashion. Buildings, food, clothing, and even the name of the country took on race-based national characteristics. What made this imagined community different from its Khmer neighbours or from the Chinese in its midst? It could reach back to the imagined, immemorial past of Ayutthaya, Sukhothai, and even Angkor and claim them as part of a teleological narrative that resolved in mid twentieth-century Bangkok. It could also be certain that it was headed to a limitless future. Its streets were wide and lined with buildings that spoke at once of its historic achievements and its modern dynamism. In its stadia and playing fields, it could encounter the bodies of its fellow citizens and be reassured that the national community was made of not only concrete and steel but the "blood and bodies of the Thai race" (**เลือดเนื้อเชื้อชาติ**).[49] The aesthetic citizens of the mid twentieth century could be assured that even if their mortal lives were short, the life of the nation for which they sacrificed was eternal, as old as the cosmic order to which the dome connected them.

The visitor to contemporary Bangkok will notice that the dome proliferates throughout the city. One way to understand the omnipresence of the dome is that it, along with other historicist idioms, was appropriated as a symbol of foreign prestige.[50] This reading is fairly uncontroversial and leaves intact a narrative about modernism that begins with in the industrialised centres of northern Europe and is assimilated mimetically at its peripheries. It is supported by an essentialising nationalist historiography that allows architects at the peripheries to "localise" universal forms that were authored in the modern "West", adapting them to the moods of various national regimes. Such narratives, however, fail to account for the lack of a unified "local" vocabulary or the complex forms of agency and imagination that are produced through the global circulation of ideas, forms and peoples in the twentieth century. If we are to take seriously the idea that areas that have been deemed peripheral to the history of modernism are also the source of truth-claims and architectural knowledge, a different picture emerges. Through a process of imperfect translation and trans-local circulation that took many unexpected detours, regional forms like the dome were incorporated into a universal language of modern architecture.

Notes

1. The romanisation of Thai words in this article follows the conventions of the General System of Phonetic Transcription of Thai Characters into Roman devised by the Thai Royal Institute, but without diacritics; the system is set out in the *Journal of the Thailand Research Society* 33, no. 1 (March 1941), 49–53. Proper names of historical figures are spelled according to the preferences of the persons, where known, or according to common usage. All translations of Thai materials in the article are the author's.
2. Andrew Spooner, Twitter post, 28 May 2013, https://twitter.com/andrewspoooner/.
3. "University Apologizes for Hitler Mural," *Bangkok Post*, 16 July 2013, http://www.bangkokpost.com/news/local/360013/chulalongkorn-university-apologises-for-hitler-mural; Rabbi Abraham Cooper, "Now Thailand Must Act Against 'Nazi Chic,'" *Huffington Post*, 17 July 2013, http://www.huffingtonpost.com/rabbi-abraham-cooper/thailand-must-act-against_b_3595882.html.
4. The associate dean of the Simon Wiesenthal Centre in Los Angeles noted that the popularity of Nazi images in the region was due to "sheer ignorance", Tibor Krausz, "Bangkok's 'Hitler chic' trend riles tourists, Israel envoy," *Travel CNN* 17 February 2012, http://travel.cnn.com/bangkok/life/hitler-chic-trend-138530/.
5. Vicha Dhitavadha, *Khon thai nai kong thap nasi* (*A Thai in the Nazi Army*) (Bangkok: Sarakhadi, 2014), 92–93.
6. In a chapter added to the original text, Anderson conceded a flaw in his earlier appraisal that official nationalism in the colonised worlds of Asia and Africa was modelled directly on the dynastic states of nineteenth-century Europe. Benedict Anderson, *Imagined Communities: Reflections on the Origin and Spread of Nationalism* (London: Verso, 1991), 163.
7. Anderson later expanded on the notion of seriality he introduced in *Imagined Communities* by describing unbound seriality, with its origins in mass media, as the open-to-the-world plurals like nationalists, anarchists and workers; bounded seriality, with its origins in governmentality, is exemplified by finite series like Asian-Americans, *beurs* and Tutsis. Benedict Anderson, *Spectre of Comparisons: Nationalism, Southeast Asia, and the World* (London and New York: Verson, 1998), 29.
8. Notable scholarship on German and Italian architecture during the fascist period includes Despina Stratigakos, *Hitler at Home* (New Haven, CT: Yale University Press, 2015), Medina Lasansky, *The Renaissance Perfected: Architecture, Spectacle and Tourism in Fascist Italy* (University Park, PA: Pennsylvania State University Press, 2004), Paul Jaskot, *The Architecture of Oppression: The SS, Forced Labor and the Nazi Monumental Building Economy* (London, New York: Routledge, 2000), and Nader Vossoughian, "From A4 Paper to the Octametric Brick: Ernst Neufert and the Geopolitics of Standardization in Nazi Germany," *Journal of Architecture* 20, no. 4

(2015). One exception to the silence around this period in Thailand is the work of Chatri Prakitnontakan. See, Chatri Prakitnontakan, *Silpa satthapatayakam khana ratsadon: sanyalak thang kan muang nai chong udomkan* (*Art and Architecture of the People's Party: Political Symbols in Ideological Aspect*) (Bangkok: Matichon, 2009) and Chatri Prakitnontakan, *Khana ratsadon chalong ratthamnun: prawatisat kan muang lang 2475 phan satthapatayakam "amnat"* (*The People's Party Celebrates the Constitution: Political History After 1932 Through the Architecture of "Power"*) (Bangkok: Matichon, 2005).

9. The term is also the title of a film and book on the history of the 1932 change in government. Pen-ek Rattanaruang and Phasakon Phramunwong, dir. *Prachatip'thai* ("*Paradoxocracy*"), Film, 2013; Pen-ek Rattanaruang and Phasakon Phramunwong, *Prachatip'thai* (*Paradoxocracy*) (Bangkok: Matichon, 2014).
10. Octavio Paz pointed out the paradox that while translation overcomes the differences between languages it also reveals them more fully; Octavio Paz, "Translation, Literature, and Letters," *Theories of Translation: An Anthology of Essays from Dryden to Derrida,* edited by Rainer Schulte and John Biguenet (Chicago: University of Chicago Press, 1992), 152–154.
11. Jacques Derrida, *Of Grammatology* (Baltimore: Johns Hopkins University Press, 1967).
12. Christopher Hill, "Conceptual Universalization in the Transnational Nineteenth Century," in *Global Intellectual History*, ed. Samuel Moyn and Andrew Sartori (New York: Columbia University Press, 2013), 135, 146.
13. Esra Akçan, *Architecture in Translation: Germany, Turkey, and the Modern House* (Durham, NC: Duke University Press, 2012), 8. Walter Benjamin pointed out that although no translation can have any significance regarding the original, the original is still closely connected with the translation, even more because it is no longer of importance to the original. Walter Benjamin, *Illuminations* (New York: Schocken, 1968), 71.
14. Cristiani and Nielsen (Thai), Limited, *Forty Years in Thailand, 1930–1970* (Bangkok: Presko Public Relations, 1970).
15. Rudolf Wittkower, *Architectural Principles in the Age of Humanism* (London: Alec Tiranti, 1952), 8–9, 27.
16. That the throne hall was used as the initial headquarters of Phibun's People's Party after it overthrew the absolute monarchy in 1932 suggests some of the continuities of the constitutionalist and absolutist projects.
17. Also, more commonly referred to as the *anda* or egg.
18. Adrian Snodgrass, *Symbolism of the Stupa* (Ithaca: Cornell Southeast Asia Program, 1985), 189, 226.
19. Ibid., 190–191.
20. Thamrongsak Phetchlertanan, *Thammasat kan muang thai jak patiwat 2475 theung 14 tula 2516* (*Thammasat and Thai Politics from the 1932 Revolution until 14 October 1973*) (Bangkok: Matichon, 2004), 42.

21. It is still not clear whether Miw Aphaiwong studied at the École in Tours or in Paris. Chatri Prakitnontakan, "Jet sip pi dom thammasastr lae kan muang" ("70 years of the Thammasat dome and politics)," *Julasan ho jotmaihet thammasastr,* 10 (June 2006–May 2007), 28.
22. As a result, Miw resigned his post as the person in charge of the building of the university in 1937. Ibid., 29.
23. Duan Bunnag, "Ruang som saem thi tham kan khong mahawityalai" ("Memo on the official repairs of the university," 3 May 1937, No. 3/2478, Thammasat University Archives.
24. Ibid.
25. "Interview with Than Phuying Phunsuk Phanomyong," *Thammasat prakatnam 70* (Bangkok: Matichon, 1974), 30.
26. Translation by author. **สิงเหล่านีทีโดมโหมจิตข้า ให้แกร่งกล้าเดือนปีไม่มีหวัน หากขาดโดม เจ้าพระยา ท่าพระจันทร์ ก็ขาดสัญลักษณ์ พิทักษ์ธรรม**
The poem was first published in *Warasan somosorn nak seuksa mahawitayalai thammasat kan muang,* no. 2, May 1952.
27. The symbolic understanding of the dome is prevalent even if there is no agreement as to its meaning. Chatri, *Khana ratsadon chalong ratthatamnun,* 94; Duangthip Woraphan, editor, *Thammasat 60 pi* (Bangkok: Thammasat University, 1994); M.R. Kukrit Pramoj, *Khon thammasat 50 pi* (Bangkok: Thammasat University, 1984); Thammasat University, *Si pi thammasat* (Bangkok: Thammasat University, 1975).
28. An anonymous peer reviewer of this chapter remarked on a superficial similarity between the relic stupa, Pa That Luang in Vientiane. Although such a precedent would underscore the two trajectories of the dome in Thai architecture, the comparison is dubious, given that Pa That Luang is four-sided. Furthermore, there is no archival evidence to support the speculative influence of regional idioms (outside of the idioms of the Thai central plains) on the Thammasat dome.
29. Chatri Prakitnontakan, "70 pi dom thammasat lae kan muang," ("70 Years of the Thammasat Dome and Politics"), *Ho cotmaihet thammasat: 72 pi ruang lao nai ngao dom* (*Thammasat University Archives Bulletin: 72 Years of Stories in the Shadow of the Dome*), no. 10 (June 2006–May 2007): 34–35.
30. Phaet ying Kannika Tanprasoet, *Phrarachawang phya thai nai wan lan ha phaen din* (*Phya Thai Royal Palace in the Days of the Five Kingdoms*) (Bangkok: Matichon, 2010), 71.
31. Watsu Potsayanan in Khana kamatikan anurak silpasatthapatayakam, *174 Moradok satthapatyakam nai prathet thai* (Bangkok: Amarin, 1974).
32. Giorgiomaria Rigotti, "Raimondo D'Aronco e Annibale Rigotti" in *Atti del Congresso Internazionale di Studi su "Raimondo D'Aronco e il suo tempo," 1/3 giugno 1981* (Udine: Istituto per l'Enciclopedia dei Friuli-Venezia Giulia, 1982), 73, cited in Richard Etlin, "Turin 1902: The Search for a Modern Italian Architecture,"

The Journal of Decorative and Propaganda Arts 13, Stile Floreale Theme Issue (Summer, 1989), 92.

33. Page of photographs, folder on the dome of Thammasat, Thammasat University Archives, 14.
34. Walter Vella, *Chaiyo!: King Vajiravudh and the Development of Thai Nationalism* (Honolulu: University of Hawai'i, 1978), 150–151.
35. Ithithepsan Kridakon, *Ruang kio kap satthapatayagam* (*On Architecture*) (Bangkok: Krom Silpakorn, 1935), 8.
36. Ibid., 49–50.
37. Translation by author. Ibid, 53.
38. There is some discrepancy as to the original number of spectators the stadium could hold. An inscription on the stadium indicated it was 40,000 while other accounts put the number at 25,000 and 30,000. An examination of early photographs, however, suggests that the original capacity was much closer to 10,000. In comparison, Jan Wils' Amsterdam Olympic stadium, built for the 1928 Olympics, had a capacity of 34,155 while Werner March's Olympiastadion (Berlin, 1933–1936), a self-conscious exercise in monumentality, could seat 76,000 following a battle of wills between March and Adolf Hitler, see Michelle Provoost, editor, *The Stadium: The Architecture of Mass Sport* (Rotterdam: Netherlands Institute of Architecture, 2000), 79, 74, 27.
39. Ministry of Education, "Ruang kio kap nayobai haeng chat" ("Memo on National Policies"), National Archives of Thailand, ศธ 0701.29/5; Thamsook Numnonda refers to them as cultural mandates in Thamsook Numnonda, "Phibun Songkhram's Thai Nation-Building Programme during the Japanese Military Presence," *Journal of Southeast Asian Studies* 9, no. 2 (1978): 234–247.
40. The first *rathaniyom*, for instance, was only legislated after it was issued, and was passed after some debate by the National Assembly, see *The Bangkok Times*, 28 August 1939.
41. Thak Chaloemtiarana, editor, *Thai Politics: Extracts and Documents, 1932–1957* (Bangkok: Social Science Association of Thailand, 1978), 246–247; *100 ekasan samkhan sapsara prawatisat thai* (*100 Important Documents: The Substance of Thai history*), (Bangkok: Chulalongkorn University Press, 2552BE), 257.
42. Translation by author. Office of the Prime Minister, "Ruang hai kuadkhan hai tangkai hai riabroi lae hai raksa khwam sa-ad khong ban ruan" ("Memo on the restrictions on orderly dress and maintaining domestic cleanliness"), NA, (3) สร. 0201.55/2 folder 2 (73–126).
43. The majority of revenues from natural resources like logging remained in the hands of European companies even after the 1932 change in government, leading the new constitutionalist state to continue to develop the Siam Cement Company as a national enterprise, see Phinai Sirikitatkul "Na thi ni mai mi khwam suam:

thanon rachadamnoen pho so 2484-2488," *Na Jua: History of Architecture/Thai Architecture* 6 (Sep 2009–Aug 2010): 41–42.

44. Chatri, *Khana ratsadon chalong ratthatamnun*, 94.
45. Scot Barmé, *Luang Wichit Wathakan and the Creation of a Thai Identity* (Singapore: Institute of Southeast Asian Studies, 1993), 154.
46. Translation by author. Luang Wichitwathakan, *Patokatha lae kham banyai khong phontri Luang Wichitwathakan* (*Lectures and Talks of Major General Luang Wichitwathakan*) (Bangkok: Cremation volume for Khunying Chan Thepprachum, 1937), 120.
47. Hailed as the "father of Thai modern art", Silpa Bhirasri began his career under the absolutist reign of King Vajiravudh (r.1910–1925) but created most of the anthropomorphic ornamentation and sculpture for the People's Party, including the friezes on the Democracy Monument (Pum Malakun, Bangkok, 1939). Born in Florence in 1924, he became a Thai citizen in 1944 and referred to Thailand in his writings as "our country". He echoed state-based accounts of the Thai as excellent adaptors who borrowed the best elements of other cultures. He echoed Mussolini in his calling for the importation of technology from the "West" but preserving Thai intellectual and spiritual spheres. He made no mention of Mussolini in his writings, although his views on agrarianism and autarchy coincided with Mussolini's. These views were shared with political leaders in Siam before and during World War II who considered Mussolini to be a "great hero".
48. Churan Thepasdin, editor, *Democratic Thailand,* (Bangkok: Government Tourist Bureau, Public Relations Department), 2.
49. Ithithepsan, *Ruang kio kap satthapatayagam*, 53.
50. An anonymous peer reviewer noted that the dome also appears in Bangkok as the *qubba* of its numerous mosques. The domed *qubba* is, in fact, a later addition to Thai mosque architecture that begins to proliferate in the city's mosques after 1932 but its history is beyond the scope of this essay. See Ammar Mas-oo-di, *Wiwathanakan satthapatayakam masyid nai krungthep mahanakhon (1782–2010)* (*The Evolution of Architectural Styles of Mosques in Bangkok (1782–2010)*) (MA thesis, Chulalongkorn University, 2010) and Adis Idris Raksomoni, *Masyid nai krungthep* (*Mosques in Bangkok*) (Bangkok: Matichon, 2014).

CHAPTER 3

Cultivating Bali Style: A Story of Asian Becoming in the Late Twentieth Century

PETER SCRIVER AND AMIT SRIVASTAVA

In current usage, the term "Bali Style" signifies a surprising diversity of things. Initially limited to descriptions of the bungalow- or villa-type resort dwellings pioneered in Bali in the second half of the twentieth century, it is now ubiquitous throughout Southeast Asia. Today the term extends to a much wider spectrum of design products and experiences that embody a shared aspiration for luxurious and leisurely tropical lifestyles, but which have jumped species from the substantive architectures of residential and corporate developments to the decorative ephemera of themed social functions and community events.

Ungoverned by any rigorous archaeological or ethnographical definitions of style, the impact of this popular term has been far reaching, having entered into critical academic discourse on the architecture of the region as well as a whole sub-industry of glossy publications targeted at both design professionals and amateurs.[1] Whilst debating its accuracy in representing the historical styles of Bali, architectural scholars questioned the authenticity of Bali Style in emulating genuine vernacular architectures which, arguably, are continuously emerging and evolving in response to the actual needs and living traditions/practices of the Balinese people. From the postcolonial perspective of the critical discourse on the contemporary architectures of Asia, Bali Style has been criticised, therefore, as a variant of a consciously contrived regionalism.[2]

Notwithstanding these critical issues, this chapter will consider how Bali Style has also been a significant political and economic tool that, since its inception, has enabled certain agents to assume control of the debate and reposition themselves not only locally but on a transnational and increasingly global stage.

Considering the development of Bali Style within the bounds of the postcolonial condition and the fraught power relationship between a re-emergent Asia in this period and the post-imperial West, the debate on authenticity has tended to focus on the issue of Asia as "other", and the implications of the characterisation of Asian material culture in the desiring outsider's gaze as a commodity for consumption.[3] On the other hand, regionalist interpretations tend to regard Bali Style as a particularist variation or a regional hybrid in the global expansion of an essentially Western conception of the Modern.[4] Indeed, the historical roots of the contemporary phenomenon – Bali Style – were deeply entwined with the cultural politics of modernity through various aesthetic and countercultural demonstrations of resistance to it earlier in the twentieth century. As we will presently recount in greater detail, some of the earliest and most influential manifestations of Bali Style can be traced to a small number of Western expatriates who retreated to Bali, before and after World War II, consciously regarding themselves as a cultural and intellectual avant-garde. Unlike later interlopers and interlocutors, however, they were not yet burdened with a critical consciousness of their implication in lingering Orientalist constructions of Bali as a tropical paradise, and the concurrent identity politics that emerged from the process of decolonisation that was unfolding across the region over this same period.[5]

However, to attribute – critically or otherwise – responsibility for the subsequent development and propagation of Bali Style as a phenomenon of contemporary cultural production to the colonial-modern circumstances of its birth would completely miss the point of the argument we wish to develop here. Bali Style was neither imported, nor imposed.[6] As this chapter will seek to demonstrate, the emergence and subsequent cultivation of Bali Style is the outcome of an Asian condition, or rather a global condition that repositions Asia in a new place or stance, culturally and economically, which was more favourable to exercising its own prerogatives and self-determination. Thus, whilst it may be argued that Bali Style is not necessarily from or even of Bali in the end, it is still, nevertheless, as Asian in its pedigree as any uncritical beholder of its myriad manifestations might presume. However, this may only be fully appreciated when we are capable of apprehending Asia beyond its former colonial and prevailing conceptual entanglement with the West.

The following sections trace the gestation of Bali Style as it emerged in its first mature statements in the form of alternative Balinese resorts in the 1960s; its subsequent rise to wider influence in the following decade within a repositioned Asian economic discourse in which the rapid growth of international tourism was playing a significant new role; and, finally, the reframing of Bali Style as a method through which Asian entrepreneurs ultimately exercised direct agency in the global flows of capital and architectural services.

The Emergence of Bali Style: Asia as a Meeting Ground of Transnational Actors

The story of the emergence of Bali Style, as articulated by previous commentators, has invariably located the development of the architectural typology to a nexus of transnational aesthetes and professionals that came to be centred in Bali in the 1960s.[7] As we excavate further into the details of this confluence of cosmopolitan expatriate and local actors, it is also important to remember the particular sociopolitical context within which this network developed. As a result of the post-war decolonisation process across Asia, economic power was shifting from expatriate colonial capital to the local entrepreneurial elite. Whilst political emancipation had in many cases been achieved with surprising speed, full economic freedom was to be much slower in coming, and these local elite remained initially dependent on their social and economic ties with ex-colonial collaborators. This delayed process of economic development further allowed for new networks between the newly decolonised nations to emerge and the cosmopolitan nature of this network transcended the colonial relationship. The earliest impact of this transnational economic and professional transfer within the decolonised nations of Asia is most clearly evident in the tourism industry, where Western exoticisation was nevertheless responsible for a largely homegrown business endeavour. The efforts of these entrepreneurial elite helped develop the extended transnational disciplinary and cross-disciplinary networks that have continued to define and further spread the influence of Bali Style and similar phenomena. It is within this context of an economically emergent Asian elite and greater transnational exchange within and across Asia that we will trace the arrival and meeting of a charmed set of local and expatriate bohemians on the shores of the island of Bali. We will argue that their efforts in developing and promoting Bali Style were directly connected to the possibilities Asia now afforded for a lifestyle that was increasingly at odds with the abstract aesthetics of international modernism and its universalising assumptions about human existence, needs and desires.

At the centre of this story about the emerging nexus of transnational aesthetes and entrepreneurial elite, is the chance meeting of Australian artist Donald Friend and Indonesian entrepreneur Wija Waworuntu. Donald Friend (1915–1989) is recognised today as one of the more significant Australian artists of the mid twentieth century.[8] Yet, when Friend quit Sydney in 1966 and ultimately settled in Sanur on Bali's eastern beaches the following year, he and his art had fallen out of favour with the contemporary art scene. A masterful draughtsman in an age of abstraction, with what was disparaged as a "decadent" taste for the decorative in art,[9] the middle-aged Friend was attracted to the salubrious, visually and culturally vibrant tropical island, much as Gauguin – one of his inspirations

– had been drawn away from early modern Paris to French Polynesia half a century earlier.

Friend was a worldly traveller whose attraction to the exotic had already been well established, but in an earlier seemingly more genteel age when perceptions of scale and distance were still formed from the deck of a ship, and lasting friendships could be forged over long sea journeys and sojourns in between. His work and wanderlust over the first two decades of his career had taken him not only to most of the expected European destinations for a budding artist, but to a number of less-frequented tropical destinations in the increasingly fluid, post-war world of the 1950s, from the South Pacific all the way to West Africa.[10] Significantly, Friend's sybaritic ideals of tropical paradise had been shaped most profoundly by an extended earlier period of residence (1957–1961) in newly independent Ceylon (now Sri Lanka), where he had also enjoyed the neocolonial comforts of house-servants and social privilege as a guest of Bevis Bawa, the aristocratic and wealthy older brother of the (later) celebrated architect, Geoffrey Bawa (1919–2003).[11]

Comparable to Ceylon in obvious respects as another tropical island paradise, Bali had also attracted Friend as the haven of an earlier cluster of reclusive expatriate Western artists and other cultural aesthetes during the interwar years. These had included German-Russian émigré painter, Walter Spies, Canadian ethno-musicologist, Colin McPhee, and the American anthropologists Gregory Bateson and Margaret Mead, among others.[12] They had coveted Bali's idyllic isolation and cultural autonomy as a unique outlier of Indo-Malay civilisation that had been little touched by either of the relatively more modern Islamic and colonial-European cultural and political orders that dominated the rest of the Southeast Asian archipelago. This bohemian attraction of Bali was also enhanced for Friend, who was openly gay – as were Spies and several other members of his Ubud-based artists' "Group" – by its relative tolerance of homosexuality. As early as the 1930s, Bali had become known in international gay circles as a place where the local culture accepted the fluidity of sexuality, and "where a little money could buy a grand lifestyle".[13]

On his initial trip to Bali, in 1966, Friend met Wija Waworuntu, a sophisticated local antique dealer, filmmaker, and erstwhile architect, in whose humble but tasteful neo-vernacular guesthouse on Sanur Beach Friend made his first residence. The growing friendship and shared interest in the vernacular aesthetic would encourage Friend and Waworuntu to collaborate on several architectural projects in the coming years. Friend's first project, a house he built for himself nearby, also showed a sense of continuity with the immersive aesthetic and ethnographic projects of his expatriate predecessors, reproducing the most innovative feature of the neo-vernacular villa that Walter Spies had lived in near Ubud in central Bali – a pagoda-like double-height verandah-cum-living room.

The house demonstrated a readiness to experiment freely with the vernacular as a passionate amateur. But Friend's agency exercised in his own expert mediums of drawing and painting, in which his discriminating eye for architectural form and detail privileged a particular way of seeing and framing the character of place, inspired him and others to continue to experiment with the vernacular.

Waworuntu and Friend were both incensed by the aesthetic insult to Sanur's quiet coconut-grove milieu of the eleven-storey Miami-style Bali Beach Hotel (Figure 3.1) that had recently been built for the Pan American Airlines-owned Intercontinental Hotels chain just a short distance up the beach.[14] The two therefore decided to work together to mount a gentle insurgency against further such high-rise construction, beginning by incrementally developing Waworuntu's guest house into an expanded yet sensitively integrated low-rise complex of cottages. Inspired by the local vernacular and stylishly appointed with Waworuntu's collection of antique Balinese furniture and sculpture, the intimate boutique hotel known as the Tandjung Sari soon became the chic upmarket alternative to the generic international-standard modern accommodation offered by the Bali Beach and other large-scale developments aimed at the rapidly growing volume of overseas tourists. In addition to a steady stream of visitors from Donald Friend's international social circles, the Tandjung Sari also attracted a reputation as a discrete and inconspicuously exclusive hotel in which

Figure 3.1: The eleven-storey international style Bali Beach Hotel at Sanur Beach, Bali, Indonesia, completed in 1966. Source: the authors, 2014.

international celebrities, from royalty to rock stars, could quietly enjoy a break from the spotlight.[15]

Friend, with his draughtsman's eye for architectural texture and character, was also influential in inspiring and attracting other collaborators from within the architectural profession. During his previous residency in Ceylon, Friend's art had been a distinct influence on a number of young architects and artists associated with Geoffrey Bawa. By the early 1960s, this circle had already begun to look at the tropical vernacular architecture of Ceylon with new respect. Emulating Friend's draughtsmanship, which was saturated equally with architectural and botanical detail, they went on to develop the signature magic-realist house-style of drawings for which the Bawa practice would eventually be famous.[16] Although the Australian artist and the Sri Lankan architect had never, evidently, become very close socially, it was at Friend's invitation that Bawa would later come to Bali in a professional capacity, and play a direct part in the framing of a contemporary Bali Style tradition.[17]

Bolstered by both the qualitative and financial success of the Tandjung Sari, but now all the more anxious to preserve and enhance the character of its immediate milieu, Waworuntu and Friend had, by 1970, acquired a substantial package of additional beachfront property on which they were keen to design and build a larger-scale resort, as well as a separate, exclusive residential enclave, the Batujimbar Estate (Figure 3.2), which was to incorporate Friend's villa and

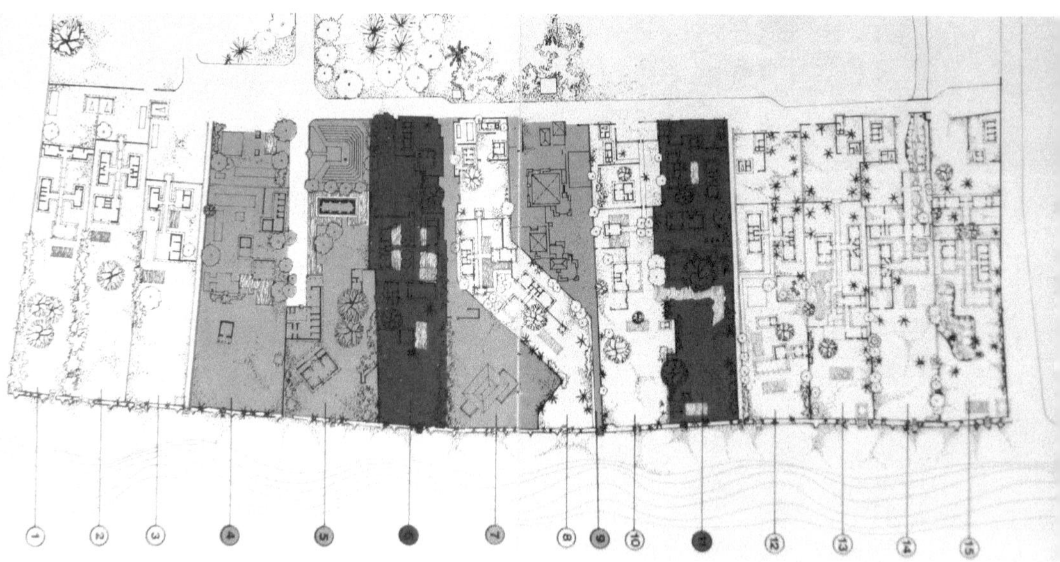

Figure 3.2: Subdivision and layout of garden villa compounds at Batujimbar Estate on Sanur Beach, Bali, Indonesia, designed by architect Geoffrey Bawa, 1972. Source: Batujimbar Estate Promotional Brochure, photographed by the authors, 2014.

thereby protect it from neighbouring developments. Their vision called for the Balinese architectural patterns and principles that they had begun to experiment with at Tandjung Sari to be extended and further developed on both of these new sites with the guidance of sympathetic architectural design consultants.

Bawa was to come in 1972 with the brief to master-plan and design a series of garden villas at the Batujimbar Estate. Fifteen of these were planned in all, each a custom-designed garden comprised of different botanical, landscape and building elements in which the typical dwelling functions – living/dining, bedrooms, guest rooms, food preparation – were distributed, in a Balinese manner, among the separate structures of the compound. The array of elements that Bawa gathered into these picturesque compositions included distinctively Balinese-style split-gateways, and even the diminutive private temples of traditional Balinese residential compounds seen in many parts of the island. Far from a pseudo-vernacular pastiche, however, the primary emphasis was on the spaces between the elements, and the possibilities to articulate and refine the order latent in the traditional patterns.[18] Although only three of Bawa's designs were faithfully executed in the end, including a small pavilion-museum to house Friend's own growing collection of Balinese sculpture, the Bali project was as influential for Bawa as it was for the nascent notion of "Bali Style". As one of Bawa's very first overseas commissions, undertaken in parallel with a cluster of others in India and Mauritius in the early 1970s, this opportunity to mine new sources of vernacular architectural elements and ideas reinforced and clarified a tendency within Bawa's work toward a "bricolage" of elements, found and designed, which was inherently hybrid and cosmopolitan rather than "traditional" in any conservative or authentic sense of the term (Figure 3.3).[19]

Ultimately Waworuntu and Friend's most influential collaboration with an architectural professional was for the earlier and more ambitious project for the resort hotel with architect Peter Muller (b.1927). Friend had already been close to Muller and his wife Carole socially for some time when he persuaded them to come to Bali in 1970, and take on the commission. An established Sydney-based architect, Muller had recently been working on the design for a hotel in Tahiti, but Friend apparently regarded Muller's more established reputation for sensitive landscape-integrated residential designs in the "organic" modernist tradition of Frank Lloyd Wright as equally relevant experience. Now in mid-career, Muller was also ready to take an extended break from his Australian practice, and was to spend the better part of the next two decades working in Bali and beyond, where subsequent commissions were to lead him.[20]

What was to have been called the Matahari (Figures 3.4 & 3.5) was a hotel reconceived as a Balinese village complete with narrow walled streets and a village market square following forms, principles and local design methods that Muller had been inspired to research more closely. Although some of the earliest

Figure 3.3: "Bricolage" of traditional built elements, found objects and horticulture composed with a modernist sense of asymmetrical spatial disposition in one of Bawa's garden villa designs for the Batujimbar Estate, Sanur Beach, Bali, Indonesia. Source: the authors, 2014.

theoretically grounded research about the everyday architecture of Bali was being undertaken by Australian academics at the same time, little of any direct use to practitioners had yet been published, obliging Muller to conduct his own survey and investigations directly.[21] Whilst the original Matahari scheme never came to fruition, when the changing economic climate of the early 1970s scuttled the Australian backed financing, Muller's shift to Bali proved to be serendipitous nevertheless. What had initially been undertaken in 1972 as a small commission on the side for a private residence and guest accommodation at Seminyak, on Bali's western beaches, ultimately evolved into a more ambitious but still distinctively intimate scheme for a small resort that enabled many of the ideas and principles that Muller had developed for the unbuilt Matahari project to be successfully demonstrated. This venture, known as the Kayu Aya (Figure 3.6), had also come close to failing due to the breakdown of the original business partnership that had financed it.[22] Fortunately, the purchase of the incomplete project in 1977 by the Indian-owned Oberoi chain of luxury hotels brought Muller back into the project to restore and extend the resort. Muller's re-engagement in Bali at this juncture was all the more fortuitous and timely as the completed resort, now called the Bali Oberoi, became the paradigm for the discrete and discerning luxury resort that Oberoi was seeking to brand, not only in Bali, but across its rapidly expanding Afro-Asian business empire. Through this new professional relationship, Muller found himself venturing further and further into this larger Asian theatre of operations and opportunity. Now, well beyond the relatively small and insular circle of cosmopolitan bohemians through which he had developed his initial

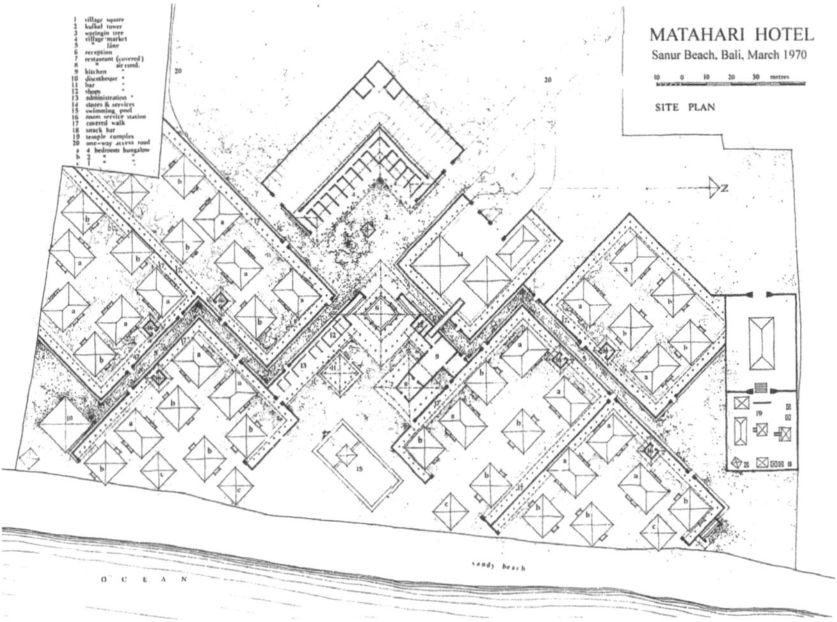

Figures 3.4 & 3.5: Balinese village-inspired site plan (*top*) and perspective sketch of Central Square (*bottom*) for the proposed Matahari Resort, by architect Peter Muller, 1970. Source: Peter Muller Archive, Walsh Bay, Sydney.

Figure 3.6: Aerial view of Kayu Aya Resort, Seminyak Beach, Bali, Indonesia, c.1977.
Source: Peter Muller Archive, Walsh Bay, Sydney.

engagement with Bali, he was part of a new transnational network of architects and designers who were crafting the design culture for the forthcoming boom in exotic hedonism that was to define the hotel and tourism industry across the region in the next decade.

Through their work in Bali, both Muller and Bawa also had a seminal influence on the early career of another architect of future pan-regional significance in the hotel sector, Kerry Hill. As a recent graduate in architecture from Western Australia, Hill had been working in Hong Kong for the large corporate architectural practice of Palmer & Turner (P&T) when that firm was commissioned to design Bali's next major international hotel.[23] Having seized an opportunity to join the Bali Hyatt project as the site architect and construction supervisor for P&T, Hill had also relocated to Bali by the time that Muller and Bawa were both working there in 1972. Contact between the young architect and these more experienced expatriate peers was perhaps inevitable given the fact that the new Hyatt was being built on the same site on Sanur Beach that had originally been intended for the Matahari Resort. Once welcomed into Waworuntu and Friend's cosmopolitan social circle, however, Hill was soon converted to their vernacular sympathies and the new design possibilities that such *arrière-garde* aesthetics presented. The low-rise configuration of the P&T designed hotel already reflected new planning controls, spearheaded by Waworuntu and Friend's advocacy, that limited new development to the height of a coconut tree.[24] But Hill was emboldened by Muller and Bawa's approaches to further soften the hard geometries of the brutalist-style concrete hotel by draping its terraced guest blocks with hanging gardens, and by incorporating traditional Balinese building materials and elements in the fitting-out of the extensive public areas and poolside amenities that had been left to the site architect and gardeners to design and build. Years later, as Hill's biographer has suggested, Bawa's much acclaimed design for the Kandalama Hotel in the jungles of central Sri Lanka, with its cascading screen of suspended foliage, was further evidence of the recurring echoes of these fruitful early encounters in Bali in the later work of this emerging professional network of "old Bali hands".[25]

The Rise of Bali Style: Asia as an Emerging Centre for Global Capital

While the initial development of the Bali Style can be explained, as we have just outlined, as the mutual invention of a particular confluence of individuals and local entrepreneurial context, the subsequent rise of Bali Style would not have been possible without a particular change in the global economic climate, and the new role that Asia was to play in it. By the mid 1970s, following on from the initial shift of power from expatriate colonial capital to the local entrepreneurial elite, in parallel with economic recession in the West, substantially new patterns of exchange would develop in Asia. An early instance of such emergent transnational networks within the postcolonial context was the rise of an international tourism and hotel industry exploiting the new possibilities of affordable air travel, and Western fascination with the exotica of Asia and the hedonistic pleasures of the recent colonial past. Within this context, the rise of a pan-Asian tourism industry headed by the Asian elite opened the doors for the idea of an idyllic island retreat to be cultivated as an economic tool that could be applied beyond Bali's shores. A new pattern of architectural patronage emerged, and as we will demonstrate, the rise of certain Western architects and designers who were later associated with the high point of the hotel industry in the 1980s would not have been possible without this earlier patronage by Asian entrepreneurs.

International tourism of the new "mass" order had not yet fully arrived in Bali by the time that Friend made his initial beachhead in 1966. Whilst the volume of tourists had increased almost thirty-fold since the pre-war days of weekly port calls by KPM steamers, when there had been only one hotel on the island, there were still fewer than 30,000 foreign tourists visiting per year. But a sea change was about to be experienced in the rates of tourism growth and associated property development over the next two decades. By 1988 foreign tourist arrivals were approaching 600,000 per year, a further twenty-fold increase since the opening of Bali's own international airport in 1969. These tourist volumes were projected to more than double again by the early 1990s, prompting the hotel capacity to increase from 13,000 rooms in 1988 to 20,000 by 1993.[26]

The new international airport, just a few kilometres south-west of Sanur, was still two years from completion, when Friend returned to stay in 1967. But his first impressions a year earlier of the seemingly uncanny perfection of an island paradise still untrammelled by mass tourism need to be put in the harsher light of that particular historical moment. Only months before, between September 1965 and mid 1966, Bali had been a hotspot in nationwide violence precipitated by an anti-communist purge by the Indonesian army, which subsequently resulted in the replacement of President Sukarno by General Suharto as the head of state. In a bid to rid the island of communist party members and their sympathisers, among whom Chinese Indonesians and their material culture were inordinately targeted, the purge had effectively erased most evidence of the heterogeneity of the local populace, reinforcing the notion of the purity of the Balinese culture.[27] To protect "Bali" from the hybridising threat of other local cultures had, in fact, been government policy ever since the colonial Dutch administration had determined to preserve the Hindu-Javanese culture against the spread of Islam following the Java War (1825–1830). By the early twentieth century, protecting the purity and preserving the order of an idealised island culture putatively harmonious with nature and cosmos, that was safe for tourist consumption, was already becoming a state enterprise. Therefore, the Australian discovery of this idealised Bali in the mid 1960s was hardly the first of such politically constructed touristic romances. In the immediate aftermath of the events of 1965–66, however, the circumstances were particularly ripe to consummate it. The purge had not only substantially erased the Chinese cultural presence on the island, but with it the potential competition of the local Chinese business community in subsequent tourism development. Accordingly, small entrepreneurs like Waworuntu and Friend were able to take advantage of this opportunity to acquire property and cultural artefacts to develop their introverted vision for an idyllic tourist village.

The launch of the Waworuntu–Friend venture was additionally serendipitous in the context of larger national-level policy initiatives where the Indonesian government, along with other postcolonial governments of the time, had begun to engage tourism as an essential part of the national strategy for economic development.[28] Suharto's "New Order" regime was one of the first among postcolonial Asian nations to anticipate the radical opening up of a market economy to entrepreneurship, and the liberalisation of international investment in the tourism industry allowed for a shift from the xenophobic attitude towards foreigners that had been harboured in the initial ideologically charged period of postcolonial nation-building preceding the coup. Over the coming years, this policy further allowed for the monolithic patronage of the socialist-nationalist state under Sukarno to be replaced by a form of disorganised capitalism and associated networks for exchange. By the start of the 1970s, a new national policy on tourism was well established and Bali served as the centre point of this strategy, already incorporated in the 1969–1974 five-year plan as an essential part of the process of cultural commodification. On a global scale, the United Nation's establishment of the World Trade Organisation (UNWTO) in 1970 encouraged international support, and by 1971 a World Bank-backed project had engaged a French consultancy to prepare the "Masterplan for Development of Tourism in Bali".[29] Moreover, international seminars held in Bali debated the implications of these policy interventions, positioning the island at the centre of the discourse on cultural tourism.[30]

It is within this renewed political environment that we observe the arrival of a new breed of entrepreneurs that would succeed the homegrown attempts of the likes of Waworuntu and Friend. As indicated earlier, these new business elites no longer originated from ex-colonial Western nations but from within rapidly growing business circles in Asia. In illustrating the impact of this emergent Asian elite, and the greater transnational exchange across Asia within which they were now operating, the case of the Indian hotelier M.S. Oberoi is of particular relevance. Mohan Singh Oberoi (1898–2002) recognised early on that rather than building conventional accommodation based on rote patterns and practices, he could utilise his nimble management expertise and style to develop a hotel business distinguished by its focus on delivering exceptional experiences for its guests.[31] Perceiving that increasingly efficient and affordable air travel would make India and other former colonial countries promotable new destinations for both business and leisure, he and his now publicly listed company already had a major stake in the new flight services and catering market in India by the late 1950s. Oberoi, now in collaboration with his sons, concentrated through the 1960s on securing a significant market share of the mainstream modern luxury hotel business in India. Moreover, by the early 1970s they were already well ahead of the curve in investing as well in the anticipated renewal of the old "Orientalist" allure, for jaded post-industrial Western consumers, of the exotica of the "East". As opportunities presented themselves, they were ready to expand internationally and exploit the profitability of their business principles and foresight on a broader regional stage, and in different cultural contexts.

Having attempted to expand their operations outside of India with the management of the Soaltee Hotel in Kathmandu in 1969 and subsequently the Imperial Hotel in Singapore in 1970, the Oberoi Hotel group was ready to engage in greater capital works with new construction and restoration projects. Constructed between 1973 and 1975, Oberoi's spanking new Colombo hotel would be the first overseas opportunity to plan and build a major new hotel from scratch. This was particularly important as Oberoi had initially sought to engage Minoru Yamasaki, architect of the Twin Towers for the World Trade Center in New York, to design it, but settled for no less than Skidmore, Owings and Merrill (SOM). Engaging SOM, the large corporate-style practice that was the most definitive architectural purveyor of the image of modern American corporate hegemony associated with Hilton and other important hotel brands, was a coup for the Indian entrepreneurs. By the late 1970s, the further expansion of the chain – which now stretched from the Gulf region and eastern seaboard of Africa all the way to Australia, including hotels in Baghdad, Cairo, Aswan, Zanzibar and Adelaide – had allowed the Oberois to connect with new sources of design expertise and ideas relating to cultural tourism, and these felicitous encounters further defined seminal Oberoi developments across the region, including Bali.

In Egypt, where, in 1971, the Oberois had the fortuitous opportunity to acquire Mena House, a former royal lodge adjacent to the Pyramids at Giza, they displayed a particular approach to artistic and architectural patronage in developing a new focus on architectural heritage restoration, and the reconstruction, thereby, of authentic cultural experiences. The next most obvious successor to Mena House, in an emerging portfolio of classic nineteenth-century hotels, was the acquisition and restoration of the Windsor Hotel in Melbourne, Australia (1980–1984), in which the Oberois were to invest millions of dollars in the best local professional design and conservation advice and craftsmanship.[32] These projects demonstrate the increasingly conscious cultivation of a distinctive new sensibility in hotel design across the intervening decade, with the conviction and commitment to invest in seemingly anachronistic values and tastes that, nevertheless, would prove to be prescient of highly marketable future trends.

Distinct from the period recreations of the palatial exclusivity of Mena House and the Gold Rush opulence that Oberoi aimed to restore to the Windsor Hotel, the company's first major stake in the luxury hotel experience that would rely on a more culturally embedded approach to architectural design and place-making came with the 1977 acquisition of the Kayu Aya hotel in Bali.[33] This was the small boutique hotel that had recently been design-built from scratch by Peter Muller, employing traditional Balinese building and planning principles (Figures 3.7 & 3.8). However, it had not been completed, and was now partially vandalised following a dispute between its original owners. Muller was immediately re-engaged by the new owner-management partnership, and the restored and expanded resort, The Bali Oberoi, would come to define a new breed of resort architecture recognised as Bali Style. Now appropriated into the exclusive portfolio of exceptional places and experiences that defined the Oberoi brand, the Indian hotel chain ultimately enabled Bali Style to be successfully demonstrated and thereby influence the design culture of the forthcoming boom.

Figures 3.7 & 3.8: Private villa courtyard gateway (*top*) and reception pavilion (*bottom*) at the Bali Oberoi (originally Kayu Aya) showing use of traditional Balinese design elements and local construction materials. Source: the authors, 2014, and Peter Muller Archive, Walsh Bay, Sydney.

Before engaging Muller, the Oberois had already been involved for over a decade with another Australian architect and former associate of Muller's, Alan Gilbert. Gilbert was engaged as an interior designer for the Oberois through the Hong Kong-based interior design practice of Dale Keller & Associates (DKA), which had come to define the hotel interior scene of the 1960s and 1970s in Asia (Figure 3.9).

Expat American designers, Dale and Patricia Keller, had come to Hong Kong in 1961, via Japan, to design the interiors for the new Hong Kong Hilton.[34] Building on the success of that flagship project for the Hilton empire in Asia, they subsequently established Hong Kong as their base for what was to rapidly become one of the most prolific and global interior design firms in the world, with the emerging market for luxury hotels across Asia and the Middle East as their prime territory. Graduate studies in Asian art and architecture undertaken in post-war Japan in the 1950s had created passionate and knowledgeable connoisseurs of the Kellers, and their subsequent approach to interior design was informed by their vision of the modern luxury hotel as the international traveller's initial primer in cultural tourism. Securely ensconced within the

Figure 3.9: Lobby view of the Oberoi Sheraton, Bombay, c.1973, designed by Alan Gilbert for Dale Keller & Associates, showing redeployment of traditionally crafted decorative elements and textures within a modernist conception of interior space and modular furniture layouts. Source: Alan Gilbert Archive, WSU Centre for Cultural Studies, Sydney.

modernist certainties of the contemporary international-style architectural exteriors typical of such hotels, interiors were a way to bring the colour, textures and tectonic riches of local and regional building culture safely inside the fortress-like shell of the hotel building and grounds, in an environmentally benign yet experientially immersive manner.

These initial attempts at incorporating local cultural references into otherwise modernist architectural shells became highly successful in the 1960s, as the changing political climate and affordable jet travel brought a new type of tourist in ever greater numbers to these destinations. Soon the older ranks of Western travellers were joined by regional tourists moving within Asia, and with no particular affiliation to the modernist architecture of the Hiltons they valued these cultural references differently. Accordingly DKA were able to formalise the process into a new design method, and the practice of collecting and cataloguing local artefacts and cultural imagery as a means to develop a thematic concept for the interior was successfully applied by Alan Gilbert and others right across Asia.

Alan Gilbert was part of a small group of Australian architecture graduates who had become pioneers in engaging with Asia at a time when the White Australia policy had kept Australia insular and disconnected from its immediate neighbours in Asia. Gilbert and a former classmate in architectural studies at the Sydney Technical College, Adrian Snodgrass, had both worked on and off with Peter Muller in the 1950s and early 1960s as two of his earliest and closest associates in the Sydney practice. Unusual for an Australian of his generation, Snodgrass had decided to travel to Asia in the mid 1950s to seek alternative cultural knowledge, and spent time living and studying with spiritual guides in Sri Lanka and Japan, respectively, for several years in each case. Alan Gilbert followed in his footsteps in 1963 when he travelled to Hong Kong, Japan and eventually China, as a freelance filmmaker and photojournalist documenting vernacular traditions and China's Cultural Revolution. Gilbert eventually landed back in Hong Kong in 1967 where he resumed his professional design career with DKA.[35] Drawing on his earlier documentary filmmaking and photojournalistic experience, Gilbert helped DKA with regional cultural research needed to inform their design practice. However, as these research projects became more complex, he sought the expertise of his old friend Adrian Snodgrass, who was commissioned by DKA to write a major report on the "Handcrafts of Bali".[36] This and a similar report on the crafts of Sri Lanka produced by Snodgrass along with other members of DKA were subsequently engaged by the respective national governments as part of their tourism policy documentation. Arguably, Snodgrass, who later pursued a full-time academic career, was the intellectual muse and critical thinker of this group of fellow Asia enthusiasts, responsible for igniting the curiosity of Gilbert and ultimately Muller himself in the opportunities for both personal and professional growth inherent in a deeper cultural understanding of their regional neighbours.[37]

By the late 1970s this extension of interest in cultural and ethnographic research, applied to the growing demands of the tourism industry, prompted Snodgrass, Gilbert and Muller to regroup with additional expert associates to form a new type of multidisciplinary professional consultancy that they were subsequently to brand and promote under the name "Regional Design and Research" (RDR).[38] Reflecting on the body of pioneering design work and research that they had produced independently over the preceding decade or so, primarily in Bali, Sri Lanka and India, the RDR collective recognised that what connected this work in novel and valuable ways was a common strategy – the "ethno-technological" survey of design as a cultural practice and product, which they were exploring through a broad array of unconventional strategies and tactics in the fast-changing development scene of modern Asia (Figure 3.10).[39]

Defined and further developed, it was this method itself that RDR, as acknowledged regional experts, could now package and deliver as their unique professional service. In addition to the hands-on research-based architectural and interior design work that they would continue to produce, RDR also contributed more directly to policy. RDR-produced reports on indigenous building techniques

Figure 3.10: Selection of interior details employed in the design of hotels across Asia in the 1970s, which were developed through the ethno-technological research on Asian crafts by RDR (Regional Design and Research). Source: RDR Promotional Brochure, c.1978, courtesy Adrian Snodgrass.

and crafts, for example, that not only examined their economic and commercial potential as forms of cultural commodities in the new tourism-driven economy, but also explored how such technology could be sustained and managed in the context of modernising building industries, while incorporating international standards of quality control. Tourist impact studies for both government and private developers were another area in which this method gave RDR an original and competitive perspective as expert consultants in this expanding pan-Asian tourism industry, with further commissions that were to extend their services to projects in the Philippines, China and elsewhere in Asia.[40]

Conclusion: Bali Style as Method

"Bali Style" has always been a somewhat ad-hoc phenomenon. If we trace it back to the origins of its contemporary architectural manifestation, as we have in this chapter, it emerged not so much by design, but as an expression of a critical resistance or counterpoint to the universalising norms and forms of mass tourism that the cosmopolitan entrepreneurs, Waworuntu and Oberoi, began to cultivate in Bali in the 1970s in collaboration with Friend, Muller, Bawa and other sympathetic providers of design expertise. This ostensible "style" was never a strictly prescribed set of formalisms, but by the late 1980s, we may now conclude, it had become more obviously what it is today: an open-ended creative design "method" for producing exquisite and distinctive experiences, not least through sensitive interpretation of the tectonic cultures of place in a spatially, texturally and sensorially immersive manner.

In 1988, less than two decades since the initial Bali Style resort prototype had been conceived in the scheme for the unbuilt Matahari resort, Peter and Carole Muller were back in Bali to design and build an exquisite new boutique resort, this time near Ubud in the picturesque rice-terraced interior of the island, where Spies and his circle of artists had made their idyllic home in the 1920s and 1930s. Once again, the Mullers were invested professionally, financially and, if anything, even more physically than they had been in the earlier Bali projects. Whilst Carole focused on the interiors, Peter Muller (now approaching his 60s) threw himself again into the actual labour of design-building this project through hands-on collaboration with local craftsmen. But the difference this time was that this value-adding approach to the crafting of the buildings was no longer just a speculative and cost-saving experiment, but a proven method. What the project's backers were investing in was not just the value of the site, and tourist growth projections, but this particular way of crafting an architecturally rich and intimate environment of retreat and repose. This was the key to an exclusive niche market that was now clearly established for those like the owner of the new Aman Group,

Adrian Zecha, who could appreciate this architectural distinction and develop it to the next level.

Czech-Indonesian businessman and former journalist, Zecha, was yet another cosmopolitan Asian entrepreneur who was well ahead of the curve in his transnational vision for the future of the Asian hotel and leisure industry.[41] Having recently sold his multi-million dollar stake in another international group of more conventional luxury hotels (The Regency Hotel Group), Zecha understood that architecture itself was the principal cultural commodity in which he would need to invest carefully to build the particular brand of hotel he sought to create. The Amandari, as Muller's new villa-hotel would be called, was one of three such exclusive boutique resorts that were then being developed simultaneously in Bali by the Aman Group. The second, the Amanusa, was being designed by Muller's former protégé, Kerry Hill, on a site on the south-eastern tip of the island while the third, the Amankila, was the work of Paris-based American architect, Ed Tuttle. Tuttle had also produced Amanpuri, the inaugural project of this new chain of ultra-exclusive small hotels, near Phuket in Thailand the previous year. Amanpuri had actually been inspired by director-owner Zecha's personal experience of the Batujimbar Estate in Sanur where he owned and occasionally lived in one of the Bawa-designed villas. But in order to create new and unique experiences comparable to but not just reproducing the earlier inventions of Bawa and Muller at Sanur, he understood that he would need to cultivate not only the equivalent pedigree of architects, but also those committed to the architectural crafting not just of designed spaces and objects, but of living cultural projects and experiences that anticipated maintenance and potential for further development and change.

Zecha's subsequent parallel engagements with Tuttle, Muller and Hill in the development of Aman's Bali hotels, and the sheer confidence in initiating three of these projects simultaneously on the same small island, indicated an altogether more intentional and clarified vision for this emerging new resort chain relative to his entrepreneurial predecessors. Empowered and mobilised by his appreciation of Bali Style as a method of place-making rather than just a particular look, Zecha would now deploy the method in further innovative developments within and beyond Bali's shores.[42] Whilst the Amandari was to be Peter Muller's last major work in Bali, this was just the beginning of a relationship that Zecha and Kerry Hill were to develop through a series of further resort and urban hotel projects for the Aman group and its subsidiaries across Asia, all the way from Japan to India (Figures 3.11 & 3.12).

Bali Style is not a historical style, but it has a history. As the preceding outline of that story has hopefully established, Bali Style cannot be dismissed reductively as merely a formal aesthetic style, but nor can or should it be attributed authority as authentic cultural practice in any form. Understood within the context of its

Figures 3.11 & 3.12: Continuation of Bali Style as method in the design of subsequent generations of hotels. The Serai Manggis (now Alila Manggis), Bali, Indonesia, by architect Kerry Hill, 1992–94 (*top*), and Alila Villas Uluwatu, Bali, Indonesia, by architects WOHA, 2009 (*bottom*). Source: the authors, 2014.

emergence in the 1960s, and the subsequent rise of culture-focused mass-tourism in Asia in the 1970s and 1980s, we have tried to articulate how this architecturally modest if not inconspicuous facet of recent cultural production was nevertheless engaged in broader political and economic changes at the regional and even global scale, which contributed directly to the subsequent resurgence of Asia as an economic and cultural powerhouse.

Equipped with the critiques and metaphors that subsequent analyses of postmodern/late-capitalist cultural production have furnished, it is tempting in retrospect to offer a more theorised representation of these historically specific developments. Could these be explained, for instance, in terms of a dialectic between what might be characterised as "hyper-traditionalism" in the design and conceptual construction of other-worldly leisure experiences, and what Fredric Jameson calls "postmodern hyperspace"; seamlessly commodified, as he has illustrated, in the new typology of mega-hotels that John Portman and other architects enamoured of his ersatz neo-futurist style began to design and propagate worldwide in the mid 1970s?[43] An extended and more discerning comparative analysis of the evolving typologies of the tropical resort in the era of increasingly deregulated transnational flows of capital and tourist-consumers, that followed the seminal early developments that we have examined here, could surely be fruitful. It is also apparent, however, that the paradoxical similarities between the neo-liberal corporate imperialism of hotel development in the expanded (post-national) field of late-capitalism, and the logic of cultural tourism and other modes of cultural (re)production that applied in the not-so-distant colonial era complicate and limit the applicability of "postmodern" cultural theories, as such, to the "postcolonial" developments that we have considered here.

It may be useful simply to consider the efficacy of "Bali Style" in terms of the metaphor of a "black box", the internal complexities and contradictions of which have remained concealed as long as it continues to succeed as a viable mode of cultural production. Opening the box, as critical historians, to examine developments in the architectural history of the recent past reveals important threads of cultural and aesthetic production pertinent to our critical understanding of Asia's transformative political and economic development in the twenty-first century that may be traced back to the middle decades of the previous century, if not well before. Understanding how architectural thinking and making has also contributed directly, in its own terms, to such significant changes is, we believe, not just important for the architectural and allied design disciplines to appreciate, but revealing of the deeper architectures of power in which society, culture and values are invested, and the capacity of creative design agency to change these, just as readily as they might be reproduced.

Notes

1. A selection of popular professional references and coffee-table books continues to propagate "Bali Style", see for instance: Rio Helmi and Barbara Walker, *Bali Style* (New York: Vendome Press, 1995); Gianni Francione and Luca Tettoni, *Bali Modern: The Art of Tropical Living* (Singapore: Periplus Editions, 2000); Gianni Francione and Luca Tettoni, *Bali Houses: New Wave Asian Architecture and Design* (Singapore: Periplus Editions, 2003); Gianni Francione, Masano Kawana, and Kim Inglis, *Bali Living: Innovative Tropical Design*, (Singapore: Periplus Editions, 2008); Kim Inglis, *Bali Home: Inspirational Design Ideas* (Singapore: Tuttle Publishing, 2010).
2. The style, as its historical beginnings discussed through the course of this chapter will reveal, has possible regional modern affiliations but could just as easily be characterised as what Ronald Burnskill terms "polite" architecture. See, Roland Burnskill, *Illustrated Handbook of Vernacular Architecture* (New York: University Books, 1970). For a more critical discussion of vernacular processes in contemporary Bali see Amanda Achmadi, "Beyond Traditional Bali Architecture," in Peter J.M. Nas (ed.) *The Past in the Present: Architecture in Indonesia* (Rotterdam: NAi Publishing, 2007), 85–96.
3. See Amanda Achmadi, "The Architecture of Balinisation: Writings on architecture, the villages, and the construction of Balinese cultural identity in the 20th century" (PhD diss., University of Melbourne, 2007). See also, Amanda Achmadi, "The Architecture of Balinisation," in Peter Herrle and Erik Wegerhoff (ed.) *Architecture and Identity* (Munster: Verlag, 2008), 73–90; and Philip Goad, Anoma Pieris and Patrick Bingham-Hall *New Directions in Tropical Asian Architecture* (Balmain, NSW: Pesaro Publishing, 2005).
4. See Philip Goad, *Architecture Bali: Birth of the Tropical Boutique Resort*, (Singapore: Tuttle Publishing, 2003); David Robson, *Geoffrey Bawa: The Complete Works* (London: Thames & Hudson, 2002); and Oscar Rieda Ojera (ed.) *Kerry Hill: Crafting Modernism* (London: Thames and Hudson, 2013).
5. For discussions of tropical imaginings see David Arnold, *The Problem of Nature: Environment, Culture and European Expansion* (Oxford: Blackwell, 1996). See also Jiat-Hwee Chang, *A Genealogy of Tropical Architecture: Colonial Networks, Nature and Technoscience* (New York: Routledge, 2016).
6. As the planning historian Stephen Ward has observed, there can be very different modes and degrees of knowledge transfer in transnational exchanges of professional and technical expertise, and the relative balances of power entailed. See Stephen V. Ward, "Re-examining the International Diffusion of Planning," in *Urban Planning in a Changing World: The Twentieth Century Experience*, R. Freestone (ed), (London: Taylor and Francis, 2000), 40–60.
7. Goad, *Architecture Bali*.

8. See Barry Pearce, *Donald Friend, 1915–1989: Retrospective* (Sydney: Art Gallery of New South Wales, 1990), 16–17; see also, Barry Pearce, "Interrupted Genius: Donald Friend as Artist," (paper presented at "An Inventive Magic: Donald Friend and his Diaries" conference of the National Library of Australia, Canberra, February 23–24, 2001), accessed 9 October 2016, http://www.nla.gov.au/events/donaldfriend/papers/bpearce.html.
9. Donald Friend, *The Diaries of Donald Friend*, vol. 4 (Canberra: National Library of Australia, 2006).
10. John Moyle, "Donald Friend in Bali," (paper presented at "An Inventive Magic: Donald Friend and his Diaries" conference of the National Library of Australia, Canberra, February 23–24, 2001), accessed 9 October 2016, http://www.nla.gov.au/events/donaldfriend/papers/jmoyle.html.
11. See Robson, *Geoffrey Bawa*.
12. See Adrian Vickers, *Bali: A Paradise Created* (Hong Kong: Tuttle, 2012).
13. See Moyle, "Donald Friend in Bali". The construction of this ideal in the interwar years, and its relative fragility in reality, for Spies in particular, is explored in Vickers, *Bali: A Paradise Created*, 113–184.
14. See Diana Darling, *Tandjung Sari – A Magical Door to Bali* (Singapore: Editions Didier Millet, 2012).
15. Notable guests included Ingrid Bergman, Mick Jagger and Margaret Mead. Mead had returned to Bali late in life as one of the intellectual heroes of the Woodstock generation that was finding its way to Bali by the 1970s as the last stop on the Asian hippie trail, in search of the idyllic, sexually liberated culture that Mead had described in her influential early work of the 1930s. See Darling, *Tandjung Sari*.
16. The circle included painter Laki Senanayake, architect Ismeth Raheem, and textile artist Barbara Sansoni. Danish architect, Ulrik Plesner, Bawa's unofficial professional partner in the early years of his practice, was another early champion of this vernacular focus. See, Robson, *Geoffrey Bawa*, 55, 141.
17. See David Robson, *Beyond Bawa: Modern Masterworks of Monsoon Asia* (London: Thames & Hudson, 2007).
18. This observation is attributed to the Australian architect Kerry Hill, whose own important relationship with Bawa we will return to presently. See Geoffrey London, "The Nature of Practice," in Ojera, *Kerry Hill: Crafting Modernism* (London: Thames and Hudson, 2013), 21.
19. Robson, *Geoffrey Bawa*, 24–27. "Bricolage" is the term that Robson uses, but we believe our respective interpretations of Bawa's encounter with Bali are somewhat distinct in their nuances and implications.
20. Details of Peter Muller's involvement in Bali are extracted from a series of conversations with the authors between 2014 and 2016. See also: Jacqueline C. Urford, *Peter Muller: The Complete Works* (Sydney: Walsh Bay Press, 2008).

21. See, for example, Douglas I. Fettling, *The Balinese Building Codes and Their Application to Domestic Architecture in South Bali*, (Melbourne: University of Melbourne School of Architecture, 1971).
22. When Muller had originally taken on the Kayu Aya project in 1972, the project was meant to be a series of cottages for its American owner Charles Osborn and his friends. Over the course of construction the client's demands kept changing and more cottages were added until it became a larger complex. As such the original complex was not planned, but grew organically.
23. See Ojera, *Kerry Hill*.
24. See Emanuel Jehuda De Kadt, "Tourism – Passport to Development?," World Bank Research: Perspectives on the Social and Cultural Effects of Tourism in Developing Countries, Volume 65 (1979).
25. London, "The Nature of Practice," 25.
26. Michel Picard, "'Cultural Tourism' in Bali: Cultural Performances as Tourist Attraction", *Indonesia*, 49 (April 1990): 37–74.
27. See Adrian Vickers, *A History of Modern Indonesia* (Cambridge: Cambridge University Press, 2005). See also Geoffrey Robinson, *The Dark Side of Paradise: Political Violence in Bali* (Ithaca NY: Cornell University Press, 1995); and Jean Gelman Taylor, *Indonesia: Peoples and Histories* (New Haven CT: Yale University Press, 2003).
28. See Michel Picard, *Bali: Cultural Tourism and Touristic Culture* (Singapore: Archipelago Press, 1996).
29. De Kadt, "Tourism – Passport to Development?"
30. Picard, "Cultural Tourism in Bali," 41.
31. See Bachi J. Karkaria, *Dare to Dream: A Life of M.S. Oberoi* (New York: Penguin, 1992). Also see, Gita Piramal and Margaret Herdeck, *India's Industrialists*, vol.1 (Washington DC: Lynne Rienner, 1985).
32. See details in Karkaria, *Dare to Dream*. Also see relevant newspaper articles in *The Age*, June 11, 1980 and *The Age*, 18 February 1982.
33. Peter Muller in conversation with authors, 2014–2016.
34. Details of Dale Keller & Associates are based on a series of conversations between Dale Keller and the authors over 2015. See also, "Dale and Pat Keller," accessed 9 October 2016, http://www.nealprince-asid.com/id165.html.
35. Alan Gilbert Archive, UWS Centre for Cultural Studies, Sydney, accessed October, 2016.
36. Adrian Snodgrass in conversation with authors, 2013–2016. See also, "RDR: Regional Design and Research," promotional brochure (Sydney: RDR, no date c.1978).
37. Adrian Snodgrass, e-mail message to authors, 4 January 2009. Peter Muller had also been inspired in his affinities for Asian culture and philosophy by Peter Kollar, a Sydney-based architectural academic who had a deep intellectual interest in the

"Traditional" (or "Perennial") philosophy of the comparative-cultural scholars, Rene Guenon and Ananda K. Coomaraswamy. See Stanislaus Fung, "The 'Sydney School'?", in A. Leach, A. Moulis, and N. Sully (eds), *Shifting Views: Selected Essays on the Architectural History of Australia and New Zealand* (Brisbane: University of Queensland Press, 2008), no.12, 191–192.

38. The collective included Chris Carlisle, a former British diplomat based in the Middle East who coordinated finance and contracts, and, unofficially, Snodgrass's ethnographer wife, Judith. At this point in his career Muller had parted ways with his wife, Carole, who was also a cultural ethnographer, but the couple was to regroup and collaborate again on later projects.
39. "For each of its design projects RDR undertakes a research programme that covers a much wider scope than usual architectural research. Before commencing design for a project, RDR sends a research unit to the region, including trained ethno-technologists and anthropologists. This team travels extensively throughout the cultural area collecting samples, recording information, and assessing standards, availability, feasibility and fitness of materials, building and craft techniques, the arts, building forms, and design themes; codifies relevant economic, environmental and geographical data and collects in-depth information on various aspects of the culture, religion, customs and outlooks of the people." In "RDR: Regional Design and Research," 2.
40. Adrian Snodgrass in conversation with authors, 2013–2016, and "RDR: Regional Design and Research".
41. Details of Adrian Zecha's involvement in Bali have been extracted from conversations with Peter Muller, Adrian Snodgrass and Kerry Hill, in discussion with authors over the 2014–2016 period. For further details of the Bali projects see Peter Muller, *Amandari: Design and Build* (Sydney: Walsh Bay Press, 2012). For details of Amanpuri see "Amanpuri, Phuket Island" *Mimar* 36 (1990): 40–45.
42. Contemporary practitioners continue to extend the reach of Bali Style. The late landscape architect Michael White, for example, (yet another Australian expatriate in Bali, who adopted the indigenous name of Made Wijaya), enjoyed the patronage of celebrity clients around the world. These included David Bowie, for whom he designed an exclusive Bali-style retreat on Bowie's own private island in the Caribbean. See Made Wijaya, "Out of Bali: the 'Bali-style' brand continues to influence tropical resort development," *Urban Land* 65, no. 11, (2006); and —, "The Rise and Rise of Bali Style: Expatriate Dream Homes in a Post Industrial Paradise," *East Magazine* (July 2000), accessed 9 October 2016, http://www.ptwijaya.com/media/2000-east/east2000.html. See also Sophia V. Schweitzer, "Building Bali-Style," *Hawaiian Style* 5, no. 3: 123–131.
43. For a discussion of "hyper-traditionalism" in contemporary tourism studies, see Daniela M. Peluso, "'For export only': Ayahuasca tourism and hyper-traditionalism." Working Paper Series: Hyper-Traditions and "Real" Places

189 (2006), 482–500. Viewed 27/08/17 at: https://kar.kent.ac.uk/9131/. For "postmodern hyper-space" in the case of the Bonaventure Hotel, Los Angeles, see Frederic Jameson, "Postmodernism and Consumer Society" (1988). In Frederic Jameson, *The Cultural Turn: Selected Writings on the Postmodern, 1983–1998*. London: Verso, 1998.

Section Two

EPISTEMOLOGY

CHAPTER 4

Conservation Diplomacy and the Narratives of Material Antiquity

TIM WINTER

Introduction

The focus of this chapter is on antiquity and its political economies of scholarship in Southeast Asia. Structures found at Angkor, Borobudur, Vat Phou, Sukhothai, Ayutthaya, and Mỹ Sơn are critically important to our understanding of Southeast Asian history. Within scholarly accounts of the past, these ruins sit somewhat uneasily between architecture, archaeology and art history. The focus here is on the shifting landscapes of scholarship that have framed them over the last century and a half, read in relation to the broader political economies within which particular modes of knowledge production have occurred. In order to discern between an era of colonial research, the formation of expert networks in the mid twentieth century and more recent changes therein, the chapter foregrounds the idea of heritage diplomacy as its explanatory frame. Specific attention is given to Bagan in Myanmar, as it is suggested the site represents an important signpost to some likely shifts in the way Southeast Asia's antiquity will be framed, narrated, valued and symbolically coded over the coming years. In that regard, the chapter takes up the question of futures, a theme that comes with the usual risks and caveats.

At the time of writing, the archaeological site of Bagan is moving towards nomination for world heritage listing. As the capital of the first Burmese empire from the eleventh to the thirteenth century CE, the city is located on the east bank of the Irrawaddy in central Myanmar. Over the course of three centuries, somewhere in the order of 3,000 Buddhist shrines and stupas were constructed on the site, with the largest and most ambitious commissioned by successive kings. The application for world heritage listing centres around identifying its significance and value as a cultural, architectural, religious or historical site. More specifically, this means identifying the "criteria" by which Bagan holds "outstanding universal value" (OUV): the benchmark of world heritage designation.[1] Like elsewhere in Myanmar, recent political reforms mean the level of international attention garnered on Bagan is now increasing. It would be safe to assume, given multiple precedents elsewhere in the region, that this will continue to accelerate as the site moves toward and beyond world heritage nomination. At the time of writing, the dossier for nomination is in the early stages of preparation, with the UNESCO Bangkok office providing assistance in the form of expert round tables, meetings and guidance on process. Given the historical size and scale of Bagan the likelihood of listing is high. As Kai Weise, an architect involved in the process noted in late 2014: "Bagan is of outstanding universal value. So it's a question of going through a process. As a site you can say it should be on the World Heritage List."[2]

But much like other sites seeking world heritage status, nomination and assessment is a tense undertaking, not least because the level of conservation work undertaken in recent times poses a particular conundrum. Since the early 1990s, significant reconstruction of the brick shrines has taken place, such that, and as we shall see in greater detail later, it is estimated in excess of 2,000 monuments have been rebuilt and otherwise altered (Figures 4.1 & 4.2). In addition, a number of modern interventions, namely a 60-metre-high viewing tower and roads, have been constructed within the archaeological area. Such (re)construction has been the subject of heavy criticism from experts in the international conservation community, with the prominent archaeologist Pierre Pichard describing the situation as "catastrophic"[3], and Christian Manhart, a programme specialist in Bangkok suggesting "a Disney-style fantasy version of one of the world's great religious and historical sites is being created by the government".[4] Such criticism stems from a concern that large-scale reconstruction has led to a loss of authenticity, with the insular Myanmar government failing to abide by today's international norms of conservation and heritage governance. But as Chapman notes, closer inspection reveals a more complex scenario, one in which funding and support for reconstruction has flowed into Myanmar from around the Asia region.[5]

The situation at Bagan thus speaks to wider debates within Asia's heritage profession concerning the validity of different approaches. Within the region there has been a sustained and growing unease about philosophies and practices of cultural conservation imported from the West. Asia, it is claimed, requires something distinct, as the region is materially, culturally and historically different to "the West". Those advancing such a critique have argued that less emphasis is placed on the "authenticity" of original material fabric and its preservation.

Figure 4.1: Pagoda including reconstructed elements, Bagan. Source: the author.

Figure 4.2: "Before" and "After", Bagan. Source: the author.

The ideas underpinning the 1994 Nara Declaration, a document that has proved highly influential in advancing this debate by foregrounding intangible heritage and the importance of understanding relative context, were renewed in October 2014 via a major international conference and fresh declaration: *Nara + 20: On Heritage Practices, Cultural Values, and the Concept of Authenticity*.

Whilst the origins and factors driving this debate are beyond the scope of discussion here,[6] it is worth acknowledging the critical role European colonialism has played in shaping the governance of the region's classical material culture and narration of its associated histories. The legacies of colonial scholarship linger on, and, as the following section illustrates, to understand the consequences of this it is necessary to situate earlier studies of Southeast Asia's antiquity within the broader political economies of the period.

Framing Antiquity: Between Art and Science

> If such a civilisation as Bagan emerged suddenly, the argument went, surely the stimulant was external. No doubt, Theravada Buddhism was a major factor in the emergence of Bagan and migrations were plausible. Yet the adoption of these interpretations, even if tentative, left some of us uneasy. In both explanations, the questions themselves assumed a sudden change, probably because of our biases for linear history and because the period before Bagan was so devoid of information. Yet there were a few tantalising pieces of evidence for the existence of a well-developed urban civilisation prior to Bagan that bothered us.[7]

In contrast to the architecture constructed in the last century or so, the far greater temporal distance between buildings of antiquity and the present day changes the relationship between memory, history and material culture. In particular, time spans stretching over millennia profoundly alter collective memories, as things become lost, reworked and reinvented between generations. Critically, there are few if any "historical" texts – such as newspapers, books, plans or diaries – that bear testimony to the importance of a particular site or building, and how it contributed to the "society" that gave birth to its construction. Over time then, stories, tales and even myths, supersede accurate recollections and factual knowledge. Antiquity in Southeast Asia, much like other parts of the world, has thus become synonymous with the idea that history needs to be unearthed, excavated, reclaimed, even rediscovered. Whilst the literal and metaphorical usage of such terminology has become fundamental to the discourse of archaeology, as concepts these terms also evoke the sense that the past needs to be retrieved, even reconstructed for wider audiences. And it is in this shared understanding of antiquity we see something critical. Unlike buildings of the print and industrial ages, the task of recovering and unearthing the history of antiquity can only be undertaken by a select few. Only scholars, those holding the expert knowledge are in a position to excavate and reclaim in ways that authoritatively speak of significance and those timelines and events, which together constitute the narratives of "history". In Southeast Asia, European exploration and subsequent structures of colonialism meant those in the privileged position of undertaking such tasks were primarily foreign. The gatekeepers of the past as "History" were mostly European. By implication then, the consolidation of scholarship into particular fields, together with the symbolic associations Europeans held towards landscapes, would prove critical to the ways in which Southeast Asia's distant past was interpreted.

As the cultural, artistic and intellectual changes brought about by the Renaissance filtered across Europe, ruins of antiquity captured the imagination. Framed as art, metaphor, allegory and as virtuous landscape, they physically embodied feelings that tied Europe's immutable pasts to its tumultuous presents.[8] The arrival of the Picturesque movement in the 1800s gave vernacular architecture, gnarled trees and ivy-covered ruins greater prominence within European visual and literary culture. An aesthetic category of both contemplation and beauty, the Picturesque celebrated ideas of decay and abandonment. As Woodward identifies, it was an aesthetic whereby "nature could be improved by the eye of the artist, who adds living trees and rocks, sunlight, water and old ruins to the palette".[9] The Picturesque was oriented by the desire of poets, philosophers and visual artists to capture the subjective and layering of the past and its memory. For writers such as Byron, Ruskin, Diderot and Shelley, the ruin became further mythologised as an icon of both lament and optimism. But as the ideals of Romanticism spread across Europe, the movement took on a political dimension, most tangibly within a post-revolutionary France. For those intellectuals committed to liberty, equality and fraternity, the notion of decaying, tree-covered structures of antiquity served as a powerful motif for "human pride, greed and stupidity".[10] In her analysis of the artist Hubert Robert, for example, Dubin argues his paintings of urban ruins in Paris represented a critique of the greed and structural and psychological uncertainties created by rapid urban transformation and the speculative accumulation of capital wealth that accompanied it.[11] Considering such changes in broader terms, Green has argued important shifts in the perception of nature occurred in the nineteenth century due to the rise of metropolitan culture and urban development.[12] In effect, an urban, industrialising modernity fostered a new aesthetic structure to nature, such that "another modernity" could be realised through encounters with ruins and other landscapes. It is within this frame that Woodward describes how the Italian city of Ninfa – destroyed and abandoned in the late fourteenth century – emerged as a place of evocation for travellers half a millennium later: "in the air humid with malaria the vegetation grew with a feverish vigour, as if exhilarating in the absence of human life. The ruins became a jungle, and as a jungle it was discovered by Romantic travellers."[13] The important point to note here then is how the Picturesque movement thus provided an aesthetic sensibility for early debates about the conservation of ruins and structures of antiquity. In Britain John Ruskin and William Morris proclaimed the virtues of leaving ruins untouched, such that we could more wholly feel the "truth", "beauty" and "memory" of the landscape.[14] In contrast, in France, Eugène Viollet-le-Duc advocated an approach towards conservation that facilitated greater amounts of reconstruction.

But in post-enlightenment Europe, ruins would also be the subject of an altogether different reading, one characterised by the values of objectivity, rationality and scientific rigour. From the seventeenth century onwards the Grand Tour encouraged individuals to travel for the study and appreciation of Europe's sites of antiquity, most notably the classical civilisations of the Greco-Roman Mediterranean. As debates in the arts and sciences shifted and evolved, notions of objectivity and empirical "verification" became the pivots around which the paradigm of scientific enquiry secured its dominant position in the hierarchy of knowledge production. Rationality, universality and the ordering of the physical world – ideals which elevated the scientific approach – would all come to bear upon the ways in which the ruins of antiquity were understood and interpreted. A form of enquiry that gathered evidence, privileged discovery and classification, and sought to deduce verifiable truths, influenced fields of scholarship as diverse as anthropology, architectural history, archaeology and epigraphy as they sought intellectual and institutional identities from the late eighteenth century onwards.[15] The emergence of formal archaeology in the mid to late nineteenth century for example involved drawing insights from empiricism and approaches developed in geology to construct scientific methodologies towards objects, buildings, artefacts and inscriptions: the texts of antiquity.[16] In effect, and as I have elaborated upon in more detail elsewhere, what we see is the consolidation of a scientistic materialism in the study and conservation of antiquity and the cultural past more broadly.[17]

Crucially here, it was a scholarly and aesthetic framing of antiquity that was exported from Europe and transposed to the landscapes and ruins of Asia. As Clarke reminds us, those romantics travelling out from Britain, France and the Netherlands were in search of a "vision of wholeness ... a oneness with nature, and for a reunification of religion, philosophy and art which had been sundered in the modern western world".[18] But by the mid nineteenth century this would also be accompanied by a desire to capture, record, classify and delineate Asia's material past in more rigorous, systematic ways. As archaeology found its feet, techniques and technologies for documenting, excavating and reconstructing ruins via anastylosis provided the means for reclaiming and unearthing the region's distant past. Seminal publications by Bruce Trigger in the 1980s helped open up space for more critical readings of the links between archaeology and the ideologies of imperialism, and the contribution they played in the production of non-European nationalisms.[19] In a similar vein, Benedict Anderson also explored the appropriation of the material legacy of glorious pasts as part of nation-building processes in nineteenth-century Southeast Asia; a transition towards newfound "imagined communities".[20]

Since then such themes have been examined in greater detail by other scholars working within the critical frame of postcolonial studies. In the case of India, for example, Cohn argues that over the course of the second half of the nineteenth century objects of antiquity were put to work and "transformed" as part of an evolving Indian historiography:

> India was to be provided with a linear history following a nineteenth century positivist historiography. Ruins could be dated, inscriptions made to reveal king lists, texts could be converted into sources for the study of the past. Each phase of the European effort to unlock the secret of the Indian past called for more and more collecting, more and more systems of classification, more and more building of repositories for the study of the past.[21]

Tapita Guha Thakurta has added considerable detail to this picture, via an account that traces the parallel emergence of archaeology and architectural history.[22] Pioneering British scholars such as James Fergusson and Alexander Cunningham were instrumental in fashioning an antiquarian past, featuring ruins, monuments and those "lost" cultural pasts in need of restitution. Rigorous description and documentation became a process of "extracting history from the ruins".[23] For Fergusson, India's long cultural past could be traced through shifting architectural styles, and, as Bohrer demonstrates, the co-development of archaeology and photography enabled the documentation of both changes and continuities across time and space through an "objective" visual means.[24] Such efforts contributed to a spatial articulation of India's historiography; a knowledge that would subsequently become critical to assertions of an Indian nationalist rhetoric. But as Guha Thakurta elaborates, Fergusson's reading of India's architectural past was heavily mediated by an aesthetic of the Picturesque imported from Britain. Indeed, for Fergusson, India's mountain ranges, craggy rocks, sun-baked plains, torrential waterfalls and haunting wilderness was altogether more "exotic" than England's landscape, with its tame, domesticated rolling hills and rivers. Interestingly, these features of nature provided the evocations of a cultural past characterised by decay and degeneration. Soon after his return to London, Fergusson published *Picturesque Illustrations of Ancient Architecture in Hindostan* in 1848. His depictions of the subcontinent's monumental past combined the romantic, evocative aesthetic of the Picturesque with an attempt to convey an authenticity through order and meticulous detail. Guha Thakurta argues that by proclaiming certain structures as exemplars of classical Buddhist art or high points of a Tamil Hindu culture, a chronologically ordered history was outlined, one oriented around racial and religious categories. Accordingly, Buddhist art was read in terms of its age and the integrity of its artistic and architectural style; characteristics that were contrasted with the "less refined" hybridity of Jainism. Over the following years Fergusson formulated a North/South, Aryan/Dravidian divide, with Buddhism associated with the purity of the former, and Tamil races in the South cited as evidence of civilisational decay. As Guha Thakurta notes, stone was not so much the material from which the past was pieced together, but instead merely acted as the evidence supporting a preconceived narrative of national history, and the idea that Indian civilisation had been in long-term decline.[25]

Further east, Southeast Asia presents us with a similar story. In 1860 the French botanist Henri Mouhot visited the temples of Angkor, located in what is today northern Cambodia. The serialisation of his diaries in *Le Tour du Monde* three years later told the story of abandoned architectural wonders and mysterious lost civilisations, an enigmatic Indochina in need of excavation and restitution. Taking up such tasks, researchers based at the École française d'Extrême-Orient (EFEO) would subsequently undertake painstaking studies of monuments across the region. As temples were cleared and mapped, a survey of stylistic and technical evolution was pursued. As Edwards has shown at length, during the early years of the twentieth century cartography, archaeology, epigraphy and anastylosis together consolidated as a broad field of scholarly research rooted in ideals of rigour, rationality, empirical verification and systemic classification.[26] Although the greatest attention was paid to the Angkor region, studies were also conducted on structures lying further afield in order to trace transitions in style, construction materials and building techniques. In addition to the architectural structures, a seemingly endless archive of freestanding statues, wall carved figurines and other ornamental features were also categorised into phases, or "styles", within an overall chronology of Khmer art.[27] Decades of study built around reading shifting architectural/artistic styles or the interpretation of bas-relief carvings and inscriptions, meant archaeologists and epigraphers provided the chronological blueprint for segmenting and categorising a Cambodian national and Khmer cultural history into a linear narrative and geo-body; such that the idea of a glorious "Angkorian Period" was set against less illustrious "pre" and "post" eras. Crucially here, Southeast Asian antiquity was also read in terms of a hierarchy of civilisations, with the region's culture understood as a derivative of the great cultures and religions of India, namely Hinduism and Buddhism. The regionalised narrative of Indianisation constructed under colonial-era scholarship reduced Southeast Asian antiquity to a story of unilinear flows and influences, with sites in Thailand, Cambodia, Indonesia and Burma all understood through the lens of a great Indian civilisation, one which had travelled southeast in multiple waves over the course of several centuries.

But here it is necessary to highlight how the political economy of South and Southeast Asia colonialism led to some clear distinctions in the modes and depths of scholarship pursued. Said has argued the accumulation of knowledge on the Orient by the French was inspired by Napoleon's ventures into Egypt and the standing of intellectual thought in French society.[28] He suggests the great institutes of learning set up in Paris, bolstered by Napoleon, would help give rigour, and a sense of honour "in the rise of archaeology, linguistics, historiography and Orientalism and experimental biology".[29] By contrast, he suggests, the British only mustered amateurish, even embarrassingly outdated attempts to understand the culture and history of the East. Whilst acknowledging Said's distinction, Edwards cites analyses of colonial knowledge production in British India by Nicholas Dirks and Keith Orr to add depth to this picture, arguing that archaeology and history came to be supplanted by anthropology from the mid nineteenth century onwards.[30] Unlike in India however, in Burma much of the emphasis remained on "antiquarian archaeology", rather than "anthropological archaeology", given the privileged position of texts and their translation via epigraphers.

As Chapman notes, for various reasons, the British dedicated considerably less time to Burma's temples, compared to the lavish attention they paid to monuments located in other parts of the Indian subcontinent.[31] The Asiatic Society of Bengal was set up as far back as 1784, with subsequent institutions such as the Delhi Archaeological Society and the Archaeological Survey of India established in 1847 and 1871 respectively. During this mid nineteenth-century period Henry Yule, an officer with the Bengal Engineers, was the first to undertake a detailed survey of Bagan, identifying nearly 1,000 shrines. Chapman suggests however that the Swiss Pali specialist Emanuel Forchhammer "was the first to study the monuments in depth" producing a number of publications on temples.[32] Burma would have to wait until 1902 before it hosted its own Archaeological Survey. Its initial director, or superintendent, would be a Burma-born individual of Chinese descent, Taw Sein Ko, described by Penny Edwards as a "cultural interlocutor" mediating between worlds of Confucian tradition, British colonialism and a Burmese ethnocultural past.[33] Over the subsequent fifteen years or so, his annual report would provide the definitive overview of activities. In 1910, the French archaeologist and amateur historian Charles Duroiselle linked up with Taw Sein Ko surveying Bagan and other ruinous sites across the country. This period would also see a consolidation of epigraphy as the principal mode of historical interpretation, as Chapman explains:

> Succeeding Taw Sein Ko as director in 1915, Duroiselle attempted to outline the history of each of the monumental sites, relying especially on inscriptions. His work owed much to Louis Finot of the EFEO, with whom he maintained a correspondence. He also worked closely with Malay-based linguist Charles Otto Blagden in the compilation of a catalogue of "lithic and other inscriptions" published in the Epigraphia Birmanica, a multivolume record begun by Taw Sein Ko.[34]

Given the number of shrines at Bagan, efforts were dedicated to conserving, collecting and documenting the material culture found above ground, rather than trying to excavate that which might be found below the surface. The arrival of G.H. Luce in Rangoon in 1912 would prove to be an important point in the historiography of Burma. An expert in Pali, Sanskrit and subsequently Old Burmese and Mon, Luce dedicated years to translating the inscriptions of the early Bagan period. Chapman notes how Luce travelled to the EFEO in Paris to learn from the epigraphist Louis Finot and Sinologist Paul Pelliot. Using the inscriptions, but "with little knowledge of architecture and concepts of art or architectural history", Luce set about classifying the "monuments by period and type, creating the first sound chronology of Burmese temples".[35] Somewhat critical of this dependence on text-based sources Aung-Thwin reflects on how "volume after volume of (mainly unedited) inscriptions ... were published under the auspices of the Archaeological Survey".[36] In the chronicles of Burma's classical past, what we see here then is the privileging of texts and the aesthetics of architecture and artistic style, over those other forms of cultural knowledge harnessed by the methodologies and frameworks of anthropology, ethnology and excavation archaeology.

Although Burma received less attention than other sites in South and Southeast Asia, it is evident that the study of Bagan was still very much contingent upon the broader structures of European colonialism within which it emerged over time. As we have seen, to some degree, the historiography and epistemologies of Burma's antiquity were characterised by an entanglement of the French and British approaches, noted earlier. This "political economy of scholarship", as Thongchai Winichakul referred to it, would shape how the classical past was not just excavated, both physically and historically, but also how it was intellectually deciphered in the narration of cultural and historical significance for both the Burmese and their emergent geo-body. In the governmentality of British imperialism, the monuments of Bagan would come to play a key role in the construction of a national imaginary built around a history of classical grandeur, former imperial power and high artistic achievement.

Decolonisation and the New Geopolitics of Heritage Diplomacy

In the aftermath of World War II, decolonisation in Asia and other parts of the world would herald a new era of international governance in the culture and heritage sectors. As we shall see, the core-periphery dynamics of empire remained a feature of the international relations of the period, but decolonisation and the search for political stability and international peace saw the the creation of new institutions and new networks of cooperation. The founding of UNESCO in November 1946 represented a landmark moment in fostering an international dialogue around the role of culture in international relations. It would form part of an emergent international civil society from the late 1940s onwards that was charged with rectifying the immense destruction inflicted on the cultural past by two world wars, and the task of finding mechanisms for ensuring it wouldn't happen again. The International Council of Museums (ICOM) established in 1946, was followed by the International Centre for the Study of the Preservation and Restoration of Cultural Property (ICCROM) in 1959, and the International Council on Monuments and Sites (ICOMOS) in 1965. Within this new framework much optimism was placed in science, culture and education as the bases for international cooperation and more peaceful forms of intercultural dialogue.

Indeed, across a number of intergovernmental agencies set up at that time, the hegemony of scientific knowledge would be maintained. As the multi-chaptered volume *Sixty Years of Science at UNESCO* illustrates, science underpinned many of the activities of the agency and its ethos of peace and international cooperation.[37] As various commentators have observed, in the postcolonial decades between the 1940s and 1960s, the scientific paradigm continued its ascendency in the international arena, even in the domain of culture. An ideology of universality enabled European knowledge to sidestep the postcolonial critique, including accusations of its role in unjust imperial rule. Wallerstein argues that the pursuit of "new, complicated and expensive technology in the operation of the modern world-system", together with the soul-searching of humanists created by the collapse of previous Orientalist certainties, ensured science pulled further ahead.[38] Crucially, scientific knowledge was also entwined in notions of social betterment and progress, a situation that maintained the idea that the West was home to the most developed, modern societies.[39] The post-war language of "development" would reinforce this hierarchy, wherein a nexus between science and social progress was linked to programmes and theories of modernisation for those "underdeveloped" countries of the non-West. Accordingly, Kennedy suggests organisations such as the United Nations helped internationalise the idea that little or no social and cultural progress could be achieved without a robust economic environment.[40]

It was within this context that the post-war landscape of built environment conservation took shape. Like other areas, heritage conservation was shifting to a structure of networks of cooperation; between states and states, and between states and a growing number of intergovernmental and nongovernmental players. The *Venice Charter for the Conservation and Restoration of Monuments and Sites* and World Heritage Convention of 1964 and 1972 respectively provided the intellectual, legal and governmental infrastructure for the heritage conservation industry as it expanded its frontiers internationally. Looking back, it is now widely accepted that they overwhelmingly prioritised a "fabric"-centric concept of conservation.[41] In the case of the 1972 convention, this extended beyond cultural sites to include natural sites as well. It was a prioritising of the materiality of culture and nature, and the subdividing of these two, that not just depended upon, but actually extended the reach of certain scientifically oriented discourses and the Western institutions that espoused such ideas. In Southeast Asia, heritage conservation of key archaeological and architecture sites continued to be driven by a privileged group of experts, the majority of whom came from Europe. Britain, France and the Netherlands viewed culture and heritage as a productive means for maintaining ties with former colonies. In that respect the study and conservation of Southeast Asia's antiquity frequently continued to be influenced by the ties and bonds established under colonialism, with the material culture of the region often acting as a catalyst for diplomacy. In the early 1970s, UNESCO's Save Borobudur campaign for example, was reliant upon considerable financial support from the Netherlands government and assistance from Dutch engineers, stone experts and biologists. In addition to the millions of dollars provided in aid, much of the "heavy lifting" required for post-earthquake reconstruction and tourism-related damage was undertaken by NEDECO Netherlands Engineering Consultants.[42] The French government also offered assistance in the form of Jacques Durmarçay, an architect and expert on Cambodian ruins.

Two decades later, Cambodia and the site of Angkor would offer a similar scenario, albeit on a much grander scale. As I have documented at length elsewhere, in post-conflict Cambodia, Angkor became the subject of a multinational heritage diplomacy aid programme, involving nearly twenty countries.[43] Whilst a number of Asian countries – India, China, South Korea, Japan, Indonesia and Thailand – featured prominently in the reconstruction and safeguarding of Angkor, the legacies of the scientistic materialism first established in the colonial era of nineteenth-century French Cambodge critically influenced how the site was approached and governed. In this respect Angkor in the 1990s and 2000s showed little had changed, heritage conservation remained a largely material and text-centric form of knowledge production and practice in both conservation policy and the range of scholarship that amassed in the narration of antiquity.

Whilst the physical and historical parallels between Angkor and Bagan are self evident, their recent pasts are defined by marked contrast. Despite being a member of the UN since 1948, Myanmar largely remained a pariah of Western aid until the reforms initiated in late 2010. The shunning of the government by the international community for its human rights abuses was perhaps the single most important factor shaping international assistance at Bagan in the decades since independence. In contrast to the coordinated, intergovernmental structure established for Angkor, programmes at Bagan have been sporadic and small in scale, often driven by individuals or small teams. Somewhat surprisingly, the United Nations Development Programme (UNDP) and Japanese International Cooperation Agency (JICA), both of which come from the development sector, together provided the most assistance. In the wake of an earthquake in 1975, the UNDP supplied in the region of US$1 million for repairs and community development. The need to rebuild arches, towers, domes and terraces also led to bilateral assistance from France, Italy, Japan and Yugoslavia (Figure 4.3). UNESCO subsequently commissioned an inventory of Bagan's structures, undertaken over a number of years by the French architect Pierre Pichard and his colleagues. Since the 1980s, agencies such as ICCROM have also undertaken a number of missions, providing small-scale assistance in training and conservation. In replicating their approach from elsewhere in Southeast Asia, JICA produced schemes intended to more directly link the cultural infrastructure to economic development. Their proposed master plans have centred around the construction and upgrading of roads, sewerage, electricity production and a local airport. Over the first half of the 1990s, international recognition of Bagan's significance advanced, with the site being added to the World Heritage Tentative List. Criticism over modern interventions and temple reconstruction, however, led to the withdrawal of the nomination by the Myanmar government.

Interpreting Bagan: Towards World Heritage

To give context to this period of reconstruction, Denis Byrne's notion of "counterheritage" is helpful here.[44] Through a focus on popular religious practice, one that is contrasted with the archaeological and conservation practice of international heritage, Byrne neatly identifies some of the key tensions over materiality:

> Whereas heritage conservation works to prevent the fragmentation and dispersion of heritage fabric, these same processes are likely to be seen by believers in popular religion as evidence of the "natural" propensity of numinous material to radiate. The belief that a fragment of a holy object contains a distillation of its power explains why followers of popular Buddhism in Thailand have often sought fragments of ancient stupas as talismans. The decay of a religious structure can occasion the radiation of its physical fabric and thus a spatial expansion of the field of its radiant magical force.
>
> The stand that heritage practice takes against dispersion is matched by its opposition to the accretion of new on old fabric. We see this in the conservator's removal of sedimentations of dirt and recent over-painting from old paintings of gods on the walls of Chinese temples. Popular religion, by contrast, favours the piling up of fabric upon fabric, renovation upon renovation, according to the logic that spirits and deities are honoured by the labour and funding expended in the renewal and elaboration of the fabric of their temples and shrines. Whereas heritage conservation seeks to stabilise built fabric, popular religion cannot seem to abide stasis.[45]

It is a distinction that speaks to the tensions over shrine reconstruction in Bagan. Byrne argues the practice of "restoring" stupas and shrines in Southeast Asia stretches back to at least the sixth century. The addition of new layers of brick or stone, together with the application of stucco or cement for resurfacing exteriors constitutes a practice of "encasement".[46] The life of a stupa is therefore "one of disintegration and accumulation". The critiques towards material permanence and attachment within both Hinduism and Buddhism mean stupas embody the unstable and impermanent. Decay, the dispersal of fragments and the practice of repair or encasement, thus constitutes its sacred power. But as the excerpt above illustrates, the sacred is also spatialised as radial power, a dimension enhanced by the dispersal of fragments. Byrne suggests then that the empowerment of stupas comes from a union of tension; between practices of fragment dispersal on the one hand and practices of spatial containment via encasement on the other. With both underpinned by a belief in meritorious acts, this tension is sustained because "both dispersion and containment stem from the same belief in the divine power and magical efficacy of a stupa's physical fabric, the ultimate source of which is the Buddha".[47] Stupas lying in a ruinous state thus speak of abandonment and the loss of sacred power. Byrne reminds us that the re-establishment of a temple site involves its reactivation, rather than the reconstruction of the physical fabric to a previous form. The decayed materiality of ruins, together with a renewal of veneration that comes from the addition of new materials and structures thus enables monasteries and local populations to accrue merit; vital if they are to be good citizens in the cosmology of Buddhism.

Byrne's reading of popular conservation practice demands we look at the reconstruction of Bagan in ways that acknowledge its cultural and religious context. It suggests we move beyond the discursive framings that have been handed down from an era of colonial scholarship via the networked governance structures established in the wake of World War II. It also helps us culturally "locate" the rebuilding of Bagan that has taken place over recent decades. But as we saw earlier, with donations for reconstruction – or to be more precise, reactivation – coming from Buddhist groups across Asia, the importance of viewing sacred power in transnational terms is also clearly evident. To understand how the controversy surrounding stupa reconstruction might play out at Bagan we need to return to the political economies within which scholarship is produced. The matrix of aid that formed around Angkor in the 1990s showed little had changed. As noted above, the internationalisation of Angkor in the 1990s reproduced a tradition of conservation and scholarship oriented towards the material and textual, such that the regime of value applied was primarily one of artistic and architectural merit. The argument for a possible different future at Bagan centres around two distinct shifts now taking place in the arena of international heritage governance in Asia.

The first pertains to the search for a paradigm for conservation and cultural interpretation that departs from approaches proclaimed as Eurocentric.[48] Reconstructions and their appropriateness have been a key point of contention within a debate carried out in both academia and the professional sector concerning the supposed "difference" between "Western" and "Asian" approaches to heritage conservation. In addition to conferences and publications dedicated to the topic, a series of charters and declarations has been produced in an effort to conceptualise a vocabulary for the region.[49] Since the initial Nara Declaration of 1994, the China Principles (1998), Shanghai Charter (2002), Indonesia Charter (2003), Yamato Declaration (2004), Okinawa Declaration (2004), Xi'an Declaration (2005), Seoul Declaration (2007) and Hoi An Protocols (2009) have all proclaimed the need to recognise alternative curatorial practices and forms of cultural governance for a number of heritage contexts, including cities, museums and intangible heritage.[50] Despite the diversity of applied context, coherence across these charters comes from a commonality of themes, namely community, spirituality, intangibility and relative authenticity.

It is a discursive positionality that, in large part, constitutes a postcolonial response to the paradigm of scientistic materialism established in the late nineteenth century. The stress on community values, local cultural expressions and so forth, represents an effort to give voice to the subjective, the irrational, the emotive, the unverifiable and the vernacular. It is also a discourse that needs to be read as a process of negotiation and resistance to particular conservation practices and methodologies which travelled geographically via the political structures of empire and subsequently proclaimed universality within the post World War II networks of global governance as outlined above. But perhaps more critically here, it is a paradigm of culture that opens up space for the themes identified by Byrne, and breathes air into the reading of antiquity as a site of culture, past and present. By foregrounding culture as practice, rather than immutable beauty, the religious comes into view, and thus for sites of Buddhism, enables a spatialised reading of significance that moves beyond the physical boundaries of archaeological remains into the reaches of the transnational.

The question thus arises concerning the degree to which such notions might gain traction within the internationalised structures of today's cultural policy. In an attempt to address this we need to turn to the second factor, that of the changing political and economic environment within which international heritage conservation takes place. Today heritage conservation is fast emerging as a component of the intra-regional economic and political ties that bind states in the region. As noted above, for a number of decades Japan has successfully utilised culture and cultural heritage as a mechanism for advancing its foreign policy and soft-power strategy in the region. Within South and Southeast Asia alone, Japan now has heritage related projects in Afghanistan, Bangladesh, Cambodia, China, India, Laos, Mongolia, Myanmar, Nepal, Pakistan and Vietnam. Today, however they are far from alone in folding heritage diplomacy into their bilateral and multilateral programmes of cooperation and aid. China, India, and South Korea are among those spending heavily on heritage diplomacy to secure influence in the region. South Korea is investing in a number of institutions designed to provide expertise both domestically and overseas (Figure 4.4). The National Research Institute of Cultural Heritage now includes a division dedicated to international exchanges. Through a focus on Buddhist archaeological sites, collaborations with Mongolia, China and Japan have been underpinned by a discourse of shared heritage. Since 2005, the institute has been running a series of training programmes, with participants travelling from more than fifteen Asian countries.[51] The Cultural Heritage Administration of Korea (CHA), an independent government agency since 1999, has also moved beyond its original domestic remit by signing nearly sixty bilateral agreements with organisations in fourteen countries over the last decade or so. In Doha in July 2014, representatives of the Ministry of Foreign Affairs and Korea ICOMOS, also used the opportunity

Figure 4.3: Modern "stele" indicating Japanese support for reconstruction. Source: the author.

Figure 4.4: Reconstruction and support from South Korea, Bagan. Source: the author.

of the World Heritage Committee meeting, attended by nearly 190 countries, to showcase a new strategy for international cooperation centred around embedding heritage into existing official development assistance (ODA) strategies.

India is similarly expanding its cultural interests in Southeast Asia. For a number of years, India has provided assistance to Indonesia, Thailand, Cambodia and Laos in an array of heritage sectors, including archaeology, textiles, museums and modern urban architecture. More recently, however, such forms of cooperation have been more explicitly mobilised as a mechanism for promoting economic and diplomatic relations, with Myanmar offering a case in point. Concerned by the growing influence of China in the country, the Indian government began integrating archaeology into its official diplomatic visits from 2010 onwards, invoking ideas of mutual pasts to build trust and diplomatic ties. The Archaeological Survey of India (ASI) offered assistance at Bagan, declaring it to be a sacred site "whose architecture is similar to temples in Bengal and Orissa".[52] With the opening up of Myanmar's economy, the Indian government stepped up its trade and assistance packages, with Manmohan Singh being the first Indian prime minister to visit the country in twenty-five years in May 2012. While much of the talk focused on bilateral trade and cooperation in the agriculture, transportation and energy sectors, such proposals were couched in a bigger context of cultural and political affinities, as the following excerpt from a speech given by Manmohan Singh in Yangon reveals:

> India and Myanmar share age-old cultural and civilisational ties. Merchants, monks and maritime traders carried influences and traditions from one to the other … Our common Buddhist heritage is an even stronger spiritual bond among our peoples … During our independence movements, our leaders shared ideas and thoughts on the freedom struggle … In the early years following independence, India and Myanmar were deeply sympathetic and supportive of each other. Today, we again have an opportunity to work as equal partners to revive the ancient links between our two countries and rediscover the immense possibilities of cooperation that exist between our two countries … We need to work with each other and with other countries of our region to build prosperity, promote openness of thought and facilitate trade and movement of goods, people and ideas.[53]

Further examples could be cited, but the key point here is how the embedding of heritage aid is occurring in tandem with a rise in intra-regional aid and trade. The economic and political ascendency of the region over the last decade or so, most notably in East Asia and India, has been accompanied by a growth in intra-regional aid and soft loans, supplanting previous arrangements with governmental and nongovernmental bodies located outside the region. As the volume by Dent and Dosch notes, a discourse of development driven primarily by bilateral and multilateral agencies headquartered in Europe or North America, is being complemented, and in some cases replaced, by new forms of intra-regional cooperation.[54] As a result, the cartographies of influence and power across the networks of heritage diplomacy are steadily shifting. To invoke the terminology of international trade, various countries across Asia are moving from being net importers of cultural aid and assistance to being net exporters.

The key implication here centres around the ways in which this trend is transforming and altering the "political economy of scholarship" for sites like Bagan. In contrast to previous decades, countries such as India and Korea now have the political and economic platform they require to more forcefully enact their vision of heritage conservation. Clear evidence of this can be found at the temple complex of Ta Prohm at Angkor, where previous approaches that prioritised the preservation of material fabric with minimal reconstruction are being replaced by a reconstruction programme conducted by the ASI, oriented by the notion of restoring religious and cultural continuity.[55] The encasement of Bagan's stupas has, in part, been funded by donations from Buddhist associations located around the region. The critical issue will be the degree to which governmental and nongovernmental agencies from these same countries adopt a similar approach. The various charters and declarations noted earlier provide the intellectual foundation for implementing alternative, even counter-readings of heritage. Or, will they merely reproduce the scientistic materialism established by previous generations of researchers and conservators? A regional-based funding structure of research and conservation also raises interesting questions about the new regionalisms it might produce. It was noted earlier how a political economy of colonial scholarship constructed a regional narrative of Indianisation for Southeast Asia, founded upon a hierarchical reading of civilisations. It is highly likely that the presence of India, in the form of the ASI, will reinforce this narrative further. In this regard we see the remnants of another legacy of colonialism, that of the Greater India vision, which took shape in India from the 1930s onwards. As Kwa Chong-Guan's excellent volume illustrates, the links between European scholarship and domestic cultural politics in colonial India filtered through archaeology, religion, literature and heritage conservation right through the twentieth century, and continued to orient projects conducted by the ASI in Southeast Asia.[56] Indeed, advancing the notion of a "greater India" sits quietly behind the strategy of using archaeology as a mechanism of soft power for India today.

At the same time however, the involvement of Buddhist countries from East Asia also suggests a more multidirectional regional narrative will emerge. Reconstruction programmes funded by Buddhist associations in South Korea and Japan speak to, and give visibility to, histories of pilgrimage, trade and cultural exchange that have hitherto been marginalised in the narrative framings of Southeast Asian antiquity. This new political economic of scholarship thus opens up a space for the establishment of a more plural, multidirectional history of connections and influences, one that reconnects Southeast Asia with East Asia and South Asia.

To conclude then, is, in large part, not to conclude at this point. The observations offered here point towards flux in the narratives of the past, and in the scholarly enmeshing of the material culture of Southeast Asian antiquity. In this respect the current situation at Bagan lies in its promise of potential futures. The production of knowledge about peoples and the past under conditions of colonialism, and the residual affects this has in forms of cultural governance today is a rich vein of academic enquiry. The analytical persuasion of critiques to date has typically been oriented towards the presence of continuity, such that organisations like UNESCO are accused of perpetuating the high modernist ideals of empire and their hierarchies of culture, class and civilisation, what Michael Herzfeld defines as "the global hierarchy of value".[57] Postcolonial states, Herzfeld argues, continue to reinforce this structure, where the vestigial affects of Western colonialism are the disguised forms of power and political culture that constitute a form of cryptocolonialism.[58]

This paper points to alternatives and other pathways, not of a totalising or revolutionary change that overthrows or sweeps away the legacies of colonial knowledge production, but to the spaces in between, the cracks that are now appearing and allowing counterheritages to find their feet. A recent history of conservation and curatorial practice that lies outside existing prescriptions of "best practice" and standards at Bagan, together with a new political economy of scholarship represents, I would suggest, an important space for mobilising new narrative framings. By returning to an era of colonialism, we have seen in the course of this paper how particular framings of Southeast Asian antiquity have emerged from and been shaped by their sociopolitical conditions. Shifts in the latter thus presuppose possible changes in the former. But for a counterheritage to take hold it will need to place material authenticity in another realm of cultural significance, one that disturbs the privileging of style, artistic grandeur and high art that is implicit in the critique of recent reconstruction projects at Bagan as "shoddy" or "Disney". The forms of heritage diplomacy currently emerging in Asia represent important possibilities for reframing antiquity towards understandings of religious practice, and the ongoing veneration of relics and the encasement of stupas. It is a set of possible futures that mean what is at stake in the reconstruction of Bagan's stupas is far more than merely a question of conservation. Rather it's about a politics of history, competing narratives of antiquity, and the unearthing of what lies in the ruins of culture.

Notes

1. For further details of the ten criteria see: http://whc.unesco.org/en/criteria/.
2. Cited in Paul Vrieze, "Bagan on Course for World Heritage Listing: UNESCO Expert," *The Irrawaddy*, 13 September 2014. http://www.irrawaddy.org/burma/bagan-course-world-heritage-listing-unesco-expert.html.
3. Richard Covington, "Sacred and Profaned: Misguided Restorations of the Exquisite Buddhist Shrines of Bagan in Burma May Do More Harm Than Good," *Smithsonian Magazine*, December 2002. http://www.smithsonianmag.com/people-places/sacred-and-profaned-72955322/.
4. Cited in Thomas Crampton, "Concrete Overlay for an Ancient Burmese Landscape," *The New York Times*, 22 April 2005. http://www.nytimes.com/2005/04/21/world/asia/21iht-burma.html?pagewanted=all&_r=0.
5. William R. Chapman, *A Heritage of Ruins: The Ancient Sites of Southeast Asia and their Conservation* (Honolulu: University of Hawai'i Press, 2013).
6. See Tim Winter, "Beyond Eurocentrism? Heritage Conservation and the Politics of Difference," *International Journal of Heritage Studies* 20(2014): 123–137.
7. Michael Aung-Thwin, *Burma Before Bagan: The Status of Archaeology Today* (Honolulu: University of Hawai'i Press, 2011), 2.
8. Simon Schama, *Landscape and Memory* (London: HarperCollins Publishers, 1995).
9. Christopher Woodward, *In Ruins* (London: Chatto & Windus, 2001), 119.
10. Ibid., 157.
11. Nina L. Dubin, *Futures & Ruins: Eighteenth-Century Paris and the Art of Hubert Robert* (Los Angeles: Getty Research Institute, 2010).
12. N. Green, *The Spectacle of Nature* (Manchester: Manchester University Press, 1990).
13. Woodward, *In Ruins*, 78.
14. J.L. Bradley (ed.), *John Ruskin: The Critical Heritage* (London: Routledge, 1995); and Chris Miele, *From William Morris: Building Conservation and the Arts and Crafts Cult of Authenticity, 1877–1939*, (New Haven: Yale University Press, 2005).
15. Nicholas Stanley-Price, M. Kirby Talley Jr. and Alessandra Melucco Vaccaro, *Historical and Philosophical Issues in the Conservation of Cultural Heritage* (Los Angeles: Getty Conservation Institute, 1996).
16. Jukka Jokilehto, *A History of Architectural Conservation* (Oxford: Butterworth-Heinemann, 2002); and Salvador Muñoz Viñas, *Contemporary Theory of Conservation* (Oxford: Elsevier Butterworth-Heinemann, 2005).
17. Tim Winter, "Clarifying the Critical in Critical Heritage Studies" *International Journal of Heritage Studies* 9 (2013): 532–545.
18. J.J. Clarke, 1997, *Oriental Enlightenment: The Encounter Between Asian and Western Thought* (London: Routledge, 1997), 55.

19. Bruce G. Trigger, "Alternative Archaeologies: Colonialist, Nationalist, Imperialist," *Man* 19 (1984): 355–370; and Bruce G. Trigger, *A History of Archaeological Thought* (Cambridge: Cambridge University Press, 1989).
20. Benedict Anderson, *Imagined Communities: Reflections on the Origin and Spread of Nationalism* (Ithaca: Cornell University Press, 1991).
21. Bernard S. Cohn, *Colonialism and its Forms of Knowledge: The British in India*, (Princeton: Princeton University Press, 1996), 80.
22. Tapati Guha-Thakurta, *Monuments, Objects, Histories: Institutions of Art in Colonial and Postcolonial India* (New York: Columbia University Press, 2004).
23. Ibid., 4.
24. F. Bohrer, *Photography and Archaeology* (London: Reaktion Books, 2011).
25. Guha-Thakurta, *Monuments, Objects, Histories*, 18.
26. Penny Edwards, *Cambodge: The Cultivation of a Nation 1860–1945* (Honolulu: University of Hawai'i Press, 2007).
27. M. Giteau, D. Guéret and T. Renaut, *Khmer Art: The Civilisations of Angkor* (Paris: ASA: Somogy, 1997); and H. Stierlin, *Angkor and Khmer Art* (Paudex: Parkstone, 1997).
28. Edward Said, *Culture and Imperialism* (London: Chatto & Windus, 1993).
29. Ibid., 99.
30. Penny Edwards, "Relocating the Interlocutor: Taw Sein Ko (1864–1930) and the Itinerancy of Knowledge in British Burma," *South East Asia Research* 12 (2004): 290.
31. Chapman, *A Heritage of Ruins*.
32. Ibid.,173.
33. Edwards, "Relocating the Interlocutor", 279.
34. Chapman, *A Heritage of Ruins*, 176.
35. Ibid., 179–180.
36. Aung-Thwin, *Burma Before Bagan*, 2.
37. UNESCO, *Sixty Years of Science at UNESCO, 1945–2005* (Paris: UNESCO Pub., 2006).
38. Immanuel Wallerstein, *European Universalism: The Rhetoric of Power* (New York: New Press, 2006), 78.
39. Sandra Harding (ed.), *The Postcolonial Science and Technology Studies Reader* (Duke University Press: Durham, 2011); and Arturo Escobar, *Encountering Development: The Making and Unmaking of the Third World* (Princeton: Princeton University Press, 1995).
40. P. Kennedy, *The Parliament of Man: The Past, Present, and Future of the United Nations* (New York: Vintage, 2007).
41. Jokilehto, *A History of Architectural Conservation*; and Dawson Munjeri, "Tangible and Intangible Heritage: From Difference to Convergence," *Museum International* 56 (2004): 12–20.

42. Caesar Voute, "The Restoration and Conservation Project of Borobudur Temple, Indonesia," *Planning: Research: Design, Studies in Conservation* 18 (1973), 118–120.
43. Winter, *Post-Conflict Heritage, Postcolonial Tourism.*
44. Denis Byrne, *Counterheritage: Critical Perspectives on Heritage Conservation in Asia*, (New York: Routledge, 2014).
45. Ibid., 4.
46. Ibid., 85.
47. Ibid., 87.
48 A number of architectural conservation projects in the region have been controversial for their level of reconstruction. In Seoul, for example, the "preservation" of *hanok* or traditional homes, has been the subject of critique for the high levels of restoration and modification. China has been widely criticised in the West for the demolition and reconstruction of *hutong*, or traditional neighbourhoods, in its cities. In Beijing, the "reconstruction" of the Yongdingmen gate – originally constructed in 1552 – was torn down in the 1950s and then relocated again in readiness for the 2008 Olympics. In Luang Prabang, Laos, local approaches to preserving temples and domestic structures have been deemed by UNESCO as "well-intended but ill-informed efforts to beautify" (UNESCO 2004, 45).
49. See, for example, Timoticin Kwanda, "Western Conservation Theory and the Asian Context: The Different Roots of Conservation." Paper given at International Conference on Heritage in Asia: Converging Forces and Conflicting Values, Petra Christian University, Surabaya, Indonesia, 8–10 January 2009. http://petra.academia.edu/TimoticinKwanda081334249185/Papers/475444/Western_Conservation_Theory_and_the_Asian_Context_The_Different_Roots_of_Conservation; and S. Silapacharanan and J. Withaya Campbell, "Research Conference Proceedings on Asian Approaches to Conservation." Faculty of Architecture, Chulalongkorn University Bangkok, Thailand, 2006.
50. The full titles for these are: Nara Document on Authenticity; Principles for the Conservation of Heritage Sites in China; Shanghai Charter 2002: Museums, Intangible Heritage and Globalisation; Indonesia Charter for Heritage; Yamato Declaration on Integrated Approaches for Safeguarding Tangible and Intangible Cultural Heritage; Okinawa Declaration on Intangible and Tangible Cultural Heritage; Xi'an Declaration on the Conservation of The Setting of Heritage Structures, Sites and Areas; Hoi An Protocols for Best Conservation Practice in Asia; Seoul Declaration on Heritage and the Metropolis in Asia and the Pacific.
51. See, for example, http://www.korea.net/NewsFocus/Policies/view?articleId=121427. Accessed 5 November 2014.
52. Quoted in www.telegraphindia.com/1100722/jsp/frontpage/story_12712529.jsp. Accessed 5 November 2014.

53. Manmohan Singh, "PM's Speech at the Banquet Hosted by President of Myanmar," Speech given in Yangon, 28 May 2012. http://pmindia.nic.in/speech-details.php?nodeid.1178.
54. Christopher Dent and Jörn Dosch (ed.), *The Asia-Pacific: Regionalism and the Global System* (Cheltenham: Edward Elgar, 2012).
55. See Winter, "Beyond Eurocentrism?"
56. C.G. Kwa, (ed.) *Early Southeast Asia Viewed from India: An Anthology of Articles from the Journal of the Greater India Society*, (New Delhi: Manohar, 2013).
57. Michael Herzfeld, *The Body Impolitic: Artisans and Artifice in the Global Hierarchy of Value* (Chicago: University of Chicago Press, 2004).
58. Denis Byrne, "Archaeological Heritage and Cultural Intimacy: An interview with Michael Herzfeld," *Journal of Social Archaeology* 11(2011): 144–157.

CHAPTER 5

Thinking Beyond the Nation: Repositioning National and Regional Identities Through Architectural Discourse

ANOMA PIERIS

Introduction

Efforts by Duanfang Lu and by William Lim and Jiat-Hwee Chang have recast modernism as a heterogeneous and dialogic regional phenomenon that melded Cold War ideologies with national development goals.[1] They reveal how decentred forms of modernism helped shed colonial globalisation and dignified national cultures via alternative epistemes. Yet nation-building processes have also produced culturally hegemonic majoritarian positions that are increasingly empowered by market forces. Neo-liberal economic policies are not necessarily wedded to democratic change. Architecture as an agent of power and capital is complicit in inequitable neocolonial social relations. De-nationalising undemocratic curricula and democratising perspectives of globalisation are critical intellectual tasks.

This chapter proposes to investigate current discursive trends based on hybrid forms of education, fieldwork, publication and dissemination in which comparative, intersectional and regional studies deviate from and counter nationally embedded research. The prism of Anglophone scholarship on architecture and urbanism in Malaysia and Singapore is used to investigate these issues. The chapter argues that fealty to national funding and investigative frameworks have constrained intellectual inquiry in many Asian nations, retarding their leadership of global intellectual platforms. Although comparative methods have fertilised the discursive capacity of this scholarship, its bilateral approach to regional issues strengthens the objects of sovereignty. Postcolonial geopolitical borders are seen as normative.

This chapter borrows from new theories on "border thinking", both across geopolitical site-lines and at the social margins, as positions from which to interrogate statist scholarship.[2] By "statist" I mean approaches where the congruence between the state (defined by a government and political system), the society (projected as the culture of the majority) and a spatially demarcated geographical territory are taken for granted. Peter Taylor in his 1996 critique of the social sciences described an "embedded statism" implicit in scholarship, which I argue persists in architectural studies today.[3] State-centric approaches stretch place associations across local, national, regional and global spatial scales and read transnational phenomena as interactions rather than intersections. In challenging these assumptions, this chapter identifies discursive platforms that cross spatial boundaries as critical for profession-oriented spatial disciplines that act within the national grid. More recently this grid has encompassed globally networked urban centres as representative spaces of national interests. Such umbilical attachments, conceived during an era of cultural recovery and decolonisation, have implications for contemporary research curricula. Their uncritical and superficial embrace of globalisation and resistance to associated forms of democratisation are among this chapter's core concerns.

The reasons for national attachments are complex and pronounced in public tertiary institutions, which remain dominant throughout Asia. Knowledge production is dependent on institutional frameworks and pathways. The integrity and accumulation of local, language-based, culturally particular knowledge supersedes politically sensitive forms of critical inquiry. There is tension between advocates of Western-style liberal democracy and its critics. The politicisation of tertiary institutions or gagging of nationally sensitive topics has periodically silenced dissenting voices and encouraged self censorship. In architecture, the competing intellectual positions may be as diverse as essentialised and sentimental notions of precolonial cultural and geographic belonging; latent anti-colonial (anti-Western) sentiments and defensive forms of national hubris; culturally sensitive and politically aligned intellectual inquiries and acultural approaches that blindly apply Western methodologies. Critical interpretations, political voices, hermeneutic methods and socially engaged topics remain marginal in professional programmes in which explicitly research-based curricula are under supported.

The evasion of socially sensitive topics in architecture reflects the biases and anxieties of a profession dependent on the market for its livelihood. The spatial disciplines too often incline towards the advocacy of professional careers, institutionalised programmes or market-led developments, and discourage or even punish their critics. In Asia, public forums for challenging new developments are poorly supported by state processes, and if they do emerge, they are largely found in erudite urban centres. Developmental ideologies frequently overturn local concerns. While such processes are equally evident in many post-industrial nations, the economic and cultural heterogeneity of Asian societies, the fragility of supportive governmental structures and unevenness of literacy and education limits access to legal instruments. For these reasons, professionals, arguably, should foster social responsibilities.

Given its social and political constraints and the increasing desire for intellectual freedom, how do scholars in architecture and related professional disciplines respond? What are the exploratory pathways that might serve as checks and balances? How might architecture's methods and processes compete with other research-led disciplines? This chapter traces significant developments in architectural historiography and the possible contribution of southern theoretical frameworks such as postcolonial and inter-Asian cultural studies, read against the perceived crisis in area studies. It argues for interregional and interdisciplinary cross fertilisation. The need for socially equitable forms of urbanisation is a strong feature of this argument. This discussion is followed by observations on gender, labour and aboriginal environments as areas of relative neglect in architectural scholarship. The vigilance displayed by postcolonial studies over twentieth-century decolonisation provides the intellectual entry point.

Beyond the Nation

Genealogically linked across two generations of scholars who extended Edward Said's (1978) Orientalist critique to the aesthetic and spatial aspects of colonial epistemes, sociopolitical analyses of Asian architecture and urbanism present the colonial or imperial city as a site of modernity and a modernist experiment. They reveal how the ideals of enlightenment and democracy were conveyed to colonised subjects via an economically exploitative, racist culture supported by superior military power.[4] This structural alterity translated as class was reproduced via postcolonial nationalism's modernisation programmes, largely achieved through urban development and institutional decolonisation. In many postcolonial nations, undemocratic majoritarian entitlements were established to counter colonial social neglect and reduce the advantages afforded to metropolitan minorities. The nationalist cultural alignment of architecture, power and knowledge, and the continuing influence of former colonisers reinforced these asymmetries.

For example, early postcolonial nationalist projects were avenues for embedding foreign expertise in former colonial territories. Their variously derivative, hybrid, innovative and enabling modernist aesthetics prolonged hierarchies of colonial energy and authorship. Eurocentric modernism, its postcolonial routes and acultural manifestations were geopolitically stratified. Comparative studies were used to determine developmental hierarchies. However, as the twentieth century progressed and identity politics dominated social agendas, indigenisation emerged as a resistant counter force, politically linked to socialist policies and village republics. A rich internal vein of intellectual scrutiny, less concerned with form, function and aesthetics but invested in constructing national dignity, indigenised architectural discourse, democratising the sources, agents and topics that were researched.

Geographer Tariq Jazeel asserts that the postcolonial approach is most useful for revealing the colonial origins of material and geographic spaces and our more subjective geographical imaginations of these spaces.[5] He describes it as a tool for undoing received geographical knowledge, "particularly in order to interrogate inequalities, power and privilege".[6] Postcolonial studies (PCS) provides a discursive framework for decolonising Euro-American historiographical traditions, including canonical texts in architectural history.[7] As best articulated by Dipesh Chakrabarty, PCS dislodged Europe as the central referent for our understanding of modernity, the modern disciplines and the production of knowledge.[8] This subversive intellectual deterritorialisation helped reconceptualise power and territory, two instruments of nation-building supported by architectural production.

The marginal place of Southeast Asia in PCS gestures at gaps and omissions within this postcolonial historiography in which scholarship on India and Anglophone former colonies dominate. However, long before China and India rose to economic and political dominance, heated imperial competition over its territories and resources, wartime Japanese occupation and Cold War tensions precipitated decolonisation in Southeast Asia. Non-alignment, marketised, illiberal democratisation and securitisation were first tested in this region. Bilateral regional relationships were forged to resist the pressures of neighbouring political giants and enabled easy cross-border trade and labour mobilities. Southeast Asia was a fertile site for border thinking. These other imperialisms, World War II and Cold War histories neglected by PCS are critical for understanding globalisation in the Asia Pacific. Consequently, architecture's focus on postcolonial Southeast Asia is narrow but resilient.

Architectural historian Gwendolyn Wright's work on French colonial urbanism first initiated the discussion of the spatialisation of colonial power in Southeast Asia; however, it was the edited volume, *Postcolonial Space(s)* by NUS-based (National University of Singapore) academics, Gülsüm Baydar Nalbantoğlu and Wong Chong Thai that provided the catalytic opening for theoretical thinking.[9] Since then, a number of architectural/urban scholars have explicitly or implicitly engaged with postcolonial theoretical schema; the most prominent being Abidin Kusno.[10] Kusno's work offers a multidimensional exploration of the capacity of socio-spatial data in theorising power, technocracy, memory, violence and nationalism in Java and Jakarta. His work additionally spans colonial and postcolonial periods. In addition to Kusno, postcolonial foci such as colonisation, nationalism and the spatial/material and physical constitution of power is examined by several architectural scholars including: Gerard Lico for the Philippines; Koompong Noobanjong and Ross King for Thailand; Eka Permanasari for Indonesia; Jiat-Hwee Chang for Singapore and Ross King and Chee Kien Lai for Malaysia.[11] Like Kusno, they too are preoccupied with capital city production; their critique of the centre deconstructs national hegemony, however, they operate within the geographical delineations of national historiography. These area studies compartments accept the modern nation state as a defining spatial framework and source of cultural subjectivity. While a bilateral comparison across a number of volumes builds a narrative of the region, they accept and represent geopolitical spaces as normative cultural constructs. There is greater cross-border movement in the humanities and social sciences.

A pattern emerges where subjects of national focus are compared critically in regional collections. A few periodicals have successfully advanced this approach. The *Journal of Southeast Asian Architecture* (*JSEAA*) published by NUS (since 1996) is the region's more established Anglophone intellectual forum for architectural history; Nalbantoğlu's advocacy of a critical break from received theories of the non-West in its inaugural volume setting the tone.[12] *JSEAA* filled the void created after *MIMAR* (1980–1992), the journal of the Aga Khan Trust for Culture (AKTC), ceased publication in 1992. Whereas *MIMAR*'s focus on professional practice precluded deeper theoretical exploration, *JSEAA* extended these intellectual boundaries. Other noteworthy journal issues published in 2010 and 2011 are "Changing Asia", *Journal of Architectural Education*; "About Asia", *Fabrications*; "Crossing Boundaries", *Review of Indonesian and Malaysian Affairs* and "Tropicality in Motion", *Singapore Journal of Tropical Geography*.[13] The publications of the Singapore Planning and Urban Research Group (SPUR 65/67 and 68/71) are very early architectural manifestos with collections of essays, a tradition explored shortly.

The unresolved disjunct between a sociopolitically astute research culture and developmental and market orientation of professional programmes has inhibited greater intellectual rigour within the discipline. Consequently, many valuable contributions on Asian topics by architectural scholars tend to be published outside its purview in humanities and social science journals. The very few examples described here reveal the urgent need for research journals produced in Asia about Asian architecture. The reasons for their paucity are part of a broader problem.

The Problem of Historiography

Questions of modernity, professionalisation and democratic institutions are critical for architectural pedagogy, which has inherited exogenous curricula patterned on and accredited by British institutions (the Commonwealth Association of Architects and Royal Institute of British Architects). Decades-long exportation of Eurocentric and mimetic professional cultures and curricula to former colonies has reinforced networks of patronage disengaged from more urgent social, political and cultural realities. These neocolonial economic asymmetries reconstitute architecture as an elite practice. Postcolonial reluctance to sever metropolitan connections, the desire for validation by former colonisers and the lack of robust and institutionally supported research frameworks likewise constrain local Asian institutions. Reflective historical research achieved via field trips, measured drawings, heritage conservation studies or text-based dissertations, which are critical, pedagogical tools, are often undertaken as instrumental analyses. In fact, professional services are largely evaluated on purely aesthetic or functional terms, as evident in the self-promotional monographs commissioned by contemporary architects.

Most Asia-based studies in local languages remain peripheral to the largely Anglophone architectural canon and are consequently excluded from global discourse. This asymmetry is evident in the relative strength of the Anglophone Singapore and Hong Kong universities, where postcolonial legacies, metropolitan affluence and repatriation of overseas-educated staff have enabled comparatively reputable international standing. In the broader professional culture, vanity publications and commercial periodicals that uncritically orientalise aesthetic representations forestall discursive decolonisation. Meanwhile, dependence on, subservience to, and suspicion of Western scholarship also produce damaging strains of intellectual inertia.

Scholars of architecture adopt different positions across this pedagogical terrain. When addressing the profession they often accept the parameters of design advocacy and celebrate the elite materialities on display. The critiques that remain muted in professional forums are deferred to interdisciplinary platforms more hospitable to social and political critique. In these extra-disciplinary spaces they encounter broader academic tensions over-determined by postcolonial legacies.

There has been a tendency for scholars to identify as insiders and outsiders based on global research hierarchies. The dominance of Western scholarship, the Western location and distribution of journals and publications and the emergence of Western institutions as centres of expertise on Asia has presented a formidable bulwark against revisionist local histories. Local scholars have consequently claimed essentialist positions based on location and cultural affinity. However, penetration of these systems and processes by individual scholars during the late twentieth century has opened up Western institutional spaces whether through education, employment, exchange or fieldwork. The resistance and competition across academic networks has become increasingly deterritorialised. The major work of this generation has been to deconstruct inherited knowledge systems and to create alternative regional epistemes.

Architecture's Visionaries

As argued by Lu, and Lim and Chang, a particular Western-centric global hierarchy of modernism denied discursive space to alternative, sometimes resistant, modernist trajectories.[14] A quick survey of manifestos on topics of environmentalism, urbanisation and identity highlights the modernist countercultures that emerged during the 1960s. The Orientalist discourse on climate was initially dehistoricised as a techno-scientific tropical architecture pedagogically reproduced through programmes in London and Melbourne (during the 1950s and 1960s) and channelled to former colonies as foreign expertise. Its multiple translations and appropriations have been analysed by a number of scholars in the *Singapore Journal of Tropical Geography*, issue 32.[15] These strains are also evident in new techno-scientific discourses on sustainability by Tzonis et al., and Bay and Ong that reterritorialise regionalist postcolonial identity politics.[16] The most recent academic critique of this protracted climatic discourse by Jiat-Hwee Chang traces its colonial genealogy.[17] Yet the profession also appropriated environmentalism for postcolonial critiques of national development, such as the advocacy of the "intelligent tropical city" and "rubanisation" (questioning the rural-urban dichotomy) by Tay Kheng Soon.[18] The work of Ken Yeang takes the techno-scientific discourse to its inevitable conclusion in the bio-climatic skyscraper, a global product exportable to the West.[19] Regional climatic features that render Southeast Asia legible and different (to Westerners) are thus domesticated for identity construction.

Meanwhile, the economic rise of East Asia and its imperial and cultural dominance has channelled alternative urban visions of Southeast Asia based on non-Western imperial centres. Japanese Metabolist mega projects tested in Singapore (Peoples Park Complex 1973 and Golden Mile Complex 1974), and the exploration of their social vision in the writings of the Singapore Planning and Urban Research Group, produce an equivalent lineage, again via Tay and Lim (see also Chapter 8 in this volume).[20] Lim's "ethical urbanism" includes a concerted defence of Singapore's complexity against the damaging accusation of tabula rasa raised by Rem Koolhaas.[21] Lim argues that Singapore is not homogeneous and hyperreal, but that at every phase of its development its negotiation of the conflicting forces of colonialism, socialism, communism and capitalism was inscribed in its built environment. In *Asian Alterity* he repositions Asia's heterogeneous translations and adaptations of Western modernism.[22] Lim's arguments coincide with the shift in cultural studies towards an Asia-centric discourse and a political desire, traceable through independence, non-alignment and the creation of the Association of Southeast Asian Nations (ASEAN), to build an alternative identity for Asia.

Since the 1990s rise of tiger economies, an affluent group of nations dominated by East Asian values have maintained cultural autonomy from the West. Yet this decentring discourse is predicated on alternative progressive but largely undemocratic histories of imperial and postcolonial political development. The desire for historical autonomy is further culturally encoded by resistant (sometimes rural) utopian visions of nationalism that divide metropolitan from rural constituencies.

A resistant vision of Southeast Asia's rural communities and cultures was cultivated by the Geneva-based Aga Khan Trust for Culture (AKTC) the architectural and pedagogical programmes of which, operating under the rubric of a non-Western and broadly Islamic architecture, successfully elided the Eurocentric/post-industrial/metropolitan discursive canon. The dilemma this posed for affluent Southeast Asian nations was debated at the AKTC's 1983 regional seminar, "Architecture and Identity", held in Kuala Lumpur.[23] A number of Southeast Asian architects, including Tay Kheng Soon, Sumet Jumsai, Hijjas Kasturi, Jimmy Lim, Ken Yeang and William Lim engaged in panel discussions, aimed at constructing a regional cultural identity where, as articulated by Tay, cultural heritage recovery might be reconciled with technological progress.[24] He advocated that committed local architects aware of internal regional dynamics should develop an architecture derived from "geo-psychology" (an understanding of geography, climate, culture and heritage). Foreign aesthetic traditions and expertise were marginalised.

The resistant, community-based and heritage-sensitive professionalisation championed by the AKTC was not applicable across Southeast Asia, particularly metropolitan Singapore and Malaysia, despite their being the hub of AKTC publications and home to its most prominent editors, Hassan Uddin-Khan and Robert Powell. The organisation had achieved democratisation by dignifying *mimar* – the craftsperson in Farsi and Arabic – although elite architects frequently mediated that relationship. Both Singapore and Malaysia were importing construction labour from within the Asian region. The idealised issues of cultural authenticity unwittingly reproduced new social hierarchies and metropolitan Orientalist imaginings.[25] The AKTC's awards and publications became alternative avenues to internationalisation and architectural prestige.

Architecture's reterritorialisation through regional cultural heritage had several advocates such as Chen Voon Fee (2007), Lim Chong Keat (1986) and Sumet Jumsai

(1990) who ventured beyond traditional representations providing a broader view of history.[26] Meanwhile explicitly vernacular derivatives such as those applied by Sri Lankan architect Geoffrey Bawa, in Batujimbar Estate in Bali (see also Chapter 3 in this volume), saw the genesis of celebratory elite/expatriate architectures.[27] Their hybrid aesthetics were featured in the series of "House" books by Robert Powell, in which the "tropical" climate and "Asian" identity remained recurrent themes.[28] As dehistoricised cultural signifiers, explicitly cultivated for the Western gaze, such representations reproduced Orientalist traditions of appropriation.

This period of radical debate was followed by decades of intellectual apathy, while the second generation of architects built their metropolitan careers. Lim, Tay and Yeang were isolated voices in a conformist profession. Meanwhile ASEAN, established in 1967, was reconfiguring regional identification beyond the Cold War dialectic and the early movement for political non-alignment.[29] As independent nations embraced marketisation, they were incorporated into this new geopolitical identity, a collaboration substantiated by architectural historiography.[30] The resultant hybrid development model is best exemplified by Singapore where welfare agendas, free-market forces and undemocratic politics have producing a mixed architectural heritage. Technocratic governmental systems and progressive urbanisation have flourished. By encouraging marketisation while limiting democracy and maintaining internal securitisation, such nations modelled early exceptions to free-market, liberal democracy.[31] Limitations to participatory democracy inhibited public discourse, civic resistance and policy change. The ongoing struggle to retain heritage environments against state-led development and market forces illustrate these limits.

Meanwhile, the democratisation of tertiary education and creation of local schools of architecture both decolonised and indigenised professional participation. Their greatest challenges were in dismantling technocratic systems that empowered government authorities, constrained private practitioners and obviated public participation. But, whereas the first generation of architects found radical dialectics, mixed economies and import substitution discursively fertile, affluence and neo-liberalism appeared to silence subsequent professional dissent. The brightest stars in the professional firmament deftly negotiated corporate design cultures monopolising opportunities and networks. The themes they adopted of identity, environment or technology lacked political impact.

Metropolitan Dominance

With the rise of the tiger economies of the 1990s, the profession seemed ill-equipped for democratisation through market reform. This was the period of intense professional proliferation into rural hinterlands, where the metropolitan biases of colonial and nationalist pedagogy colonised the periphery. Simultaneously, from the late 1980s until the Asian economic recession in 1997, globalisation, receding welfarism and the proliferation of private practices saw a populist shift towards celebratory developer-led architectures. New urbanist expansion and resort tourism uprooted former plantations, encouraging suburban sprawl. Gated residential communities, high-rise condominiums and resort hotels dominated architectural publications signalling the further economic insulation of elites and expatriates. The environmental costs of such developments were rarely acknowledged in the green aesthetics of many practitioners. The nascent discourse on regionalism, rescripted via sustainability, now serviced cultural tourism's excesses. Meanwhile, the insular nationalisms of an earlier era lost their salience and capacity to produce national objects. Ahistorical appropriations of culture produced revivalist strains of indigenous and colonial aesthetics. Their aesthetic worth was evaluated very differently by politicians, tourists, locals and architects. The latter shuttled between abstractions of regional traditions (regarded modernism's sophisticated legacy) and the parochial regionalist styles adopted for institutional buildings and resorts.

The historically grounded counterpart to this surfeit of acultural-cultural production was urban heritage practice, invigorated, internationalised and regulated by UNESCO, the International Council on Monuments and Sites (ICOMOS) and the Asian Academy for Heritage Management, key concerns of which were outlined in William Logan's *The Disappearing Asian City*.[32] Logan highlights their imbrication in the politics of nation-building and the calibration of relative local or global advantages. A most insightful observation is the increasing influence of Asian member states, following the Nara Document of Authenticity drafted in 1994, and regard for sociocultural and intangible heritage. Although originating in Orientalist notions of antiquity, heritage consciousness in architecture introduces historicity as an alternative means for making socio-spatial claims. Despite vulnerability to political, social and market forces, heritage practice provides the critical grounds for public advocacy and civic activism against indiscriminate urban development.

Best practice examples of heritage discourse are found in the vigilance of the Singapore Heritage Society (1986), Badan Warisan Malaysia (The Heritage Trust of Malaysia, including the Chen Voon Fee resource centre) (1985), The Sarawak Heritage Society (2006), The Penang Heritage Trust (1986) and the many publications of Areca Books. They respond to the heritage casualties of expedited development and multicultural commodification. The founding dates of these organisations coincide with the 1985 recession when Southeast Asian governments were forced to rethink their development strategies. Although their discourses and tactics are predominantly metropolitan, the imaginary of the kampung (village) remains a nostalgic symbol of emplacement for heritage activism. The future of the kampung is indeed imperilled. Adaptive reuse of buildings, tourist facilities, resorts and theme parks have introduced hybrid architectures and metropolitan imaginaries into rural contexts. The reciprocal provision of metropolitan amenities invites specular consumption of local sites and drains local resources. It produces new discourses of class. Such motions are increasingly linked to changing regional economies, a growing middle class of Asian tourists and relaxed border controls.

The dissolution of economic borders and resultant transnational investment has produced new forms of upward social mobility, placing the Southeast Asian region within global networks of consumption. Metropolitan centres compete directly for investment, labour and tourism, sometimes circumventing national controls. Depoliticised local and regional architectures have been commodified for cosmopolitan travellers who replicate former colonial networks of mobility. Social programmes have likewise assumed a new global dimension with the internationalisation of post-disaster housing, adding international non-governmental organisations to this traveller demographic. Urban Asia has become the all-consuming intellectual focus, objectifying and networking individual cities.

This cult of urbanisation and its message of progress is steering Southeast Asia in the new millennium, as the new stage for liberal markets and measure of development. Competing urban centres construct new regional alliances and determine cultural trends. Cities have centres and peripheries, cosmopolitan districts and refugee borderlands that translate national cultures in economic terms. They produce new territorial alliances that are economic and epistemic. Yet, the desire for metropolitan linkages and global cosmopolitan cultures reproduce and even internalise colonial relationships. How might their spatial politics be theorised?

New Spatial Theories

The unification of Europe at the end of the Cold War prompted many intellectual positions that explored the critical and epistemological significance of the periphery. The dissolution of nations shifted interest to the geopolitical space of the border, sovereignty and violence, marginalised subjectivities and human mobilities. New theoretical explorations on marginal socialities such as "border as method" and "border thinking" diverted intellectual attention to spaces in the Global South.[33] While these were not entirely new ideas, their theoretical and methodological approaches diversified globally applicable interpretations.

Such thinking was not new to Southeast Asian studies. As argued by Thongchai Winichakul in 1999, the declining hegemony of modern nation states and challenges from plural perspectives internal and external to the nation suggests the need for writing history "at the interstices" – both a "history of the margins and history of the localisation of transnational elements".[34] In endorsing this method he identified what he describes as "home scholars" – those who have an ontological affiliation with a particular country, region or location when compared to those who study the homes of others. He observes that "[Such self-identification with a specific location] allows for various subjective claims of, more or less, intimacy or knowledge of the place thought of as home" – claims that he acknowledges are open to dispute but are invested in the discursive political culture of the home society. This is not an issue of authenticity but of commitment to situated identities. If extended to the region, it identifies a group of scholars who take intellectual responsibility for the discursive constructions in which they collectively participate.

Introducing this approach in *New Terrains in Southeast Asian History*, Abu Talib Ahmad and Tan Liok Ee ask several questions that destabilise the area studies perspectives adopted by some of the contributors to their collection, such as the problem of assuming static national spaces across historical time, and thereby obscuring overlapping or changing political, spatial and cultural territories.[35] They ask if the histories of diverse peoples can be constructed via a single narrative. They argue that, "When the nation is consistently placed at the centre of historical research, the result often is an inward-looking perspective that displaces or diminishes the attention given to broader issues or stories that cross national boundaries."[36] Winichakul observes that as the anti-colonial impetus that has shaped many national histories loses force, other narratives of non-national subjects and their spatial identities might emerge.[37] He writes,

> History at the interstices traverses along the margins of national identity and national history, looking for the "in-between" locations of encounters. It would inevitably expose the edges and limits of the national domain and record the changing configurations of national identity along its borders. At the interstices, differences, hybrids, and mixtures come into play.[38]

Such questions have preoccupied recent area studies efforts at shifting the West-dominated focus of Southeast Asian studies to a more regionally inclusive platform.[39] As outlined by Goh Beng-Lan, the crisis of area studies in the Western academe (due to its failure to transcend Western power hierarchies and disciplinary divides), is not necessarily relevant within Southeast Asia, where regional scholarship can continue to denaturalise American or Eurocentric visions.[40] Energies must be directed towards cultural relativism and the contingency of knowledge production.[41] Consequently the most noteworthy change has been the greater integration of Southeast Asian scholars in regional and international discourses during the late 1990s and early 2000s, including sociologists and geographers influenced by the "spatial turn" in the humanities.[42] Geographer Brenda Yeoh's work on colonial Singapore and her many subsequent edited anthologies, several with Lily Kong, form a bulwark of such explorations.[43] Sociologist Chua Beng Huat has a similar legacy of work on public spaces and social housing in Singapore.[44] In fact, Singapore's built environment is over-represented, due to the (strength of its academic research and publication culture, and) urgent need to sustain spatial knowledge against imminent erasure. Studies of less-contingent colonial urban pasts are relatively few.[45] This is also true for Indonesia and Vietnam which have attracted a small number of scholars. [46] Goh Beng-Lan and Eric Thompson, respectively, explore urbanism and rural urbanism in Malaysia.[47]

Although still largely defined by nation-state boundaries, these scholars draw on marginal histories and histories of the localisation of transnational elements advocated by Winichakul. More importantly they privilege the complex plural (multi-ethnic) social contexts initially produced through the colonial encounter and subsequently via regional flows of capital and labour. In the decade following Winichakul's observations, minority positions have entered broader and spatially overlapping (and temporally) postcolonial, national and cosmopolitan discourses.[48] Indeed the most revealing examples of Southeast Asian territoriality are found in comparative anthologies such as *Postcolonial Urbanism*, *Theorizing the Southeast Asian City as Text*, *The City in Southeast Asia* and *Critical Reflections on Cities in Southeast Asia* which are interregional, interdisciplinary and draw liberally from both postcolonial and globalisation theory.[49] In these anthologies we find examples of interstitial approaches whereby multiple local scenarios are gathered under common themes. However, there are certain temporal evasions around government policies during decades of intellectual censorship. Comparative regional studies help fill these forced silences, by borrowing external examples to expose internal injustices. They pre-empt a new theoretical focus and desire for inter-Asian research.

Intellectual Autonomy Through InterAsian Cultural Studies

Taiwanese cultural theorist Kuan-Hsing Chen offers a useful framework for analyses of geopolitical transformations across Asia in his seminal book, *Asia as Method* arguing that "decolonising", "de-Cold War" and "de-imperialising" are part of the same historical process that must proceed together to achieve both the reintegration of Asia and greater reflexivity.[50] He writes, "... the task is for the colonizing or imperializing population to examine the conduct, motives, desires and consequences of the imperialist history that has formed their own subjectivity".[51] Using the modern period in East Asia and the region's globalisation as intellectual starting points, Chen demonstrates that the theoretical and methodological gravitas typically attributed to Euro-American histories can be applied to Asian topics using other Asian nations as referents. *Asia as Method* poses the very different histories of imperialism that influenced Taiwan and Korea as an analytical counterpoint to European colonialism and its dominant epistemes. Although problematic in its Asia-centricity, Chen escapes the dogged alterity of postcolonial theory. His interregional approach denationalises these histories, challenges area studies at the national level and facilitates collaboration across Asia. It obviates many of the inequities arising from Western intellectual and institutional hegemony. The Inter-Asia Cultural Studies (IACS) journal and reader bring East Asian imperialism into focus, critically reinvigorating the scope of cultural studies while filling a gap in regional research.[52] Nevertheless, in placing East Asia at the discursive centre there is considerable risk of displacing European imperialists with their neo-imperial competitors. The marginality of other Asian regions in the IACS discourse has more to do with their relative economic and political standing than their cultural diversity. While Eastward reorientation is a critical move, economic and political models remain Western derivatives.

Each of the theoretical platforms discussed here are departures from a world order in which Western scholars, publications and research cultures determine intellectual trends. They create regional spaces within which local knowledges can explore alternative methodologies. These spaces are intellectually hybrid due to the movement of scholars between Western and Asian institutions, and between Asia and the West for education and for fieldwork. Publication cultures have likewise expanded as Western publishers seek global partners and markets. It is within such environments that we find the most strident critiques of the West. However, this scholarship is increasingly oriented towards phenomena internal to the region more broadly defined as the Asia Pacific. This Pacific orientation reflects a US-led worldview, an East Asian dominance and decline of Europe's global political authority. However, the major global publishing houses remain Europe-centred as do their journals and, for now, their Asian subsidiaries or partners have a limited impact. Meanwhile the growing economic strength of China and India and their market potential infiltrates and transforms these discourses.

The East Asian model of urbanisation, suburbanisation and globalisation has provided a popular paradigm for urban development. Globalisation theory scrutinises phenomena as disparate as super-modern corporate towers and informal settlements and is keenly aware of transnational networks and flows. The dominance of China has impacted and marginalised other postcolonial debates. Gayatri Spivak's description of Jakarta as a "megacity", addresses these "other Asias".[53] Indeed, regional complicity or impoverishment due to the emergence of China and India may provide material for new postcolonial spatial critiques.

Despite their intention to democratise pedagogy and foster cultural diversity, the spectres of India and China linger in both PCS and IACS. Within PCS, India acts as an alternative post-imperial centre that adapted, redefined and translated the terms of coloniality – while Indian scholars based in India or the West move fluidly between these two poles. Indian intellectual hegemony is evident in South Asian studies. Similarly, IACS expands on the links created by Chinese diasporic movements that have always straddled the tensions between region and nation. The place of Hong Kong, Taiwan and Singapore in this network suggests that veins of intellectual inquiry flourish in these in-between zones. Such interstitial identities help denationalise scholarship through attention to globalisation's trace. However, they also create exclusive groupings based on political histories of colonisation or Asian geographic locations that have been given ideological agency through these very intellectual framings. Terms like Asian and postcolonial, "Asianising" or Asian perspectives reduce a heterogeneous region to a uniform agency based on geographic proximity. These strategic geopolitical essentialisms presume East–West alterities that divert attention from internal conflicts.

So how might we address urgent but marginalised social equity concerns within national pedagogy? How do we frame or understand inter-Asian conflict? As argued by University of Sydney sociologist Raewyn Connell, diverse perspectives on sociology from the Global South, described by her as "Southern Theory", offer convincing alternatives.[54] While critiquing the subservience to Euro-American modernity in modern disciplinary frameworks, she reassesses the transformative value of other non-Western and Indigenous perspectives as distinct frames of thinking. Connell argues that political and economic transformations of geographical areas, previously classified as Third World dependencies – the legatees of colonialism, the Commonwealth and Cold War imperialisms – might inform a south-south discourse. Three theoretical movements identified by Connell are particularly significant. Feminism and intersectional social theory within third-wave feminism expose discourses of power and patriarchy normalised in regional structures.[55] Subaltern studies, a group within postcolonial studies identifying with the work of Antonio Gramsci raise resistant histories from below.[56] The critique of colonial anthropology in Australian Indigenous studies challenges national sovereignty and its assimilatory strategies. All three of these minority constituencies created by gender, class and ethnic discriminations operate across a range of complex social intersections that are spatially inscribed. These are useful positions for critiquing structural elitism and systems of oppression within architecture.

Alternative Subjectivities

Such alternative intersectional investigations across gender, class and ethnicity have the capacity to transform architectural discourse in Southeast Asia where labour mobility, education and professionalisation of women have accelerated social change since the 1990s. The convergence of various systems of oppression is particularly evident in the metropolitan reconfiguration of traditional rural identities and women's navigation of masculinised public spheres.[57] Third-wave feminist discourses have reconceptualised home-space through discussions of transnational domestic labour, diasporic estrangement and familial transformation, and explored embodied socio-spatial practices that engage contested sexualities.[58] Few architectural publications venture into this socially complex terrain. An issue of *Gender, Place and Culture*, edited by Gulsum Baydar, has focused on sexualised productions of space, destabilising gender binaries and challenging Western-centric tropes, within which regional issues are highlighted.[59]

Social intersections across class and through labour mobility have reterritorialised Southeast Asia producing highly gendered human flows across sovereign borders.[60] Female domestic guest workers employed in Singaporean and Malaysian homes and sharing their employers' spaces and nurturing their children, create uneven transnational labour dependencies.[61] Colonial period divisions of industrial labour inform architectural and urban studies – for example the role of Samsui women or penal labour in the construction industry discussed by Kelvin Low or Pieris, respectively, or Khoo Salma Nasution and Abdur-Razzaq Lubis's work on the Kinta Valley mining industry.[62] Although the metropolitan emergence of Asian cities (whether in the colonial period or neo-liberal present) is largely contingent on the affordability, economic exploitation, depoliticisation and temporary mobility of racially differentiated contract workers from poorer Asian nations, these "guest workers" remain largely unacknowledged.[63] These extraterritorial and depoliticised labourers, ubiquitous in the Singapore and Malaysia construction industries, shadow the movements of privileged metropolitan subjects as an imported underclass. Short-term contractual arrangements absolve the industry of the responsibility of training them.

The final category, the artificial separation of indigenous and modern values, is perhaps the most critical for demonstrating internal hierarchies and racist overtones. As argued previously, the forces of indigenisation – vernacular and regionalist architectures – were conceptualised as critical and resistant positions. Yet regionalism's internal hierarchies preserve monumental architectures for institutional designs while deploying the vernacular tradition for tourist theme parks. Within this differentiation is a troubling distinction between civilisational and Aboriginal identities untenable in politically self-conscious Australasian scholarship.[64] This difference is evident in the work of Australia-based architectural scholars.[65]

An extension of Orientalist ethnography (staged in imperial expositions) and collections of tribal architectures in nationalist theme parks reproduce a problematic uncontaminated (by colonialism) "authenticity" and yet are demoted within nationalist discourse. They compete for representation against the urban or rural vernaculars of cultural majorities and regional settlers.[66] The role of Taman Mini Indonesia Indah in authenticating President Suharto's New Order has been discussed by Kusno and John Pemberton.[67] However, the challenge posed by Aboriginal/Indigenous communities to the politics of national belonging is ignored. Internationally, since the UN Declaration on the Rights of Indigenous Peoples (2007) invigorated their cause, transnational forums have used cultural centres and museums as reconciliatory spaces. The museums of ethnology in Hanoi, Osaka and Taipei embrace this discourse. Elsewhere, regional collections or outdoor ethnographic museums foreground troubling tourism practices that are manipulated for nation-building goals.[68] Their marginality is compounded by nationalist land entitlements and postcolonial language policies that naturalise regional settlers with institutionalised literary and religious traditions (for example, the Malay bumiputra – sons of the soil – of Malaysia) over Aboriginals. Conversely, the complex Indigenous identities of Balinese architecture with its synthesisation of Hindu and tribal practice has been globalised through resort tourism and, as argued by Amanda Achmadi, prompting Orientalist reconstitution for the traveller's gaze.[69] Metropolitan cultures, forms and amenities injected into remote areas transform aboriginal settlements into variations of suburban sprawl.

Although engaging with the spatial experiences of subaltern subjects and groups and highlighting their diverse social and political intersections, a large part of this scholarship focuses on people rather than the spaces that they occupy. The structural disruption of rural agrarian polities, subsistence or local economies and abandonment of former colonial agricultural systems for urban industries underscore these intersectional histories. The transformation of domesticity, mobilisation of rural labour and commodification of rural vernaculars are the most vulnerable aspects of contemporary urbanisation discourse. Tariq Jazeel argues that

> [G]eographically there is much to gain from treating subalternity not just as a reference to subordinate subjects and/or groups, but also as a more figurative reference to geographies occluded by the hegemonic conceptualizations of space that pervade our discipline.[70]

He proposes identifying spaces through their subjectivity, a theme explored by Nihal Perera in *People's Spaces*, in which he focuses on the everyday activities, spatial appropriations, negotiations and transformations of ordinary people.[71] Within it lies a sustained critique of the urban disciplines, their Eurocentricism and their social neglect. Although these scholars focus on Sri Lanka, their positions are applicable to Southeast Asian urban studies.

Against Urbanisation

Southeast Asian urbanism has been dominated by geographers including T.G. McGee, Peter Rimmer and economic historian Howard Dick.[72] Notable exceptions from architecture, such as Johannes Widodo, Yat Ming Loo and Ross King, explore aspects of Chinese settlement and resultant ethnic politics using very different methodological approaches.[73] King also presents revisionist analyses of self-colonisation in his study of Bangkok.[74] Ole Johan Dale provides an analysis of urban planning strategy extending to the postcolonial period, the cultural complexities of which are articulated by Lim.[75] Conferences such as modern Asia Architecture Network (mAAN) and "Great Asian Streets" have published proceedings investigating modernism, heritage conservation, mega projects and megacities.[76] Consequently the scholarship is uneven, comprised of heterogeneous approaches based on quantitative and qualitative methods from urban design, planning and architecture as well as internal or external cultural perspectives on the region. There are also numerous spatial analyses by state organisations.[77]

The most successful critiques of Asian urbanisation advocate resistant strategies such as the civic activism and guerrilla public spaces studied by planning historian, Jeffrey Hou.[78] They draw on and refer to subaltern studies perspectives, popular histories and "weapons of the weak".[79] As argued by sociologist, Daniel Goh, re-urbanisation within globalisation is a critical political practice where official strategies, civic activism and collective memories compete.[80] Underlying these forces is the colonial legacy of urban apartheid: legislated metropolitan privileges that persisted as national urban policies.[81] Resistant, largely Marxist, positions on spatial justice and the city counter the planners' view with alternative concepts such as "Asianising" or "People's Spaces" advocated by Nihal Perera.[82] These ephemeral materialities become central to discussions of urban degradation, post-disaster accommodation and refugee environments, where the much-celebrated mobility of transnational subjects is contrasted with the abjection of impoverished urban populations, migrants and refugees.[83]

The social damage caused by rampant urbanisation, highlighted in such scholarship, is revelatory. It questions the social power attributed to transnational networked forms of globalisation by advocates of the city-centric lens.[84] As revealed by Chua Beng Huat in his chapter in *Worlding Cities*, when global city and nation state combine successfully in the case of Singapore, undemocratic politics underwrite globalisation.[85] The absence of a hinterland that erodes their socio-spatial congruence makes these darlings of globalisation – Hong Kong, Dubai and Singapore – spatial anomalies. Their exportation and replication as a measure of "successful" development validates their formulas for social engineering. To what extent do we internalise these conditions as measures of Asian progress? To what degree are nations being modelled after city states? As demonstrated in this chapter, scholarship on Southeast Asian architecture has developed in tandem with accelerated urbanisation often supporting its imagination and imperatives. The city is consistently reproduced as a celebratory object and subject of research. In the political-economic sphere this intellectual imbalance has polarised national constituencies with troubling consequences.[86] While supporting the social democratisation promised by urban processes we must be wary of their growing hegemony.

Notes

1. Duanfang Lu, *Third World Modernism: Architecture, Development and Identity* (New York: Routledge, 2011); William Lim & Jiat-Hwee Chang, *Non West Modernist Past: On Architecture & Modernities* (Singapore: World Scientific Pub., 2012).
2. Sandro Mezzadra, *Border as Method* (Durham: Duke University Press, 2013); Walter Mignolo, *Local Histories/Global Designs: Coloniality, Subaltern Knowledges, and Border Thinking* (Princeton, N.J.: Princeton University Press, 1999).
3. P.J. Taylor, "Embedded Statism and the Social Sciences: Opening Up to New Spaces", *Environment and Planning A* 28 (1996): 1917–1928.
4. Edward Said, *Orientalism* (New York: Pantheon Books, 1978). For an overview on the impact of Said's work in architectural scholarship see Anthony D. King, "Writing Colonial Space: A Review Article," *Comparative Studies in Society and History* 37, no. 3 (1995): 541–554; Anoma Pieris, "South and Southeast Asia: The Postcolonial Legacy," *Fabrications*, 19, no. 2 (2010): 6–33; Peter Scriver, "Constructing Colonial and Contemporary South Asia: A View from Down Under," *Fabrications*, 19, no. 2 (2010): 34–57. The relationship between colonialism, modernity and modernism is discussed in Peter Scriver & Vikramaditya Prakash, *Colonial Modernities: Building, Dwelling and Architecture in British India and Ceylon* (London: Routledge, 2007); Jane Jacobs, *Edge of Empire: Postcolonialism and the City* (London: Routledge, 1996); Mark Crinson, *Modern Architecture and the End of Empire* (Aldershot: Ashgate, 2003); Mark Crinson, *Empire Building: Victorian Architecture and Orientalism* (London: Routledge, 1996).
5. Tariq Jazeel, "Postcolonialism: Orientalism and the Geographical Imagination," *Geography*, 97, no.1 (2012): 4–11.
6. Ibid., 4.
7. Sibel Bozdogan, "Architectural History in Professional Education: Reflections on Postcolonial Challenges to the Modern Survey," *Journal of Architectural Education*, 52, no. 4 (1999): 211 and 214; Gülsüm Baydar Nalbantoğlu, "Toward Postcolonial Openings: Rereading Sir Banister Fletcher's 'History of Architecture'," *Assemblage* 35 (1998): 6–17.
8. Dipesh Chakrabarty, *Provincializing Europe: Postcolonial Thought and Historical Difference* (Princeton, N.J.: Princeton University Press, 2000).
9. Gwendolyn Wright, *The Politics of Design in French Colonial Urbanism* (Chicago: University of Chicago Press, 1991); Gülsüm Baydar Nalbantoğlu & Wong Chong Thai, ed., *Postcolonial Space(s)* (New York: Princeton Architectural Press, 1997).
10. Abidin Kusno, *Behind the Postcolonial: Architecture, Urban Space, and Political Cultures in Indonesia* (London: Routledge, 2000); Abidin Kusno, *The Appearances of Memory: Mnemonic Practices of Architecture and Urban Form in Indonesia* (Durham, NC: Duke University Press, 2010); Abidin Kusno, *After the New Order: Space, Politics, and Jakarta* (Honolulu: University of Hawai'i Press, 2013).

11. Gerard Lico, *Edifice Complex: Power, Myth and Marcos State Architecture* (Manila: Ateneo Press, 2003); Koompong Noobanjong, *The Aesthetics of Power: Architecture, Modernity, and Identity from Siam to Thailand* (Bangkok: White Lotus Press, 2013); Ross King, *Reading Bangkok* (Singapore, NUS Press, 2011); Eka Permanasari, *Constructing and Contesting the Nation: The Use and Meaning of Sukarno's Monuments and Public Places in Jakarta* (Saarbrücken: Lambert Academic Publishing, 2010); Anoma Pieris, *Hidden Hands and Divided Landscapes: A Penal History of Singapore's Plural Society* (Honolulu: University of Hawai'i Press, 2009); Jiat-Hwee Chang, *A Genealogy of Tropical Architecture: Colonial Networks, Nature and Technoscience* (New York: Routledge, 2016); Ross King, *Kuala Lumpur and Putrajaya: Negotiating Urban Space in Malaysia* (Singapore: Asian Studies Association of Australia in association with NUS Press and NIAS Press, 2008); Chee Kien Lai, *Building Merdeka: Independence Architecture in Kuala Lumpur, 1957–1966* (Kuala Lumpur: Galeri Petronas, 2007). See also, Iwan Sudradjat "A Study of Indonesian Architectural History" (Unpublished dissertation, University of Sydney, 1991).
12. Imran bin Tajudeen, "Review, Journal of Southeast Asian Architecture, Vol. 1 1996 to Vol. 11 2009," *Fabrications*, 19, no. 2 (2010): 177–179, 177.
13. Abidin Kusno et al. ed., "Changing Asia," *Journal of Architectural Education* 63, no. 2 (2010); Anoma Pieris & Paul Walker ed., "About Asia," *Fabrications* 19, no. 2 (2010), Lilian Chee, Jiat-Hwee Chang & Bobby Wong ed., "Tropicality in Motion, Performing Tropical Spatialities," *Singapore Journal of Tropical Geography*, 32, no. 3 (2011), and John Ting and Campbell Macknight ed., "Crossing Boundaries, Review of Indonesian and Malaysian Affairs," 44, no. 2 (2010).
14. Duanfang Lu, "Entangled Histories of Modern Architecture," in *Non-West Modernist Past*, ed., Lim & Chang, 59–68, Chang and Lim, "Non West Modernist Past: Rethinking Modernisms and Modernities beyond the West," in *Non West Modernist Past*, 7–22.
15. See, Chee Kien Lai & Anoma Pieris, "Post-Tropical/Post Tsunami: Climate and Architectural Discourse in South and Southeast Asia," *SJTG*, 32, no. 3 (2011): 365–381, and Kusno, "Green Governmentality" in *After the New Order*, 119–138.
16. Alexander Tzonis, Liane Lefaivre & Stagno ed., *Tropical Architecture: Critical Regionalism in the Age of Globalization* (Chichester; New York: Wiley-Academic, 2001); Joo-Hwa Bay & Boon Lay Ong, *Tropical Sustainable Architecture: Social and Environmental Dimensions* (Oxford; Burlington, MA: Architectural Press, 2006).
17. Chang, *A Genealogy of Tropical Architecture*.
18. Akitek Tenggara website, Rubanisation. Accessed at: http://www.rubanisation.org/autobiography.
19. Ken Yeang, *Bioclimatic Skyscrapers* (London: Ellipsis, 2000); William Lim, *Asian Ethical Urbanism: A Radical Postmodern Perspective* (Singapore: World Scientific Pub., 2005).

20. Tay Kheng Soon, *Mega-cities in the Tropics: Towards an Architectural Agenda for the Future* (Singapore: Institute of Southeast Asian Studies, 1989); William Lim, *Asian Ethical Urbanism: A Radical Postmodern Perspective* (Singapore: World Scientific Pub., 2005).
21. William Lim, "Architecture, Art, Identity in Singapore: Is There Life After Tabula Rasa?" in *Asian Ethical Urbanism*, 133–214, in reference to Rem Koolhaas,"Singapore Songlines: Portrait of a Potemkin Metropolis … or Thirty Years of Tabula Rasa," in *S,M,L,X,L*, ed., Rem Koolhaas & Bruce Mau (New York: Monicelli Press, 1995), 1009–1089.
22. William Lim, *Asian Alterity: With Special Reference to Architecture + Urbanism Through the Lens of Cultural Studies*, vol.1 (Singapore: World Scientific 2007).
23. Robert Powell, ed., *Architecture and Identity* (Singapore: Concept Media, 1983).
24. Tay Kheng Soon, "Case Study 3, Singapore, Cultural Identity in Architecture as Seen from a Singapore Viewpoint," in *Architecture and Identity*, ed., Robert Powell, 46–51.
25. Samer Akkach, "Identity in Exile: The Aga Khan's Search for Excellence in Islamic Architecture," in *On What Grounds? Conference Proceedings* ed., S. Pickersgill & P. Scriver (Adelaide: Society of Architectural Historians of Australia and New Zealand, 1997), 1–8; Akkach, "Expatriating Excellence: The Aga Khan's Search for Muslim Identity," in *Building Dwelling Drifting: Migrancy and the Limits of Architecture*, proceedings of the 3rd "Other Connections" conference (Melbourne: University of Melbourne, 1997), 1–8.
26. Sumet Jumsai, *Naga: Cultural Origins in Siam and the West Pacific* (Singapore: Oxford University Press, 1990); Chen Voon Fee, *Encyclopedia of Malaysia: Architecture, Vol. 5* (Singapore: Archipelago Press, 2007); Lim Chong Keat, *Penang Views*, 1770–1860 (Penang: Penang Museum and Summer Times Pub., 1986).
27. David Robson, *Beyond Bawa: Modern Masterworks of Monsoon Asia* (London: Thames and Hudson 2007).
28. The first in the series was Robert Powell, *The Tropical Asian House* (Singapore: Select Books, 1996).
29. ASEAN website, Overview, http://www.asean.org/asean/about-asean, accessed 2 October 2014.
30. Jon Lim ed., *Transforming Traditions: Architecture in the ASEAN Countries: Brunei, Malaysia, Indonesia, Philippines, Singapore, Thailand* (Singapore: ASEAN Committee on Culture and Information, 2001).
31. Aihwa Ong, *Neoliberalism as Exception: Mutations in Citizenship and Sovereignty* (Durham, N.C.: Duke University Press, 2006).
32. William Logan, ed., "Introduction: Globalization, Cultural Identity and Heritage," in *The Disappearing Asian City: Protecting Asia's Urban Heritage in a Globalizing World*, ed., Logan (Hong Kong; Oxford: Oxford University Press 2002), xii–xxi, 1–3.
33. Sandro Mezzadra, *Border as Method* (Durham: Duke University Press, 2013); Walter Mignolo, *Local Histories/Global Designs*.

34. Winichakul first broached these ideas at the "Conference on Southeast Asian Historiography since 1945", Penang, 30 July to 1 August 1999. It was subsequently published as Thongchai Winichakul, "Writing at the Interstices: Southeast Asian Historians and Postnational Histories in Southeast Asia" 3–29, in Abu Talib Ahmad and Tan Liok Ee eds, *New Terrains in Southeast Asian History* (Singapore: NUS Press, 2003), 6.
35. Ahmad and Tan, "Introduction" in *New Terrains*, ix–xxv. Many of the contributors identify through nation spaces such as Singapore and Malaysia.
36. Ibid., xvii.
37. Winichakul, "Writing at the Interstices", 9.
38. Ibid., 23.
39. Goh Beng-Lan, *De-centring & Diversifying Southeast Asia Studies: Perspectives from the Region* (Singapore: Institute of Southeast Asian Studies, 2011), 1.
40. Ibid., 1.
41. Laurie J. Sears ed., *Knowing Southeast Asian Subjects: Critical Dialogues in Southeast Asian Studies* (Seattle, WA: University of Washington Press, 2007), 4.
42. Ibid., 18.
43. Brenda Yeoh, *Contesting Space: Power Relations and the Urban Built Environment in Colonial Singapore* (Kuala Lumpur: Oxford University Press, 1996); Lily Kong & Brenda Yeoh, *The Politics of Landscapes in Singapore: Constructions of "Nation"* (Syracuse: Syracuse University Press, 2003).
44. Chua Beng Huat, *Political Legitimacy and Housing: Stakeholding in Singapore* (London: Routledge, 1997).
45. Stephen Dobb, *The Singapore River: A Social History, 1819–2002* (Singapore, NUS Press, 2003); Pieris, *Hidden Hands*; Yeoh, *Contesting Space*; Chang, *A Genealogy of Tropical Architecture*; Freek Colombijn & Martine Barwegen, *Under Construction: The Politics of Urban Space and Housing During the Decolonization of Indonesia, 1930–1960* (Leiden: KITLV Press 2010); Rudolph Mràzek, *Engineers of Happy Land* (Princeton, N.J.: Princeton University Press, 2002).
46. Jean Taylor, *The Social World of Batavia: European and Eurasian in Dutch Asia* (Madison, Wis.: University of Wisconsin Press, 1983); Marieke Bloembergen, *Colonial Spectacles: The Netherlands and the Dutch East Indies at the World Exhibitions, 1880–1931* (Singapore: Singapore University Press, 2006); and William Logan, *Hanoi: Biography of a City* (Sydney: UNSW Press, 2000).
47. Beng-Lan Goh, *Modern Dreams: An Inquiry into Power, Cultural Production, and the Cityscape in Contemporary Urban Penang, Malaysia* (Ithaca: Cornell SEAP, 2002); Eric Thompson, *Unsettling Absences: Urbanism in Rural Malaysia* (Singapore: NUS Press, 2007).
48. See, for example, Joel Kahn, *Other Malays: Nationalism and Cosmopolitanism in the Modern Malay World* (Singapore: ASAA, Singapore University Press and NIAS Press, 2006); Tim Bunnell, *Malaysia, Modernity, and the Multimedia Super Corridor: A*

Critical Geography of Intelligent Landscapes (New York: RoutledgeCurzon, 2004) Robbie Goh, *Contours of Culture: Space and Social Difference in Singapore* (Hong Kong: Hong Kong University Press, 2005).

49. Ryan Bishop, John Phillips & Wei Wei Yeo ed., *Postcolonial Urbanism* (London; New York: Routledge, 2003), Robbie Goh & Brenda Yeoh, *Theorizing the Southeast Asian City as Text* (Singapore: World Scientific, 2003) Peter Rimmer & Howard Dick, *The City in Southeast Asia: Patterns Processes, Policy* (Honolulu,: University of Hawai'i Press, 2009); and Tim Bunnell, Lisa Barbara Welch Drummond & Ho Kong Chong, ed., *Critical Reflections on Cities in Southeast Asia* (Singapore: Times Academic, 2002).
50. Kuan-Hsing Chen, *Asia as Method: Towards Deimperialization* (Durham, N.C.: Duke University Press, 2010).
51. Ibid., 4.
52. Kuan-Hsing Cheng & Chua Beng Huat, *Inter-Asia Cultural Studies Reader* (London: Routledge, 2007).
53. Gayatri Chakrovorty Spivak, "Megacity," *Grey Room*, 1 (Autumn, 2000): 8–25. Reprinted as chapter 5, "Megacity – 1997: Testing Theory in Cities," in *Other Asias*, (Oxford: Blackwell, 2008), 161–174.
54. Raewyn Connell, *Southern Theory: The Global Dynamics of Knowledge in Social Science* (Cambridge: Polity, 2007)
55. Gillian Howie, Stacy Gillis, and Rebecca Munford, *Third Wave Feminism: A Critical Exploration* (Hampshire; New York: Palgrave Macmillan, 2004). The concept of intersecting categories of discrimination was introduced by Kimberlé Williams Krenshaw, within Critical Race Theory. Kimberle Williams Crenshaw, "Mapping the Margins: Intersectionality, Identity Politics, and Violence Against Women of Colour", *Stanford Law Review* 43, no. 6 (1991): 1241–1299.
56. Ranajit Guha & Gayatri Chakrovarty Spivak ed., *Selected Subaltern Studies* (New Delhi; New York: Oxford University Press), 1988.
57. Krishna Sen & Maila Stivens, *Gender and Power in Affluent Asia* (London; New York: Routledge, 1998); Aihwa Ong & Michael Peletz, *Bewitching Women, Pious Men: Gender and Body Politics in Southeast Asia* (Berkeley, CA: University of California Press, 1995); Theresa W. Devasahayam & Brenda S.A. Yeoh, *Working and Mothering in Asia: Images, Ideologies and Identities* (Singapore: NUS Press 2007).
58. Sonita Sarker & Esha De, *Trans-status Subjects: Gender in Globalization of South and Southeast Asia* (Durham, NC: Duke University Press, 2002).
59. Gulsum Baydar, "Sexualised Productions of Space," *Gender, Place and Culture* 19, no. 6 (2012): 699–706. See also Lilian Chee, "The Domestic Residue: Feminist Mobility and Space in Simryn Gill's Art," *Gender, Place and Culture* 19, no. 6 (2012): 750–770 and Chee, *The Third Archive: Architecture, Anecdote and Encounter at the Raffles Hotel*, forthcoming.
60. Devasahayam & Yeoh, *Working and Mothering in Asia*.

61. See Brenda Yeoh, Shirlena Huang and Joaquin Gonzalez III, "Migrant Female Domestic Workers: Debating the Economic, Social and Political Impacts in Singapore," *The International Migration Review* 33, No. 1 (1999), 114–136.
62. Kelvin E.Y. Low, *Remembering the Samsui Women: Migration and Social Memory in Singapore and China* (Vancouver: UBC Press, 2014); Pieris, *Hidden Hands and Divided Landscapes*; Khoo Salma Nasution & Abdur-Razzaq Lubis, *Kinta Valley: Pioneering Malaysia's Modern Development* (Ipoh: Perak Academy, 2005).
63. Anoma Pieris, "Plural Politics and Transient Labour: Reflections on the Sunday Map,"*South Asian Diaspora*, 4, no. 1 (2012): 57–76.
64. See Paul Memmott & James Davidson, "Indigenous Culture and Architecture in the South Pacific Region: 25 Years of SAHANZ Research,"*Fabrications*, 18, no. 1 (2008): 74–117.
65. John Ting, "The Egalitarian Architecture of the Iban Longhouse," in "Celebration – Proceedings of the 22nd Annual Conference of the Society of Architectural Historians, Australia and New Zealand," ed., Andrew Leach & Gill Matthewson (Napier, New Zealand: SAHANZ 2005); David Beynon, "The Contemporary Iban Longhouse: The Sustenance and Applicability of a Socio-spatial Culture", *International Journal of Social Sustainability in Economic, Social, and Cultural Context* 9, no. 1 (2013): 87–99.
66. Ronald Knapp, *Asia's Old Dwellings: Tradition, Resilience, and Change* (New York: Oxford University Press, 2003); Roxana Waterson, *The Living House: An Anthropology of Architecture in South-East Asia* (Singapore; New York: Oxford University Press, 1990); Paul Oliver, *Dwellings: The Vernacular House Worldwide* (London: Phaidon Press, 2003).
67. John Pemberton, *On the Subject of "Java"* (Ithaca, NY: Cornell University Press, 1994), 152–161; Abidin Kusno, *Behind the Postcolonial*, 77–78.
68. Michael Hitchcock & Nick Stanley, "Outdoor Ethnographic Museums, Tourism and Nation Building," in *Heritage Tourism in Southeast Asia*, ed., Michael Hitchcock, Victor T. King & Michael Parnwell (Copenhagen, NIAS Press 2010), 72–82; Kathleen Adams, "Museum/City/Nation: Negotiating Identities in Urban Museums in Indonesia and Singapore," in *Theorizing the Southeast Asian City as Text*, ed., Robbie Goh & Brenda Yeoh (Singapore: World Scientific Pub Co Inc., 2003), 135–158.
69. Amanda Achmadi, "The Architecture of Balinization," in *Architecture and Identity*, ed., Peter Herrle, Erik Wegerhoff (Berlin: Technische Universität Berlin, Habitat Unit 2008), 73–90.
70. Tariq Jazeel, "Subaltern Geographies: Geographical Knowledge and Postcolonial Strategy", *Singapore Journal of Tropical Geography* 35 (2014): 88–103, 88.
71. Nihal Perera, *People's Spaces: Coping, Familiarizing, Creating* (Oxon; New York: Routledge, 2015).

72. T.G. McGee, *The Southeast Asian City: A Social Geography of the Primate Cities of Southeast Asia* (London: Bell, 1967); Rimmer & Dick, *The City in Southeast Asia.*
73. Johannes Widodo, *The Boat and the City: Chinese Diaspora and the Architecture of Southeast Asian Ccoastal Cities* (Singapore: Marshall Cavendish Academic, 2004); Yat Ming Loo, *Architecture and Urban Form in Kuala Lumpur: Race and Chinese Spaces in the Postcolonial City* (Burlington: Ashgate, 2013); King, *Kuala Lumpur to Putra Jaya.*
74. King, *Reading Bangkok.*
75. Ole Johan Dale, *Urban Planning in Singapore: The Transformation of a City* (Shah Alam, Selangor Durul Ehsan, Malaysia; Oxford: Oxford University Press, 1999). Lim, *Asian Ethical Urbanism.*
76. Chye Kiang Heng, Boon Liang Low & Limin Hee, ed., *On Asian Streets and Public Space* (Singapore: Ridge Books, 2010).
77. For example the Urban Redevelopment Authority in Singapore publishes a range of instrumental analyses for policy recommendations.
78. Jeffrey Hou, *Insurgent Public Space: Guerilla Urbanism and the Remaking of Contemporary Cities* (London: Routledge, 2010). This book has been influenced by Jim Holston, *Insurgent Citizenship: Disjunctions of Democracy and Modernity in Brazil* (New Jersey: Princeton University Press, 2009).
79. In reference to James Scott, *Weapons of the Weak: Everyday Forms of Peasant Resistance* (New Haven: Yale University Press, 1985).
80. Daniel Goh, "History, Heritage and the Re-urbanisation of Asian Cities," public lecture, University of Melbourne, 22 October 2014, accessed 19 October 2014, http://public-cultures.unimelb.edu.au/event/public-lecture-visiting-scholar-daniel-goh.
81. Mike Davis, *Planet of Slums* (London; New York: Verso, 2006), 51–53.
82. David Harvey, "The Right to the City," *New Left Review* 53 (2008): 23–40; Nihal Perera ed., *Transforming Asian Cities: Intellectual Impasse, Asianizing Space, and Emerging Translocalities* (Oxon; New York: Routledge, 2012); Perera, *People's Spaces.*
83. See Tamaki Endo, *Living with Risk: Precarity and Bangkok's Urban Poor* (Singapore: NUS Press; Kyoto, Japan: Kyoto University Press, 2014).
84. Peter J. Taylor, "Embedded Statism and the Social Sciences 2: Geographies (and Metageographies) in Globalization", *Environment and Planning A* 32 (2000): 32, 1105–1114, 1113.
85. Beng Huat Chua, "Singapore as Model: Planning Innovations, Knowledge Experts", in *Worlding Cities: Asian Experiments and the Art of Being Global*, ed. Ananya Roy and Aihwa Ong (Chichester: Blackwell Publishing, 2011), 29–54.
86. For example, the recent political rifts in Thailand, between the United Kingdom and the European Union, and within the United States.

Section Three

POWER

CHAPTER 6

"Manila Beautiful": Urban Hygiene and Colonial Architecture in the Age of American Imperialism (1898–1942)

GERARD LICO

Manila Under the Stars and Stripes

The ambitious imperial venture of America to colonise the Philippine archipelago commenced in the city of Manila at the turn of the twentieth century. After the surrender of Manila in August 1898, the Americans took up their positions in the city and commenced to govern Manila. In the process of the takeover, Manila as a new American colonial city, received massive urban transformation to restructure its urban built environment as a model colonial outpost. Charged with imperialist agenda, this urban overhaul was initiated to facilitate efficient colonial governance and to signify the power and prestige of the new colonial order.

When the civil government was established, enormous power to shape the urban space was concentrated in the hands of the Municipal Board. As legislating body, it was a colonial agent charged with deploying the technologies of power such as town planning regulations and police supervision to categorise and control the indigenous population. In the process, urban planning became the mechanism by which colonial adjudications of cleanliness, civility and modernity were realised from the ground up. The Municipal Board's vision of urban life was strictly guided by a mandate codified in detail in the City Charter of Manila, which conjured spatial and environmentalist metropolitan strategies that mimicked those of the metropole. These ranged from the prevention of conflagrations to the construction of public infrastructure; from abating public nuisance to the maintenance of social hygiene. Under the charter's provision, the Board was empowered to take on the supreme role of a social architect responsible for shaping the urban built environment of the colonial metropolis. The sense of entitlement of the colonist to transform the space was driven by the rhetoric of manifest destiny, an idealistic and benevolent rationale that aimed to bring freedom and democratic order across the globe, whether it was wanted it or not. Coupled with this belief was a perceived notion that Manila was a pathologic space, a city brimming with infective agents brought about by the unsanitary habits of its native inhabitants. The colonial municipal authorities initiated an extensive site clearance and stern urban cleansing of spaces in Manila. This was a harsh prerequisite of colonial hygiene and spatial disinfection, which the Filipinos had to endure so that the site could be prepared for the building of monumental edifices that signified the American democratic and civilising mission.

Medicalisation of Space

In the period's medical texts and commission reports, the image of the Filipinos was constructed as reservoirs of latent infection. Through the lens of the American sanitary gaze, the space inhabited by Filipinos was viewed as "filthy to the extreme",[1] and Americans must necessarily avoid contact with it. The sanitary measures encouraged by colonial authorities focused on cleaning up the islands and reconstructing the image of the Filipino as a clean, white individual. The colonial officials aimed at submitting the social body to an encompassing administrative gaze that was to discipline the physical body and the people's life world and supervise the native's physical reproduction in view of labour force and colonial productivity.

The new spatial order required negotiations of power between the municipal authorities and the native population in shaping, representing and using the urban built environment in colonial Manila. The ordering of the built environment in the Philippines under the American colonial authorities necessitated a radical approach to social and urban planning policy, the implementation of which was to achieve sanitation, mass housing, and urban aesthetics – all the physical consequences of colonialism's tactic of framing the colonial subjectivity. Colonial modernity, which conflated altruism and intimidation was made more palpable in the transformation of the urban space and the building of colonial infrastructure necessary to carry out the cultivation of the indigenous population for what was termed by Paul Rabinow as "techno-cosmopolitanism",[2] a premise asserting that society must be designed, planned and organised through the technologies of both art and science.

The early years of American occupation were plagued by a succession of epidemic diseases attributed to the unhygienic domestic practices of the Filipinos at that time. Building ordinances were issued to prevent the outbreak and spread of diseases. In the context of Manila's epidemic-stricken urban terrain, and allegedly filthy native customs, habits and spatial practices were singled out as the causes of the proliferation of various tropical diseases that threatened the equilibrium of the hygienic colonial order. A sweeping colonial urban programme was designed by the American colonial authorities, conscripting the expertise of imperial physicians, sanitarians, planners, architects and engineers with disciplinary strategies to "cure" the unhealthy colonial environment by excising its dangerous and disorderly elements and reforming the unwholesome native spatial practices. American colonial urbanism crafted the geometry of spatial regulation, instilling new disciplinary technologies by controlling social behaviours though indirect impositions encrypted in spatial and built forms.

Epidemics justified the medicalisation of space, both public and private, and biopolitical reinvention of native spatial behaviours through the alliance of tropical medicine, sanitary science and urban design. The native bodies thus became a biopolitical object under constant surveillance, submitting themselves to the supervisory actions of the colonial state, which infiltrated the private and intimate details of the native's everyday spatial practices under the guise of sanitary activism and reform.

The colonial Board of Health had been subjected to severe and long-term strain by the presence of bubonic plague in the city of Manila at the time of its organisation in 1898, and more so when the cholera epidemic commenced in Manila on 20 March 1902. The successive outbreaks of bubonic plague and cholera were heuristic moments in the galvanisation of a new sanitary order in the Philippines. Apart from the application of therapeutic medicine, the hygienic interventions instituted by colonial health authorities were directed towards socio-spatial surveillance of the natives. For Foucault the modes of state intervention during times of epidemic outbreak were neither therapeutic nor medical in the strictest sense. Rather, they were concerned with modes of life, food, dwelling and environment. The regulations applied in times of epidemic were derived from "emergency plans" used in plague-infected towns.[3] Matters of spatiality and surveillance of the population soon became the obsession of the colonising state. Moreover, the moment of epidemic emergency gave rise to disciplinary diagrams (*schemas disciplinaires*), a socio-spatial schema requiring strict spatial portioning, careful surveillance, detailed inspection and order. Foucault[4] teases spatial description of a quarantine at the height of an epidemic:

> This enclosed, segmented space, observed at every point, in which the individuals are inserted in a fixed place, in which the slightest movements are supervised, in which all events are recorded, in which an uninterrupted work of writing links the centre and periphery, in which power is exercised without division, according to a continuous hierarchical figure, in which

> each individual is constantly located, examined and distributed among the living beings, the sick and the dead – all this constituted a compact model of the disciplinary method.

While Foucault's language painted a grim picture of the mechanism of power into which this model of surveillance would develop, these practices and others instituted during this time marked a certain rigour of observation and attention to detail that would set the tone for the implementation of medico-sanitary surveillance. The American method of colonial hygienic surveillance was implemented in the same disciplinary logic explicated by Foucault. Such policies of compartmentalisation and surveillance in combatting epidemics of plague and cholera were highly meticulous and militaristic: sanitary squads moved through the city, street-by-street, quarter-by-quarter, house-by-house, accounting the daily census of the living and dead, arresting suspected and infected native bodies for medical incarceration, cleansing or burning contaminated nipa (thatch) houses, and removing and disposing of the dead by cremation.

The Onslaught of Epidemic

This moment of sanitary warfare coincided with the American campaign to win the Philippine–American war. Such intersection prompted many scholars of Philippine history to consider the cholera epidemic of 1902 as a watershed event in the genesis of American sanitary order in the Philippines – a time "when the war against cholera and the 'pacification' of Filipinos were barely differentiated, when medico-sanitary measures and popular resistance to such, were continuing acts of war".[5] The decision to declare a medical emergency and to grant broad interventionist powers to health officials was political, not medical. The campaign against the plague infection and cholera outbreak represented the severity of American colonial therapeutics, "necessitating the use of force in the administering of medicine"[6] and justified the aggressive overhaul of the physical urban space and the native practices that occurred within its domain. Sanitary controls affected traditional practices such as visits to the sick, attendance at funerals, burial practices, and indigenous curative and therapeutic regimen. As David Arnold elaborated in *Imperial Medicine and Indigenous Societies*: "seeing itself as rational, scientific and universalistic, western medicine defined itself in opposition to the presumed irrationality and superstition of indigenous medicine. The customs and beliefs of the people were treated as obstacles to be overcome, obscurantism to be brushed aside by the new scientific knowledge."[7] These controls deprived the indigenous community of valuable tools used by people everywhere to ease social tensions in times of traumatic illness, death and mourning. But on a larger urban scale, the spatial consequence of the bubonic plague was urban vigilance, and campaigns against rodents, strict maritime quarantine, and rat-proofed architecture were codified in the Manila's new building code. At the same time, the cholera epidemic birthed the concept of sanitary relocation sites appropriately called "sanitary barrios", modern water infrastructure, piped water systems, underground networks of sewage conduits, and the medicalised domestic architectural prototype called the "Sanitary Model House". Epidemics in Manila, therefore, triggered the installation of infrastructural systems of colonial modernity.

The knowledge of disease etiology generated from the experience of urban epidemics resulted in the consolidation and legislation of a colonial building code, known as Ordinance No. 78, the provisions of which were embedded with medico-sanitary prescription to assure the salubrity of the future constructions in Manila. In the long run, the imposition of hygienic maneuvers by the colonial state to contain the epidemic and prevent its recurrence yielded a legacy of spatial technologies embedded in the colonial building code that would forever alter the Filipino domestic and urban spheres.

The swift sanitary response of the American military hygienist to arrest the onslaught of bubonic plague before it could result in a massive death toll was lauded in the May 1903 issue of *National Geographic* in an article titled "The Conquest of Bubonic Plague in the Philippines". It recounted the wholesale eradication of bubonic plague in the Philippines, which had "no precedent in the history of plague". The erasure of the plague pathogen from Manila was attributed to the "tireless vigilance and ceaseless war on rats and filth by Major Meacham, Chief Sanitary Inspector of Manila, and his subordinate". Without which "a wave of plague would have swept Manila and the islands as destructive ... as cholera itself".[8]

During this time, the medical world was uncertain of the mechanics of plague transmission, although scientists already suspected that rodents were involved in its etiology. The role of the rat flea as a carrier of plague existed as a theory of the Indian Plague Commission and was not verified until 1905 by the same Commission. Adopting the British anti-plague methods used in colonial India, the Manila Board of Health issued Circular Letter No. 11 on 30 June 1901 informing its sanitary officers of the modes of plague transmission. The Board of Health demanded that all clothing, bedding and furniture be disinfected and "all valueless clothing and other effects exposed to infection" be burnt. The streets should be cleaned of dust and then soaked with disinfecting carbolic acid solution to prevent the entry of germs into the cracks and wounds of the bare feet of natives and coolies. The actions taken to regulate the urban space included prohibiting the congregation of individuals at fairs, celebrations, and pilgrimages; the surveillance and supervision of markets; the inspection of soil

Figure 6.1: A cholera squad tasked with administering disinfectant during house-to-house visitations. Source: Report of the Philippine Commission to the Secretary of War, 1902, Government Printing Office, Washington.

for cleanliness; the regular removal of garbage; the inspection of habitations for cleanliness; the particular supervision of places, workshops, forges, etc., intended for occupancy by the labouring and industrial classes; the cleaning and regular disinfection of toilets, public and private; and the supervision and disinfection of latrines and cesspools.

War against Germs and Domiciliary Surveillance

Premises infested with rats were declared menaces to public safety and owners were required to make alterations such as the removal of wooden floors in basements, cellars, storerooms, etc., and their replacement with concrete and other hard materials, such as stone, tile, brick, etc.; the repair of walls and other badly constructed or decaying structures; the covering of holes, small windows and other openings on ground floors by wire netting; the abatement of all accumulations of lumber and other refuse from yards. Non-compliance with these orders meant demolition or burning of the rat-infested nipa houses. Radical remedial measures such as house burning ignited the hatred of natives – especially the poor who suffered the most – for those bearing the torches of medico-sanitary authority.

Since the appearance of plague cases in Manila, rats infected with bubonic plague bacilli had been found in over 500 houses. Lt. Colonel Maus, the president of the Board of Health, disparaged the state architecture of Manila as a contributing factor in the diffusion of plague bacillus: "The character of the buildings of Manila and their crowded condition offer every opportunity for the growth and increase of rodents. The nipa colonies within the city limits also afford a splendid place for their propagation."[9] In view of these conclusions, it became necessary for the Manila Municipal Board, at the behest of the Board of Health, to legislate an ordinance regulating the structure of buildings. Municipal Ordinance No. 5, "An Ordinance Relating to Buildings and Premises Infected with Bubonic Plague" was enacted on 16 December 1901.[10] This ordinance possessed an architectonic impact that compelled owners of plague-infected houses to remove or repair their dwellings in accordance with the architectural prescription of the Board of Health in order to deny rodents a breeding habitat. Cement ground floors were laid, double walls and double ceilings – a potential refuge for rats – were removed, defects in plumbing were remedied, whitewash was profusely applied, and, in general, nothing was left undone where plague had occurred that could render buildings safe for human resettlement. If the owner failed to adopt the prescribed rat-proofing methods, their houses would be expeditiously demolished.

As a result of this municipal ordinance over 600 domiciles were remodelled, cleaned and transformed into habitable condition, and in a number of cases the property owners expended $500 to $3,000 in undertaking the appropriate repairs and renovation.[11]

When Manila was threatened by a cholera epidemic in 1902 to 1904, the American doctors and sanitarians crusaded against disease with medico-sanitary intervention that placed much emphasis on both regulation of physical space and control of individual spatial practice. Here, environmental cleanups were deemed as important as the supervision of personal contact and social interaction.

The epidemic was introduced to Manila from Canton, China. When news reached Manila that a cholera epidemic had occurred in Canton on 3 March 1902 and in Hong Kong on 8 March 1902, the Philippine Commissioner of Public Health immediately banned the importation of vegetables from Southern China, Manila's chief supplier of vegetables. The imported produce had been found to be fertilised with infected human excreta. A cholera victim would have a medical condition of uncontrollable diarrhoea leading to rapid dehydration and death. The person's excrement is highly infectious and must be properly disposed of. For this reason, the cholera outbreak gave impetus to the politicisation of excremental matters, justifying the American colonial sanitarian's obsessive regulation of native bowel movements. A whole range of infrastructure devoted to native's excremental practices would emerge in the cityscape. In addition to general cleaning of the physical environment, the American method to suppress the cholera epidemic attempted to regulate the personal contact and the domestic and social lives of the natives as bacteriological knowledge justified this expanding medical gaze.

Right away, the colonial authority mobilised its resources and instituted rigid measures for suppressing the disease. It immediately assembled its legion of health and sanitary enforcers composed of thirty-one army physicians on loan from the Army Medical Corps who commanded a task force of 1,500 sanitary inspectors, nearly all American. The number of employees was subsequently increased until it reached 5,000.[12] Some of them worked as medical inspectors or quarantine officers; while others took charge of the cholera hospital and detention camp. Manila was divided into twelve districts for the purpose of sanitary surveillance, each placed under the charge of a medical officer who supervised a corps of thirty to sixty men in conducting house-to-house inspections (Figure 6.1). In the initial stages of the epidemic, house-to-house inspections were performed both day and night so as to prevent cases from escaping the notice of the Board. Such a vigilant measure was "necessary in order to detect cases which were being hidden by the natives, presumably to prevent being sent to the detention camp".[13] Each district was provided with a disinfecting pump and chemical disinfectants that were used to thoroughly purge the pathogens from the infected house after the cholera victim and the other contacts had been removed. After meticulous disinfection the house was closed for occupancy for five days. People exposed to the disease were sent to a detention camp near San Lazaro capable of handling 2,500 inmates, but with the increase in cases it quickly became overcrowded, so the authorities hastily set up a tent camp in the district of Santa Mesa.

Adding to the panic and fear of the disease, the forced isolation of the sick and the rounding up of household contacts to be sent to detention camps was greatly resented by the natives. House disinfection, forced detention, and compulsory quarantine infringed on the private rights, familial bonds and domestic space of the Filipinos. The military-style sanitary arrest provoked much fear among Filipino and Chinese communities in Manila as the house inspections conducted by the sanitary police brought them closer to the possibility of being confined to concentration camps, of being subjected to disinfecting baths, and of the destruction of their contaminated property. As a consequence, they made every effort to evade sanitary inspection or conceal plague cases from the sanitary inspectors to the extent that they threw their dead in rivers rather than risk the chance of having their property burned and being sent to a detention camp.[14] To deal with this situation the colonial authorities spread its huge military force over the entire urban space.

Spectacle of Site Clearing and the Burning of Farola

It was believed that Manila's cholera epidemic originated in the Farola (lighthouse) district (Figure 6.2) in Manila, a narrow tongue of land extending to the sea where Pasig River intersects Manila Bay, and "where an aggregation of overcrowded and filthy shacks presented conditions favorable to its spread".[15] The infection was attributed to a smuggled shipment of presumably contaminated cabbages and other green vegetables from Canton, via Hong Kong, which had been denied entry into the port. Due to the rejection of the produce, the crew tossed the vegetables overboard to be washed ashore, where the poor natives of Barrio Farola gathered and ate them.[16] Another theory to explain the localisation of infection in Farola was that many of its residents were stevedores, fishermen and petty smugglers who could have contracted the disease through contact with sailors from Southern China.[17]

In the belief that they could restrict the outbreak to Farola, the colonial health authorities surrounded the district with military-installed *cordon sanitaire* to quarantine its residents. This cordon failed miserably when several natives escaped the blockade by water under the cover of night. The impossibility of

Figure 6.2: The neighbourhood of Farola tagged by the authorities as the centre of the cholera epidemic of 1902, was consequently cleansed by burning. Source: Report of the Philippine Commission to the Secretary of War, 1902, Government Printing Office, Washington.

Figure 6.3: The burning of the Farola district of Manila in 1902 at the height of the cholera outbreak. Source: Report of the Philippine Commission to the Secretary of War, 1902, Government Printing Office, Washington.

disinfection impelled the Board of Health to adopt the following resolution on 26 March 1902:

> Whereas the district known as the Farola Barrio, of the city of Manila, is at present time infected with Asiatic cholera, and a center of infection for the disease, and it is therefore a menace to the public health, and is hereby declared a public nuisance, be it *Resolved*, That the houses and property in this barrio be appraised by a committee appointed by the commissioner of public health, and that such houses and property be destroyed at the discretion of the committee so appointed.[18]

Without delay, Secretary of Interior and Philippine Commissioner Dean C. Worcester ordered the execution of Government Order 66, which called for the burning of the Farola district (Figure 6.3). Colonel Maus was reluctant to set the entire slum neighbourhood ablaze but, after being commanded to do so three times, he expedited the draconian order. Just before setting fire to the area, the military forcibly removed all of its residents, whether ill or well, to a concentration camp at San Lazaro.

The anticipated burning of Farola was the subject of front-page news on the day of its destruction. *Manila Freedom*, an American-owned newspaper enthusiastically announced the forthcoming destruction of Barrio Farola and the urban relief it might bring in the course of its obliteration:

> Farola barrio, otherwise known as "Shacktown," which has been a source of considerable anxiety to the health authorities because of its cholera breed propensity, will in the course of the day or so be reduced to ashes. This district is about the worst in Manila because of its unsanitary conditions, and its removal will be a source of great satisfaction to the residents of Manila.[19]

A day before its scheduled burning, the barrio was virtually a ghost town as cans upon cans of carbolic acid were spread over the district so as to reduce the danger of the germs being spread by fire and smoke. The authorities allowed one person per house to be left behind in the barrio, to guard the property until the final conflagration.

On Good Friday morning, 28 March 1902, the "pest-breeding Farola was burned to the ground".[20] Shortly after 5 a.m. the torch was applied to the doomed village of 125 dry nipa shacks and in a matter of minutes the entire district was aflame. Liberal quantities of kerosene had been applied at intermediate points and this pungent odour, interacting with the corrosive stench of carbolic disinfectant "made life miserable for the health officers and police".[21] The unsympathetic pyro-spectacle, supervised by Major Meacham and Colonel Maus and witnessed by Commissioner Worcester himself, necessitated a "strong force of police"[22] to ensure the successful execution of the official order. Hundreds of natives gathered to watch the destruction of what health authorities decried as an urban health nuisance, the smoke from which had spread over the whole Binondo district. The blaze lasted for a short time and died as quickly as it had risen, yet this was only the beginning of a state-sanctioned house burning spree of the "unsanitary habitations" of the poor natives of Manila.

The burning of Farola was heralded by the American press in Manila as a symbolic event that "has lifted a load of great anxiety from the shoulders of health authorities. They have not relaxed their unceasing vigilance, however, but are putting forth renewed efforts towards bringing Manila back to its former healthful state."[23] The Filipino press denounced the authoritarian and coercive schemes of the Board of Health as inhumane acts of arson. Moreover, rumours were circulated among the natives that the burning of plebian houses in Farola was a part of an American real estate conspiracy to develop the dense district into an exclusive residential neighbourhood and warehouse facility for rich Americans at the expense of evicted natives.[24]

A series of nipa house burnings immediately followed the Farola fire with the issuance of a Board of Health resolution on 12 April 1902:

> Whereas all houses constructed of light materials, by reason of their construction, cannot be properly disinfected when infected with cholera, they are hereby declared a menace to the public health and a nuisance; *Resolved*, That such structures shall be entirely or partially destroyed, at the discretion of the board of health but, before such destruction, shall be appraised by the board of health.[25]

The burning of houses accomplished a three-fold agenda: first, the disinfection of urban space in order to contain the possible spread of the pathogen from the house of infectives to neighbouring districts; second, the instant erasure of decrepit architecture of poor natives and appalling urban squalour tainting the imperial metropolitan imaginary; and third, cleansing/clearance of the site rendered the urban space ready for regeneration, imperial embellishment and hegemonic social control of the unruly and diseased bodies of the modern metropolis.

Building Regulations and Excremental Control

The onslaught of epidemics had major architectural implications, which brought about many technological changes to Filipino domestic space in order to minimise the indoor pollution it generated. The municipal imaginary of salubrious urbanity had implicated the native nipa houses as foci of potential infection and launched an invasive system of policing, which encroached on the bounds of domestic privacy to expose the filthy, dark, claustrophobic and disease-harbouring domesticity obscured from the imperial sanitary gaze. The architecture of the native dwelling was radically overhauled by the municipal and health authorities who ordered the installation of latrines and other domestic services as well as structural modifications to other internal features of the urban nipa houses through congeries of military orders and ordinances. Structures were ordered to be rat-proofed in response to plague-carrying rodents.

In 1905, the city's Building Ordinance, brimming with provisions against house infections, was passed. The ordinance stringently fixed the minimum standards and stipulated medicalised guidelines for housing density, illumination, ventilation and waste disposal. The use of toilets was introduced in 1902 at the height of the cholera epidemic among the communities of nipa houses in Manila through the pail conservancy system or *cubeta* (Figure 6.4). By May 1902, the actual organisation of the pail system commenced. Overseers were immediately

Figure 6.4: The public latrine known as *cubeta* was introduced in 1902. Source: Report of the Philippine Commission to the Secretary of War, 1902, Government Printing Office, Washington.

dispatched to the districts of Santa Cruz, San Nicolas and Tondo to conduct a house-to-house inspection of the toilet arrangements and to order homeowners to make the necessary repairs to accommodate the installation of the pail system. These orders consisted mainly of providing seat covers and ventilation pipes, repairs to floors and vaults, and resealing the vaults tightly so that gases were only allowed to escape by way of ventilation pipes.[26]

In the absence of a metropolitan sewer, the system provided each household with wooden buckets, which were collected daily by the municipal excrement wagons. Public toilets were built in congested nipa districts.

By 1905, the pail-conservancy system grew to a point where the number of pails installed in private buildings had almost doubled. In July 1904, a total of 52,794 pails were cleaned, whereas in June 1905, the department handled 95,254 pails. The increase in public patronage in 1905 could be attributed to the aggressive campaign and effective enforcement of the sanitary law by the Manila police, who arrested 375 individuals for "neglecting to occupy a public station" and another 134 for "committing a public nuisance".[27]

In 1905, a latrine system was also developed based on toilet structures prevalent in the town of Antipolo. The authorities banned the use of canals or *esteros* for bathing and washing, and established a new type of communal architecture that combined the functions of toilet, bath and laundry supplied continuously with clean water. The first public bath and laundry, a one-story structure made of concrete, was built in 1913. This meticulous domestic surveillance and socio-spatial regimentation was driven to effectively cordon off the contamination discharged by native bodies and prevent it from spreading to a larger area of the city.

Establishment of Sanitary Barrios

To abate overcrowding, filth, bad ventilation and the threat of fire in light-material districts, in 1908 the Americans introduced the neighbourhood concept known as "sanitary barrios" that permitted hybridised nipa houses known as the "Sanitary Model House" to be built on highly regulated blocks of subdivided lots (Figure 6.5). Each sanitary block had a built-in system of surface drainage, a public latrine, public bath houses and laundry, and public water hydrants, which could be used by the residents free of charge. The building of these model communities marked the shift of American urban policy, which recast the image of the colonial authorities before the eyes of the Filipinos from ruthless demolisher and arsonist of indigenous neighbourhoods to altruistic community developer and urban benefactor. Imprints of these barrios can still be seen in areas of Sampaloc, San Lazaro and Vito Cruz.

The sanitary barrios followed a general template that was made up of a system of permanent street lines or city blocks laid out according to the regulated street plans of the municipality. The unit of the sanitary barrio was the sanitary block, defined by wide streets possessing a gradient that allowed for efficient surface drainage. These blocks were then partitioned into uniformly sized house lots. Every lot was oriented so that each had a street or alleyway frontage. Only a single house was allowed on each lot.[28] Blocks were cut by alleys to shorten

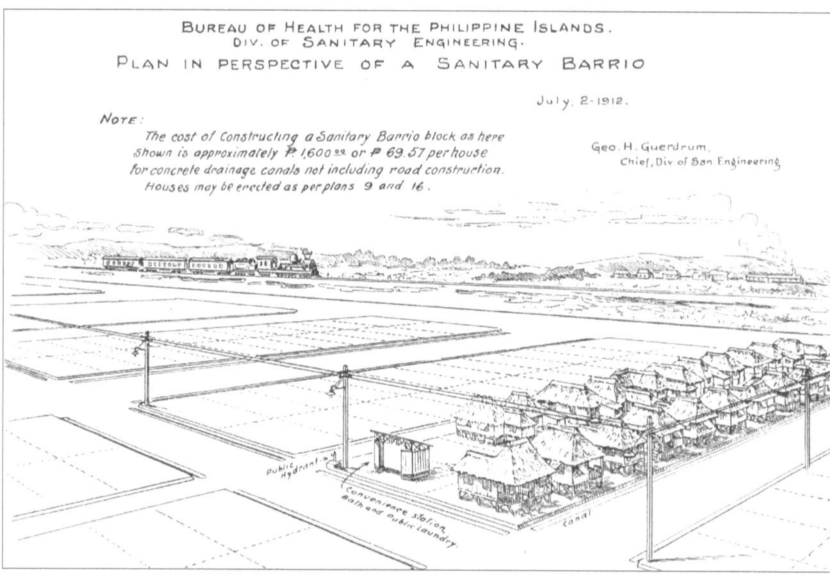

Figure 6.5: Perspective of a typical sanitary barrio drawn by the Bureau of Health in 1912. Source: Bureau of Health, Bulletin Number 10, *Philippine Habitations* (*Viviendas Filipinas*), Bureau of Printing, Manila.

the distance and travel time from the house to the public convenience station and hydrant.

The San Lazaro Estate, owned by the Insular Government and administered by the Bureau of Lands, was the first area in the metropolis to be developed as a sanitary barrio in October 1908. Shortly after, the sanitary barrio was seen as a source of great civic pride, evidenced by an overwhelming patronage from donors who offered portions of their estate to the municipal government to be developed along its reformist template.

Development of the *Tsalet*

With the success of the sanitary barrios, the American authorities focused their efforts on modernising the Filipino house known as the *bahay kubo* (Figure 6.6). The *bahay kubo*, made primarily of bamboo and thatch, was a single room dwelling with square or rectangular plan raised above the ground on stilts and capped by high pitched gable or hipped roof of nipa. This vernacular dwelling – its materials, layout, construction and services – posed myriad health issues that threatened to compromise the colonial sanitary order. Inadequate air quality, potable water and waste disposal adversely affected the medical condition of

Figure 6.6: The Filipino vernacular dwelling known as *bahay kubo*. Source: Bureau of Health, Bulletin Number 10, *Philippine Habitations* (*Viviendas Filipinas*), Bureau of Printing, Manila.

its occupants. The ineffective drainage of surface water and the inadequate treatment of human faeces before they contaminated the underground water sources were crucial aspects in the prevention of cholera, typhoid fever, dysentery and other enteric diseases. The colonisers believed that the city should be made up of houses of more permanent constitution such as stone or concrete: the vernacular nipa dwellings were appropriate in the countryside but not in the city. This architectural defamation of vernacular dwellings was the consistent trope in the colonial discourse: stone and concrete equated with permanence, affluence and civilisation, while houses of nipa and bamboo gave shelters to "innately unhygienic" people.[29] The colonial abhorrence for the materiality of the nipa house was aggravated even further in the aftermath of two epidemics to the point of expunging its presence from the urban core by effecting sweeping municipal legislation. These building regulations were to introduce architectonic strategies to revolutionise its form according to American sanitary designs. The pinnacle of the official action of the Insular Government in discouraging the use of nipa that eventually diminished its staple status in native building practice was epitomised by the passage in the Philippine Assembly Act No. 1838: "Act Granting a Prize of Fifteen Thousand Pesos to the Inventor of an Incombustible Roof to Substitute Nipa, and Creating a Technical Board to Pass Upon the Conditions of the Invention", on 29 May 1908. New materials were to be developed to replace the highly flammable nipa as the staple material for urban construction, especially after the Great Fire that engulfed Manila in 1903. Effectively, Philippine Assembly Act No. 1838 sanctioned the banishment of the nipa roof, with incombustible material as substitute. The pinnacle of this material experimentation was the development of the prototype "Ideal Sanitary House" displayed at the Manila Carnival of 1917.

The colonial architects and sanitary engineers successfully evolved a new kind of domestic architecture. In the quest for a sanitary domestic architecture, the Americans, following what the British did for the Indian bungalow, successfully developed a new kind of architecture that crossbred the tropically responsive features of vernacular buildings with modern materials and imported hygienic architectonic principles that gave premium to "light, ventilation and drainage".[30] This innovative hybrid house, hinting stylistically at a tropicalised chalet, would be simply called the *tsalet* (Figure 6.7) by the Filipinos and would influence the domestic aspirations of the Filipino middle class beginning in the 1910s and continuing even after the Pacific War. It was a single-storey structure constructed either entirely of wood or a combination of ferroconcrete and wood. The living areas were maintained at an elevation of a metre above ground, lower than the *bahay kubo* to discourage the placement of domestic animals in the underfloor area. The extended porch or verandah in front, which could be accessed by either an L-shaped or a T-shaped stair, was another improvement. These deep

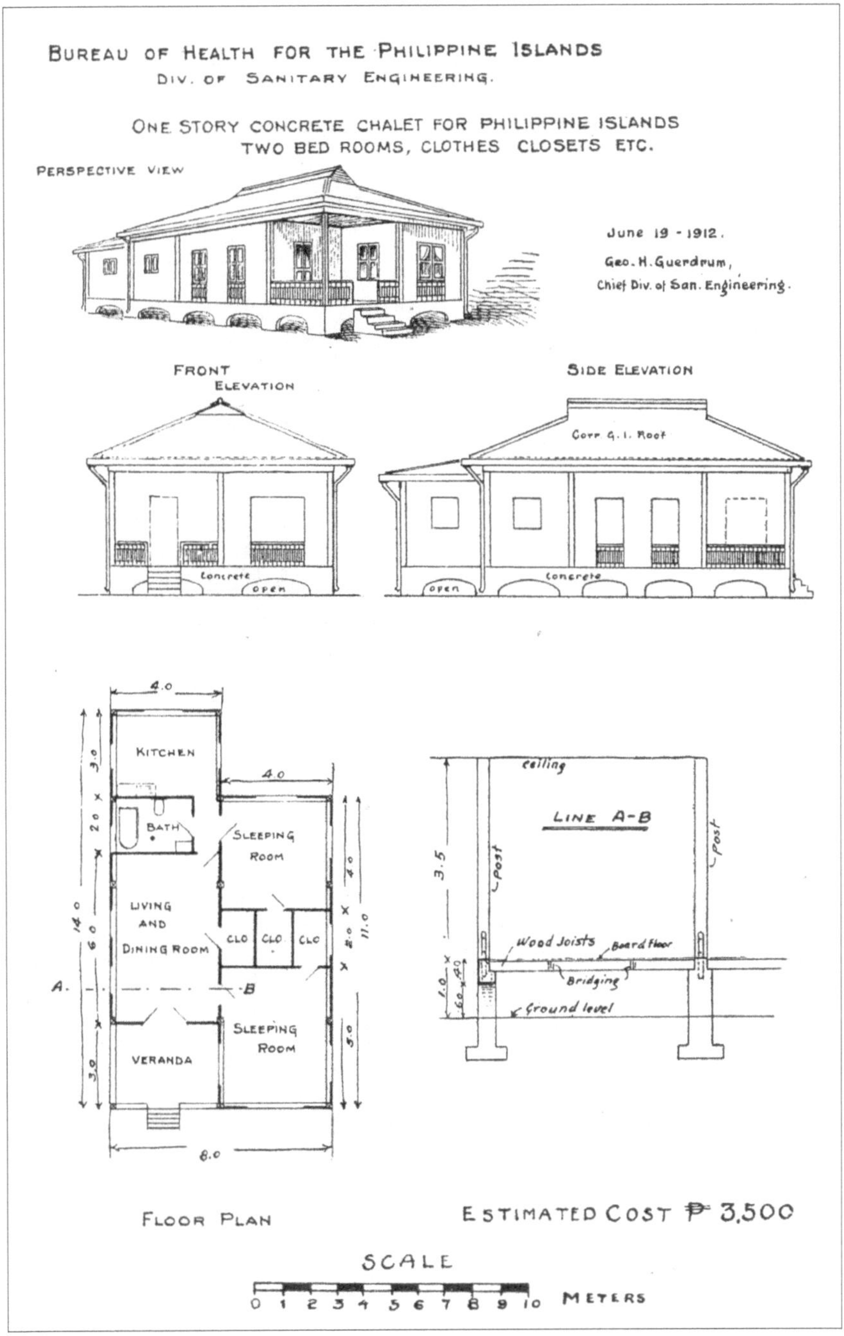

Figure 6.7: Plans for a one-storey *tsalet*, a housing type favoured by the Bureau of Health. Source: Bureau of Health, Bulletin Number 10, *Philippine Habitations* (*Viviendas Filipinas*), Bureau of Printing, Manila.

verandahs and covered balconies were essential architectural features borrowed from early sanatorium design to harness the curative effects of fresh air, a well-known treatment for tuberculosis prior to the introduction of triple-drug therapy.[31] Unlike the *bahay kubo*, the interior space of the *tsalet* was defined by wall partitions, which divided it into rooms. The bedrooms were laid out in a row on one side perpendicular to the front, living and dining rooms and the kitchen were laid out on the other side. The medical doctrine that air-borne bacillus was most transmissible in enclosed spaces empowered the revision of Filipino interior domestic space into separate room compartments to isolate the possible contagion if a household member fell ill. In addition, the spatial arrangement of the rooms was such that all rooms received natural light and ventilation through its large windows and *ventanillas*, a system of smaller windows below the main window sill, and took advantage of the disinfecting effect and regenerative beams of solar exposure.

In 1912, the Bureau of Health drew up the plans for sanitary habitations reiterating the *tsalet* prototype. These plans, drafted George by H. Guerdrum, chief of the Division of Sanitary Engineering, were disseminated to the public via Health Bulletin No. 10, *Philippine Habitations* (*Viviendas Filipinas*), written in English and Spanish, "instructing architects, builders, house owners, and occupants of houses in the few simple principles of sanitary house construction".[32] Schemes were drawn for the general types of urban house: single detached, semi-detached (duplex), and row house apartments (*accessoria*).

Urban Aesthetics: Making Manila Beautiful

The field of vision of this domestic sanitary surveillance soon expanded its coverage to include the larger public environment, propelling a systemic urbanistic change that converged both in civic design and public policy. Since colonialism was primarily about economic gain, the urban landscape was radically transformed in order to yield greater profit. The urban makeover germinated from the philosophy of City Beautiful planning the fundamental basis of which professed that physical beautification of the city and the dispensation of urban aesthetics would breathe new life to Manila's presumed diseased urban condition and bring instant social recuperation as well. The clarity and cleanliness of the public environment were crucial in representing the image of Manila, especially to foreigners and capitalists, as one which engendered civic pride and municipal vivacity.

Behind the façade, the imperial iconography and colonial modernity that the Burnham plan – designed by the foremost American beaux arts architect Daniel A. Burnham in 1905 – sought to erect in Manila was an urban "cure" conceived in the language of geometry, function, hierarchy and pathology and driven to regularise the colonial space and facilitate the orderly arrangement of native bodies within that space.

The cleared sites of pathology provided an empty anachronistic space where ceremonial straight avenues, right angles, and functional zoning prescribed by the City Beautiful master plan of Daniel H. Burnham were to be laid and made available for imperial place-making. The centrepiece of the Burnham Plan was the civic core where a grand concourse emanated from the bay and terminated in an arc further inland. Here Burnham envisioned a national capitol complex where colonnaded buildings were formally arranged around a rectangular plaza. Radiating from this civic core was a series of tree-lined boulevards superimposed on an efficient gridiron street system.

The shift from invasive domestic surveillance to public environmental regularisation was also signalled by a huge capital investment provided by the colonial officials to install infrastructural networks of urban modernity – a piped water system, a sewer system, streets and bridges, electricity, a transit system, a telephone system. The rationality of techno-cosmopolitanist logic governed this quest as a means to rehabilitate the diseased and disorderly body of Manila and maneuver urban life closer to an image of the metropole as paragon of colonial modernity.

In the pursuit of colonial modernity and scientific progress, it was necessary to install and overlay the City Beautiful master plan with technological systems such as piped water, a sewerage system, electricity, a transportation network and public infrastructure. These technologies were not merely a material element in the production of the urban image of a rapidly advancing American imperial city, but also constituted a critical dimension to the social production of space, implying connectivities between the native body and the city, between the social and biophysical systems, and between the invisible and visible aspects of the urban space. For instance, the hydrological transformation of the city represented by the synchronic construction of a modern sewerage system and piped water distribution system in Manila was both a process of physical reconstruction and social engineering within a modernising city, marked from the very beginning by a tension between the punitive and progressive hygienist discourses. The evolution of modern technological systems could thus be conceived in Foucauldian terms as part of biopolitical dynamics wherein social relations and codes of bodily conduct were increasingly subjected to indirect modes of social discipline and managerial techniques of colonial urban governance.[33]

It was at this juncture that urbanism and architecture replaced physical force and coercive strategies with rituals of civility and governmentality to solicit native obedience to the colonial state. The styling of architecture paralleled the styling of native discipline. The Philippine Commission created the Bureau of

Engineering and Construction of Public Works and the Bureau of Architecture and Construction of Public Buildings to oversee the production of colonial infrastructure and architecture. Through these agencies, which later merged as the Bureau of Public Works (BPW), the American regime deployed its resources to build public architecture such as markets, slaughterhouses, power plants, crematories, fire stations, public toilets and baths, prisons, ports, bridges, roads, public parks, transit stations, hospitals and asylums, scientific buildings and laboratories, exposition grounds, schools, official residences, and capitol buildings. It was also within the institutional framework of the BPW that Filipino pioneer architects would receive their architectural tutelage.

As the sanitary transformation of Manila shifted into high gear, insular architect Edgar K. Bourne, chief of the Bureau of Architecture, designed set-piece architecture that mimicked the style of Spanish colonial buildings – the Spanish Mission Revival. The curvilinear parapets, arched entrances, white plastered walls, pyramidal terracotta tiled roofs, and dominant *mirador* towers were architectural elements transplanted from the American Southwest, and adorned the early architecture of American rule in Manila.

For the implementation of Burnham's urban directives, beaux arts-trained William Parsons came into the picture. He was appointed as consulting architect, a new position created to replace that of insular architect. Parsons served as the longest consulting architect of the BPW from 1905 to 1914. During his tenure, he was responsible for the design of all the public buildings and parks for the entire colony.

Under the guidance of the master plan, neoclassical monumental structures slowly rose in the landscape, working to enhance the imperial image, colonial commerce and native discipline. The plan also stimulated the adoption of beaux arts as the official style of the colony for the next three decades. Neoclassical capitol buildings, the embodiment of American republican ideals, also rose in every provincial urban centre. And it was through this style that the processes of democratic apprenticeship were made more tangible in modern reinforced concrete buildings sponsored by the colonial state.

Parsons followed Burnham's advice to learn from the extant Philippine-Spanish sources and consciously orchestrated the fusion of locally derived architectural forms and the neoclassical idiom to dramatise the encounter between and coexistence of two cultures. The extensive appropriation of familiar local motifs made colonialism appear as a civilising continuity rather than a disruption of native civilisation.

Parsons' contribution to local architecture and building technology was the improvement of the quality of construction materials and technique. Of course, this was achieved with the importation of building technologies from the United States such as reinforced concrete, hollow concrete blocks, and the Kahn truss system. Perhaps, the most pervasive legacy of Parsons, which lent itself to mass-reproduction, was the standardisation of building types and plans for schoolhouses, markets, *tiendas* (stores) and municipal buildings.

Aside from Parsons, there were other American architects like George Fenhagen and Ralph Doane at BPW who contributed to the propagation of neoclassicism both in government and private practice. The influx of American capital and assimilation of the new culture allowed new building types to flourish.

Apart from receiving technical training from the offices of BPW, deserving Filipinos who aspired to be architects were given scholarships by the government under the *pensionado* system. Launched in 1903, the system allowed Filipino students to pursue university education in the United States. Upon graduation they were absorbed into the colonial bureaucracy as high-profile civil servants. The majority of *pensionado* architects received their academic training on the American east coast, the bastion of beaux arts pedagogy, in schools such as Cornell University and the Drexel Institute among others. Upon their return, the *pensionado* architects were employed at the Division of Architecture of the BPW. Their homecoming also propelled the establishment of architectural schools, where they were recruited as faculty members and consultants. Their influence both in education and practice signalled the remarkable surge in the number of structures in the neoclassical style, even more ornate than the works of Parsons. The *pensionado* system ensured the perpetuation of the beaux arts in the Philippines.

The monumental neoclassical edifices existed in a spatial logic in which imperialist time dwelled, where hybrid forms emerged from the tumult of cultural encounter and exchange. The manufacture of colonial architecture under the American regime was motivated by a hybridic framework, which consciously appropriated and integrated locally derived building motifs. This appropriation of local motifs was rendered safely within the bounds of neoclassicism in order to generate a genius loci that visibly expressed flexibility and accommodation of cultural differences as well as respect for the indigenous architectural knowledge.

This gesture of architectural associationism is an exercise that avoided the outright assimilation of colonised people into Euro-American civilisation, ensuring the native consensus and legitimation of the colonial state apparatus. Rather than impose a foreign architectural style, the technique necessitated the blending of classicist (even modernistic) forms with traditional building elements. The grafting of capiz windows (that use oyster shells as a substitute for glass), *ventanillas*, *calados* (fretwork), precast ornaments evoking tropical flora and fauna, classical statuary clad in native clothing and adornment in the neoclassical ornamentation of the building were not only visual indices of attempts at cultural sensitivity played out by the colonial architects but also an imperialist non-invasive strategy to project aesthetic reconciliation and unproblematic coexistence of indigenous and American in a lived space born from a tumult of miscegenation. This appropriation of local motifs was used safely within the neoclassical principles to produce a sense of place that visually communicated flexibility and accommodation of cultural differences, and above all, respect for the indigenous architectural knowledge, yet colonial control and domination effectively operated covertly. This encounter, as Gwendolyn Wright expressed, produced "a complex semiology of architectural messages – a certain respect and knowledge of the other, but still a clear dominance of the West".[34]

The result was a kind of architectural style that is neither indigenous nor American, but a hybrid style. The hybrid was one of colonialism's illegitimate offspring, the product of crossbreeding between the metropolitan and the colonial.[35] The consequence of hybridisation was the erasure and blurring of boundaries between stylistic appearances and the dissolution of codes of difference established by colonialism. The hybridisation of architectural forms as a consequence of the colonial building programme could be linked to Homi Bhabha's postcolonial concept of the hybrid, which "terrorizes authority with the ruse of recognition, its mimicry, its mockery".[36] The paradox of stylistic crossbreeding is that colonial practices produced hybrids even while repudiating them because of the potential to dissolve racial boundaries and perpetuate impure images. Yet it enabled the colonizers to better see, control and hold their colonial subjects through the mastery of nostalgic images of nativism and the representation of the regime's alleged benevolence and philanthropic purpose in the colonial built forms. It is in this capacity that architecture was overwhelmingly political. Architectural representation and images were processed to enable the colonising power to nurture an iconic metanarrative and consolidate the plural identities and loyalties of the natives in a collective identity constructed and sanctioned by the colonial state with the melding of native and metropolitan.

For almost half a century the implementation of colonial urban design and the production of colonial architecture created a metropolitan imagery that bears witness to America's hygienic control, altruistic building programme, colonial tutelage, and technological progress expressed along the urban grids of "Manila Beautiful" – a mythical image of urban memory prior to the Pacific War.

Notes

1. William Washburn, "Health Conditions in the Philippines," *Philippine Journal of Science 3*, no. 4 (1908): 270.
2. Paul Rabinow, *French Modern: Norms and Forms of the Social Environment* (Cambridge MA: MIT Press, 1989).
3. Michel Foucault, *Dits et ecrits 1954–1988*. ed. D. Defert and F. Ewald. (Paris: Gallimard, Four Volumes, 1994), vol. III, 727.
4. Michel Foucault, "Space, Knowledge and Power", "Panopticon", "Of Other Spaces: Utopias and Heterotopias," in *Rethinking Architecture: A Reader in Cultural Theory*. ed. Neil Leach (London and New York: Routledge, 1997), 197.
5. Reynaldo C. Ileto, "Cholera and the Origins of the American Sanitary Order in the Philippines." In *Imperial Medicine and Indigenous Societies*, ed. David Arnold, 125–48. (Manchester: Manchester University Press, 1988), 127.
6. H.A. Lindley, "Report of the Santiago Cholera Hospital, 27 April to 17 June 1902," Exhibit B to Maus Report, 390.
7. David Arnold ed., *Imperial Medicine and Indigenous Society*. (Manchester: Manchester University Press, 1989), 18.
8. "The Conquest of Bubonic Plague in the Philippines." *National Geographic* XIV (1903): 185.
9. Report of the Philippine Commission to the Secretary of War, 1902 (Washington: Government Printing Office, 1902), 337.
10. Municipal Board of Manila. *[Annual] Report of the Municipal Board of the City of Manila* (Manila: Bureau of Printing, 1902), 9.
11. Report of the Philippine Commission to the Secretary of War, 1902 (Washington: Government Printing Office, 1902), 338.
12. Dean C Worcester, *A History of Asiatic Cholera in the Philippines* (Manila: Bureau of Printing, 1909), 24.
13. Report of the Philippine Commission to the Secretary of War, 1902. (Washington: Government Printing Office, 1902), 342.
14. Ibid., 562.
15. Ibid., 268.
16. Ibid., 342.
17. Ibid., 420.
18. Ibid., 323.
19. "Governor issues proclamation," *The Manila Freedom*, 9 August 1901, 1.
20. Ibid., 12.
21. "The Burning of Farola." *Manila Times*, 30 March 1902, 8.
22. "Governor Issues Proclamation," *The Manila Freedom*, 9 August 1901, 12.
23. Ibid., 12.

24. Report of the Philippine Commission to the Secretary of War, 1902 (Washington: Government Printing Office, 1902), 271.
25. Ibid., 324.
26. Ibid., 371.
27. Municipal Board of Manila. *[Annual] Report of the Municipal Board of the City of Manila* (Manila: Bureau of Printing, 1905), 206.
28. Bureau of Health. Bulletin Number 10. *Philippine Habitations* (*Viviendas Filipinas*) (Manila: Bureau of Printing, 1912), 12.
29. Victor Heiser, *An American Doctor's Odyssey: Adventures in Forty-Five Countries* (New York: W.W. Norton and Company Inc. Publishers, 1936). In his extraordinary popular autobiography published in 1936, Victor Heiser, the commissioner of health in the Philippines, described Filipinos in the following terms: "grown-up children", "dirty", "unsanitary", "diseased", "ignorant", "unscrupulous", "superstitious", "born actors", "resigned to death", "untrustworthy", "cowards", a "nation of invalids", "incubators of leprosy" and "unhygienic".
30. Ibid., 3.
31. Margaret Campbell, "What Tuberculosis did for Modernism: The Influence of a Curative Environment on Modernist Design and Architecture." *Medical History* 49, no. 4 (2005): 465.
32. Bureau of Health, Bulletin Number 10. *Philippine Habitations* (*Viviendas Filipinas*) (Manila: Bureau of Printing, 1912), 3.
33. Michel Foucault, *Discipline and Punish: The Birth of the Prison*, trans. A. Sheridan. (New York: Pantheon Books, 1977).
34. Gwendolyn Wright, *The Politics of Design in French Colonial Urbanism*. (Chicago: The University of Chicago Press, 1991), 113.
35. Patricia Morton, "A Study in Hybridity: Madagascar and Morocco at the 1931 Colonial Exposition," *Journal of Architectural Education* 52, no. 2 (1998), 83.
36. Homi K. Bhabha, "Foreword: Remembering Fanon – Self, Psyche and the Colonial Condition" in Frantz Fanon *Black Skins, White Masks*, (London: Pluto, 1986), 176.

CHAPTER 7

Forgotten Memorials: The Constitutional Defense Monument and Democracy Temple in Bangkok, Thailand

KOOMPONG NOOBANJONG

Introduction

The architecture of the state and public space typically serve as grand symbolic devices to mediate power for diverse political regimes, whether these are military and civilian dictatorships or royalist and democratic governments. As illustrated by several studies published since 2000 on the critical histories of modern architecture in Southeast Asia and other parts of the world, the designs and meanings of these built forms, ranging from throne halls and royal temples, to government and civic buildings, shaped – and were shaped by – the social, cultural, political and economic contexts that brought them into being.[1]

The role of one particular political regime of early twentieth-century Thailand in the planning and design of public buildings may be demonstrated by two historically important public structures in Bangkok, Anusawari Phithak Ratthathammanun (the Constitutional Defense Monument) and Wat Phra Sri Mahathat, Bang Khen (the Democracy Temple).[2] Commissioned in 1936 and 1940 respectively by the People's Party or Khana Ratsadon – a group of foreign-educated military personnel and civil servants who orchestrated a bloodless revolution on 24 June 1932 that terminated the age of royal absolutism in Siam (which became Thailand in 1939)[3] – the memorial and temple conjointly operated as a statement of power, manifesting the victory of the constitutional regime over a failed attempt to restore the monarchical rule by royalist troops in 1933.[4]

However, the present physical condition of both structures indicates that the above-mentioned symbolic signification has been largely forgotten and ignored by the general public. For instance, the Democracy Temple today has been embellished by a multitude of regal paraphernalia such as royal images and emblems, thus seemingly reaffirming the omnipresent authority of the monarchical institution. In addition, the massive elevated structures for the mass transit rail running almost directly over the Constitutional Defense Monument reduce its significance to a vague vestige in the current collective memory of many Thai people.[5]

As I will show in the ensuing discussion, the obliteration of symbolic meanings and memories of the temple and memorial – which began after the demise of Khana Ratsadon in 1947 – was in fact not a coincidence. Rather, such negligence resulted from deliberate efforts by royalist advocates to undermine the cultural legacies and political legitimacy of the People's Party, while obliterating recollections of the 1932 coup promoters from public memory altogether.

Informed by critical and semiological theories, this chapter presents two thematic foci.[6] The first is the political form of architecture and public space, in which Anusawari Phithak Ratthathammanun and Wat Phra Sri Mahathat, Bang Khen served primarily as significative tools to mediate power.[7] The discourse and iconographical analyses of the memorial and temple demonstrate how they encode the People's Party's efforts to assert, legitimise and maintain their hegemonic power under the guise of political ideologies, namely nationalism and democracy. Aside from their capacity for power mediation, the two structures are also investigated for their representational roles in nation-building, namely as expressions of the national and cultural identities known as "Thai-ness" or *khwampenthai*, to reflect the ideological views of the ruling elites on the Thai nationhood, and to act as propagandistic devices to introduce political ideologies together with social policies to the masses.[8]

Second, by problematising their politics of representation, Anusawari Phithak Ratthathammanun and Wat Phra Sri Mahathat, Bang Khen are further examined through the lens of architectural and urban form politics, in terms of their semantic reappropriation for certain political agendas. On the one hand, I argue that by operating like a system of signs, both structures were interpreted by textual materials, as much as they became interpretations of other signs, leading to a slippage of their original meanings that has been exploited by successive administrations in modern Thailand since 1957. On the other hand, I also look into recent discursive practices by ordinary citizens in resisting the regime in power by turning the Constitutional Defense Monument into a kind of contested space, as evident from the citizenry's capacity to reappropriate and revive the significance of the memorial – as a tribute to Khana Ratsadon, the constitution and democratic ideology – during their political demonstration at Anusawari Phithak Ratthathammanun in 2010.

The Genesis of the Constitutional Defense Monument and Democracy Temple

Catalysed by the bloody Boworadet Rebellion during the Phot Phahonyothin administration (1933–1938), the Constitutional Defense Monument was the second public monument commissioned by the People's Party.[9] On 11 October 1933, Prince Boworadet, an ardent royalist and minor member of the royal family, staged a counter-coup issuing a list of seven demands, including a restoration of the monarchical power in political affairs. The constitutional government rejected the royalists' ultimatum, sending Plaek Khittasangkha (Phibunsongkhram or Phibun)[10] – head of the junior military faction of the People's Party – to command troops in the field.[11] Heavy fighting took tolls on both sides around the area known as Bang Khen Field in Laksi District, a northern suburb in Bangkok near Donmuang Airbase, which later became the site for erecting a memorial.

The carnage lasted until 23 October before it finally ended. Prince Boworadet fled to French Indochina. Although there was no concrete proof that King Rama VII (Prajadhipok, r.1925–1935) – the country's first constitutional monarch – supported the mutiny, the outcome was a blow to the sovereign, diminishing his prestige and authority. In the following year, the Crown departed to England and abdicated after a falling out with the military. He remained there until his death in 1940. For the next quarter of a century, the monarchy did not play a visible role in Thai society. Key members of Khana Ratsadon took turns to assume administrative positions in the fifteen-year period after 1932.[12]

The military triumph of the constitutional regime in 1933 gave rise to the passage of the Act for the Protection of the Constitution, coupled with a promise of a fully elected National Assembly when the educational level of the people permitted.[13] In order to commemorate their victory, the government organised state funerals at the Royal Field (Sanam Luang) – a large public space located at the heart of historic Bangkok – on 17–19 February 1934, to honour the seventeen government troops who perished in the Boworadet Rebellion, in defiance of King Rama VII's repeated objections.[14] Apart from proclaiming their ideological triumph over the conservative royalists, the People's Party violated the regal sanctity of Sanam Luang by erecting a temporary crematorium for commoners, signifying the endeavour by the 1932 coup promoters to shape the political landscape of the country.

Still, Khana Ratsadon yearned for something more permanent, so the Phahonyothin administration decided to construct a military memorial and a

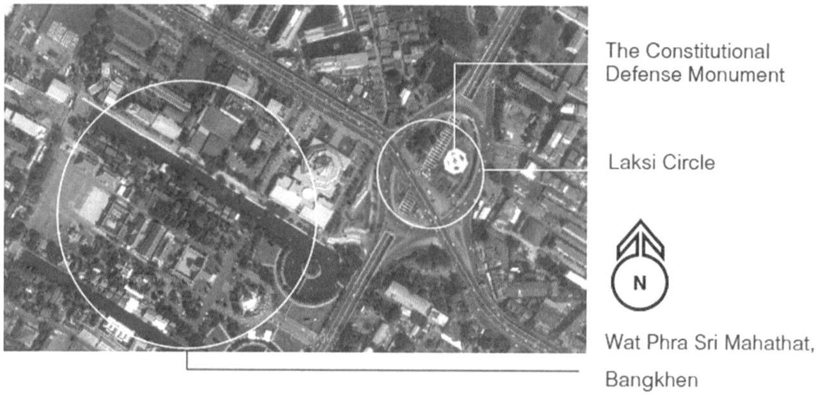

Figure 7.1: An aerial view of the Constitutional Defense Monument and Wat Phra Sri Mahathat, Bang Khen. Source: Google Maps, 2017, with notations by the author.

Buddhist temple.[15] In 1936, the Constitutional Defense Monument – initially named the Rebellion Suppression Monument (Anusawari Prapkabot) – was built.[16] The memorial was accompanied by the commission of a new monastery to be built nearby in 1940 (Figure 7.1).

Originally called Wat Prachatipthai (the Democracy Temple), it was renamed Wat Phra Sri Mahathat, Bang Khen, when a special envoy came back from India with a relic of the Buddha to be enshrined in a stupa, together with branches of the sacred Bodhi tree to be planted in the grounds of the monastery.[17] The temple was inaugurated on 24 June 1942, precisely on the tenth anniversary of the 1932 revolution to mark "the rebirth" of Siam as Thailand. Phot Phahonyothin, the second prime minister of Thailand and leader of the senior military faction in the People's Party, was the first layperson to ordain and reside at the monastery in 1941.[18]

The Constitutional Defense Monument and Democracy Temple as a Political Form of Architecture and Urban Space

Anusawari Phithak Ratthathammanun

The Ministry of Defense tasked Lieutenant Colonel Luang Naruemitr Laekhakarn (Yuean Bunsen, 1890–1955), a faculty member at the Army's Cadet School (known today as Chulachomklao Royal Military Academy), to design the Constitutional Defense Monument.[19] Unveiled to the public on 15 October 1936, its construction was entrusted to the newly reorganised

Fine Arts Department. The memorial housed the ashes of the seventeen deceased government troops, including the remains of Major Luang Amnuay Songgram, an army officer who was a 1932 coup promoter and an associate of Phibun.[20] Taking this into account, it could be proposed that Anusawari Phithak Ratthathammanun indeed functioned simultaneously as a military monument and a war memorial.

By perceiving architecture as a system of signs, it may be construed from a semiological point of view that the Constitutional Defense Monument mediated the power of the People's Party via the following means of representations. First, as indicated by the emblem of the Thai armed forces on its west façade in conjunction with the overall bullet-shaped profile of the memorial (Figure 7.2), the martial origin of Anusawari Phithak Ratthathammanun provided a source of references in depicting the People's Party as the country's sociopolitical hegemonic force.[21] Likewise, by occupying the battlefield where the royalist troops were defeated, the location of the memorial not only celebrated the military victory of the post-absolutist regime in 1933, but also reaffirmed the political legitimacy and ascendancy of the People's Party.[22]

Second, the apex of the Democracy Defense Monument featured a pair of golden offering bowls (*phanwaenfa*) supporting an image of the constitution carved in the form of a folded document (*samutthai*) (Figure 7.2).[23] The two sculptural elements portrayed the constitution – and by extension, Khana Ratsadon – as the country's leading sociopolitical authority. The said symbolic meanings originated

Figure 7.2: The north façade of the Constitutional Defense Monument. Source: the author.

from a long tradition of the Thais in using the same kind of bowls to present their offerings to the sovereigns. At Anusawari Phithak Ratthathammanun, the gift to the Crown was the folded document of the constitution, which the coup promoters forced King Rama VII to accept in 1932.[24]

In effect, the gilded bowls worked in concert with the folded constitutional document as a subversive mechanism in asserting the sociopolitical predominance of the People's Party, while contesting, negotiating and subjugating the monarchy into oblivion. Both sculptural elements conjointly stood for Prajadhipok's acquiescence to the proletarian request for a constitution, which further implied the supremacy of the constitution over the monarchical institution.[25] At the same time, their combined imagery enabled the coup promoters to depict and legitimise themselves as champions of democracy and guardians of both the constitution and Thai nation.[26]

Owing to its crucial political implications, the combined image of the dual gilded offering bowls and folded document of the constitution (*phan ratthathammanun*) was extensively used by Khana Ratsadon not only as a symbol of the democratic ideology and new age of constitutionalism, but as an emblem of the highest authority – the constitutional charter – binding the modern Thai nation together.[27] Being the first public monument to employ the offering bowls and image of the constitutional document, the Constitutional Defense Monument set a precedent for other architecture of the state, works of art, and even everyday objects created during the era of the People's Party to emulate.[28]

Prominent examples included the Democracy Monument (Anusawari Prachatipthai) in Bangkok in 1939 and many pavilions at the Constitutional Celebration fairs (*nganchonong ratthathammanun*) between 1932 and 1947, in combination with graphic design products, such as a lottery ticket in 1940 and a set of postage stamps in 1943. Even after the end of the People's Party's rule, the iconography continued to be used, especially for state agencies in the legislative branch of government, as shown by the emblem of the Secretariat of the House of Representatives today.

Third, under the pretext of paying respect to the democratic ideologies by the virtue of self-sacrifice, Anusawari Phithak Ratthathammanun was devised as a simplified form of traditional Siamese *prang* or pagoda, consisting of eight tapered façades but without a pointed spire with an orb at the pinnacle, to enshrine the remains of the seventeen troops.[29] Sitting on a large traffic roundabout, called the Laksi Circle, intersecting Phahonyothin Road – Thailand's first major highway (Figure 7.1) – the eight facets of the memorial metaphorically disseminated the dominant authority of Khana Ratsadon through the four cardinal plus the four intermediate directions (Figure 7.2).[30]

The aforementioned formal appropriation turned the Constitutional Defense Monument into a quasi-religious structure, elevating "the status of the war heroes to the supreme level of religious saint".[31] For their good deeds in defending the nation and democracy, the names and ranks of the seventeen perished servicemen were exhibited on the west side of the memorial. In bestowing a spiritual honour to these martyrs, Anusawari Phithak Ratthathammanun was adorned with a Buddhist emblem of *dharmachakra* (the wheel of law) – representing the teachings of the Buddha – on its north façade (Figure 7.2).[32]

Whereas most studies on the art and architecture of the People's Party investigated the Constitutional Defense Monument in the context of a nationalistic creation, some scholarly publications characterised the memorial as "an illustration of the artistic metamorphosis of Thai nationalistic monuments".[33] This claim was substantiated by Phibun's speech in 1936 (then the Minister of Defense) at the opening ceremony of the memorial.[34] The Ministry of Defense, Phibun announced, "dedicated this public monument to the Thai nation".[35] He then appealed for political reconciliation by stating that there was "no personal pleasure to witness the construction of the memorial".[36] Apart from being a tribute to the seventeen servicemen, the minister concluded, the Constitutional Defense Monument stood for the tragedy of the Boworadet Rebellion that caused death and destruction among Thais, serving as a reminder for Thai citizens to refrain from letting their political differences turn into hostility that would destroy the national unity once again.[37]

The patriotic and reconciliatory sentiments in Phibun's speech called for further inquiries into the manners in which nationalism together with the concept of Thai nationhood were manifested at Anusawari Phithak Ratthathammanun. According to the Six Principles of Khana Ratsadon – Independence, Security, Economy, Equality, Liberty and Education – the notion of Independence occupied the first order,[38] indicating that the idea of nation state and its sovereignty ranked among the top concerns for the 1932 coup promoters. Nonetheless, their visions of Thai nationhood were diverse, mirroring an internal rift within the group. Divided into two circles roughly identified with the civilian and military members and their respective leaders, Pridi Banomyong and Phibun, the two factions held dissimilar perspectives on the roles and purposes of the state, as well as different views on nationalism.[39]

Envisioning the nation and constitution as a new focus of public loyalty for Thai citizens, consisting of various ethnic groups, the socialist-oriented Pridi believed in a liberal version of nationalism. On the contrary, the fascist-oriented Phibun advocated a militarised one.[40] Phibun's faction promoted strong military leadership to govern a well-ordered society and a civilised nation state, populated predominantly by the Thai race. In doing so, the latter group modified King Rama VI's (Vajiravudh, r.1910–1925) concept of Thai nationhood – centring on nation, religion (Buddhism) and monarchy – but reinforced the regal institution with the notions of constitutionalism and modern egalitarianism.[41]

Figure 7.3: The south façade featuring an inscription of King Vajiravudh's poem "Siamanutsati", and the east façade displaying an image of the ideal Thai family. Source: the author.

Despite their ideological dissimilarity, both sides resorted to the value of patriotism, which was signified by an inscription of King Vajiravudh's poem "Siamanutsati" ("Conscience of Siam") on the south façade of the Constitutional Defense Monument (Figure 7.3). This semantic appropriation served as a reference to illustrate the People's Party's efforts in promoting political pacification, social reconciliation and national unity, echoing Phibun's speech at the inauguration of the memorial in 1936.[42]

The above analyses on the symbolism and iconography of Anusawari Phithak Ratthathammanun begged additional investigations on roles of the monument as a propagandistic tool to express Thai identities. Analogous to textual materials and other types of cultural artefacts, public memorials – like the Constitutional Defense Monument – were not only tangible images of the aspirations of the society that produced them, but they were an attempt to mold social attitudes.[43]

In post-absolutist Thailand, it was commonly known that key members of the People's Party were acutely aware of the importance of modern architecture to help construct their self-image as a progressive organisation.[44] Modernist buildings became objects of their aspiration that were energetic and desirable, representing symbols of pride, progress and parity with the West, while at the same time proving a "novelty of propaganda for the new government".[45]

In accordance with the modernist principles of simplicity, together with structural and materialistic expressions, Luang Naruemitr Laekhakarn rationalised that the eight *prang*-like façades of the monument appeared more geometric. Likewise, the patterns of stacking rows of lotus leaves were de-curved to fit the tectonic capability of reinforced concrete (Figure 7.3).

A number of recent investigations suggested that the geometrical simplicity coupled with minimal use of decorative elements of the memorial represented two cardinal values of the Six Principles of Khana Ratsadon – Equality and Economy – thus promoting the democratic ideology along with the idea of modern egalitarianism in built forms.[46] Aside from symbolising Thailand's engagement with modernity, the tectonic novelty of the monument not only denoted the modernisation and Westernisation processes of the country, but also differentiated the post-1932 regime as more technologically and socially progressive, and therefore "superior" to the "inferior" rule of royal absolutism.[47]

In addition, with respect to the concept of modern egalitarianism, the Constitutional Defense Monument was the second public monument commissioned by the People's Party that introduced images of ordinary people, as seen from the bronze-relief sculpture on the east side depicting the "ideal citizens". The relief portrayed an image of a Thai family consisting of a husband, wife and child.[48] Although they appeared to be farmers, the job held by the majority of the Thai population during the 1930s, their costumes demonstrated a sense of sociocultural sophistication (Figure 7.3).

Aesthetically akin to the "heroic realism" style widely adopted by many nation states in the 1930s and 1940s, these commoners represented the notions of Equality and Liberty among the populace. Consequently, the iconography of "the ideal citizens" propagated a new Thai identity.[49] With the defeat of the royalist rebels in 1933, the image of the ideal citizens symbolically demonstrated that Thai people were no longer royal subjects whose fates and livelihoods depended on mercy, preference, and whims of the rulers. On the contrary, they were citizens of a civilised and modern nation state. Their rights and duties were established and equally guaranteed by the constitution, as promulgated by the Six Principles of the People's Party embedded in its first revolutionary manifesto.[50]

Wat Phra Sri Mahathat, Bang Khen

The creation of Wat Phra Sri Mahathat, Bang Khen should be properly comprehended in connection with the commission and physical modification of Anusawari Phithak Ratthathammanun. An expansion of open space at the Constitutional Defense Monument took place in 1939, followed by the construction of the neighbouring Wat Phra Sri Mahathat, Bang Khen a year later during Phibun's first premiership (1938–1944).[51] At the urban scale, both projects reiterated the shift of power and political legitimacy away from the absolutist regime while celebrating the era of constitutional government led by the People's Party, as explained earlier.[52]

Prior to the 1932 revolution, the Bang Khen area had been rice paddies since the reign of King Rama V (Chulalongkorn, r.1868–1910), thanks to the introduction of irrigational system inaugurated by the creations of Bang Khen and Perm Prachakorn canals.[53] Following the outcome of the Boworadet Rebellion, the constructions of Anusawari Phithak Ratthathammanun and Wat Phra Sri Mahathat, Bang Khen exemplified a centre of everything progressive, by which Phahonyothin Road and the Laksi Circle connected, linking Bangkok to the upper parts of the country and at the same time expressing the sweeping authority of Khana Ratsadon. Named the Democracy Road (Thanon Prachatipthai) at first, the title was switched to Phahonyothin in 1940 to honour the second prime minister of Thailand.[54]

In actuality, the construction of this 1,005-kilometre-long highway bore a strategic importance for the People's Party as well.[55] Built mostly by the Army Corps of Engineers, Phahonyothin Road was intended from the beginning to function as a new line of communication, adding onto existing rail networks for transporting military supplies and reinforcements had another attempt to seize power of the state by means of a coup d'état, similar to the Boworadet Rebellion, been made in future.[56]

Figure 7.4: The stupa at Wat Phra Sri Mahathat, Bang Khen. Source: the author.

Considering the politics of representation at Wat Phra Sri Mahathat, Bang Khen, the temple possessed two major significative components: the *ubosot* (an ordination hall) and stupa (a dome-shaped structure erected as a Buddhist shrine) (Figure 7.4). Apart from sheltering the hallowed relic of the Buddha, this 38-metre-tall structure was actually comprised of the outer and inner stupas, separated by a 2.5-metre-wide corridor. Whereas the inner part enshrined the Buddha relic, the outer layer contained 112 niches facing towards the interior space (Figure 7.5).

Initially, there were four alternatives for the outer stupa to shelter: first, donated objects for spiritual reverence; second, chronological figures and mural paintings of the Buddha; third, statues and engravings about Thai history; and fourth, ashes of the persons deemed fitting by the government.[57] The idea of erecting a shrine for Khana Ratsadon had been envisaged by Phot Phahonyothin since the mid 1930s, but it was temporarily shelved due to the lack of available funds. Luang Wichit Wathakan, the chief ideologue and predominant cultural architect who served as the director general of the Fine Arts Department from 1934 to 1942, convinced the cabinet that the stupa at Wat Phra Sri Mahathat, Bang Khen could realise the prime minister's dream.[58]

In Wichit Wathakan's proposal, the structure should not be limited to harbouring merely the ashes of the coup promoters, but also should include those of national heroes in a comparable manner to the French Panthéon in Paris. Yet, in the end, the remains of members of the People's Party and their spouses occupied those niches.[59]

Figure 7.5: The interior space and niches at the stupa. Source: the author.

In any case, a close examination of the decorative details revealed that numerology played an important part in the design of the stupa. Unlike traditional Thai stupas, the spires of which usually employed odd-numbered tiers, Wat Phra Sri Mahathat, Bang Khen utilised a six-tiered spire for its main stupa (Figure 7.4). Several published investigations suggested that the six-tiered spire referred to the Six Principles of Khana Ratsadon, similar to other public structures erected by the People's Party such as the Democracy Monument that contained six gates at its central turret.[60]

In combination with numerology, the symbolic content of the Democracy Temple was conveyed through terminology. Although the custom of constructing Buddhist temples under the name of Phra Sri Mahathat dated back centuries, Wat Phra Sri Mahathat, Bang Khen signified the political spirit of the country following the 1932 revolution. In pre-modern Siam, Wat Phra Sri Mahathats were commissioned exclusively by the monarchy.[61] The use of this name by the People's Party set a new paradigm that the commoners like the 1932 coup promoters could also construct a Wat Phra Sri Mahathat. As architecture of the state, the temple exhibited a radical alteration in social and political authority from the royal elites to the proletariat Thais by infusing new meanings into the conventional mode of iconography for religious buildings, in combination with the uses of modern construction technique and materials, as illustrated by the *ubosot* at the Democracy Temple (Figure 7.6).

Figure 7.6: The *ubosot* at Wat Phra Sri Mahathat, Bang Khen. Source: the author.

Widely celebrated by Thai scholars as an apposite synthesis between the imported modernist concepts and traditional Thai design elements, the hybridised ordination hall has been generally recognised as a masterpiece of Thai-style reinforced concrete architecture. The architect – Phra Phromphichit (Au Laphanon, 1890–1965) – devised the edifice in accordance with the modernist principles of simplicity, massive and voluminous formal and spatial configurations, functional and rational compositions, as well as structural and materialistic expressions.[62] He organised the overall profile of the structure into simplified geometric shapes and straight lines to fit the tectonic capability of reinforced concrete. As a result, the proportions of the roofs and façades were shortened, making other architectural elements such as bracings and decorative details more volumetric and less flimsy, and at the same time fashioning a new kind of architectural characteristic for the entire ordination hall.[63]

In a nutshell, this stylistically hybridised modern Thai *ubosot* offered a discursive means of representation to the People's Party. On the one hand, with the regal code of architectural symbolism abolished and substituted with simplified and geometrical decorative patterns, the design of the ordination hall disseminated the idea of modern egalitarianism in built forms in a similar fashion to Anusawari Phithak Ratthathammanun. Such a prudent choice of materiality of the *ubosot* – reinforced concrete – indicated a logical and careful management of the country's economy by Khana Ratsadon while criticising extravagant, conspicuous, and irrational spending on luxurious goods during the royal absolutist era.[64]

On the other hand, the absence of symbolic references to the monarchy at the Democracy Temple served as a propagandistic tool to publicise a denunciation of "the divine regal authority" by the People's Party. The lack of such an iconographical allusion was clearly visible from the pediment of the ordination hall, where a figure of the deity, Aruna, (Figure 7.6) rested in place of regal emblems or seals. Some contemporary studies insisted that Aruna, personifying the dawn of the day and red colour according to the Hindu myth, implied the rise of the democratic age by bringing sunlight to disperse the political darkness during the age of royal absolutism.[65]

Taken as a whole, the above-mentioned politics of representations via the symbolism and iconography of Wat Phra Sri Mahathat, Bang Khen demonstrated a conscious attempt by the Phahonyothin administration to craft a modern image of Thailand and to convey its authority to the masses. Nevertheless, like the royal absolutism in nineteenth-century Siam, members of Khana Ratsadon still obsessed with constructing a "civilised" national and cultural identity for their regime and the country.

Between 1939 and 1942, under the directives of Luang Wichit Wathakan, the first Phibun administration embarked on the Nation-Building Programme

Figure 7.7: A poster published during the first Phibun administration promoting the "civilised" form of dress as demonstrated on the right-hand side versus "uncivilised" attire as illustrated on the left-hand side. Source: Office of the Prime Minister.

and issued a series of twelve cultural mandates – known as the *rathniyom* or State Customs – aimed to "uplift the national spirit and moral code of the nation and instill progressive tendencies and a newness into Thai life".[66] The twelve edicts instructed the people in all aspects of their social life, which were "necessarily in the interests of progress and civilisation that the world might see that Thailand was a modern nation"[67] (Figure 7.7).[68]

As evident from the use of the niches inside the main stupa, the social connection between Wat Phra Sri Mahathat, Bang Khen and the People's Party arguably portrayed the temple as a material manifestation of Thai-ness as stipulated by the *rathniyom* mandates.[69] Correspondingly, an observation could be put forward that the Democracy Temple appeared to be an integral part of the Nation-Building Programme in public recognition.[70] As shown by the modernist design philosophies, structural system, and materiality of the stylistically hybridised ordination hall, its signification of the Thai identity or *khwampenthai* seemed to operate on Khana Ratsadon's nationalistic and democratic ideologies.

In effect, these political, social and spiritual links provided a ground to elaborate that the so-called Thai-style reinforced concrete *ubosot* epitomised the capability of Thailand as a country and culture that was able to assimilate modern ideas, process, knowledge and technology from abroad and integrate them with existing practices. Accordingly, a remark may be made that the architecture of Wat Phra Sri Mahathat, Bang Khen thus exemplified the "Thai way" in negotiating modernity as required by the *rathniyom* edicts on the Thai identity.[71] Conversely, whereas the traditional forms of the stupa and *ubosot* emphasised the autonomy of the Thai nation from Western colonialism, differentiating the Thais from foreigners, the absence of any symbolic reference to the Crown rendered those royal palatial and religious structures erected before 1932 as being backward and hence "un-Thai".[72]

In addition to the regal authority, Buddhism also served as a discourse of power mediation for the post-absolutist regime.[73] Nevertheless, Wat Phra Sri Mahathat, Bang Khen symbolised the sociopolitical ascendency of the People's Party in a different manner from the accepted convention. The fact that the remains of the 1932 coup promoters and their spouses were housed inside the same structure as the holy Buddha relics exhibited the transcending authority of Khana Ratsadon that had altered a long-standing religious custom to suit its political objectives. Such a subversive, if not heretical, practice undermined the Hindu–Buddhist belief in the sacred Traiphumi cosmology,[74] which the monarchy utilised to signify and legitimise its power.[75]

Overall, although the said significative conceptions of Wat Phra Sri Mahathat, Bang Khen might sound impressive, people were kept ignorant and unable to discern between fact and fiction in the game of power politics in modern Thailand, concealed through the representational intent of the temple. By deceiving the audience into a false sense of freedom and security, the *ubosot* and stupa's references to the identification of *khwampenthai* as stipulated by the *rathniyom* mandates in fact functioned in terms of a conniving device to manage the interests and desires of the masses. Disguised by the iconography and symbolism of the Democracy Temple, both Poth Phahonyothin and his successor, Phibun (g.1938–1944), were able to appropriate the discourse of Thai-ness to mask the true nature of their administrations, which were despotic and fascist-oriented.

In a corollary view, it could be postulated that, similar to the Anusawari Phithak Ratthathammanun, Wat Phra Sri Mahathat, Bang Khen too happened to be a self-glorifying medium par excellence for the People's Party rather than a bona fide tribute to the revolutionary and democratic spirit. Without a referendum to build the Democracy Temple, not to mention a lack of public participation in the design process and site selection, the conception and development of this religious structure were entirely dictated by the personal preferences of the 1932 coup promoters. In sum, Wat Phra Sri Mahathat, Bang Khen, ironically failed to live up to its democratic connotation as Wat Prachatipthai or the temple of democracy.

As a final point, in deviating from the customary ways of architectural signification for Buddhist temples, the iconography, symbolism and stylistic expressions of Wat Phra Sri Mahathat, Bang Khen, appeared too abstract, making it difficult for the public to understand the intended messages. Not many people today realise the real meaning behind the numerology of the stupa, along with the implication of the Aruna deity at the pediment, and the rationales for the aesthetic principles of modernist tectonics and materiality in the design of the ordination hall. For that reason, the relationships between the Democracy Temple, Constitutional Defense Monument, power, identity and ideology were complicated, dialectical and contradictory, leading to a slippage of symbolic signification as well as changes and oblivions of their original meanings in public memory.

The Architectural and Urban Forms of Politics at Anusawari Phithak Ratthathammanun and Wat Prachatipthai

Phibun stepped down as prime minister a year before the fall of Japan to the Allied forces in August 1945. Yet, Thailand was saved from losing World War II by the Seri Thai (Free Thai) underground resistance, organised by Phibun's political arch-rival, Pridi, who was a former Regent of King Ananda Mahidol (Rama VIII, r.1935–1946). He became the elected prime minister in 1946.

Nonetheless, within the same year, the young sovereign was mysteriously shot dead and succeeded by his younger brother Bhumibol Adulyadej (Rama IX, r.1946–2016). Accused of being the regicidal mastermind, Pridi ran off and lived in exile. He was demonised by the military and royal apologists as a monarchy-destroying communist to intimidate those with liberal ideas.[76] In short, it could be concluded that within two decades of the termination of the absolutist rule, the People's Party regime met its demise after long and bitter vying for political domination between the military and civilian factions that resulted in an expatriation of Pridi in 1947.

In contrast, Phibun was brought back to power by the armed forces in 1948. During his second term in the office (1948–1957), he promoted democracy in place of fascism, and ultranationalism as an ideological façade. Even though defending its forms, the premier suppressed democratic yearnings among the masses.[77] In spite of the fact that the power precariously remained in his hands, Phibun survived as a national leader by skillfully manipulating prominent members of the ruling elites against each other, while obtaining support from his American patrons. He abandoned the Western style of leadership and adopted a paternalistic image, harping on compassionate guidance, family values and religious piety.[78]

Domestically, whereas Phibun relied on the army as his power base, the exiled Pridi still enjoyed the navy's backing. Although Pridi's remaining supporters made significant attempts to oust Phibun in 1948, 1949 and 1951, leading to heavy fighting between the army and navy, the field marshal and his military clique prevailed.[79] During this tremulous decade, key administrative positions in the cabinet were occupied by the military officers of the "coup group", or *khana rattaprahan*. These younger men mostly held conservative views and were supporters of the monarchy.[80] With the rising influence of the royalist advocates, the cultural policies of Thailand in the 1950s reverted to King Rama VI's ethos of preserving and promoting traditional artistic expression and practice[81] under the rhetoric of "anti-communism" and "pro-Americanism".[82]

The coup d'état that brought down Phibun in 1957 proved to be another crucial turning point in modern Thai history, since it bolstered the return of royalist advocates in national politics occasioned by the internal rift in the People's Party which began during World War II. The former premier escaped to Japan and never set foot on Thai soil again.

Up to the mid 1970s, Thailand was mostly governed by a series of military dictators, beset with coups and counter-coups.[83] Phibun's successors, field marshals Sarit Thanarat (g.1959–1963) and Thanom Kittikachorn (g.1963–1973), were traditionalists. Espousing orderliness, cleanliness and conformity, the nationalist principles of these locally educated strongmen embraced Vajiravudh's concept of Thai nationhood – and by extension, the Thai identity – dwelling on the triad values of nation, religion and monarchy in place of exogenic and intangible ideas like constitutionalism and democracy as propagated by Khana Ratsadon.[84]

In order to legitimise and maintain his authoritarian rule, Sarit utilised the monarchical institution as both the focus of loyalty for the citizens and the source of legitimacy for maintaining his regime of "despotic paternalism".[85] He resuscitated the role of the king along with many ancient Hindu–Buddhist royal customs, while enacting the lèse-majesté law. Aside from reviving royal ceremonies, Sarit maintained a very public allegiance to the monarch and the royal family. The restoration of the monarchy elevated King Bhumibol to an omnipotent and sacrosanct status, which was a far cry from Ananda Mahidol's powerless figurehead position.[86]

Contrary to the regal reinstatement, Sarit and his royalist collaborators portrayed the People's Party and its members as anti-monarchist and hence "un-Thai". In their collective efforts to negate the political legitimacy of the 1932 coup promoters, the People's Party was depicted as a group of inept intelligentsia who prematurely brought democracy to Thailand.[87] By the same token, the art and architecture sponsored by Khana Ratsadon was criticised by influential royalist advocates – such as Kukrit Pramoj, a conservative scholar and a prime minister of royal descent (g.1975–1976) – as the most degraded form of aesthetics.[88]

Correspondingly, the concept of the Thai nationhood along with the discourse of Thai-ness were reinterpreted and transformed. Whereas the juntas retained some aspects of the People's Party's Nation-Building Programme – chiefly the modernisation process – they abolished and/or amended most cultural policies and social practices of their predecessors, namely the *rathniyom* edicts. With Khana Ratsadon's fall from power, architecture of the state along with other cultural artefacts commissioned by the government between 1932 and 1947 faded into symbolic obscurity. As the military government suppressed all commemorative activities for the 1932 revolution, royal functions regained priority in social festivities and state ceremonies.[89]

Moreover, due to the fact that the physical modifications of existing public structures commissioned by Khana Ratsadon was technically difficult and prohibitively expensive, the junta regime largely preferred to reappropriate and reconstruct their meanings by displacing the framework of representations, as evident from the Democracy Temple and Constitutional Defense Monument after 1957. Under the authoritative umbrella of the royal-nation historiography, the original significations of these built forms either became a vague vestige in public memory, or were reinterpreted in a negative view as shown below.

From a Proletarian Heaven to a National Crematorium

Throughout the Cold War and armed conflicts in Indochina, Thailand was a staunch ally of the US. Because of its anti-communist commitment, the junta enjoyed support from the West. Under the pretence of safeguarding national security, the military regime often prosecuted their critics without trial, casting them as communist sympathisers.[90] During this period, the Communist Party of Thailand (CPT), joined by left-wing intelligentsia and disgruntled peasants, initiated their insurgency, assisted by China and the USSR to counter the American influence in Southeast Asia.

As the fighting continued, the military government employed Wat Phra Sri Mahathat, Bang Khen, as an official crematorium for perished armed personnel and government officials who lost their lives in the line of duty. Apart from honouring the fallen "national heroes", the funerals at the temple were intended to muster public support and approval for participating in the war in Indochina, as well as curbing the internal communist insurgency. The funerals became a state affair, presided over by King Bhumibol and the royal family. As a consequence, Wat Phra Sri Mahathat, Bang Khen, was re-semanticised to propagate a new sense of nationalism and democracy under the regal authority, coupled with the power of the military rule.

Although there is no substantial account to verify the reason behind the government's selection for this particular religious structure in such a capacity, it is not too far-fetched to suggest that its original name: Wat Prachatipthai (Democracy Temple), and militaristic history might have played an important part in the choice to utilise this religious structure as a state crematorium to honour those who died protecting democratic ideology and Thai nationhood. Regardless of whether this was the reason, the Royal Thai Air Force continued to use Wat Phra Sri Mahathat, Bang Khen, as an official crematorium, even after the war in Indochina and the communist insurgency ended.

Obviously, such semantic refashioning occurred through a reinvention of religious ritual – the state funerals – in place of a physical modification. Here, the concept of sacred kingship was revised and merged with a modern practice of constitutional monarchy under the royal-nation historiography, eventually eclipsing the People's Party's idea of egalitarian democracy and Phibun's vision for *khwampenthai*. By rearticulating the discourse of Thai-ness, the ascendency of the royal-national history rendered any symbolic identification of Wat Phra Sri Mahathat, Bang Khen, with Khana Ratsadon in a negative light, whereas the original meaning of the temple became obscured in public memory.

Regarding the national historiography, the aforementioned politics of representations served as a reminder that the narratives of Thai national history featured abundant stories of benevolent leaders, self-sacrifice, struggle for liberty, etc. Yet at the same time, the same history was full of irrational, accidental and ironic moments, including ideological as well as psychological excuses and deceptions.

From a Tribute to Democracy to a Traffic Obstacle

Changes in architectural significations at Anusawari Phithak Ratthathammanun took a longer course with more twists and turns than those at Wat Phra Sri Mahathat, Bang Khen.[91] After 1947, the Constitutional Defense Monument had increasingly been portrayed in a negative light by royalist advocates, mainly because of its close identification with Phibun and his cult of leadership, as well as due to the political decline of Khana Ratsadon. Telling evidence of such renditions can be witnessed from a number of published examples.

In 1949, Chamlong Ittharong wrote that the memorial was indeed a disgrace to the dignity of Thailand because it stood for a sad chapter in the modern history of the nation when Thais slaughtered each other in 1933. In combination with its name as the Rebellion Suppression Monument (Anusawari Prapkabot), the enshrinement of human remains at this public structure comprised exclusively of those of the victors, he went on, would result in animosity from the vanquished for further revenge.[92]

Lui Khiriwat offered a more disapproving assessment in 1950. He charged that Anusawari Phithak Ratthathammanun was the first and only public memorial in the country that was built without any underlying principle or logical explanation. Lui pointed out that unlike other public memorials, the representational contents of the Constitutional Defense Monument did not comply with the triad values of the Thai nationhood. On the contrary, by signifying hostility among Thais, the memorial became a public shrine to which nobody voluntarily paid respect, except those servicemen who were forced to do so once a year.[93] Even after the end of the junta regime in the mid 1970s, such negative interpretations continue to stigmatise the memorial until the present day.

Contrary to the demise of the People's Party, the royalists re-established the regal authority as the supreme sociopolitical arbitrative force since the 1970s, ushering the country into the so-called era of "Hyper-Royalism".[94] The most obvious evidence, perhaps, could be seen from King Rama IX's interventions during the student uprising in 1973 and the urban bourgeoisie's revolt in 1992 (the so-called Black May incident) against military dictators, which twice averted the prospect of civil war in Thailand. Nonetheless, the Crown and the royal family distanced themselves from the atrocious massacre of students and left-wing social activists on 6 October 1976 at Thammasat University at the heart of the capital city.[95]

In the 1980s and early 1990s, Thailand was once again riddled with military coups d'état, successful or otherwise. It was not until after the Black May incident that the country's sociopolitical situation could be somewhat stabilised. The aftermath of the 1992 uprising not only brought a fifteen-year hiatus to military involvement in politics, but also sweeping political and legislative reforms. Despite the devastating effects of the 1997 economic crisis, Thailand enjoyed robust sociopolitical developments, wherein elections were regularly held until 2006, when the country experienced a rude awakening from its false sense of democratic stability.[96]

Realising the stain of silence from the massacre of students in 1976, the government initiated public relation campaigns to salvage the image of the regal authority, and to negate the legacy of the youth revolution. These objectives were accomplished by several measures, for example, revising school textbooks, and popularising patriotic songs, plays and literature. They were reinforced by a depiction of the sovereign by the mass media as the "father of the nation", who had worked tirelessly through his networks of charitable foundations and social organisations for the socio-economic betterment of his subjects.[97]

In addition, via comprehensive state-sponsored public relation campaigns, the promotion of regal authority worked hand in hand with the efforts by royalist advocates to erase the legacy of the People's Party from public memory. In the built environment, such vindictive practices could be seen from the demolitions of several structures commissioned by Khana Ratsadon in Bangkok – that is Chaloemthai Theater in 1989[98] and the Supreme Court Building in 2012 – coupled with a series of physical alterations of the Constitutional Defense Monument as examples.[99]

In order to relieve traffic problems in the northern Bangkok area, the Department of Highways (DOH) transformed the Laski Circle to an intersection in 1993. With its large open space replaced by traffic lanes, Anusawari Phithak Ratthathammanun was seriously deprived of its representational ability, as its pedestrian access was taken away. In spite of this drastic undertaking, the traffic situation did not improve, and heavy traffic became a common sight at the intersection.

In 2005, the DOH decided to build a tunnel along Phahonyothin Road. Prior to the construction, the memorial was dissembled and rebuilt in a new location, situated away from the centre of the intersection, which was converted into a traffic roundabout for a second time. These modifications occurred without the comprehensive collaboration of all of the state agencies involved – namely the DOH, Bangkok Metropolitan Administration (BMA), and Fine Arts Department (FAD) – to preserve the monument, resulting in a barren landscape that further incapacitated its symbolic signification.[100]

Even after the tunnel became operational, traffic congestion within and around the Laksi area continued to worsen. In 2011, construction works began to erect a massive vehicular bridge passing almost on top of the Constitutional Defense Monument. Thirty months later, the project was completed. Once again, irrespective of opposition from some concerned citizens, academics and professionals, including an objection from the FAD's director of Archaeology Office to move the monument to make way for the flyover,[101] the memorial was taken apart and reconstructed 50 metres away from its previous location.[102]

In mid 2010, an official from the DOH clarified that the agency organised public hearings and secured permissions from the FAD before relocating and rebuilding the monument. Although registered as a historical site, this public structure was not listed as an archaeological site. So, there was no legal issues with its relocation.[103] The director of the Office of Transport and Traffic Policy and Planning at the Ministry of Transportation offered a bolder justification, saying that the relocation of Anusawari Phithak Ratthathammanun should not be considered disturbing by the general public. The memorial was not a religious structure, but rather a representation of political ideology in built form.[104]

Standing now in an obscure spot, the representational ability of the Constitutional Defense Monument is close to nil.[105] Nevertheless, at the end of the first decade of the new millennium, the original meaning of the memorial has been revived and reappropriated by members of the National United Front of Democracy Against Dictatorship (UDD). Members of the UDD wear red attire and are referred to as the "Red Shirts".

In 2010, the monument was utilised by UDD protesters as a staging area for political rallies against the Abhisit Vejjajiva government (2008–2011). With his Democrat Party (Phak Prachathipat) siding with the elite establishment and backed by the military, Abhisit was appointed prime minister of Thailand in late 2008,[106] after the Constitutional Court removed Prime Minister Somchai Wongsawat from office.[107] The new premier was perceived by the Red Shirts as lacking the popular mandate to lead. He came under intense pressure from them to dissolve the parliament and hold a new general election. The demonstrations culminated in urban riots in Bangkok that resulted in ninety-one deaths and 1,378 injuries.[108]

The UDD political movement first appeared in 2006 in opposition to a coup d'état that deposed the popularly elected but very controversial and corrupt Thaksin Shinawatra administration (2001–2006).[109] During the demonstration on 12 March 2010, the Red Shirts adorned the Constitutional Defense Monument with the national colours, red flags (the Thai national flag is composed of red, white, and blue stripes), Buddhist emblems, pictures of the royal family, together with patriotic and democratic banners. Taken together, the proletariat genesis in combination with the iconography and symbolism of the memorial enabled the leaders of the Red Shirts to assert that their protests were intended to advance the cause of the 1932 revolution.[110]

Through these representational means, the UDD's allusions to the democratic ideology and Khana Ratsadon turned Anusawari Phithak Ratthathammanun into a kind of a contested space, symbolising the Thais' struggle for democracy and self-empowerment. As demonstrated by their political rhetoric, the Red Shirts' leaders embraced the Six Principles of the People's Party. Core members of the UDD frequently cited the notions of Independence, Security, Economy, Equality, Liberty and Education in their speeches. As a result, by ideologically associating themselves with Khana Ratsadon, the Red Shirts gained sympathy from people who opposed the 2006 coup and its ramifications, but were not necessarily political allies of Thaksin.[111]

In spite of the UDD's discursive efforts, the past significations of the memorial could still not be fully awakened in the present collective memory. Both the historical and political importance of the Constitutional Defense

Figure 7.8: The construction of the BTS extension near the Constitutional Defense Monument in November 2017. Source: the author.

Monument, however, seemed to firmly register with neither the state authorities nor public perception at large. On the contrary, owing to the recent and upcoming construction projects at the Laksi Circle area, the original meaning of the memorial continued to be largely ignored. In 2012, the Mass Rapid Transit Authority of Thailand (MRTA) unveiled a plan to erect gigantic elevated structures to accommodate two overlapping passenger stations and their associated rail-based mass transit systems, the size and location of which would render the memorial even more unrecognisable. Since 2015, this has become increasingly perceptible as the construction works progress, particularly on the Bangkok Mass Transit System (BTS) (Figure 7.8).[112]

In short, the miserable and undignified fate of the Constitutional Defense Monument raised the following fundamental questions on the politics of representations in built forms in Thailand. For instance, regarding the country's current political climate that appears to be at the pinnacle of Hyper-Royalism,[113] could a similar physical modification be imposed on any royal monument, even if the rationale to do so was the same: to alleviate Bangkok's traffic jams? If not, why? If the geneses together with iconographic programmes of the Constitutional Defense Monument and the Democracy Temple justify the Thai military's involvement in the country's political affairs, then what should be the proper role of the armed forces in a civil and democratic society? Do these stylistically hybridised structures represent a modern way of expressing Thai identity, or a Thai way of engaging modernity? Neither? Both? What exactly is *khwampenthai*? What constitutes the Thai identity? What do the mediation of power coupled with signification of Thai-ness at the memorial and temple really mean for Thai people, culture and society?

Conclusion

The preceding critical and analytical investigations disclose that the original significations of Anusawari Phithak Ratthathammanun and Wat Phra Sri Mahathat, Bang Khen, were generated, manipulated, altered and disregarded by power politics. Despite being nearly forgotten in the present collective Thai psyche, the meaning of the memorial and temple – as physical marks of the military triumph of the constitutional regime led by the People's Party over the royalist Boworadet Rebellion – was not totally disremembered but was revived by a discursive practice of symbolic reappropriations by the UDD in 2010 as a case in point.[114]

In essence, the survey of the politics of representation at the Constitutional Defense Monument and Democracy Temple demonstrates that both public structures signified a certain intended original meaning, while also accruing various interpretations as shown by critical and negative appraisals of the memorial and temple after 1947. Aside from mediating and legitimising the authority of the People's Party, Anusawari Phithak Ratthathammanun and Wat Phra Sri Mahathat, Bang Khen, served as a material manifestation of the 1932 coup promoters' endeavours to define public space, to create public memory and shared mentality, to reflect their ideological views on the Thai nationhood, to express the Thai identity, and to commemorate the trauma of the loss of lives in 1933. Following the political demise of the People's Party, however, the very same public structures have been characterised by royalist advocates not only as symbols of misguided nationalism and ill-prepared democracy, but also as relics of a discredited and defunct regime.

In addition, as much as the ruling authorities in modern Thailand and their politics of representations shaped the aesthetics and significations of the memorial and temple, the hybridised designs of these built forms provided them with a means of power meditation, a symbolic device for the creation and revision of *khwampenthai*, a medium to express their ideological views on the Thai nationhood, and a propagandistic instrument to prescribe political ideologies along with social practices for the populace.

The hybridity of the Constitutional Defense Monument and Democracy Temple was, thereby, the state's tactic to appropriate Western/modern material culture to suit their own political agendum, by reciting the concept of Thai nationhood through the built environment. Operating as a means to reframe the Thai-self, Anusawari Phithak Ratthathammanun and Wat Phra Sri Mahathat, Bang Khen, became a spiritual-cum-secular tool to locate the Thai cultural and national identities along with and/or against the Western-initiated projects in the name of a modernisation process. Their hybrid modern Thai designs testified that the Thai identity was indeed a product of modernity, which had been hybridised in various aspects. In other words, the identification of *khwampenthai* was an outcome of a historically rooted and culturally grounded system of knowledge and power production, which had been defined and redefined over the course of the Westernisation and modernisation processes in both Siam and Thailand.

In sum, the Constitutional Defense Monument and Democracy Temple exemplified that, apart from representing the Thai identity and reflecting the Thai worldviews on the West and modernity, the discourse of Thai-ness had uncovered the uncertainty and anxiety among Thais over their own modernisation and Westernisation processes. As exhibited by the hybridised characteristics of the memorial and the *ubosot* at Wat Phra Sri Mahathat, Bang Khen, perhaps the most important contribution from the West and modernity to the making of the Thai-self may be seen in its role in the production of hybrid knowledge and power.[115]

Nonetheless, Khana Ratsadon's espousal and fascination with the West and modernity – as epitomised by their commissions of hybrid modern Thai architecture like the Constitutional Defense Monument and Democracy Temple in combination with implementations of the conceptually schizophrenic mandates on *khwampenthai* – revealed a dilemma faced by the Thais in constructing their national and cultural identity, which was syncretic, inconsistent, ambiguous and even self-contradictory. The aforementioned inherently intricate dynamism and paradoxical nature of Thai-ness were subjected to more appropriations and contestations, resulting in the slippage of the symbolic significations in built forms, as evidenced by the transformations of meanings and memories of Anusawari Phithak Ratthathammanun and Wat Phra Sri Mahathat, Bang Khen.

Overall, these changes further indicate that the architecture of the state in Thailand has been in a perpetual evolution. Their significations are caught between the polarities of a conservative force tending to preserve the existing meanings and a revolutionary force striving for the rise of new meanings. Whereas the conservative force led to stability of meanings and institutionalisation of forms, its revolutionary counterpart replaced old meanings and forms with new ones. The forms remained the same, but the meanings were in flux.[116] Both the creation and signification of architecture and urban space in Thailand thus involved the ebb and flow of life rather than the stabilisation of identities and/or conditions.[117]

At the time of this writing in mid 2017, I and my fellow Thai citizens have found ourselves governed by a military regime for the second time since 2006, when the Yingluck Shinawatra administration (2011–2014) was removed from office by another coup d'état in May 2014. The latest takeover by the armed forces – whose rule is entering its fourth year – was an outcome of a decade-long political conflict that has bitterly polarised the nation.

Notwithstanding the constitutional referendum on 7 August 2016, the current situation in Thailand under the oppressive rule of the National Council for Peace and Order (NCPO) is still unsettled and could become socially explosive.[118] On 13 October 2016, King Rama IX – who acted as the country's supreme stabilising force for many decades – passed away, and has been succeeded by his only son Vajiralongkorn (King Rama X, 2016–present). Once again, not only is the future of Thai nationhood hanging in the balance, but also that of Thai democracy. How the upcoming developments would affect the politics of representations at the Constitutional Defense Monument remains to be seen.

To close, I would like to give notice that another development in the politics of representations in architecture and urban space in twenty-first-century Thailand took place in early April 2017 when the brass plaque that signposted the pivotal moment of the country's transformation from absolute monarchy to parliamentary democracy was mysteriously removed from its location and replaced by a new plaque. Fit into the road surface near the King Rama V's equestrian statue at the Royal Plaza in Bangkok's Dusit district, this memorial plaque marked the site where the coup promotors read their revolutionary manifesto on 24 June 1932.[119] The original plaque read, "At this place, on the dawn of 24 June 1932 we the People's Party have birthed the Constitution for the nation's progress."

In stark contrast to Khana Ratsadon's revolutionary zeal, the replacement plaque conveyed a message asserting a nation at ease. "Long live Siam forever! Happy, fresh-faced citizens build up the power of the land!" Circling the new plaque were proverbs of the ruling Chakri Dynasty. "Loyalty and love for the Triple Gem, one's clan and having an honest heart for one's king is good. These are the tools to make one's state prosper!"[120]

Finally, while many scholars and activists cried foul over the removal of the historic artefact, the incumbent junta administration insisted that it had nothing to do with its disappearance.[121] Irrespective of who took it, the removal of Khana Ratsadon's plaque signified a new turn in the politics of representations through the art and architecture of the People's Party during the reign of King Rama X.[122]

Notes

1. Examples of such scholarly publications include Abidin Kusno, *Behind the Postcolonial: Architecture, Urban Space, and Political Cultures in Indonesia* (New York: Routledge, 2000); Mark Crinson, "The View from Penang Hill: Modernism and Nationalism in Malaysia," in *Modern Architecture and the End of Empire* (Burlington, VT: Ashgate, 2003); Gerard Lico, *Edifice Complex: Power, Myth, and Marcos State Architecture* (Quezon City: Ateneo de Manila University Press, 2003); Helen Grant Ross and Darryl Leon Collins, *Building Cambodia: New Khmer Architecture 1953–1970* (Bangkok: The Key Publisher, 2006); Chee Kien Lai, *Building Merdeka: Independence Architecture in Kuala Lumpur, 1957–1966* (Kuala Lumpur: Gelari Petronas 2007); Jiat-Hwee Chang and William S.W. Lim (ed.), *Non-West Modernist Past: On Architecture and Modernities* (Singapore: World Scientific, 2011); and Koompong Noobanjong, *The Aesthetics of Power: Architecture, Modernity, and Identity from Siam to Thailand* (Bangkok: White Lotus Press, 2013).
2. The romanisation of Thai words in this chapter follows the conventions of the Royal Thai General System of Transcription (RGTS), devised by the Royal Institute of Thailand but without diacritics. The system is set out in the *Journal of the Thailand Research Society* 33, no. 1 (1941): 49–53. Proper names of historical figures are spelled according to the preferences of the persons, where known, or according to common usage. All translations of Thai materials in the article are the author's.
3. My utilisation of the term "Siam" refers to the absolutist kingdom whose monarchical rule ended in 1932, while that of "Thailand" denotes the democratic nation after the 1932 revolution, notwithstanding the fact that the constitutional government continued to use "Siam" as the name of the country until 1939.
4. According to the convention, whereas a "monument" is a structure, statue or a building commissioned to honour someone notable or a special event, a "memorial" is a structure or a statue erected to remember a dead person or a group of people who died in an important past event. Although I recognise such a difference in architectural significations, the two terms are used interchangeably in this research. Because Anusawari Phithak Ratthathammanun was constructed to commemorate the victory of the People's Party government in crushing the Boworadet Rebellion in 1933 and to honour the seventeen fallen government troops who perished during the incident, it essentially operated in both capacities as a military monument and a war memorial. See Phibun Hatthakitkoson, "Anusawari Thai: Kansueksa Naichoeng Kanmueang" [Thai Monument: A Political Study], (Master's Thesis, Chulalongkorn University, 1984), 73.
5. A similar vein of argument had also been put forward by some contemporary publications in Thai language on the art and architecture commissioned by the People's Party between 1932 and 1947. For instance, see Chatri Prakitnondhakarn,

Kanmueang Laesangkhom Naisinpa Sathapattayakam Sayamsamai Thaiprayuk Chatniyom [Politics and Society in Architecture: Siamese Era, Applications in Thai Designs, and Nationalism] (Bangkok: Matichon, 2004); *Sinpa Sathapattayakam Khana Ratsadon: Sanlakthang Kanmueang Naichoeng Udomkan* [*The People's Party's Art and Architecture: Ideological and Political Symbolism*] (Bangkok: Matichon, 2009).

6. According to philosopher Jürgen Habermas, critical theory contained two overlapping academic disciplines. In sociology and political philosophy, "critical theory" (or "social critical theory") described a form of self-reflective knowledge and assessment of society and culture, involving both understanding and theoretical explanations that aimed to liberate human subjugation to systems of domination or dependence. In literary studies and literary theory, the term (also called "literary critical theory") referred to a system of knowledge via interpretations to understand the meanings of human texts and symbolic expressions, thus associating with the field of semiology (or studies of signs). See Jürgen Habermas, *Erkenntnis und Interesse* [*Knowledge and Human Interests*], trans. J. Shapiro (London: Heinemann Educational Books, 1972).
7. Because critical theory, on the one hand, sought to engage in reflexive assessments and critiques of society and culture – including the productions and consumptions of cultural products such as architecture and languages – it provided a theoretical ground for this research to explore the Constitutional Defense Monument and Wat Phra Sri Mahathat, Bang Khen, through their relationships with the social, political and cultural contexts. On the other hand, the philosophical connection between critical and semiological theories offered a conceptual framework to examine the linguistic principles by which the memorial and temple obtained, transformed, relinquished and regenerated their symbolic meanings.
8. A number of recent studies argued that the nation of Siam (and by extension Thailand) was a concept completely alien to the Thais. It was, in fact, invented during the nineteenth century as an outcome of the Thais' experience from encountering Western colonialism. In antagonising the Europeans' encroachment in Southeast Asia to retain their hegemonic powers, King Mongkut (Rama IV, r.1851–1868) and later his son – King Chulalongkorn (Rama V, r.1868–1910) – transformed the kingdom of Siam into a modern nation state via the processes of Westernisation and modernisation. For example, see: Craig J. Reynolds, ed., *National Identity and Its Defenders* (Chiang Mai: Silkworm Books, 2002), 19–20.
9. The first was the Monument of Thao Suranari at Nakhon Ratchasima province, commissioned in 1934. See Ka F. Wong, *Visions of a Nation: Public Monuments in Twentieth-Century Thailand* (Bangkok: White Lotus, 2006), 108.
10. With the exception of the bibliographic references, this chapter follows the convention in Thai studies in terminology that Thai people are referred to by first names, as opposed to Westerners who are referred to by their surnames.

11. Sarunyou Thepsongkraow, "Anusawari Prapkabot Kapkanramluek Wirachon Phuphithak Kanpatiwat 2475" [The Rebellion Suppression and a Recollection for the Defenders of the 1932 Revolution], *Silpawatthanatham* 34, no.12 (2013): 105.
12. Sinlapachai Chanchaloem (Nai Hon Huay), *Chaofa Prachathipok Rachan Phunirat* [*Prajadhipok: The Exiled Monarch*] (Bangkok: Poh Sampand Panich, 1987), 485–486.
13. Wong, *Visions of a Nation*, 56.
14. National Archives of Thailand, The Prime Minister's Office, Sor. Ror. 0201.26/6, "Baibanthuek Rueangraingan Rueangthonngan Thakthuang Kankho Praborromrachanuyat Plongsopthahan thithongsanamluang" [Reports on King Prajadhipok's Objection to Grant the Royal Permission for the Cremation of the Soldiers at the Royal Field], 5 January 1934; The Prime Minister's Office, Sor. Ror. 0201.26/6, "Chotmai Ratmontriwakan Krasuangwang Rian Nayokratthamontri Wanthi 6 Mokkarakhom Por. Sor. 2486" [Letter from the Minister of the Royal Household to the Prime Minister], 6 January 1934.
15. Hatthakitkoson, "Anusawari Thai," 73.
16. Anusawari Phithak Ratthathammanun (the Constitutional Defense Monument) was called by different names, such as Anusawari Prapkabot (the Rebellion Suppression Monument), Anusawari Sipchet Thahanlaetamruat (Memorial of the Seventeen Soldiers and Policemen), Anusawari Luang Amnuay Songgram (Luang Amnuay Songgram's Memorial), or simply Anusawari Laksi (Laksi Monument). Thepsongkraow, "Anusawari Prapkabot," 113–114.
17. Prakitnondhakarn, *Kanmueang Laesangkhom Naisinpa Sathapattayakam*, 387–388.
18. National Archives of Thailand, Ministry of Education, Sor. Tor. 0701.46/1, "Rueang Anchoen Phraphuthotsihing Painaiphithi Upsombot Naiphontho Praya Phahon Phonpayuhasena" [Relocation of Phraphuthasihing Statue of Buddha to the Ordination Ceremony of Lieutenant General Phahon Phonpayuhasena (Phot Phahonyothin)], 1941.
19. *San Anuson Nganphraratthan Phloengsop Phantho Luang Naruemitr Laekhakarn* [*Cremation Volume for Lieutenant Colonel Luang Naruemitr Laekhakarn*] (Bangkok: Thaikasem Printing, 1957), 20.
20. Wong, *Visions of a Nation*, 56.
21. See Hatthakitkoson, "Anusawari Thai," for more detailed explanations on the historical developments of the Boworadet Rebellion and its relationships with the Democracy Defense Monument.
22. Ibid., 73.
23. Some scholars suggested that the use of the double offering bowls (*phanwaenfa*) in conjunction with the folded constitutional document (*samutthai*) – collectively known as *phan ratthathammanun* – might indeed be considered as a representation of a compromise between the old and the new powers as well as a part of the People's Party's political propaganda. A recent example of such an argument could be seen

in Thanavi Chotpradit, "From 24th June to 10th December: The Political Life of the Ananta Samakhom Throne Hall in 1932," *NAJUA: History of Architecture and Thai Architecture* 13 (2016), 20–32.

24. Nidhi Eoseewong, *Chat Thai, Muang Thai, Baebrean, Lae Anusawari: Waduay Watthanathamratt Lae Rupkarnchitsamnuek* [*The Thai Nation, Thai Nationhood, Textbooks, and Public Monuments: On State-sponsored Culture and Forms of Consciousness*] (Bangkok: Matichon, 1995), 117.
25. Ibid.
26. Noobanjong, *The Aesthetics of Power*, 171–174.
27. Wong, *Visions of a Nation*, 57.
28. Prakitnondhakarn, *Sinpa Sathapattayakam Khana Ratsadon*, 136–142.
29. By appropriating the formal composition of a traditional Siamese *prang* and housing the remains of the deceased soldiers, the Constitutional Defense Monument followed King Rama VI's architectural precedent in combining a Buddhist shrine with the idea of militarism (and by extension, nationalism), as evident from the Monument of the First World War built in 1918. See Wong, *Visions of a Nation*, 52.
30. Also see Thepsongkraow, "AnusaowariAnusawari Prapkabot," pp. 115–116.
31. Wong, *Visions of a Nation*, 56.
32. Be that as it may, contemporary sources offered dissimilar interpretations on the utilisation of this icon. Some interpreted that the *dharmachakra* denoted the peaceful and united Thailand after the Boworadet Rebellion. See Thepsongkraow, "Anusawari Prapkabot," 116. Others suggested that the wheel was indeed employed as a symbolic discourse by the People's Party to justify their military triumph in 1933 in terms of a rightful defense of the Thai nation, constitution and democratic ideology, which was morally equivalent to an act of protecting the *dharma*. See Wong, *Visions of a Nation*, 52–53, 56. In this regard, it might be construed that the emblematic reference to the Buddhist wheel of law empowered Khana Ratsadon to establish their righteous place and authoritative position in the history of the nation, aside from depicting the royalist rebels as national enemies. See Thepsongkraow, "Anusawari Prapkabot," 120.
33. For instance, see Wong, *Visions of a Nation*, 58.
34. The opening ceremony of the Constitutional Defense Monument was a major state affair in 1936, presided over by representatives of King Rama VIII's (Ananda Mahidol, r.1935–1946). After Buddhist services at the Ministry of Defense in the afternoon of 14 October and in the morning of the next day, the remains of the soldiers were transported via an armoured convoy, escorted by battalions of guards of honour to the memorial site. Contained in artillery shells, the ashes were enshrined inside the monument in the afternoon of 15 October 1936. Following Buddhist and military burial rites, the ceremony concluded with a flyby of fighter planes from the air force. In the evening, musical and theatrical performances were

also organised to commemorate the occasion. See Prachachat, 17 October 1936, 5; Thepsongkraow, "Anusawari Prapkabot," 118.

35. National Archives of Thailand, The Secretariat of the Cabinet, (2) Sor. Lor. Kor. 3.37/1, "Rueang Sang Anusawari Prapkabot Laksi" [Constructing the Rebellion Suppression Monument Laksi], 19 January 1933–6 November 1943.
36. Ibid.
37. Ibid.
38. Khana Ratsadon (The People's Party), "Prakat Khana Ratsadon Chabapthi Nueng," [The First Manifesto of People's Party], 24 June 1932, http://enlightened-jurists.org/directory/84. Accessed 9 September 2016.
39. Chris Baker, and Pasuk Phongpaichit, *A History of Thailand*, 3rd Edition, (Port Melbourne: Cambridge University Press, 2014), 120.
40. Ibid., 128.
41. Ibid., 137.
42. The Secretariat of the Cabinet, (2) Sor. Lor. Kor. 3.37/1, "Rueang Sang Anusawari Prapkabot Laksi."
43. Spiro Kostof, *A History of Architecture: Settings and Rituals* (New York: Oxford University Press, 1995), 19.
44. Nonetheless, a caution must be heeded as well. The connection between modern architecture and ideologies – especially nationalism – was neither unique to Siam before 1932, nor post-absolutist Thailand. Such a practice was indeed a global phenomenon, due to the popularity of modernism during that time. Between the 1920s and 1940s, modernist design principles and elements were widely adopted for architecture of the state by governments around the world, ranging from the Italian fascist, British colonialist, to American capitalist and Russian communist rules. Regardless of their ideological diversity, those regimes shared one peculiarity that served as a framework of references for modernist structures, the notion of nationalism albeit operating under dissimilar definitions.
45. Wong, *Visions of a Nation*, 58.
46. For instance, see Prakitnondhakarn, *Sinpa Sathapattayakam Khana Ratsadon*, 17.
47. Ibid., 12–19.
48. As stated earlier, the first was the Monument of Thao Suranari at Nakhon Ratchasima province, commissioned in 1934. Ibid., 108.
49. Historically, Siamese monarchs institutionalised a code of cultural consumption (*thananusak*) indicating a person's social status. Derived from the Indic caste system, certain ranks in the sociopolitical hierarchy were entitled to specific designs of cultural artefacts, e.g. architecture, costume, language and custom, while particular qualities were reserved for the monarchy. For instance, a nine-tiered parasol was reserved exclusively for a king. Violating the codes amounted to committing a high crime on the lèse-majesté charge. After the 1932, the People's Party abolished this code along with other royal-related practices, customs and traditions, deemed

as obstacles in promoting sociopolitical equality among Thai citizens. Also see Prakitnondhakarn, *Sinpa Sathapattayakam Khana Ratsadon*, 10–11.

50. The meanings of Anusawari Phithak Ratthathammanun were conveyed through public rites, rituals and ceremonies as well. See Malinee Khumsupha, *Anusawari Prachatipthai Kapkhwammai Thimongmaihen* [*The Democracy Monument and Its Unseen Meanings*] (Bangkok: Wiphasa, 2005), 76–77. The annual commemorative event and the memorial became an integral part in preserving a collective memory to remind the populace that the battle against Boworadet rebels was conducted by the People's Party on behalf of their best interests to counter a return of the royalist rule. See Thepsongkraow, "Anusawari Prapkabot," 120.

    On 14 October the Ministry of Defense organised the annual commemoration marking the day when a decisive battle happened in 1933. Acting as a self-glorifying ritual for Khana Ratsadon, the commemoration was regarded as an important public event, especially from 1939 to 1943. Attended by high-ranking officials, commanders of the armed forces, and royal representatives, the activities started in the afternoon with a Buddhist ritual of merit making for the seventeen deceased servicemen performed by an equal number of monks, followed by a military ceremony. Being an amalgamation of a religious ritual, military rite and civic festivity, the ceremony began in the afternoon, followed by musical performances and movie shows in the evening, drawing a significant number of spectators to the memorial thus allowing the government to cultivate popularity among people. See National Archives of Thailand, The Prime Minister's Office, Sor. Ror. 0201.97.5/3, "Rueang Wanthiraluek Thahanlaetamruat Anusawari Laksi" [The Day of Commemoration for the Fallen Soldiers and Policemen at Laksi Monument], (8 October 1939–12 October 1943).

51. National Archives of Thailand, The Secretariat of the Cabinet, (2) Sor. Lor. Kor. 3.19.1/23, "Rueang Thidin Samrapkhayai Anusawari Tambonlaksi" [Land Acquisition for Expanding the Monument at Laksi Sub-district], 19 December 1939–9 September 1943.

52. Thepsongkraow, "Anusawari Prapkabot," 120. Also see Prakitnondhakarn, *Sinpa Sathapattayakam Khana Ratsadon*, 100–117.

53. Sansani Wirasinchai, *Chuebann Nammueang Nai Krungthep* [*Names of Buildings and Places in Bangkok*] (Bangkok: Matichon, 2003), 81–82.

54. Also see Suphaphit Ngamwitrot, "Naiya Thangkanmueang Khong Thanon Phahonyothin Bonphuenthi Bang Khen" [The Political Significance of Phahonyothin Road for the Bang Khen Area], *KU History Club Journal* 3 (2011), 51–72.

55. The Prime Minister's Office, "Phraratchabanyat Waduaikanchatsue Thidinlae Asangharimmasap Yanguen Phueakhayai Laetatthanonchueam Krungthepmahanakhon Kapdonmuang Laephueasang Anusawari Thahanprapkabot Phutthasakkarat 2486" [The Act of Land Acquisitions and

Other Kinds of Real Estates to Enlarge the Road linking Bangkok and Donmuang and to Construct the Rebellion Suppression Monument 1934]," in *The Royal Thai Government Gazette* 50 (11 February 1934), 951.

56 National Archives of Thailand, The Secretariat of the Cabinet, (2) Sor. Lor. Kor. 3.19.1/23, "Rueang Thidin Samrapkhayai Anusawari Tambonlaksi;" (2) Sor. Lor. Kor. 3.37/1, "Rueang Sang Anusawari Prapkabot Laksi."

57. National Archives of Thailand, Ministry of Education, (2) Sor. Tor. 0701.46/1, "Rueangkhokwamdamri Rueangchaichong Naichedi Wat Phra Sri Mahathat" [Request for Opinion on the Usage of the Niches inside the Stupa at Wat Phra Sri Mahathat, Bang Khen], 22 April 1941, 1–2

58. Ibid.

59. Prakitnondhakarn, *Sinpa Sathapattayakam Khana Ratsadon*, 107.

60. Ibid., 109.

61. See the previous note on the code of cultural consumption (*thananusak*) in pre-modern Siam.

62. Somchat Chungsiriarak, "Chitwinyan Baepthai Samaimai: Khongngan Sathapattayakam Baep Modernism Khong Phra Phromphichit" [The Spirit of Modern Thai: Architectural Works in the Modernist Style by Phra Phromphichit]," *Muangboran* 27 (2001), 114.

63. The stylistic amalgamation of the ordination hall also arose from the fact that during that time, modernism was extensively employed for architecture of the state in "civilised" countries throughout the world in spite of their political orientations.

64. Noobanjong, *The Aesthetics of Power*, 157.

65. For instance, see Prakitnondhakarn, *Kanmueang Laesangkhom Naisinpa Sathapattayakam* 397–399.

66. National Archives of Thailand, 0701.22.1/7, "Sunthoraphot Khong Nayokratthamontri Nueangnai Aphilaksakhitsamai Haengngan Chaloemchalong Wanchat 24 Mithunayon 2483" [The Prime Minister's Speech to Celebrate the National Day on 24 June 1942], as cited in Manit Nuan la-or, *Kanmueangthai Yuksanlaksathai* [*Thai Politics during the Era of the Thai Symbolism*] (Bangkok: Rungruangrat Printing, 1997), 83.

67. Ibid.

68. National Archives of Thailand, The Prime Minister's Office, (2) Sor. Ror. 0201.45, "Phraratniyom Lae Rathniyom" [The Royal and State Customs], 1936, as cited in Suwimol Phonchanthorn, "Kromkhotnakan Kapkankhotna Udomkan Thangkanmueang Khongrat (B.E. 2476–2487)" [The Department of Public Relations and Its Propaganda for State Ideologies 1933–1944], (Master's thesis, Thammasat University, 1988), 101.

69. The twelve edicts required Thai citizens to know the national anthem, use Central Thai dialect as the lingua franca, eat with spoon and fork, buy Thai products, and dress in modern (meaning Western) fashion. People were also forbidden

from consuming four meals per day, and from chewing betel nut. Later edicts instructed husbands to treat their wives with respect, including kissing them both before leaving for work and when arriving home. Any kind of physical abuse was prohibited as well. Ibid.

70. Be that as it may, Phibun's cultural mandates on *khwampenthai* – the *rathniyom* – proved to be conceptually schizophrenic since several measures taken to define the new Thai identity were as much Western as Thai. The most vivid example is the name of the country, changed in 1939 from Siam, a native word signifying an ancient absolutist regime, to Thailand, a hybrid Thai-English term meaning "land of the free" and a modern democratic nation state. See Charnvit Kasetsiri, "The First Phibun Government and Its Involvement in World War II," *Journal of the Siam Society* 62, no.2 (1974): 25–88.

    In any case, "Thailand" also denoted a close kinship with Tai-speaking populations in Southeast Asia, reflecting the premier's vision of creating "the Great Thai Empire", a terra firma for all Tai-speaking ethnic groups to dwell in unison. See Barend J. Terwiel, "Field Marshal Plaek Phibunsongkhram," (MA thesis, University of Queensland, 1980), 133–151.

71. In addition to the commissions of several monumental structures, the state employed mass media and the educational system to popularise a new history, filled with prideful ethno-national rhetoric, as well as tales of great saviour-leaders, ancient empires and glorious wars. Wichit Wathakan's historical narratives deliberately emulated contemporary Western history books, intended to provide the nation with an organic-historical link to its "golden past", to promote a new "tradition" drawing on obscure folk customs and a variety of other practices. Despite their relatively recent origins, many of these so-called "national traditions", including the verbal "*sawasdee*" greeting, are still accepted today as authentic constituents of Thai culture. Joseph Wright, *The Balancing Act: A History of Modern Thailand* (Bangkok: Asia Books, 1991), 102–104.

72. Nevertheless, a counter-argument could also be made that rather than exemplifying the ability to reconcile with modernity while subverting Western hegemony, architecture of the state erected in the mid nineteenth century in Siam and twentieth-century Thailand inadvertently resulted in a subjugation to an alternative form of Western domination: the so-called crypto-colonisation, notably in cultural and intellectual terms. For instance, the stylistic hybridisation of the ordination hall at Wat Phra Sri Mahathat, Bang Khen, was an exception rather than the norm. Most government offices, as well as public and civic buildings commissioned both before and after 1932 were devised in Western and modern styles, thus casting doubt on the validity of the claim by the Thais to have successfully appropriated Westernisation and modernisation processes in a selective manner. See Michael Herzfeld, "The Absent Presence: Discourses of Crypto-

Colonialism" *The South Atlantic Quarterly* 101 (2002), 899–926; "The Conceptual Allure of the West: Dilemmas and Ambiguities of Crypto-colonialism in Thailand." in *The Ambiguous Allure of the West: Traces of the Colonial in Thailand*, R.V. Harrison and P.A. Jackson (ed.), (Chiang Mai: Silkworm Books, 2010), 173–186.

73. Furthermore, Wat Phra Sri Mahathat, Bang Khen, was aimed from the onset to serve as a model for constructing an ideal monastery in which monks from two major orders of *theravada* Buddhism in Thailand: the *mahanikaya* and *dhammayuttika nikaya* (the reformist movement) could co-tenant. In pacifying their doctrinal discords, the creation of this temple allegorically accused King Mongkut of causing a schism in Buddhism by establishing and sponsoring the *dhammayuttika nikaya* as a separated order from the *mahanikaya*.

    In contrast, however, the commission of Wat Phra Sri Mahathat, Bang Khen, by Khana Ratsadon expounded the reconciliatory effort by the post-1932 regime as being meritorious and auspicious in practical term for bringing peace and prosperity to the nation. For that reason, the temple epitomised the predominant power of the state over the *sangha* council (the Buddhist clergy administration), and by extension over ordinary Thai citizens.

74. Regardless of the fact that *khwampenthai* discourse was created in the early twentieth century, it incorporated many ancient beliefs from both Hinduism and Buddhism that supplied forms of consciousness as well as modes of actions. Among the most influential ones was the concept of Traiphumi cosmology. A fourteenth-century manuscript known as "The Three Worlds According to King Ruang" or "Traiphumi Phra Ruang" – composed from over thirty Buddhist doctrines under the sponsorship of King Lithai of Sukhothai in 1345 – described the three realms of existence: heaven, earth and the underworld. Divided into thirty-one sub-domains, all the three universes were in a shape of circular discs. The human domain was located in the earthly realm, at the centre of which stood the Mount Meru – the vertical axis of the universe – surrounded by four continents, sixteen mountain ranges, and vast oceans, which were metaphysically and symbolically represented by a series of circles and squares in typical *mandala* diagrams. See King Lithai, *Traiphumiktha* [*On The Three Realms of Existence*] (Bangkok: ASEAN Committee on Culture and Information, 1985), 66, 74, 248, 376.

75. Buttressed by the practice of god-king or *devaraja*, the ruling Siamese authorities traditionally employed the Traiphumi sacred cosmological model – embodied in the designs of the built environment – to attain, legitimise and preserve their political power over the masses. Bound with the concept of Traiphumi, Siamese architecture was infused with cosmological symbolism. Religious structures such as temples and monuments were conceived as microcosms of the sacred universe. Likewise, the sovereign realm of the king, its centre and his sacred residential space were devised according to the cosmographic order, around which a consolidation

of power took shape and a hierarchy of social agents revolved. See Clarence Aasen, *Architecture of Siam: A Cultural History Interpretation* (Kuala Lumpur: Oxford University Press, 1998), 20–21.

76. Marc Askew, "The Ineffable Rightness of Conspiracy," in *Bangkok, May 2010: Perspectives on a Divided Thailand*, ed. M. J. Montesano, P. Chachavalpongpun, and A. Chongvilaivan (Singapore: Institute of Southeast Asian Studies, 2012), 73.

77. Judith Stowe, *Siam Becomes Thailand: A Story of Intrigue* (Honolulu: University of Hawai'i Press, 1991), 228–283.

78. During his second term as the premier, Phibun portrayed himself and his administration as fervid fighters against communism. He took this position not only to advance a militaristic right-wing political agenda, but also to decimate the remaining support for the socialist Pridi, while at the same time seeking approval from the United States and Western Europe to use violence to suppress left-wing activists.

    By doing so, Phibun became the preferred choice for the US to contain the People's Republic of China's influence in the Southeast Asian region. When the Korean War broke out, the prime minister ordered a contingent of Thai troops to join the UN's multinational force led by the Americans. He also implemented several discriminatory socio-economic measures against ethnic Chinese in Thailand. See Daniel Fineman, *A Special Relationship: The United States and Military Government in Thailand* (Honolulu, University of Hawai'i Press, 1997), 12–16.

79. Nonetheless, by the latter half of the 1950s, Phibun was criticising America's overwhelming influence in Thai politics, and sent two of the children of his closest advisor to Beijing to establish a secret diplomatic channel. He even tried to reconcile with Pridi to counter the growing clout of the rightist elements in the armed forces. Ibid.

80. With their growing political clout, the *khana rattaprahan* commanders pushed for a more visible and authoritative role for the monarchical institution in Thai society through the politics of representations in architecture and urban space, especially public monuments commissioned by the People's Party. For instance, in 1952, the cabinet proposed to replace the central portion of the Democracy Monument with a statue of King Rama VII. See National Archives of Thailand, Ministry of Interior, Mor. Tor. 1.1.3.3/1, "Rraingan Kanprachum Khanakamkan Damnoenkansang Anusawari Phrabatsomdet Phrapokklao Chaoayuhua" [Meeting Reports of the Committee Overseeing the Construction of King Prajadhipok's Monument], 31 January 1952, 56. The project did not materialise, since Phibun did not sanction it, citing a lack of available funds as the main reason. See National Archives of Thailand, Ministry of Interior, Mor. Tor. 1.1.3.3/1, "Rueang Anusawari Phrabatsomdet Phrapokklao" [King Prajadhipok's Monument], 14 February 1953, 1.

81. The Oxford-educated King Rama VI took a conservative position on Westernisation and modernisation processes. Although a staunch critic of the West, Vajiravudh collaborated with a small circle of foreign educated intellectuals and resorted to nationalistic ideology in constructing the Thai identity. The sovereign found the Fine Arts Department (FAD) in 1912 to preserve and control all the productions of cultural artefacts in Siam. See Walter Vella, *Chaiyo! King Vajiravudh and the Development of Thai Nationalism* (Honolulu: University of Hawai'i Press, 1978), 205.
82. Thak Chaloemtiarana, *Thailand: The Politics of Despotic Paternalism* (Bangkok, Thailand: Thammasat University Press, 1979), 81–91.
83. Thawatt Mokarapong, *History of the Thai Revolution: A Study in Political Behavior* (Bangkok: Thai Watana Panich, 1972), 229.
84. Chaloemtiarana, *Thailand*, 96.
85. Ibid.
86. Mokarapong, *History of the Thai Revolution*, 283–293.
87. See Natphon Chaiching, "Kanruesarang 2475: Fanching Khong Nakutmokti Namngoenthae" [Deconstructing 2475: Genuine Dreams of the True Blue-blooded Idealists], *Silpawatthanatham* 27, no. 2 (2005): 113–114.
88. Kukrit Pramoj, Opening Speech on Modern Art, in *A Proceeding for Seminar on the Post-1932 Art*, (Bangkok: Thai Khadi Research Institute, Thammasat University, 1985), 2–14.
89. Chaloemtiarana, *Thailand*, 161–166.
90. Somsak Jeamteerasakul, *Prawatsat Thiphoengsang* [*Recently Constructed History*] (Bangkok: Hok Tula Rumluek, 2001), 34–36.
91. Some published scholarly works contended that the transformations indeed first started when the People's Party was at the height of its power during the first Phibun administration, for instance, see Thepsongkraow, "Anusawari Prapkabot." From 1938 to 1944, an observation could be made that Phibun "had played the role of kings as had no man in living memory, and as such no man could even hope to replace him". See Thongchai Winichakul, "Thai Democracy in Public Memory: Monuments and Their Narratives," (Paper presented at the 7th International Conference on Thai Studies, Amsterdam, 4–8 July 1999), 9. Under the ideological cover of nationalism and constitutionalism, Phibun fashioned a militaristic state, concentrating on a process of modernisation. Seeing military leadership as a suitable model for Thailand during World War II, he assumed the role of a "strong and principled leader to whom the Thai elite had historically turned to arbitrate differences". See Wright, *The Balancing Act*, 88–104.

    In fact, even before ascending to the premiership, Phibun published articles on the global crisis in the Ministry of Defense magazine calling for a strong leader in Thailand, as "an animal herd needs its leader". See Charnvit Kasetsiri, "The First Phibun Government and Its Involvement in World War II," *Journal of the Siam Society* 62, no. 2 (1974): 35.

Moreover, facilitated by Luang Wichit Wathakan, Phibun's chauvinistic cult of leadership and fascist-oriented nationalistic vision were popularised by songs, plays, dances and novels, as well as were institutionalised by public events and state ceremonies. As exhibited by the annual at the Constitutional Defense Monument in 1941 as an example, the Ministry of Defense extended its invitation to the prime minister to attend the event together with the regal representatives. The commemorative service was presided over by Phibun, who commanded the combined armed forces that defeated the Boworadet Rebellion in 1933. See Thepsongkraow, "Anusawari Prapkabot," 122.

Through this mode of self-ascription, the martial connotation of the Constitutional Defense Monument was appropriated to become a discursive discourse to promote Phibun's cult of leadership, depicting him as a saviour of the Thai nation. In the social arena, Phibun's cult of leadership was reinforced by the promotion of the Code of National Bravery in 1944, illustrating Thailand as "a nation of capable warriors", who were "harsh to their enemies" and would deliberately "follow their leader". See National Archives of Thailand, Department of Public Relations, Sor. Bor. 9.2.1/5, "Wiradharma" [Code of National Bravery], 1944. Inspired by the Japanese Bushido warrior code, many paramilitary and educational organisations, such as the *yuwochon thahan* (Militaristic Youth Movement), were established by the state during the late 1930s. They further disseminated the warrior spirit and military gallantry, accompanied by Phibun's chauvinistic cult of leadership propagated by the constructions of war memorials throughout the country. See Stowe, *Siam Becomes Thailand*, 85.

Finally, it was widely known that Phibun was an admirer of European dictators of the same age, namely Mussolini and Hitler, notably the ways in which Il Duce and der Führer transformed their nations through architectural and urban designs. Aside from commissioning several new public monuments and civic structures, the Thai premier pushed for the legislation of the Act of National Monument Protection, which encompassed the rules and regulations for maintenance and protection of Anusawari Phithak Ratthathammanun. Yet the enactment process was eventually shelved after Phibun resigned from the premiership in 1944. See National Archives of Thailand, The Secretariat of the Cabinet, Sor. Lor. Kor. 3.37/9, "Rueang Kankhumkhrong Anusawari Haengchat" [The Protection of National Monuments], (3 July 1943–1945).

92. Chamlong Ittharong, *Lakhonkanmueang* [*Political Drama*] (Bangkok: Sahaupakorn Printing, 1949), 322–324.
93. Lui Khiriwat, *Prachatipthai Sipchetpee* [*Seventeen Years of Democracy*] (Bangkok: Odeon Store, 1950), 226–230.

94. In Thailand, the term "Hyper-Royalism" denoted a hegemonic ideology intended to identify and chastise potential antagonists of the monarchical institution, while providing justification for the believers to take such actions. Hyper-Royalism strengthened the sacrosanct status of the kings and royal families – both in the past and present – as the most sacred, untouchable and inviolable institution. Consequently, the belief that the monarchy must be defended at all costs has been indoctrinated into the Thai consciousness. Hyper-Royalism also legitimised the practice of punishing those who failed to display love and respect for – as well as those who criticised or insulted – the monarchy with harsh social sanctions and legal means, namely through draconian lèse-majesté law. Since 2006, the ideology had provided a discourse for the royal apologists to justify their use of actions and policies, which were incompatible with democratic principles, against their political opponents. See Thongchai Winichakul, "Hyper-royalism: Its Spell and Magic, Its Origin and Possible End," Area Studies Seminar Lecture, Institute of Developing Economies, Japan External Trade Organization, Chiba, Japan, 28 June 2013.

95. In 1973, Thai vocational and college students orchestrated a series of massive protests against the Thanom Kittikachorn military regime, which developed into the 14 October uprising that brought down the regime. On that day, about 400,000 demonstrators staged a huge rally at the heart of the capital city, demanding a release of political activists and student leaders from prison. Their peaceful demonstration erupted into vicious street fighting when riot police and infantrymen, backed by tanks and gunship helicopters, opened fire on unarmed protestors the following morning. See Wright, *The Balancing Act*, 198–200.

As the number of casualties increased over the next few days, King Rama IX decided to intervene by asking Thanom and his accomplice, Field Marshal Prapas Jarusathien, to go into an exile and appointing a provisional government headed by Professor Sanya Dharmasakti (g.1973–1975). Bhumibol later granted permission to cremate the seventy-seven fallen protestors at the Royal Field. See Winichakul, "Thai Democracy in Public Memory," 11. The subsequent three years saw a period of chaotic democracy. In 1976, panicked by the fall of Indochina to communism, coupled with the rise of socialist-oriented ideology in Thailand, ultra right-wing elements in the armed forces seized power and massacred students at Thammasat University in Bangkok on 6 October, eliminating the political activities of the youth. Many surviving students fled; others joined the Communist Party of Thailand (CPT) to wage a revolutionary war. Despite the atrocities, the massacre of students and left-wing social activists at Thammasat University has largely been ignored by the post-1976 administrations. King Rama IX distanced himself from the incident as well. The anti-government struggles intensified throughout the country, causing unprecedented animosity among Thai people and claiming thousands of lives. It went on until the conclusion of the Cold War in the late 1980s. See Baker and Phongpaichit, *Thailand*, 298–310.

Yet, as the progress of Thai Democracy appeared quite promising at the beginning of the 1990s, in 1991 General Suchinda Kraprayoon deposed a civilian administration, elected two year earlier. Fearing the return of another junta rule, the urban middle class organised large-scale protests against Suchinda and his supporters in Bangkok in early May 1992, drawing a crowd of 100,000 people and marking the rise of the urban bourgeoisie in Thai politics. See David Murray, *Angels and Devils: Thai Politics from February 1991 to September 1992: A Struggle for Democracy?* (Bangkok: White Orchid Press, 1996), 257–269.

Although the rallies began peacefully, the military high command ordered a crackdown on the night of 17 May, leading to the Black May uprising. Bloody urban fighting between heavily armed troops and protestors persisted for some days, but stopped when the general, at Bhumibol's request, left the prime minister post. The total death toll is still unknown, but is estimated to range anywhere from 50 to over 200. See Human Rights Watch, "Human Rights Development in Thailand," *Human Rights Watch World Report 1993*. http://hrw.org/reports/1993/WR93/Asw-11.htm# P397_166328. Accessed 15 March 2007.

96. On 19 September 2006, Thai people found themselves under military rule, when the popularly elected but very controversial Thaksin Shinawatra administration (the so-called Thaksin Regime, 2001–2006) was removed from office by a coup d'état. The 2006 coup plunged the country into an ongoing sociopolitical crisis, creating bitter division and resentment between the anti- and pro-Thaksin groups across the socio-economic spectrum and down to the household level (or the "Yellow versus Red Shirts" phenomenon). See Jonathan Head, "Rift behind Thailand's Political Crisis," *BBC News*, 27 August 2008, http://news.bbc.co.uk/2/hi/asia-pacific/7584369.stm.
97. Winichakul, "Hyper-royalism."
98. In his polemical essay published in 1989, Kukrit Pramoj justified his endorsement for the removal of Chaloemthai Theater via an allusion to the triad foundations of *khwampenthai*. The modernistic Chaloemthai, he castigated, was totally alien to the Thai identity. The fact that the People's Party constructed this building that had a Western origin and secular purpose to obscure the exquisite Ratchanatdaram royal temple reaffirmed that the 1932 coup promotors valued neither Buddhism nor traditional Thai art and architecture, not to mention the Crown. So, by eliminating such an eyesore, Kukrit wrote, the majestic splendour of Rachadamnoen Avenue was restored. For that reason, citizens of the Thai nation should rejoice, and press for demolitions of Khana Ratsadon's architectural heritage from Bangkok altogether. Kukrit Pramoj, "Column Soi Suanplu" [Suanplu Newspaper Column], *Siamrath*, (17 January 1989).
99. Prakitnondhakarn, *Sinpa Sathapattayakam Khana Ratsadon*, 200–208.
100. Noobanjong, *The Aesthetics of Power*, 373.

101. Lamphai Intathep and Amornrat Mahitthirook, "Dept Blocks Laksi Monument Relocation," *Bangkok Post*, 19 June 2010. https://pressreader.com/thailand/bangkok-post/20100619/textview.
102. Ministry of Transportation. "Kromthangluang Rueyai Satharanupaphok Gorsangkronggan Gorsangsapanloitee Anusawari Laksi," [The Highway Department to Demolish and Relocate Infrastructures in Preparation for Constructing an Overpass at the Laksi Monument]. 184/2553, (2011). http://dip.mot.go.th/ MOTC/News_MOTC/public/show_file.jsp?motc_number=184&motc_=2553. Accessed 1 May 2014.
103. Intathep and Mahitthirook, "Dept Blocks Laksi Monument Relocation."
104 "Maison Klumanurak Tanrue Anusawari!" [No Attention Given to the Opposition of the Disassembly of the Monument], *Thansarasetkit* 2543, 27–30 June 2010, http://skyscrapercity.com /showthread.php?p=75375351&langid=6.
105. Lawrence Chua, "Review of The Art and Architecture of the People's Party," *New Mandala Book Reviews*, 12 August 2010, http://asiapacific.anu.edu.au/newmandala/2010/08/12/review-of-art-and-architecture-of-the-people-party-tlcnmrevix/.
106 "Abhisit Vejjajiva Endorsed as Thailand's New Prime Minister by King," *Xinhua News Agency*, 17 December 2008, http://news.xinhuanet.com/english/2008-12/17/content_10519661.htm.
107. Thomas Bell, "Thailand's Prime Minister Ousted after Weeks of Protests," *The Daily Telegraph*, 3 December 2008, http://telegraph.co.uk/news/worldnews/asia/thailand/3542674/Thailands-prime-minister-ousted-after-weeks-of-protests.html.
108. Damien McElroy and Ian MacKinnon, "Bangkok in Flames as Protesters Refuse to Back Down," *The Daily Telegraph*, 19 May 2010, http://telegraph.co.uk/news/worldnews/asia/thailand/7741635/Bangkok-in-flames-as-protesters-refuse-to-backdown.html.
109. Motivated by the UDD leaders' promises to restore true democracy by eliminating social injustice and political disenfranchisement, the Red Shirt supporters were mainly liberal academics and activists, coupled with rural people and the urban poor, especially the northerners and northeasterners who benefited from Thaksin's populist policies in relieving their poverty and promoting socio-economic advancement. Also see Nirmal Ghosh, "Clash of the Thai-tans," *The Straits Times*, 2 September 2008, http://blogs.straitstimes.com/2008/9/2/clash-of-the-thai-tans/.
110. "Pro-Thaksin Demonstrators Reach Bangkok ahead of Rally," *BBC News*, 13 March 2010, http://news.bbc.co.uk/2/hi/asia-pacific/8565658.stm.
111. "Smiling for the Cameras: Thailand's Political Deadlock," *The Economist*, 31 March 2010, http://economist.com/node/15819472.

112. Mass Rapid Transit Authority of Thailand (MRTA), "Kronggan Rotfaifa Saiseekiew Chuangmorchit – Saphanmai" [The Green Line Construction Project Morchit-Saphanmai Section], *Pink Line Project*, 25 August 2013, http://pr-cr-mrta.blogspot.com/2013/08/blog-post_ 1017.html.
113. Also see Pavin Chachavalpongpun, "The Monarchy in Thailand: At the Critical Royal Transition," in *SEARC Working Paper* 145 (June 2013). http://cityu.edu.hk/searc/Resources/Paper/14061614 _145%20-%20WP%20%20Dr%20 Pavin.pdf.
114. Taken together, two conflicting yet coexisting interpretations on Anusawari Phithak Ratthathammanun emerge. On the one hand, the Red Shirts' selection of the monument as a site for symbolic projections indicated further instances of power struggles in the twenty-first century, leading to more semantic reappropriations that generated additional layers of significations. On the other hand, those proposed construction projects at Laksi Circle testified that the original meanings along with historical importance of the memorial had continued to be disregarded by the state.
115. Correspondingly, a remark can be made that the otherness in the hybridised designs of both structures indeed fell into the well-established Occidentalising project initiated since the reign of King Mongkut. See Edward Said, *Orientalism* (New York: Penguin Book, 1978), 252–253. Because both the Siamese and Thai ruling elites regarded the Western model of modernisation as the sources of and methods for achieving a respectable status among the civilised countries, the Occidentalising project furnished them a new and refined self-identity through their consumptions of material culture, while framing their worldview about the West and modernity itself, by historical and cultural experiences with and/or against Western powers and modern world. See Thanet Aphornsuvan, "Morbradlaykub American Orientalism Naisayam" [Dr Bradley and American Orientalism in Siam], *Silpawatthanatham* 25 (Jul 2004): 96–105. Maurizio Peleggi, *Lords of Things: The Fashioning of the Siamese Monarchy's Modern Image* (Honolulu: University of Hawai'i Press, 2002), 10–11.
116. Juan Pablo Bonta, *Architecture and Its Interpretation: A Study of Expressive Systems in Architecture* (New York: Rizzoli, 1979), 29.
117. Clarence Aasen, *Architecture of Siam*, 2–3.
118. Michael Peel, "Thai Junta Cracks Down on Opposition ahead of Constitution Vote," *Financial Times*, 28 April 2016, http://ft.com/intl/cms/s/0/20f029ae-0cfa-11e6-9cd4-2be898308be3.html#axzz47noqn0md.
119. The original plaque bore an inscription reading: "Here at dawn on 24 June 1932, Khana Ratsadon brings into being the constitution for the sake of the country's prosperity." It was replaced by a new commemorative metal roundel bearing the inscription: "May Siam be blessed with prosperity forever. May the people be happy and cheerful and become the strength of the country." Furthermore, the

rim around the surface of the new plaque also bore another inscription reading: "The respect for *phra ratanattaya* (The three jewels of *Buddha*, *dharma*, and *sangha*), the state, one's family, and the faithfulness towards one's king will all contribute to the prosperity of one's state." See Nattaya Chetchotiros, Wassana Nanuam, and Prangthong Jitcharoenkul, "You Say You Want a Revolution Plaque – Well, It's Gone," *Bangkok Post*, 16 April 2017, http://bangkokpost.com/news/politics/1232906/you-say-you-want-a-revolution-plaque-well-its-gone.

120. Todd Ruiz, "1932 Democratic Revolution Plaque Removed," *Khaosod English*, 14 April 2017, http://khaosodenglish.com/featured/2017/04/14/1932-revolution-plaque-removed/.
121. According to some historians, the memorial plaque was made about nine years after the 1932 revolution when the government at the time designated 24 June as National Day (ibid).
122. In fact, one famous ultra-royalist academic earlier made a public threat to destroy the plaque for the reason that it symbolised the treason against the monarchy by the 1932 coup promoters. See Teeranai Charuvastra, "Why Was the 1932 Revolution Plaque So Important?" *Khaosod English*, 15 April 2017, http://khaosodenglish.com/politics/ 2017/04/15/1932-revolution-plaque-important/.

CHAPTER 8

People's Park Complex: The State, the Developer, the Architect and the Conditioned Public, c.1967 to the Present

EUNICE SENG

People's Park Complex strikes a commanding presence in Singapore's city centre. As the first of several urban renewal projects built by private developers in the late 1960s through to the 1970s that front Eu Tong Sen Street, the residential slab-tower sitting atop a commercial podium and parking garage can be seen from the streets and alleys of old Chinatown. From the podium rooftop, one can see the contiguous rows of terracotta-tiled shophouse rooftops to the southeast bounded by Eu Tong Sen Street, Cross Street, South Bridge Road and Kreta Ayer Street, capped by the government-built Kreta Ayer Centre (now renamed Chinatown Complex) to the southwest (Figure 8.1). Further beyond is the Pinnacle at Duxton, a public housing project of six fifty-storey slab blocks connected by sky parks, rising from the site of the first urban renewal housing blocks. Looking past the government-built People's Park Hawker and Food Centre, Yue Hwa Building (previously Nam Tin Building) and OG Building in the northeast, one can see the taller People's Park Centre across Upper Cross Street. To the west, lie Pearl's Hill City Park (previously Mount Stamford) and the Pearl Bank Apartments completed in 1976. All these buildings and places play an integral role in a narrative of exemplary projects under the national urban renewal programme.

The visitor who enters People's Park Complex will find the Overseas Emporium, an anchor tenant in the shopping complex since 1971.[1] Offering 20,000 square feet of "authentic Chinese goods", its presence today is but a

Figure 8.1: View of old Chinatown from the podium roof of People's Park Complex. In the centre are the remaining shophouses that were conserved. Behind them stands the twenty-one storey Chinatown Complex. Source: the author, 2015.

shadow of its heyday in the 1970s. This is due to the emergence of competitors like the more upmarket Yue Hwa Chinese Products Emporium, which opened next door in 1996 with 50,000 square feet of retail space, the ubiquitous accessibility of Chinese goods and changing market tastes.[2] The reinforcement of what is "Chinese" nonetheless is symptomatic of the embedded narratives that underscored the national urban renewal programme to reconstruct the central area, within which Chinatown is situated. The founder of Overseas Emporium Lim Djit Sun – a native of Futsing in China's Fujian province, and chairman of both the People's Park Complex association of businesses and the Futsing Association in the 1970s – was a strong advocate for Chinese culture.[3] There were over twenty regional clans, dialect associations and temples in Chinatown, most of which were formed in the nineteenth century. Many key members were entrepreneurs like Lim.[4] By the time the urban renewal programme was set into motion in 1967, there was already a group of entrepreneurs and developers whose interests aligned with the national agenda for economy-triggered social development.[5] They anticipated an urban public defined by shopping. In People's Park Complex, this consumer public converges with the one planned for by the state and designed for by the architect.

Building (An)other People's Park

The historical significance of People's Park reaches back to Singapore's founding in 1819, where the section of the city south of the Singapore River was allocated to the Chinese population of mostly immigrants from South

China. Chinatown evolved out of such a form of colonial containment that identifies the Chinese as a diaspora, not allowing their demographic advantage to dominate the culture. Under the British, the containment created through segregation produced a historic template for a constricted mixed-use neighbourhood where the domestic and commercial coexisted in the form of continuous rows of back-to-back shophouses with an alley in between.[6] Public space within this urban rubric was limited to the street, market, temple, river, residual fields and vacant lots. Designated as a public open space for leisure, People's Park functioned as the Chinese counterpart to the Padang in the civic district north of the Singapore River – a green field designated by the British government for colony-wide celebrations, parades and recreational sports like cricket and lawn tennis.[7]

At the foot of Pearl's Hill on Eu Tong Sen Street was an open public park, 10 acres of land inaugurated as People's Park in 1886 by the governor and presented to the public in exchange for the part of Dunman Green that was occupied by the Police Courts[8] (Figure 8.2).The public here is tellingly identified in a speech by then Municipal Officer Tan Keong Saik who thanked the governor for dedicating "so much land for the Chinese". The naming of the park was in line with the British idea for the "People's Park" which would have the same features as "a People's Park anywhere else" but embodying different "ideas, manners and customs" in each place.[9] In the early 1890s, People's Park contained fairground attractions including an electrically illuminated carousel. It saw mostly British and European visitors at the opening but quickly became an attraction for the Chinese in the area.[10] From 1896, the Park was one of three designated sites for weekly band performances intended to cater mainly to Chinese audiences. By this time, Chinese hawkers selling mostly food and drinks had begun to appear in these public grounds. After vehement protests from the Straits Chinese Recreation Club against the "filthy" presence of hawkers in the adjoining Hong Lim Green, the municipal government set up a portion of People's Park as a commons for the sale of "all those things that the Chinese heart delights" in order to keep the turf of the Esplanade and Hong Lim Green "free".[11]

By the early 1900s, People's Park was known as the "recreational grounds for the Orientals". It contained playgrounds and a band performance space; it was home to all kinds of vendors and petty trades peddled by the lower working class, and crowds gathered there to watch firework displays during Chinese festivals.[12] The opening of the People's Park Station in 1907 (previously a switchback station in 1889) as part of the extension of the Singapore–Kranji railway line brought even more people in from beyond Chinatown, as did the number of streets that multiplied around the Park.[13] Briefly in the 1910s, it was the public meeting place for the local supporters of Sun Yat-sen, a Chinese revolutionary who became the first President of the Republic of China.[14]

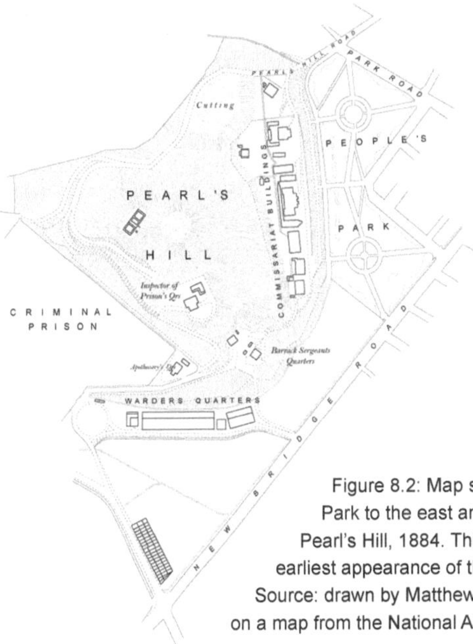

Figure 8.2: Map showing People's Park to the east and south of Pearl's Hill, 1884. This was the earliest appearance of the survey map. Source: drawn by Matthew Chan based on a map from the National Archives, UK.

By then, the Park space was shared by licensed and unlicensed hawkers, sheltered illicit activities – theft, gambling and prostitution raids were frequent occurrences – and accommodated police and civil guard parades held in front of the barracks by the foot of Pearl's Hill.[15]

The tensions between the Chinese market and the need for municipal open space defined the public discourse on People's Park in the 1920s. A hawker shelter that was built there had witnessed rampant overcrowding, cheating and poor levels of sanitation. In 1924, in what was identified by a municipal health officer as "the hawker problem", the government attempted to abolish street hawking.[16] It implemented hawker bylaws, dug new drains, installed water and power supply and fenced up the hawker shelter to prevent the hawkers from spilling back onto the street.[17] The *Singapore Free Press*, calling for more sports fields and playgrounds, expressed that the municipal government's decision to allow People's Park to be an open air market "crowded with eating sheds, stalls and impedimenta" had led to the loss of open space, free air and unimpeded views on the ground.[18] As the actual and representational space of the Chinese, People's Park was the site of confrontations between different entities: Europeans and Chinese, colonialists and communists; and the Chinese and the Sikhs in the fire brigade and police force during the tram workers boycott in 1927.[19]

The opening of the Great Southern Hotel (in Nam Tin Building) in 1927 and the Tian Yien Moi Toi (Tin Yin Dance Stage) next to it in 1928, at the eastern corner of People's Park, signified a new phase of Chinese representation among the Chinese themselves and to the colonial community.[20] Built by the wealthy Guangdong-born merchant Eu Tong Sen, the six-storey boutique hotel with its rooftop garden restaurant was the tallest in Asia. The theatre next door offered twice the seating capacity as the colonial Victoria Theatre.[21] Designed by architectural firm Swan & Maclaren, both buildings were white boxes with strong horizontal lines, angular arches and cornices, that aligned with the streamline moderne aesthetic of the period. Grills and railings with Chinese ornamental motifs and metal windows punctuated the hotel façade. The theatre was clad with tiles depicting Cantonese opera scenes, and shiny multicoloured mosaics fashioned into flying dragons. Neon-lit and installed with modern equipment, the buildings stood in contrast to the rest of Chinatown, which had been undergoing municipal improvements with the opening of back lanes and open spaces in the shophouse tenement blocks. The municipal government withheld the hotel proprietors' application for first-class licensing status until it made the recommended alterations to the sanitary arrangements.[22] Designed for the higher class Straits and China-born Chinese, the appearance of the two new buildings meant the removal of hawkers from the streets fronting them[23] (Figure 8.3).

The hawker situation in People's Park reveals the complex contestations in space and identity beyond those between the colonial government and the Chinese at large. The "war on the hawkers" continued into the 1930s. The municipal police saw the overall environs of People's Park as an uncontrollable

Figure 8.3: Majestic Theatre on the left and Nam Tin Building, which housed the Great Southern Hotel, on the right, at the junction of Eu Tong Sen and Upper Cross streets, c.1950. Source: courtesy of the National Archives of Singapore.

site that was "little short of a disgrace to the town".[24] In early 1938, anti-Japanese protests took place near People's Park Market and loudspeakers were installed the following year throughout Chinatown for updating the people on the war news and broadcasting air raids up till the eve of the Japanese occupation in 1942.[25] The Tian Yien Moi Toi (renamed Queen's Theatre when the Shaw Brothers took over the tenancy in 1938 to screen blockbuster Cantonese films) was renamed the Tai Hwa Opera House and screened Japanese propaganda films.[26] Shortly after the occupation ended in 1945, the Majestic Film Theatre took over the premises and renamed it Majestic Theatre.[27]

When the British returned to the colony at the end of the occupation, Chinatown remained the most densely populated area in Singapore.[28] The municipal government embarked on a process of resettlement and development that included the construction of an additional 300 hawker stalls in People's Park to accommodate the demolition of other markets and to relocate the hawkers from the overcrowded streets in Chinatown.[29] Between December 1949 and November 1950, People's Park was at the centre of negotiations between the municipal government and the hawkers, represented by the Hawkers Union, to reprieve a ban on hawking within a 1.5 mile (2.4 kilometre) radius of the Park.[30] The Hawker Inquiry Commission was set up to address the problems related to hawking and a report was released in November 1950. It highlighted how the streets in Chinatown were rampant with illegal and itinerant hawkers, and advocated for municipal action to rebuild Chinatown to deal with "the appalling overcrowding".[31] Amongst the recommendations that the municipal government adopted was the building of small "fixed pitched hawker shelters" on the side streets so that "instead of one People's Park, there would be hundreds of little 'peoples' parks' wherever people needed them".[32] In the 1958 Master Plan for the central area, the site, extending to the whole of Chinatown, was predominantly zoned for commercial and community purposes, with literally no residential allocation. The residents were presumably to be relocated in the new high-rise blocks and housing estates at the city's periphery.

The colonial government dissolved in 1959, before any development plan was enacted. In the transitional years before self-government, big roadside stalls had sprung up along the five-foot way in front of People's Park.[33] The Hawkers Department began demolishing unauthorised structures found inside People's Park.[34] By then, it was evident that the stakeholders invested in Chinatown were far from a homogeneous group that had been in direct confrontation with the colonial government. While the early migrants were traders, coolies, sojourners and re-migrants, it was the peasant- and coolie-turned traders that had become the economic strength in twentieth-century Singapore.[35] Clan, dialect and temple associations, in offering Chinese mass education and social networks, played a substantial role in galvanising the Chinese and providing them an identity in the decades leading up to independence. The Chinese-educated elite group that emerged became the champions of the Chinese community within the multi-ethnic polity of postcolonial Singapore.[36]

"*Sin Chew Pasah*" and "People's Park Market"

By the 1950s, People's Park Market was known as "Sin Chew Pasah" to the Chinese, which was translated in English as "the peoples' market".[37] The pairing of "Sin Chew", which referred to colonial Singapore in the southern Chinese dialect and "pasah", which meant "market" in Malay, is significant in the context of the emerging discourse on Malayan nationalism in the 1950s.[38] The replacing of "Sin Chew Pasah" with the post-independence urban renewal project of People's Park narrates the unfolding of events from the late 1950s through independence. Up till 1959, the meaning of the "nation" referred to an independent nation free from colonialism, jointly formed by Malaya and Singapore. It reflected the shift from competing discourses of multiculturalism in the 1950s and 1960s to a post-independence politics of neutral meritocracy that swiftly became the hegemonic model.[39] When the People's Action Party (PAP) became the ruling party in 1959, the multiculturalism that expressed the "Malayan consciousness" was downplayed to enhance the chances of merger with Malaysia.[40] The PAP's post-independence ideology on multiculturalism is synonymous with multiracialism, which regards society, culture, race, language, ethnic community and the individual as interchangeable.

By independence in 1965, efforts at social integration and marketisation were often conflicted. For the new government keen on jump-starting its massive urban renewal programme, the remaking of Chinatown began with the rebuilding of its most visibly representative public space – People's Park Market. When a fire broke out on Christmas night of 1966 and wiped out most of the makeshift structures, it reopened the space for the reimagination of a People's Park under the rubric of nation-building. The new incumbent PAP government began a systematic process of reallocation, reconstruction and reinvention of People's Park as a modernised public space still predicated on commerce, or the activity of shopping. On the site of the old market later rose People's Park Complex. Privately owned, interiorised and air-conditioned, it was no longer a residual space to contain the itinerant and harbour the unwanted. Reinstalled as the new nexus of Chinatown, it was an urban design project based on market principles, co-financed, planned and co-managed by the state. The continued use of the English name "People's Park" and the renaming of the Chinese name to "珍珠坊" (Pearl Square), which takes its direct reference from Pearl's Hill behind the site, was symptomatic of the Chinese identity shaped by the post-independence political ideology following the sociopolitical turmoil and Malayanisation politics of the 1950s and early 1960s, which produced the retreat to cultural Chineseness and capitalism in the 1970s.[41]

This apparent contradiction was resolved within the state's idea of multiculturalism. The sociologist Chua Beng Huat contends that for a post-independence Singapore that was ideologically "severely impoverished", capitalist economic modernisation was the obvious candidate to ground the reason of the new state.[42] Under the "hegemony of the economic", politics and political life became the rational basis for organising the new nation. Within the rubric of capitalist growth as the raison d'être of the state, presented as "survival", the ideological exclusion of the economy-determined everyday life as culture is facilitated by foregrounding the "cultures" of the three main races through the concept of "multiracialism as cultural policy". Race is officially essentialised strictly by patriarchal descent and therefore one's culture is predetermined. As culture is assumed to be embedded in the language of the race, compulsory school instructions as a "mother tongue" language (second language), after English as the common national language (first language) ensured continued existence of racial distinction. Chua asserts that the set of discursive processes which constitute individuals into distinct racial groups radically reduced differences among the population. These three discursively produced groups of "Chinese", "Malays" and "Indians" became the relevant administrative racial categories that are used to rationalise government policies and political practices. These groups are distinguished and made "observable" through their "cultural" activities. As he describes, this freezing of the "cultures of Singaporeans" into three respective traditions is an effect of official "multiculturalism" promoted by the government. In a subsequent essay, "Culture, Multiracialism, and National Identity in Singapore", Chua argues that the processes of nation-state formation in Singapore erase hybridity, as the newly invented Asian identity based on the purported ethos of multi-ethnic society is not produced through the cultural practices of everyday life. He details how this is done first through the erection of racialised boundaries and the subsequent homogenisation of the racialised population to arrive at a definition of Singapore as an "Asian" nation.[43]

Foreshadowed by the complexity of multiculturalism in multiracial politics and the accompanying anxiety, the new People's Park Market and subsequently the People's Park Complex were conceived and developed in tandem with the reconsolidation of Chinatown. In 1970s Singapore where three quarters of the population were ethnically Chinese, a self-conscious recentring of the city's identity emerged that was differentiated from the colonial imagination of the Chinese people and their place in the city. How was the paradox of a model for social integration within a development schema played out in the two People's Park buildings, especially in the privately developed Complex? To consider the instrumentality of the project in the formulation of a Chinese middle class whose collective identity was perpetually and publicly reinforced by its proponents – the state, the developer and the architect – this chapter shall focus on the three mostly incompatible visions of public space that quickly came to a condition of mutual accommodation.

The State's Public Space

Urban renewal began as a programme combining slum clearance and public housing. The implementation of a new public housing programme in 1960 oversaw the completion of 50,000 housing units by 1966. Chinatown remained the targeted site under the government's inaugural urban renewal program, following the recommendation made by the team of United Nations experts comprising architect-planner Otto Koenigsberger, land and legal advisor Charles Abrams, and traffic economist Susumo Kobe, who conducted a survey of Singapore in 1963.[44] Their report "Growth and Urban Renewal in Singapore" served as the basis for the Urban Renewal Plan of 1964 and the subsequent establishment of the Urban Renewal Department (URD) in 1966.[45] In February 1964, architect-planner Alan Choe, was tasked to head the Urban Renewal team, a subsidiary of the Building Department in the Housing & Development Board (HDB), and to execute the plan.[46] It proposed to rebuild the city completely in stages, in a curated suite of multi-storey apartment blocks and car parks, commercial houses, restaurants, hotels, theatres, shopping centres, markets, schools, etc. Provision was made for a traffic circulatory system and mass transport system to accommodate 4 million people and half a million vehicles by the twenty-first century.[47]

The implementation of the plan would be a joint venture with private enterprise, "for such a gigantic task as envisaged ... maximum cooperation between the private and public sector is sine qua non".[48] In his speech on the opening of the Building Industry Exhibition in January 1965, Minister for National Development and former HDB Chairman Lim Kim San highlighted the four partners in redevelopment: government, the building industry and professional bodies, private enterprise, and the citizenry.[49] The urban renewal programme was officially described as "the rejuvenation of the old core of the city by making better use of land in the 1,700 acres of the old city bounded by Cantonment and Outram roads south of Singapore River, and Kallang Basin to the north."[50] By the end of the year, the Urban Renewal team had grown from three to seventy-six people and their plan divided the central area into twelve precincts, five in the north and seven south of the Singapore River (Figure 8.4). A scheduled programme of action was drawn up for each of the precincts based on priority. The strategic, simultaneous redevelopment of two precincts,

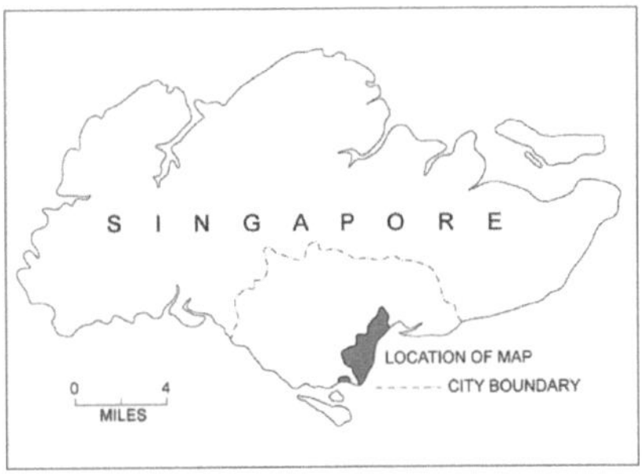

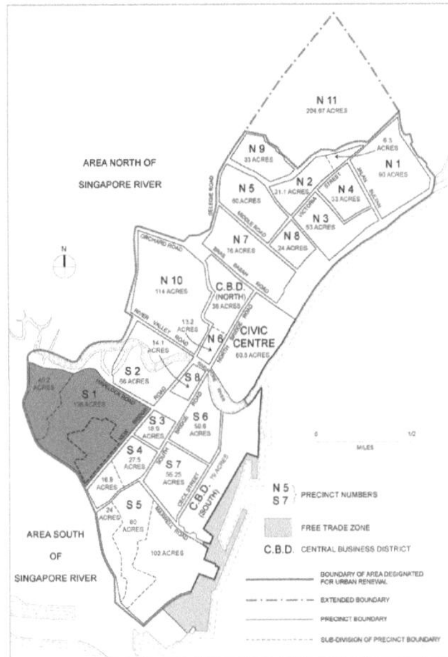

Figure 8.4: Urban renewal in the central area of Singapore. The central area was divided into five northern precincts (N1–5) and seven southern precincts (S1–7). People's Park Complex is located within Precinct South 1 (grey) under the urban renewal programme, 1967. Source: drawn by Matthew Chan based on a plan in *URA Chronicle of Sale Sites*, 1983.

one in the north and one in the south, reflected "a two prong centrifugal action of redevelopment moving from north and south towards the city centre".[51] Meanwhile, the HDB's Building Department conducted information talks and activities to educate the various groups of people on the merits of urban renewal and to garner public support for the government's "earnest intentions" in anticipation of the acquisition of public open space by private enterprise.[52]

The modernisation of Chinatown via People's Park Complex began in late 1966 with the establishment of the URD. The previous programme of clearance and reallocation was expanded to the two-prong approach from the perspective of finance, resource and enterprise. On 16 June 1967, the Minister of Law and National Development Edmund W. Barker announced a $90 million plan for fourteen urban redevelopment projects that the government would carry out with private enterprise. This was the first programme in the world of its kind in which private participation on such a scale was promoted by a government. Stating that "urban renewal, in fact, thrives on private participation", Barker also framed the role of investors drawn from Singapore and abroad as shareholders of a new nation.[53] The government provided incentives in the form of instalment payment for land purchase and property tax exemption for six months, plus one month per storey of the building to be constructed.[54] Developers could choose to carry out the sketch plans provided by the URD, amend them for submission, or submit their own. Criteria for successful tenders included the amount of premium offered, capital investment, employment generation, revenue potential and architectural merits. The URD made preliminary search planning to ensure that submitted plans would already be provisionally cleared, with certain concessions in planning parameters granted. It also worked as an intermediary between the developer and the Public Works Department (PWD) on road infrastructure, water, drainage and so on.

"[U]rban renewal is no longer a major political and social problem but one of economics, town planning and building," said Deputy Prime Minister Toh Chin Chye in 1967.[55] Repeatedly emphasising the necessity of private participation, the URD's Choe also gave talks to business and community organisations, such as the Chambers of Commerce, YMCA, Rotary Club, Lions Club and World Assembly of Youths (WAY), and the architectural society. He stated that urban renewal would be a "tandem team operation" that would undertake the planning and provision of infrastructure, while private participation would offer scope, variety and scale of development.[56] Choe was most explicit in espousing the economic imperatives behind land acquisition and the Sale of Sites. He was proud of the latter as the driver of the urban renewal programme's success, stating that it was a unique national initiative not attempted elsewhere in the world. He argued that the proceeds from the sold sites would trigger other social and economic projects to further attract private interests, which would then help pay for road improvements and resettlement of families.[57] On the ground, the people affected by the expropriation, including the many Chinese secret societies residing in the area, were taken care of by resettlement officers and the police who were tasked to uphold the stance of the "no-nonsense government". There were no consultation channels. The HDB determined how many units of housing to build, the areas in which to build housing, which areas should be redeveloped, and where to move people to ensure electoral support.[58] To that end, public opinion was led by political directive.

The Developer's Public Space

The URD's call for contemporary building types that manifested its ideals in urban development was met with responses mostly from developers who had not built such large-scale mixed-use buildings before. Each came paired with a local architectural firm led by young ambitious foreign-trained architects. Singapore glass merchant and first-time developer Ho Kok Cheong and Design Partnership Architects (DP Architects) won the tender to develop the thirty-one-storey People's Park Complex in late 1967.[59] The 2.5-acre complex was Ho's first development project in Singapore and was DP Architects' first urban project since its founding in 1967.[60] Ho explained the importance of keeping the name People's Park as it had become "legendary in the hearts and minds of the citizens of Singapore, a place of gaiety, life and activity". He envisioned that when completed, "People's Park will recapture and recreate the atmosphere on a larger and more sophisticated scale. It will also thrive and remain lit at night in keeping with its existing character."[61]

Implicit in Ho's statement was his desire to replace the old tenants with new ones deemed appropriate for the new People's Park (Complex). By then, the URD was in the process of relocating the shop owners and hawkers affected by the Christmas Day fire.[62] From the announcement of the project to the opening of the shopping and parking podium in 1970, People's Park Complex garnered so much public attention that it overshadowed the other People's Park building – a nine-storey project known as the Park Road Scheme – completed by the HDB in late 1967. Located on the site adjacent to the Complex, the $2.3 million shopping-cum-residential building comprised three floors of 290 shops, 74 eating stalls, a crèche and a kindergarten, and six floors of two- and three-room flats. Its tenants witnessed the demolition of the old People's Park Market in 1968 and then the rise of the thirty-one-storey $17 million People's Park Complex out of 2.5 acres of rubble. In place of the demolished one-storey People's Park Market rose the biggest and tallest shopping-cum-residential complex ever to be built in Singapore and the first of its kind to be built in Southeast Asia. The first phase consisting of the five-storey shopping podium and parking garage opened in 1970. It contained 15,000 square metres of rentable shops and restaurants, 5,000 square metres of rentable offices, and parking space on the fourth and fifth storeys for 700 cars.[63] Completed in 1973, the twenty-six storey residential block contained 360 flats, half of which were taken up by the business owners in the complex. In an anticipatory statement to mark the demolition, Ho said: "We want to maintain the image of a people's park."[64]

That image of a "people's park" is at once a projection and a construction. The URD worked in parallel with the developer to disperse the lower income "people" from People's Park. Choe estimated that six new low-cost dwellings nearby must be provided for every slum structure demolished.[65] He maintained that the high-rise shopping-cum-residential complex was the most appropriate building type to accommodate Singapore's projected density and was, by extension, a fitting form for the nation's social and economic development. Moreover, the Complex embodied the ideals of a more physically and economically mobile citizenry. Months before the demolition of the existing stalls, Ho promoted the People's Park project to the businesses and home-owning merchants during a three-day exhibition at the Victoria Memorial Hall, with the help of the architects who produced the scale model for display, and advised on the sales brochure.[66]

Ho's People's Park Complex was a contrast to the HDB's Park Road Scheme. Despite the architects' original intention for the atrium of the Complex to be naturally ventilated, all the commercial spaces were air-conditioned, whereas the three-storey podium of the HDB's hawker-cum-shopping centre was naturally ventilated with two open-air courtyards. The ground floor housed many of the relocated hawkers from the original market and the two floors above consisted of small shops selling sundries, textiles and clothing. On the roof of the third floor was an open play deck adjacent to the crèche, serving as a buffer zone between the bustling commercial activities below and the residences above.[67] It was the first state-provided crèche and play deck in the city centre designed in response to the rapidly rising trend of working mothers as Singapore's expanding industries turned to female labour. Choe extended this notion of buffer zones to open space and parks as transitional zones "for pedestrians to move from one precinct to another".

Ho demonstrated the idea of a "larger and more sophisticated" update of the old People's Park by inviting retail businesses like the Czech Bata Shoe Company to set up their flagship store and Eastern United Trading to set up a departmental store selling home furnishings.[68] The merchants formed an association in 1970 with its first chairman being the import/export company Southern Enterprises Singapore, Bata as treasurer, and the Gemini Chit Fund Company as secretary.[69] Ho and the merchants association celebrated the modern sanitised version of Chinatown with organised activities marking major Chinese events, such as a pugilistic show and lion dance in conjunction with a "giant sale" and fashion show to mark National Day, which became an annual event. Despite the ban on firecrackers from March 1970, it was one of 153 sites where supervised letting off of firecrackers was allowed; and the podium rooftop continued to be one of three sites in Chinatown for the fireworks display to mark the countdown of the New Year celebrations.[70] The most representative Chinese business, Overseas Emporium, hosted exhibitions on particular Chinese products to showcase the traditions, technology and culture of China.[71]

The provision of incentives was a mutual exchange. The space was frequently loaned to the government for public education exhibitions held in conjunction with the whole slew of national campaigns in the 1970s.[72] When the government decided to move to the metric system in 1972 to be more internationally viable as a business partner, a month-long exhibition "to help the public understand the use of metric in everyday life" was held at the atrium. In 1973, a Road Safety and Pedestrian Safety exhibition was held in late February to coincide with the Road Safety campaign, followed by a weeklong "Keep our Water Clean" exhibition in July and a Dental Health exhibition in late August, held in conjunction with Dental Health Week. Over the next couple of years, social and cultural campaigns were introduced. These included: a three-day "Vocational Activities and Hobbycraft" exhibition in December 1974 which became an annual event; in 1975, an arts and crafts exhibition and a photographic exhibition in conjunction with first Salvation Army week in August, a Crime Prevention exhibition and

Babycare show in September, and a two-day Welfare carnival organised by the People's Association Regional Youth Council (Central) in November. In 1976, a "Beautiful Singapore" exhibition featuring 200 photographs was held as part of Singapore's long-term plan to develop a garden city; and an eight-day health exposition titled "Nation's Wealth Through Better Health" was held to raise national health awareness, with a talent show as highlight to raise funds for medical equipment for chronically sick patients.[73]

Throughout, Ho openly concurred with the government's vision on urban renewal and policies on housing and development.[74] As part of the project, he built a covered overhead bridge across New Bridge Road (Figure 8.5). It was the first of its kind in Singapore and a gift from Ho to the people. In a national television programme "A New Environment for Singapore" broadcast months before the building's opening, the URD's Choe highlighted People's Park Complex to illustrate multi-level connections between buildings and precincts. He pointed out that not only did it exemplify urban continuity it also became an instant tourist attraction, an important aspect in the revitalisation of the central area.[75] Choe envisioned a city centre of one-stop complexes to contain all available amenities that cater to the needs of tenants, people of the locality and possibly the whole island.[76] Ho affirmed this, stating his intention to create "a new and modern Chinatown that will not only attract the local population but tourists as well".[77] The first two floors would be served by three escalators and a covered overhead bridge connecting the building to Chinatown across the street, realising CIAM 8's focus on a city for the pedestrian and Team 10's notion of urban reintegration, whereby a continuous space connects one's residence through shops and onto the rest of the city of work, leisure and more shopping.[78] Reporting on the high-rise, high-density rebuilding of the old city, William Campbell of *The Straits Times* wrote of People's Park Complex as triggering the trend of private mixed-use structures with express elevators and elevated pedestrian bridges, which would transform urban lifestyles. "More residential development, especially," he wrote, "will be promoted to ensure that the city continues to hum at night; while also having the effect of reducing commuter travel and lessening road congestion as a result."[79]

Ho's Complex was an instant success. Filled with throngs of shoppers from the day of its opening, it immediately became a model for other mixed-use developments in Singapore and Malaysia.[80] In 1971, as treasurer of the Singapore Land and Housing Developers Association, he persuaded thirty Japanese and South Korean developers to visit Singapore and showed them his newly opened shopping complex and other urban renewal projects to entice them to the prospect of investing in building projects in Singapore.[81] And as a patron of the newly founded Building and Estate Management Society (BEMS) at the University of Singapore, he urged members to recognise their "tremendous responsibility" in

Figure 8.5: Covered pedestrian bridge across New Bridge Road. In *Far East Builder*, April 1971, 22. Source: DP Architects archive.

maintaining all that had been planned and built, and to actively contribute to the growth of the city into a centre of modern office towers and commercial complexes.[82] With multiple engagements in various committees and societies, he even advocated the further development of the expertise of Singapore's builders and the establishment of a building consortium of professionals in the industry to offer its expertise in regional building projects.[83]

Between 1965 and 1975, the HDB commissioned a number of films made by Cathay Film Services with the main purpose of presenting Singapore's progress. A sixteen-and-a-half-minute documentary titled "Building a New Singapore" showed scenes of congestion, overcrowding and insanitary conditions in the city centre interspersed with new housing estates. Towards the end of the film, the models of urban renewal projects including that of People's Park Complex are presented, immediately following aerial views of old derelict buildings in Chinatown.[84] Choe had personally reviewed the film and made specific points with regard to highlighting the urban renewal programme as an imperative, especially making sure that the scenes of old Chinatown depicted only "the worst picture within the existing central area".[85] In another documentary, which had the working title of "Golden Mile and People's Park", scenes shot in 1970 and 1971 show the building progress. Although never publicly released, clips of the Complex were included in a subsequently produced nine-minute film (titled "Singapore – It's a Bargain") replete with scenes of shopping throughout Singapore, including highlights on traditional crafts in Chinatown and interiors of various shopping centres. It was an explicit showcase of shopping as a national activity and the atrium as a public space of the city. But was this the same type of public envisioned by the architects? It would seem so, although the difference lies not in the use of the public space but rather, in the process of engaging the public. The architects, despite their role as designer and collaborator in the urban renewal project, were critical of the actual lack of public engagement in the entire process.

The Architect's Public Space

People's Park Complex was the newly founded Design Partnership Architects' first response to the urban renewal programme. In mid 1967, Choe had released a proposed sketch design with an estimated cost of $10 million to demonstrate the URD's objective of developing a shopping centre with flats to minimise traffic and parking problems by bringing the residents close to their place of work.[86] He referred to this new architectural type as one that houses an entire township. The sketch model he presented showed three eighteen-storey apartment blocks sitting atop a large three-storey podium of shops. Parking was not incorporated in the complex. Design Partnership Architects elaborated upon Choe's vision for the core with "an urban architectural prototype" that would not only house workplace, home and leisure within but would be part of a network of layered traffic in the area. However, they rejected the URD's scheme and took advantage of the tax incentives by consolidating the three blocks into one massive twenty-six-storey block and increasing the shopping podium to five storeys to accommodate 700 car parking spaces.[87] The roof of the shopping complex could then be an expansive "garden" for the apartment residents living above (Figures 8.6 & 8.7).

People's Park Complex was developer Ho and Design Partnership Architects' first major collaboration even though they had previously worked on smaller projects together. Co-founded by architects William Lim, Tay Kheng Soon and Koh Seow Chuan in 1967, Design Partnership Architects proposed a design for People's Park Complex that was the result of a feasibility report produced by the young team, and based on the net floor area calculations according to

Figures 8.6 & 8.7: Urban Renewal Scheme – The People's Park Complex. Design Partnership Architects' model of the People's Park Complex (*left*). In *Far East Builder*, January 1969, 11. Artist's impression of the shopping complex interior (*below*). In *Far East Builder*, February 1968, 52. Source: DP Architects archive.

the density outlined in the 1958 Master Plan.[88] Lim attributed the project's influence to "the modernist movement spearheaded by Le Corbusier and subsequently the Team 10 members", many of whom he knew quite well.[89] As a student at the Architectural Association (AA) in the early 1950s, he was taught and greatly influenced by "brutalist architects" John Killick, William Howell, Peter Smithson, and the architect-planner Otto Koenigsberger who later founded the School of Tropical Architecture at the AA in 1957.[90] As an observer at the last CIAM meeting chaired by Team 10 members, he witnessed the debates concerning the ideological shift towards a systems-based network approach to cities – a mode of discourse that would have a lasting impact on his own intellectual production.

Lim attributed his theoretical knowledge on economic development to his teachers, land-use law professor Charles Haar and urban studies professor Lloyd Rodwin, during his year at Harvard under the deanship of Josep Lluís Sert.[91] It was also there that he met Jaqueline Tyrwhitt who recommended that he take courses in planning law, development economics and public administration. At Harvard, he developed an intellectual leaning towards social equity and justice, and first learnt about the urban ideas of Lewis Mumford, Jane Jacobs and Kevin Lynch.[92] He also studied with Charles Abrams, one of the three UN team members responsible for the 1963 Report on Growth and Urban Renewal in Singapore.[93] He explained that the feasibility report was the result of knowledge gained from his time at Harvard and that it was his partners and he who convinced the developer to pre-sell the units before the completion of the Complex to fund the project. He also revealed that not many others tendered for the project, possibly because the lot was very big.[94] Together with Tay and Koh – all three were aware of Victor Gruen's mall projects in the US – they approached the project with the attitude of looking "for our own solution".[95]

While this idea for People's Park Complex may sound similar to Choe's approach to urban renewal, Lim was critical of Choe's bureaucratic style.[96] Lim, Tay and Koh, together with a group of like-minded academics and practitioners, had formed the Singapore Planning and Urban Research (SPUR) group in 1965, the year the country became independent. In a series of intensive workshops and research activity that spanned six years, SPUR produced two publications that presented the core members' collective ideas on Singapore's urbanism and papers by international affiliates such as Koichi Nagashima and Tyrwhitt.[97] Making frequent suggestions and urban proposals to the government, the group aimed for academics and professional bodies to be involved in the city's urban development through collaborative and multidisciplinary research.[98] Lim championed efforts in environmental planning, arguing for a more humanistic multi-perspective approach towards development, a position that was shared by Tay.[99]

In the first edition of *SPUR*, the editors expounded on "city ideals" in their manifesto "The Future of Asian Cities". It addressed two moves made by the government – the construction of satellite towns by the HDB and urban renewal by the URD. With regard to the former, they argued for a radical economic policy aimed at securing balanced development for the country as a whole to create a more equitable distribution of wealth between the rural and city population; and to increase and expand the social amenities to be accessible to those in the rural areas. In contrast to the URD's stance on urban renewal, they called for the preservation of "local character and identity", emphasising that cities should be congested places of and for people, not cars. They took the high-rise and high-density as a given condition for the city, and advocated planning in four dimensions including the vertical and the temporal. The manifesto concluded with the case for a linear city "free of the traffic confusion of a radial city" that could be controlled along certain lines of growth to "permit frictionless expansion and renewal when the cycle of regeneration occurs".[100] The authors concluded that, "any planning action must be accompanied by a political decision". In this regard, they engaged in various public activities promulgating the humanistic multi-scalar and multi-perspective approach to urban development.

Years before the commission of People's Park Complex, Lim had identified the design and planning of the Lijnbaan area by Johannes Hendrik Van de Broek and Jaap Bakema in Rotterdam as an innovative and successful urban environment based on a strong yet flexible framework that contained "a dynamic tension from the positive solution of apparently conflicting requirements"[101] (Figures 8.8 & 8.9). In particular, Lim pointed out that the Dutch architects used the same basic four-storey housing element but allowed for variations of height in key places that "respect the varied requirements of and freedom of expression of the individual shopkeeper while creating a disciplined urban setting".[102] Though he did not directly refer to the project in relation to People's Park Complex, the notion of flexibility in section within a more rigid framework remained a shared principle between the two projects. As for the shopping complex, it was consciously designed as a public amenity. To that end, the architects conceived the four levels of shops to be laid out around the perimeter with balcony walkways providing views of all levels across two large multi-level atria – the smaller one named the "city mall" (concourse) and the larger central one, the "city room". Shops and stalls occupying the ground floor concourse were meant to evoke the previous

Figures 8.8 & 8.9: Examples of shopping-cum-housing complexes, rigid in form yet flexible in use. Illustration of Lijnbaan Shopping Centre in Rotterdam by Van de Broek and Bakema (1955–66) (*top*). Source: Ina Wu, 2018. The People's Park Complex in Chinatown Singapore by DP Architects (1967--73) (*bottom*). Source: *PA* (1970): 23.

market of makeshift stalls. The "city room", with a sunken plaza for flash sales and bazaar events, was an arrangement of scales of spaces, levels and movement. Accessible from each of the four sides of the complex, it was designed to invite people in and to accommodate them in a variety of ways and speeds. This continuous public space is connected throughout the entire People's Park site via the paved plaza to the Park Road redevelopment project and Majestic Theatre (Figures 8.10 & 8.11).

The implication of interiorising the street into the atrium – "city room" – is two-fold.[103] On the one hand, it suggests a kind of transparent, democratic space in which the "safe" and "neutral" activity of shopping would take place. Yet it is also precisely this formal architectural gesture that produces a socially engineered public space wherein the users belong to a self-selected class of shoppers. The other people, when invited in for other events, invariably partook in the same consumption logic inscribed in the interior architecture. Initially, the architects responded to the tropical climate with a multi-level shopping atrium that they believed could be naturally lit and ventilated, especially when all the doors were open. This was also reflected in the earlier version of the project where the podium roof consisted of large skylights that could also serve as ventilation shafts.[104] But this was not the case and the roof was reworked as a stepped deck of deep box beams. Furthermore, success in drawing in the crowds resulted in the interior spaces and shops becoming unbearably warm and prompted the owners to air-condition the entire interior. The Complex filled in the rest of the original site, leaving a wide strip of paved landscape connecting Eu Tong Sen Street and the HDB's other "People's Park" building.[105] To the extent that the "city room" with multiple access doors from all directions contradicted the maintenance of an air-conditioned interior and so only partially realised the idea of an urban continuum, the perpetual return of illegal hawkers and vendors especially at night and on crowded weekends fulfilled it.

Even during the construction of the Complex, Lim was vocal and critical in his concern with the social consequences of urban renewal. In 1971, he outlined a thirteen-point criteria for urban development in which he cautioned against haste in demolition, including large areas unaffected by major roads and the single approach of removal towards slums. In terms of private development he believed, "compensation would be adequately given to the urban poor … The demolition of these buildings do[es] not and cannot solve the problems of the slum dwellers."[106] Despite the seeming ideological alignment between the state and the architects, SPUR's model for social integration differs from the development model of the nation state in that it aims to accommodate various types of legalities (even illegalities), complexity, and irrationality.[107] Lim, quoting Victor Gruen, argued for "a city of compactness, intensity of public life, and a small-grained pattern in which all types of human activities are intermingled in

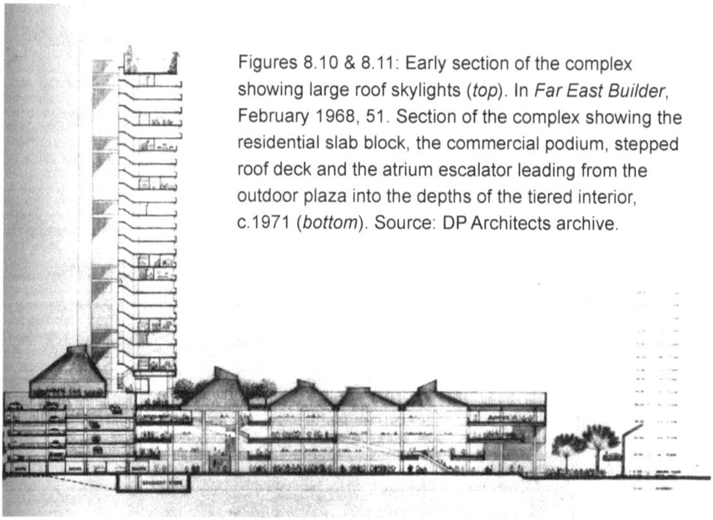

Figures 8.10 & 8.11: Early section of the complex showing large roof skylights (*top*). In *Far East Builder*, February 1968, 51. Section of the complex showing the residential slab block, the commercial podium, stepped roof deck and the atrium escalator leading from the outdoor plaza into the depths of the tiered interior, c.1971 (*bottom*). Source: DP Architects archive.

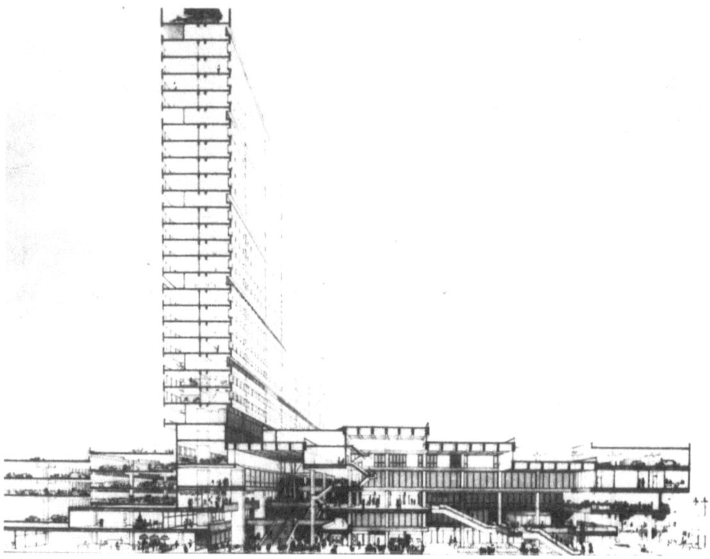

close proximity".[108] His urban ideas align more with the complex multidisciplinary systems model of Constantinos Doxiadis and the inclusive open-ended model of the Japanese Metabolists.[109] In the People's Park Complex, these ideas translate to an interior urbanism of small stores, the provision for admixture of public and private domains to accommodate greater numbers; and within the big space are nooks and crannies of intimate spaces and places.[110]

Lim's humanist planning ideas were given a platform via local media. His talks on real estate, property speculation and urban development at conferences and seminars in the 1960s and 1970s were reported in *The Business Times* and *The Straits Times*. These events were quite different from the ones at which Choe and Ho spoke. In 1973, when the residential block of People's Park Complex was completed, Lim called for the immediate implementation of a capital gains tax, equivalent to the forty per cent company tax on all land transactions, to discourage land speculators.[111] At "The Environment in Malaysia" symposium in 1978, he criticised developers in Third World countries as mercenaries who benefited from urban renewal at the expense of the poor; he also faulted the state adoption of planning theories that favoured the interest of the urban elite and financial corporations. Cautioning against impending crises, he argued for city planning to prioritise more equitable income distribution, preservation of the urban environment, and to maximise community participation: "Our priorities must be for culture, values human dignity, and relationship to the environment."[112] He went on to decry four fallacies of planning theories – urban redevelopment, road construction, housing shortage and high-rise construction – and argued for alternative urban models for Third World countries "which can provide a better framework for our cities". Speaking at a conference on "Urban Development in the Eighties" in 1980, Lim reiterated that the high density of buildings in the central business district was not based on sound planning principles but rather, was "a response to the greed [of] and manipulation by landlords and policymakers".[113]

Concurrently, the building of People's Park Complex was followed closely in regional building press, specifically the *Far East Architect and Builder* (renamed *Asian Building and Construction* in 1972). The 1967 urban renewal programme with the URD's version of a three-storey podium and three residential blocks was announced, followed in the next two years by the announcement of Design Partnership Architects' project of a six-storey podium with a twenty-five storey residential block. Tyrwhitt, during a visit to Singapore in 1970, remarked that what impressed her most about the city's architecture was the "commercialism with a human face"; she cited People's Park Complex as an exemplary urban model of a "strongly commercialised but very human business centre".[114] Her description was highlighted in the journal which also lauded the Complex as having "retained Chinatown's way of life". When the entire building was near completion, the journal published the building plans, featuring the three types of plans related to shops, apartments and offices.[115]

Since its conception, the People's Park Complex has been repeatedly and rhetorically celebrated as an exemplary urban architectural model, one that is specific to its place and historical condition where the nationalising moment and the architectural context of the 1960s and 1970s intersected.[116] Notwithstanding Lim's stance against wholesale renewal, Design Partnership Architects' People's Park Complex aligned with the URD's idea of a modern, sanitised urban environment of large self-contained buildings. The architects shared the preoccupation with architect-designed public gathering places of postwar CIAM, Team 10, Urban Design at the Graduate School of Design, and the Japanese Metabolist Group. To the readers of the architectural and building journals, the decade following Singapore's independence seemed to be a time when the architect as urban designer was given the space to translate public policy and programmatic concepts to advocate for the realisation of the urban potential through architectural design. As Fumihiko Maki commented when he visited during the project's construction, "We theorised and you people are getting it built."[117] Yet conflict, a condition common to contemporary cities, was not present in the accounts of the People's Park project by its commentators and historians, who focused primarily on celebrating it as evidence of the URD's success and as Singapore's tribute to brutalist architecture.[118] Maki, reflecting in 2006 on the first Urban Design Conference at Harvard in 1956, pointed out the value of urban design competitions as spaces for reflection on issues of reconstruction after cities experience complete or partial destruction. "As long as, and precisely because the city is incomplete," he wrote, "emphasis on any particular direction calls forth dissent and challenges that in turn open up new possibilities."[119] In the case of the enforced partial destruction of Chinatown for urban renewal, that contested space for reflection and debate was not created.

Conditioned Public, Contested Space

People's Park Complex became the prototype for accommodating the urban life of the new citizenry. From the impetus for the removal of the old People's Park and its actual demolition to the public tender, design, building, reoccupation and use, each step of the process embodied the ideologies of the new nation. It exemplified a moment of large-scale modernist visions when public and private enterprise equated urban development with the necessary removal of entire neighbourhoods and the rebuilding of "instant cities". The "instant city" of People's Park Complex is a model of a shopping centre based on a merger of commercial and humanist interests that has yet to be refuted. Together with the URD's People's Park, Design Partnership Architects' People's Park was meant to provide public spaces for the residents of Chinatown – many of them crowded the complex to "escape" their rented homes of cramped bed-spaces – and for the larger population. With all the shops and emporia under one roof in an air-conditioned space, the Complex became the instant nexus of Chinatown. Alluding to the megastructural implications of People's Park Complex, Rem Koolhaas called it "a brutal high-rise slab on a brutal podium" that is "in fact a condensed version of a Chinese downtown, a three-dimensional market based on the cellular matrix of Chinese shopping – a modern-movement Chinatown".[120]

The vision of urban integration in the form of a networked city of pedestrians on continuous overhead bridges with vehicular traffic speeding below was not quite realised within the URA's mode of state-incentivised urban design. As the first privately owned public space in Singapore, the Complex was the shopping centre for people eager to exercise their newly found economic freedom.[121] With a larger workforce employed in the new factories and companies set up under the national initiative of economic growth and efficiency, most weekend itineraries included shopping at People's Park. Chinatown was also the first of three sites developed to highlight the "Instant Asia" theme as part of the nation's multiracial agenda. Each had an ethnic focus – Chinatown to showcase Chinese culture and tradition, Geylang Serai for the Malays, and Little India for the Indians. In the mid 1990s the PWD expanded and rebuilt the Complex's bridge in a design inspired by the meandering zig-zag bridges and walkways in Chinese gardens. With two Chinese pavilions and a landscaped garden, it was a public space in itself. The bridge was further expanded to connect to the Chinatown MRT station, which opened in 2006. With that development the vision of People's Park Complex as fully integrated with the city's mobility network had come full circle.

Nothing of the previous People's Park remained, but the people of Singapore accepted their "park" as a "gift" – a public amenity – offered by the state and the developer.[122] The success of People's Park Complex formula of mixed-use commercial podium and residential tower triggered the government's issuance of a directive for major downtown commercial projects to provide at least three floors of residential space. Developers had the option of either converting at least three storeys of existing office buildings to residential accommodation or those still on the drawing board could add additional storeys before construction. The free gross floor area (GFA) was their incentive for building mixed-use developments.[123] This led to subsequent new building complexes that were even taller. In 1974, a new $40 million People's Park Centre opened across the street. Consisting of a six-storey shopping podium and car park, a seven-storey office block and a twenty-two-storey apartment block (opened in 1976), the government and the owner no longer needed to explain why "the people" of Chinatown were systematically replaced en masse. Lee Kuan Yew, in his autobiography published in 2000, reiterated Choe's 1968 statement that renewal was imperative: "When we live in high-rises ten to twenty storeys high, incompatible traditional practices had to stop."[124]

From the operations and occupancy to the maximisation of the building footprint, the rigidly delineated sectional datum of commercial and residential spaces, and the continuous shopping interior and public atrium space, People's Park Complex in its entirety is a simulacrum of the city and a miniaturisation of the state apparatus. Initiated at the end of the Indonesian Confrontation in 1966, the Complex staked Singapore's claim as an economically and culturally vibrant city in a region shrouded in political uncertainty. But the central question – at what expense? – was raised by Lim in his 1971 essay "The City Core – Heart of the Metropolis", though it was not part of the public discourse at the time.[125] Even as the focus shifted on development in Chinatown towards conservation and awareness of heritage in the 1980s, the irreconcilable conflicts of redevelopment remain.

In the most recent phase of nationalist multiculturalism, pre-independence Chinatown is showcased as a rich and diverse heritage site of Chinese culture championed by the Singapore Tourism Board (STB) as one of two focused "cultural precincts" for the implementation of place-making initiatives such as festivals and infrastructure improvements.[126] Complementary to this are the public education initiatives of the National Heritage Board in mapping the district's diversity – dialects, religions, clan associations, cuisines, crafts and architecture. On the one hand, these revisionist efforts are a timely response to the new wave of occupation by Chinese from various regions in Mainland China. Millennial People's Park Complex is described by Singaporean Chinese and regional tourists as being filled with mostly "Mainland Chinese people activities" – an observation

Figures 8.12 & 8.13: People's Park Complex from the outdoor plaza, with the People's Park Food Centre and Market on the right (*left*). One of the multilevel interior atria with makeshift stalls on the ground level, in place of national exhibition kiosks (*right*). Source: the author, 2014.

that may not be as easily picked out by other visitors.[127] On the other hand, they highlight the irreconcilable difference between the historical imagination of the diversity of the place and the present-day everyday activities of the "locals" – predominantly shopping – where one can get "the real flavour of Singapore".[128]

Within the post-independence national rubric of multiculturalism in the 1970s, "People's Park", recoded under a broader universal notion of "Chinatown", was complicit in placing a screen of "Chineseness" over the diversity of different Chinese identities and experiences. People's Park Complex, an icon of cultural "Chineseness" and capitalism contingent on an architecturally managed disappearance of diversity, stands as massive and stoic as an archival testimony to an age of nationalism. Its brutalist concrete facade is now painted in a palette of bright green and orange while its interior shows serious signs of aging (Figures 8.12 & 8.13). Exhibitions of national campaigns are no longer held within. Still, the podium roof of People's Park Complex continues to be home to Chinatown's annual Lunar New Year fireworks display. The iconicity of People's Park Complex has been concurred by the state, the developer-owner and the architects. Their mutual accommodation of the "people's" public space (of commerce) is symptomatic of the model of Singaporean governance under which the absence of the fourth vision, that of the users – "the conditioned public" – reinforces the modus operandi of post-independence Singapore.

Notes

1. Founded by Lim Djit Sun, Overseas Emporium Pte. Ltd. was incorporated in 1970 and in the ensuing years of the decade, the company expanded to include movie theatres and production. It built seven movie theatres throughout Singapore in the 1970s. The investment arm of OE was incorporated as Overseas Emporium Investment Pte. Ltd. and a subsidiary company set up in Malaysia to handle movie distribution in Malaysia and Southeast Asia. Now known as the OEGroup, which comprises five companies, it owns the emporium, property rental and redevelopment and in 2013 began specialising in digital media content and software development. Its head office is still located in People's Park Complex.
2. Yue Hwa occupied the Nam Tin Building (南天), designed by Swan & Maclaren in 1936, which previously housed the Great Southern Hotel. Complete with a few cabarets and retail shops, it was popular amongst Chinese travellers and known to locals and tourists as the "Raffles Hotel of Chinatown" because of its clientele of rich Chinese immigrants and celebrities. At six storeys, it was the tallest building in Chinatown and the first to be equipped with an elevator in the early twentieth century. The hotel ceased operation in February 1994 shortly after it was sold to the Hong Kong-based corporation who owned Yue Hwa Chinese Products Emporium as its flagship store and the building was renamed Yue Hwa Building (裕华大厦) in 1996. The public announcement of the opening of Overseas Emporium in 1970 presents its business philosophy: "Our company employs the small profits business model to serve the people wholeheartedly. Therefore the company's founding will be of great news to the majority of urban citizenry who love Chinese goods." "Overseas Emporium scheduled to open end of the month," *Nanyang Siang Pau* [*Nanyang Business Daily*], 9 November 1970, 17.
3. The Futsing Association's primary mission was "to promote Chinese Culture and tradition" and "to enhance member understanding of Chinese culture and Futsing tradition". http://www.futsing.org/futsing_eng/index.php/about/mission-a-vision.
4. The dominant dialect groups represented in the Chinese Chamber of Commerce were Hokkien, Teochew, Cantonese, Hainanese, Hakka and the Straits-born Chinese.
5. An emporium selling only Chinese goods, the Katong Shopping Centre and the Singapura Emporium located on the first floor, was officially opened by the president of the Chinese Chamber of Commerce earlier in January 1967.
6. By the turn of the twentieth century, Chinatown was singled out as the most problematic and unhygienic area that urgently needed improvement. The Singapore Improvement Trust was formally established in 1927 to clean up the most crowded parts of the city centre. Back lanes were driven into densely packed urban blocks and buildings demolished to give way to open spaces and parks.

7. After independence, the Padang continued to be used for the same purposes and was the site for many national day parades, including the inaugural one in 1966.
8. "Notes," *The Singapore Free Press and Mercantile Advertiser*, 24 July 1886, 46. An earlier plan of Pearl's Hill dated 1884 showed the criminal prison, Inspector of Prisons quarters, barrack sergeants' quarters and commissariat buildings and People's Park with a formal garden layout. The British colonial government in India had previously constructed a People's Park in Madras between 1859 and 1861, which were contemporaneous to the people's parks built in various British cities in the mid nineteenth century.
9. This idea was articulated by the Chancellor of the Exchequer William E. Gladstone, in his speech at the opening of Farnworth Park in Lancashire in 1864. "Mr Gladstone," *The Straits Times*, 17 December 1864, 2. See also *Proceedings at the Opening of Farnworth Park, Presented to the Township by Thomas Barnes. with a Report of the Oration by W.E. Gladstone* (London: General Books, 2012). The idea of a "people's park for the people's good" was already articulated by the Exhibition of 1851 Commissioners with regard to the use of Hyde Park as the site for the Great Exhibition. "London Correspondence," *The Singapore Free Press and Mercantile Advertiser*, 6 September 1890, 5.
10. "Untitled," *The Straits Times*, 3 August 1891, 2. "Tuesday, 4th August," *Straits Times Weekly Issue*, 12 September, 1891, 2.
11. "Hong Lim Green," *Mid-day Herald*, 11 September 1896, 2. In the 1918 *Report of the Government Commission*, the Botanic Gardens and People's Park, with seven acres left of open park space to serve as "lungs" rather than formal recreational grounds, were the only two parks that were able to fall under the definition of "park". "Singapore Housing: Report of the Government Commissions," *The Straits Times*, 29 August 1918, 8. "Playgrounds," *The Singapore Free Press and Mercantile Advertiser*, 20 February 1919, 115.
12. There were many reports on the thousands of Chinese who went to the park to celebrate festivals from Confucious birthday to the Lunar New Year. See for example, "Untitled," *The Straits Times*, 12 October 1909, 6. "Through the streets," *The Singapore Free Press and Mercantile Advertiser*, 31 August 1911, 139.
13. "Summary of the Week," *Straits Times Weekly Issue*, 30 September 1889, 1. First opened in 1902, the Singapore railway extended southwards from Bukit Timah to a new station at Tank Road via Pulau Saigon bridge, People's Park and Tanjong Pagar, and on to Pasir Panjang near Alexandra Brickworks. "The Singapore Railway," *The Singapore Free Press and Mercantile Advertiser*, 22 January 1907, 5.
14. "Local Revolutionaries," *The Straits Times*, 23 October 1911, 7. "Singapore and Martial Law," *The Straits Times*, 29 September, 1919, 9. They were described as "itinerant and eloquent native orators" who "preached" the gospel of revolution in the Park, coolie *bangsals* (wards) and in the *kongsis* (clan associations).

15. "The Civil Guard," *The Straits Times*, 26 January 1921, 8. "Governor to inspect Police," *The Straits Times*, 26 January 1921, 8. "The Police Parade," *The Straits Times*, 29 January, 1921, 8. "The Police Parade," *The Straits Times*, 31 January 1921, 10.
16. "The Hawker Problem," *The Singapore Free Press and Mercantile Advertiser*, 28 May 1924, 16. "Food Hawkers," *The Straits Times*, 28 May 1924, 9. The municipal government had built many cooked food shops and shelters in the few years leading up to the Report.
17. "Municipal Commission," *The Straits Times*, 11 July 1925, 10.
18. "Playgrounds," *The Singapore Free Press and Mercantile Advertiser*, 30 December 1925, 8. The editors reasoned that those living in the tropics were practically living in open air, as opposed to the Europeans who shut themselves in houses, "'fugging' over the fire."
19. "Disturbance at People's Park," *The Singapore Free Press and Mercantile Advertiser*, 28 March 1927, 16. "The Tram Boycott," *The Straits Times*, 29 March 1927, 10. "Troops called out," *The Singapore Free Press and Mercantile Advertise*, 29 March 1927, 9. "Boycott Disturbances," *The Straits Times*, 30 March 1927, 9. A Hylam (Hainanese) Chinese was arrested as the inciter of the riots.
20. "The Southern Hotel," *The Singapore Free Press and Mercantile Advertiser*, 5 February 1927, 10. The Theatre was renamed Queen's Theatre when the Shaw Brothers rented it and converted it into a cinema in 1938. It was tenanted to the Majestic Film Company when the Shaw Brother's lease ended in 1945, after the Japanese occupation, and was renamed the Majestic, which is its present name.
21. "Matters Chinese," *The Singapore Free Press and Mercantile Advertiser*, 18 February 1927, 8. "Matters Chinese," *The Singapore Free Press and Mercantile Advertiser*, 17 May 1927, 3.
22. "Licensing Justices," *The Singapore Free Press*, 22 June 1927, 11.
23. "Municipal Affairs," *The Straits Times*, 8 March 1927, 10. "… the portion of Eu Tong Sen Street in front of the Southern Hotel be deleted from the list of specified streets for hawkers." In fact, Eu already owned the street in front of the Theatre, when he previously acquired two other theatres in 1919.
24. "Why the Police Wants [sic] Parks," *The Straits Times*, 16 January 1930, 17. "Police Reconstruction Scheme Completed – Sikh Barracks opened," *The Straits Times*, 20 December 1934, 13. The police quarters were rebuilt and facilities expanded in the early 1930s.
25. "Big-scale disturbances in Singapore," *The Singapore Free Press and Mercantile Advertiser*, 10 January 1938, 1.
26. "War News for Chinatown," *The Straits Times*, 12 September 1939, 10. "News Broadcast in Singapore," *The Singapore Free Press and Mercantile Advertiser*, 12 September 1939, 3.
27. Sold to the Cathay Organisation in 1956, it was a popular venue for Hong Kong films made in Mandarin and Cantonese (and their stars) in the 1950s and 1960s.

28. The Chinese population in 1947 was 730,133, which was 75 per cent of the total population of 940,824. Khun Eng Kuah-Pearce, *Rebuilding the Ancestral Village* (Hong Kong: Hong Kong University Press, 2011), 31.
29. "Market Demolition Questions," *The Straits Times*, 25 November 1948, 7. "One mile ban on hawkers' stall," *The Singapore Free Press*, 17 December 1945, 5. "Street blocked by vendors," *The Straits Times*, 26 March 1949, 7.
30. "Hawker's plead for reprieve," *The Singapore Free Press*, 26 January 1950, 5. "City Ban on Hawkers Deferred," *The Singapore Free Press*, 17 March 1950, 5. "Chinatown Speaks," *The Straits Times*, 22 October 1950, 15.
31. "The Hawker Report," *The Straits Times*, 24 November 1950, 6.
32. Ibid.
33. "Roadside stalls spring up everywhere," *The Singapore Free Press*, 29 September 1960, 6.
34. "Shanties a hazard," *The Straits Times*, 18 July 1964, 12. A Town Cleansing and Hawkers Department set up by the municipal government was in place in the 1920s.
35. Kuah-Pearce discussed the creation of a Chinese community in Singapore based primarily on migrants from Guangdong and Fujian. Kuan-Pearce, 2011, 31. See also Wang Gungwu, *China and the Chinese Overseas*. Singapore: Times Academic Press, 1991, 3–21. Up to the 1920s, key figures amongst the more educated, multilingual and affluent Straits-born Chinese with roots in China and the region and were adept at navigating their business interests in the Mainland, Hong Kong and Malaya, took a lead in representing the public affairs of the Chinese in Singapore. See Song Ong Siang in *One Hundred Years History of the Chinese in Singapore* (Singapore: Oxford University Press, 1984). Originally, *One Hundred Years' History of the Chinese in Singapore: Being a Chronological Record of the Contribution by the Chinese Community to the Development, Progress and Prosperity of Singapore … from the Foundation of Singapore on 6th February 1819 to its Centenary on 6th February 1919* (London: Murray, 1923).
36. Kuah-Pearce, *Rebuilding the Ancestral Village*, 34. See also Yong, Ching Fatt. "A Preliminary study of Chinese leadership in Singapore 1900–1941," *Journal of Southeast Asian History* (September 1968): 258–285.
37. S. Ramachandra, "Chinese have own names for markets," *The Singapore Free Press*, 28 April 1951, 3. Ramachandra's use of "peoples'" was specifically referring to the Chinese.
38. The use of "Sin Chew" – literally means "star island" because of its small size compared to the Chinese Mainland – by the Chinese diaspora in Southeast Asia to describe Singapore predates the British Crown Colony. Ideologically, it references China as the hinterland to which it is an extension as one of its islands.
39. Among the competing discourses was the imagination of Malaya and the corresponding multicultural practices by the Chinese-educated students and

intelligentsia in the 1950s who found camaraderie with the other main ethnic groups (Malays and Indians) in their shared imagination of an independent Malayan nation state. This was discussed by Quah Sy Ren in his essay "Imagining Malaya, Practising Multiculturalism: The Malayan Consciousness of Singapore Chinese Intellectuals in the 1950s," *Inter-Asia Cultural Studies* 16, no. 1 (2015): 96–112. It was translated from an earlier Chinese version in *Renjian Thought Review* 1, (2012), by Teo Eng Hao. Another was the Anglophone version of multiculturalism associated with the English-educated Chinese, Malays and Indians (plus Eurasians) studying at the University of Malaya and Singapore.

40. This was pointed out by Michael Hill in his chapter, "Multiracialism and the Structuring of Ethnic Relations," in Michael Hill and Lian Kwen Fee ed. *The Politics of Nation Building and Citizenship in Singapore* (London: Routledge, 1995), 92.
41. Instead of a transliteration from its original name after Captain James Pearl who used to own the gambier plantations on the hill, "Pearl", as translated to refer to the object "pearl", invokes a Chinese culturalism.
42. Chua Beng Huat, "Racial-Singaporeans: Absence after the Hyphen," *Social Scientist* 24, Nos. 7–8 (1996): 52.
43. Chua Beng Huat, "Culture, Multiracialism, and National Identity in Singapore," in *Trajectories: Inter-Asia Cultural Studies,* ed. Chen Kuan-Hsing (New York: Routledge, 1998), 186–205. By the 1980s, this "Asianisation of Singaporeans", where the 'West' was cast as a single homogeneous cultural entity which embraces liberal individualism in its cultural core, saw the emergence of a simple dichotomy of morally "good" Asian communitarianism against morally "decadent Western liberal individualism". Chua saw this formulation of "Asian communitarianism" as the "threshold in the long and anxious process of a public discourse" based on the reinvention of a particular version of 'Asian' culture, which has "its objective the containment of modernisation within an 'Eastern' context". Chua, "Racial-Singaporeans,": 60–61. See also Koh Tai Ann, "The Singapore Experience: Cultural Development in a Global Village," in *Southeast Asian Affairs* (1980), Sharon Siddique, "Singapore Identity," in *Management of Success,* ed., Kernial Singh Sandhu and Paul Wheatley (Singapore: Institute of Southeast Asian Studies, 1989).
44. The three-man team was preceded by Erik Emil Lorrange, a Norwegian expert sent after the government approached the UN for help. He presented a report after a six-month long survey of the island on 1962.
45. Charles Abrams, Susumu Kobe, and Otto Koenigsberger, *Growth and Urban Renewal in Singapore: Report prepared for the Government of Singapore* (UN Program of Technical Assistance Department of Economic and Social Affairs, 1963).
46. A graduate of the University of Melbourne and the Royal Melbourne Technical College (later the Royal Melbourne Institute of Technology), Choe revealed

that Australia was the "obvious choice" for his professional training because it was closer and cheaper, and the degree was recognised by the Commonwealth and accredited in Singapore. Interview by Soh Eng Khim, "The Public Service – A Retrospection: Choe, Alan Fook Cheong" [Interview], NAS 001891-04.

47. "UN Experts go ahead for big city face-lift," *The Straits Times*, 13 August 1963, 4.
48. Housing & Development Board, *HDB Annual Report 1963* (Singapore: Government Printer, 1963), 2.
49. Press Release 22 January 1965 [MC.JA.28/65 (DEV)], National Archives of Singapore (NAS) 65024448.
50. Rejuvenating the old core of the city: most ambitious project in Southeast Asia," *The Straits Times*, 21 July 1965, 1.
51. By the end of 1966, 90 per cent of land in Precinct S.1 had been acquired and planning and preparation for the sites had begun. Housing & Development Board, *HDB Annual Report 1965* (Singapore: Government Printer, 1965), 51.
52. Housing & Development Board, *HDB Annual Report 1966* (Singapore: Government Printer, 1966), 62–64.
53. "$90m plan for a new look Singapore," *The Straits Times*, 16 June 1967, 5.
54. The instalment payment method was simply a 20 per cent down payment and the balance of 80 per cent to be spread over ten years without interest.
55. Toh Chin Chye, *Journal of the School of Architecture* 1 (1967). See also "Toh on city rebuilding," *The Straits Times*, 3 April 1967, 4.
56. "Tandem Team Operation: How urban renewal should be carried out," *The Straits Times*, 20 July 1967, 6.
57. Interview by Soh Eng Khim. "The Public Service – A Retrospection: Choe, Alan Fook Cheong." NAS 001891-09. See also "First in Asia: Choe," *The Straits Times*, 2 May 1969, 10.
58. Choe himself made this point in an interview in 1998. "The Public Service – A Retrospection: Choe, Alan Fook Cheong" [Interview], NAS 001891-13.
59. Koh Seow Chuan was the architect-in-charge for the project. The design team comprised Koh, Lim, Tay, Gan Eng Oon and Chee Soon Wah. The developer, Ho, was one of the principal owners of the glass manufacturing company Kwong Kum Sun Chan, located in South Bridge Road. Established since 1921, it made glass and aluminum sheets for the building industry.
60. Prior to his career in real estate and development, Ho had made a fortune in the business of glass and mirrors.
61. "People's Park Complex: Singapore's tallest building-to-be," *The Straits Times*, 1 December 1967, 8.
62. The hawkers were relocated first to an open space down the street and then into a HDB-built redevelopment project adjacent to the People's Park site on Park Road and to another block of flats in Outram Road, a fifteen-minute walk southwest from the site.

63. "People's Park Complex," *ASA for Architecture and Building Industry*2, no. 4 (December 1973): 34. One of the earliest *Straits Times* article on the project reported that there were to be 56 offices, 233 departmental stores and emporiums, 44 kiosks, a restaurant, a nightclub and a Chinese opera house in the five-storey shopping podium; and 98 one-room flats, 144 three-room flats and 18 four-room flats. "People's Park complex models on show," *The Straits Times*, 16 January 1968, 6.
64. "Old Landmark Goes," *The Straits Times*, 18 June 1968, 6.
65. "Choe: Slums in city centre block progress," *The Straits Times*, 18 April 1967, 6.
66. "Models of the $17m. complex at VMH show," *The Straits Times*, 12 January 1968, 4. "People's Park complex models on show," *The Straits Times*, 16 January 1968, 6. The author wishes to acknowledge Mr Koh for pointing out the existence of the sales brochure that contained English and Chinese texts. Koh Seow Chuan, interview with author, 11 August 2016.
67. HDB, *HDB Annual Report 1967* (Singapore: Government Printer, 1967), 80–81. HDB, *HDB Annual Report 1968* (Singapore: Government Printer, 1968), 79–80.
68. "New departmental store opens at People's Park Complex," *The Straits Times*, 12 December 1970, 12.
69. The Czech-owned Bata Shoe Company, with more than 140 subsidiaries worldwide in 1940, had begun its overseas mass-production operations in Malaya in the 1930s and provided jobs for thousands in Malaysia and Singapore. The Gemini Chit Fund Corporation Ltd. was founded in 1964 by war veteran Abdul Gaffar Mohamed Ibrahim, and collapsed in 1979. The company was the spotlight of what was touted as "the crime of the century" that was akin to "a national crisis". "Great chit fund Swindle," *Singapore Monitor* (12 August 1984): 4. "When chit fun bubble burst with a big bang," *The Straits Times*, 23 December 1979, 7. "Gaffar in for life for the swindle of the century," *The Straits Times*, 19 July 1973, 11.
70. The total ban on fireworks in the form of the Dangerous Fireworks Bill was enacted in June 1972.
71. These included a three-week long exhibition of "genuine medicines from China", the first of its kind in Singapore, in July 1972, and a month-long exhibition on garments worn by the people in various parts of China in March 1973.
72. "Council plans pedestrian safety campaign," *The Straits Times*, 4 February 1973, 6. "Disasters that strike in the home," *The Straits Times*, 26 March 1973, 17. "Dental Health Week opens today," *The Straits Times*, 14 October 1974, 9.
73. "Show to raise funds for the sick," *The Straits Times*, 12 April 1976, 13. "Budding artists show talent," *The Straits Times*, 28 June 1976, 10. "Talentime at exhibition," *The Straits Times*, 1 September 1976, 25.
74. "Building career loses out to social prejudice," *The Straits Times*, 2 December 1973, 4.

75. "A peep at the exciting city of the future ...," *The Straits Times*, 26 May 1969, 5.
76. See Chia Poteik, "New People's Park," *The Straits Times*, 22 June 1971, 7.
77. "Coming up fast, grandest complex in Asia," *The Straits Times*, 30 September 1969, 5. "Hey big spender, happiness is a many splendoured shopping centre," *The Straits Times*, 26 July 1970, 12.
78. CIAM 8 refers to the eighth *Congrès Internationaux d'Architecture Moderne* [Congress of Modern Architecture], titled "The Heart of the City," held in 1951 in the town of Hoddesdon, 20 miles north of London. It was significant on a number of levels, especially as one of the earliest efforts to discuss the issues of urban public space in the transformed circumstances of modern architecture after World War II. It saw the attendance of two new members from Asia – Balkrishna Doshi from India and Kenzo Tange from Japan. It was also the first instance where the work of a "non-western" architect – Tange's Hiroshima Peace Centre – was presented at a CIAM Congress. And it was in this congress that efforts began to be made to officially revitalise CIAM by turning it over to the younger members, which resulted in the formation of Team 10 after CIAM 9. The main schism that resulted in the dissolution of CIAM and Team 10's formation was the challenge of the latter on the doctrinaire approach to urbanism. The first formal meeting of Team 10 took place in Bagnols-sur-Cèze in 1960s, led by a core group of mainly Dutch and British architects, in particular, Jaap Bakema, Georges Candilis, Giancarlo De Carlo, Aldo van Eyck, Alison and Peter Smithson and Shadrach Woods.
79. William Campbell, "When you walk to work above noise and traffic," *The Straits Times*, 6 September 1973, 12.
80. These were referred to as "similar to the People's Park Complex". "Houses, shops on site of abattoir," *The Straits Times*, 9 March 1971, 7. Henry Chang, "Work starts on largest 'shop-under-one-roof' centre in Malaysia," *The Straits Times*, 20 October 1971, 14.
81. "30 here to see housing projects," *The Straits Times*, 17 July 1971, 11.
82. "Society has big responsibility to keep up rapid pace of building industry," *The Straits Times*, 13 December 1971, 9.
83. "Call for Building Consortium in S'pore to offer packaged deals," *The Straits Times*, 10 January 1972, 12. Ho was also deputy secretary of the International Real Estate Corporation and sponsor of a two-day seminar at the Shangri-La Hotel in November 1972. Choe presented a paper on the urban renewal aspect of real estate development in Singapore.
84. HDB, "Building A New Singapore" [Film], 1969, NAS Acsn No. 2010000396.
85. "Memorandam from Head of Urban Renewal to Ag. Secretary" [Letter], 11 July 1967. UR/17/10. NAS 113/5/60 S/004/87. An excerpt of his letter to the acting secretary of the Ministry of National Development (to be conveyed directly to the film producer) revealed clearly the agenda for the film, which was meant to be circulated within the country and regionally, even worldwide:

"On commentary Nos. 11 to 22, elaboration should be made highlighting the problem of overcrowding, chaos, congestion and uneconomic land usage. There should be greater emphasis on the defects of the present city centre and shots should be made highlighting such defects which causes decay of the city centre. Such shots could include traffic jam, roads being used for eating shops, etc. (other than the use it was designed for), children playing dangerously on roads because of lack of playground, unhygienic and insanitary living conditions within the cubicles, the degree of overcrowding and lack of light and ventilation within the building; refuse dumps being resultant all over the central area and also close-up shots showing structural defects in too many of the buildings that are ripe for demolition and therefore constituting a danger to life and health of the residents. There should be many more such shots depicting the worst pictures within the existing central area in order to highlight how we can improve the area for urban renewal."

86. "New People's Park," *The Straits Times*, 22 June 1967, 7.
87. Lim suggested that Choe had disagreed with them on this point and so they brought the matter up to the then permanent secretary. William Lim, email response to author, 3 May 2013.
88. According to Koh, the architects convinced the developer Ho that since net floor area also meant net rentable floor area, the spaces in the multi-level atrium would command a higher value than if the spaces were separate and enclosed without an atrium. Koh Seow Chuan, interview with author, 11 August 2016.
89. William Lim, email response to author, 3 May 2013.
90. It became the Development Planning Unit of the University College London where he moved to until his retirement in 1978. Lim took William Howell's design studio at the AA and learnt of the latter's concern with integrating building programmes with social needs. Both Killick and Howell was part of the team of architects in the London County Council Housing Department responsible for the design of Alton West estate at Roehampton. J.M. Richards, rev. Catherine Gordon, "Howell, William Gough [Bill] (1922–1974)," *Oxford Dictionary of National Biography*. See, John R. Gold, *The Practice of Modernism: Modern Architects and Urban Transformation, 1954–1972* (London; New York: Routledge, 2007). See also Eric Mumford, *The CIAM Discourse on Urbanism, 1928–1960* (Cambridge, MA: The MIT Press, 2000), 238–265.
91. See Richard Marshall, "Josep Lluís Sert's Urban Design Legacy," in *Josep Lluís Sert: The Architect of Urban Design, 1953–1969*, ed. Eric Mumford and Hashim Sarkis (New Haven; London: Yale University Press, 2008), 130–143. Koolhaas emphasised the influence of Maki and the Japanese Metabolist Group in making a case for the project being demonstrative of the emergence of a "non-white avant-garde" in the 1960s. Rem Koolhaas and Bruce Mau, *S,M,L,XL* (New York: Monacelli Press, 1995), 1054, 1067.

92. William Lim, email response to author, 3 May 2013.
93. William Lim, email response to author, 30 May 2013.
94. William Lim, email response to author, 30 January 2013.
95. Ibid.
96. Koh qualified, however, that because Choe shared the agenda of public space and national identical, he was, more often than not, prepared to take up the architects' ideas to the government. Koh Seow Chuan, interview with author, 11 August 2016.
97. Jacqueline Tyrwhitt, "Town Planning Notions – Some Rethinking. Talk to SPUR members, January 1971," *SPUR 68–71* (Singapore: Eurasia, 1971), 66–68. Lim was chairman of the group from 1965 and succeeded by Tay in 1971. Koh took over as chairman in 1972.
98. They referenced the Ekistics Group formed in the late 1950s by Doxiadis and Tyrwhitt.
99. "In search of a new ethic," *New Nation*, 6 May 1971, 7. A version of this paper was presented at the Student Christian Movement conference. "New ethic keystones," *New Nation*, 7 May 1971, 7.
100. These ideas resonated with Kenzo Tange's Plan for Tokyo of 1960. Lim had met Tange in some of the CIAM and Team 10 meetings during his student days and had heard the latter present his urban theories. SPUR. "The Future of Asian Cities." *SPUR 65–67* (Singapore: Eurasia Press), 4–12. First published in *Asia Magazine* (May 1968).
101. William S.W. Lim and A.F. Rutter, "'Undertones': Reflections on the 1955 I.U.A.," *AAJ* (1954): 107–108.
102. Ibid.
103. Fumihiko Maki's "city room" was a reference for the interior urban space. Koh recalled a pamphlet published by Maki's office that contained descriptions of the ideas of the city room. Koh Seow Chuan, interview with author, 11 August 2016.
104. Koh Seow Chuan, interview with author, 11 August 2016.
105. The building was later named the People's Park Food and Shopping Centre.
106. William Lim, "The City Core – Heart of the Metropolis," *SPUR 68–71* (Singapore: Eurasia, 1971), 37–40.
107. See for example, "Pirate Taxis in Singapore" which gives an idea of SPUR's position towards the existing elements of the city. Rather than complete removal by regulation as was the government's tendency, they recommended a multi-perspective approach to framing the problem and a multi-prong solution instead of simply getting rid of them. This attitude is consistently maintained as evidenced in subsequent position papers by Lim. For example, his paper presented to the Southeast Asian Study Group for Architecture and Urbanism in Singapore. Lim, "A Plea for Complexity and Irrationality in Architecture," *Cities for People: Reflections of a Southeast Asian Architect* (Singapore: Select Books, 1990), 30–38.

108. William Lim, "The City Core – Heart of the Metropolis," *SPUR 68–71* (Singapore: Eurasia, 1971), 41.
109. Constantinos Apostolou Doxiadis (b. 1914, d. 1975) was a Greek architect and urban planner, who proposed *ekistics* as the multidisciplinary study of human settlements, including regional, city, community planning and dwelling design. He propagated the theory through the formation of the World Society of Ekistics and its annual Delos Symposium; and with the help of the British urbanist Jacqueline Tyrwhitt, founded the *Ekistics* journal in 1955, first as a newsletter and by the 1960s, it became the platform for research and design projects and papers that demonstrated the scope, aims, intellectual framework and relevance of *ekistics*. Articles by members of SPUR began to appear in *Ekistics* from the late 1960s. See, Tay Kheng Soon, "Housing and Urban Values – Singapore," *Ekistics* 27, no. 158, Housing by the People for the People (January 1969): 27–28. Also, T.T.B. Koh and William S.W. Lim, "Planning Law and Processes in Singapore," *Ekistics* 30, no. 176 (1970): 42–48.
During this time, since Kenzo Tange's first participation in CIAM 9 and later in the final meeting in 1959, post-war architecture received its first international exposure and at the Tokyo World Design Conference in 1960, a group of young architects and designers, including Kiyonori Kikutake, Kisho Kurokawa and Fumihiko Maki, presented the publication of a manifesto, "Metabolism: The Proposals for New Urbanism," that established the name of the group and the architectural movement that propagated large-scale architecture based on principles of organic biological growth.
110. Ibid., 37–40.
111. "Unhealthy trend in property boom," *The Straits Times*, 22 August 1973, 9.
112.. "When a city is not a home," *The Business Times*, 25 September 1978, 2.
113. "Copied ideas may not work in Third World," *The Straits Times*, 21 November 1980, 11.
114. "Town expert sees S'pore as centre for expertise," *The Straits Times*, 21 December 1970, 7.
115. "People's Park Shopping and Flats Complex," *Far East Architect & Builder* (February 1968): 49–52. "Tenders for People Park's Project," *Far East Builder* (January 1969): 10–11. "Space for all in People's Park Complex, " *Far East Builder* (April 1971): 21–24. "Multipurpose Complex in Downtown Singapore," *Asian Building & Construction* (October 1972): 5. "Singapore Project Retains Way of Life," *Asian Building & Construction* (April 1975): 13–15. "People's Park Centre Residential Block," *Asian Building & Construction* (March 1976): 8.
116. See, for example, Tan Kok Meng, "After tabula rasa: nodal city Singapore," *Lotus International* 108 (2001): 21–29. Also, Wong Yunn Chii, *Singapore 1:1 City: A Gallery of Architecture & Urban Design* (Singapore: Urban Redevelopment Authority, 2005). Norman Edwards and Peter Keys, *Singapore – A Guide to Buildings, Streets, Places*

(Singapore: Times Books International, 1996). Prior to these, Rem Koolhaas situated this project as avant-gardist in his essay "Singapore Songlines: Portrait of a Potemkin Metropolis … or Thirty Years of Tabula Rasa," in Koolhaas and Mau, *S,M,L,XL*, 1008–1089.

117. William Lim, *Cities for People* (Singapore: Select Books, 1990), 8.
118. The URD was replaced by the Urban Redevelopment Authority (URA) in 1974, a statutory board under the Ministry of National Development of the Singapore government.
119. Fumihiko Maki, "Fragmentation and Friction as Urban Threats: The Post-1956 City," *Harvard Design Magazine – The Origins and Evolution of Urban Design* (Spring/Summer 2006): 46.
120. Koolhaas and Mau, *S,M,L,XL*, 1067.
121. "Sarawak team tours two Housing Estates," *The Straits Times*, 9 June 1971, 9. "Hey big spender, happiness is a many splendoured shopping centre," *The Straits Times*, 26 July 1970, 12.
122. "The people like their new Park," *The Straits Times*, 3 February 1970, 6.
123. "Homes in the new office buildings in city," *The Straits Times*, 3 April 1971, 4. Such an overarching schema to populate the commercial core was met with scepticism by many architects. The general sentiment amongst them was that the People's Park Complex was a unique case where its location ensured the daily presence of crowds of shoppers, whereas this was not necessarily so at many other sites.
124. Lee Kuan Yew, *From Third World to First* (New York: Harper Collins, 2000), 182.
125. At least not until the late 1980s. Following the unveiling of the government's plans to conserve Chinatown and other historic parts of the city in December 1986, William Lim founded the Singapore Heritage Society to "channel public opinion and to start a dialogue with the authorities on how best to give our children a sense of their history". "April Date for Heritage Society," *The Straits Times*, 30 March 1987, 1.
126 See Singapore Tourism Board – Placemaking. https://www.stb.gov.sg/about-stb/what-we-do/Pages/Placemaking.aspx.
127. See, for example, visitors' reviews of People's Park Complex on tripadvisor.com.hk, which reflect the current sociopolitical dynamics of the Chinese diaspora and the Mainland Chinese. https://en.tripadvisor.com.hk/Attraction_Review-g294265-d8015306-Reviews-People_s_Park_Complex-Singapore.html.
128. Ibid.

CHAPTER 9

Women's Prayer Space: A Feminist Critique of Southeast Asian Islamic Architectural History

TUTIN ARYANTI

Introduction

Existing studies on Southeast Asian mosques mostly treat mosques as material entities produced by powerful princely patronage, spanning from the end of the fifteenth century to the end of the nineteenth century. The existing scholarship emphasises aesthetics and style to represent regional Islam, authoritative patronage, and the mosque's role in Indonesian city formation. Studies by Hugh O'Neill, Bagoes Wiryomartono, and Bambang Setia Budi, to name a few, are valuable in that they focus on the local formal idioms as a product of cultural hybridisation in colonial Southeast Asia, particularly Java.[1] Abidin Kusno's study explores the way architecture has served as a political tool in postcolonial Indonesia.[2] These sources are immensely useful for understanding the formal history of Southeast Asian architecture, but the insistence on form as the primary object of investigation leaves an important area of meaning unexamined: the interaction between the space and the user. Architecture has been the primary focus of attention but the presence and characteristics of the users have been virtually ignored. Indeed, in such an object-centred framework, the actual users of mosques are either overlooked or assumed to be a homogeneous group. There is no consideration of gender or other forms of difference. The mosques are therefore perceived as static monuments, used by a homogeneous group of users.

Unlike in many parts of the Islamic world, where women are not allowed to attend the mosque together with men, many mosques in Southeast Asia provide women with prayer spaces. Most of those spaces are part of a mosque that is used by both the male and the female congregation. However, these women's spaces are very rarely mentioned in Islamic architectural history.

This article discusses the way women and their prayer spaces are marginalised in mosque architectural history. I conducted archival investigation and ethnographic research to find out how women's prayer spaces are used and seen by the public. This study shows that the visibility of their spaces to the public mirrors society's patriarchal way of looking, which tends to overlook women because they are considered insignificant, or their eyes are trained not to look at women as taught and embraced in Islamic traditions.

The selection of Yogyakarta, which was the capital of the Yogyakarta Sultanate (1755–1945), as the site of research is based on two major reasons. First, the city, like other prominent Javanese Islamic kingdoms, has been a centre of Islamic teaching since the religion's introduction to Java in the fifteenth century. Like other Javanese sultanates, the Yogyakarta Sultanate built a sultanate state mosque as an integrated element of the four state facilities, consisting of a palace, a market, a mosque, and a city square, at the city centre, and a number of sultanate community mosques to support the spread of Islam and to maintain a consistent religious interpretation of the Islamic law across the sultanate's territory. The sultanate mosques have served as a model of the typological traditional Javanese mosque. Second, Yogyakarta is the home to the Muhammadiyah organisation (established in 1912 by Ahmad Dahlan). Contending for Islamic "purification", the organisation has been known for its "modern" interpretation of Islamic law and has been one of the two most prominent Islamic organisations in Indonesia. Muhammadiyah, through its female wing, the 'Aisyiyah organisation (established in 1917), was also the first Islamic organisation in Indonesia to struggle for gender equality in Islamic practices.[3]

The research was conducted at two sites: Kauman Village and the larger *keputren* (harem) of the Sultan's palace (Figure 9.1). Kauman Village is historically important to the establishment of Yogyakarta Sultanate as a new Islamic centre and the founding of the Muhammadiyah and 'Aisyiyah organisations. Such a neighbourhood, which is typically found in historical sultanate capital cities in Indonesia, was once reserved for the sultanate religious officials and servants and their families but has changed into a diverse Muslim community today. Confirming Pijper's observation in the 1930s,[4] my research showed that Kauman has strong Islamic characteristics generated by its vibrant Islamic activities and devout Muslims.

I focus on the women's mosques in Yogyakarta, consisting of Masjid Keputren (nineteenth century), which is located inside the sultanate palace, Musalla 'Aisyiyah (1922), and Musalla Ar-Rosyad (1951) and a women's prayer space in a mixed-gender mosque, Masjid Gedhe Kauman (1773), all of which are situated

Figure 9.1: The research sites. Source: Google and Digital Globe.

in Kauman Village, to discuss the way the women's prayer spaces and women's appearance are arranged to be less visible to the public eye. My selection of these mosques serves to demonstrate their invisibility to architectural historians despite their significance in providing women with prayer space and, more importantly, in contributing to promoting gender equality in Muslim society. Musalla 'Aisyiyah was the first women's mosque in Indonesia, built in 1922 by the 'Aisyiyah organisation. Affiliated with the 'Aisyiyah organisation, the *musalla* (a small community mosque) has been a model for women's mosques in the country and a centre of women's social and religious activities for the organisation. Another women's mosque in Kauman Village is Musalla Ar-Rosyad, built by Nyai Zaenab Humam (1900–1985), a well-known Kauman female Islamic scholar, in 1951. The purpose was to accommodate Islamic teachings for women and children. This mosque has been another women's Islamic centre, in addition to the Musalla 'Aisyiyah, in the city of Yogyakarta.

In addition to the mosques that were built by the community, there are also mosques that were built by the Yogyakarta Sultanate. Masjid Keputren, built in the nineteenth century, is a palace mosque that is reserved for use by royal women and their female attendants. Masjid Keputren is important because it facilitates royal women's prayer and learning of Islam outside their home, albeit in a limited public territory. Additionally, the sultanate also added a women's prayer space, called the *pawestren*, in 1839 to its sultanate state mosque. Although it was not the first *pawestren* in a Javanese sultanate mosque, the *pawestren* of Masjid Gedhe Kauman has served as the model for a typical women's prayer room in a mixed-sex mosque on the island and, for this reason, it is architecturally important.

Studies on Islamic architecture in the Middle East, North Africa, and South Asia can be easily found, but the international scholarship knows very little about that in Southeast Asia. Failing to consider the fact that Islam has grown immensely across the region, the existing studies have generally ignored the area and seen it as peripheral to the primary body of knowledge. Moreover, we know even less about women in Islamic architecture. Thus, this chapter contributes to filling the gap and to enriching both studies on Islamic architecture in Southeast Asia and the discourse of gender in Islamic architectural historiography, which can also be applicable to the writing of history in general and other fields.

The Southeast Asian Mosque and Women's Prayer Space in Islamic Architectural History

In the last three decades, scholars have produced important studies on Southeast Asian mosques. Focusing discussions on major mosques, particularly state mosques or mosques built by Islamic saints, most of these works reveal the critical role of architecture in reflecting a cultural hybridity that adapted the cultural elements of Islam with preexisting local cultures in the region. It is not surprising because major mosques usually served as the centre of Islamic teaching.

Ismudiyanto and Parmono Atmadi,[5] focus their study on Masjid Agung Demak (1482), Masjid Menara Kudus (1537), and Masjid Astana Mantingan (1559), all of which are in Central Java, and G.F. Pijper[6] demonstrates that early Javanese mosque architecture resembles the Hindu-Javanese temples in terms of spatial sequence, floor levelling, forms, and ornamentation. Masjid Agung Demak (1482), as also argued by Hugh O'Neill and Bambang Setia Budi,[7] has served as a model of Javanese mosque typology. The Javanese mosques' prayer halls are basically rectangular or square in plan and, like Hindu temples, covered with a triple- or – in smaller mosques – double-tier pyramidal roof that is supported by columns that serve as the master pillars (*saka guru*). The number of columns vairies, it is most commonly four, sometimes six, and very rarely there is just one column.

The resemblance is not only reflected in the architectural forms and ornaments but is also found in the traditional urban layout. Bagoes Wiryomartono's seminal study shows that the traditional Javanese cities under the Islamic kingdoms from the late fifteenth century to mid twentieth century have adopted Hindu spatial arrangement, centralised in the city square, surrounded by the sultanate or regency state mosque (previously a Hindu temple), the palace, and the market.[8]

Several works further explore Southeast Asian mosque architecture as society's sociocultural and ecological product. Mohamad Tajuddin Mohamad Rasdi[9] finds that Malaysian Islamic architecture embraces forms and styles throughout time in response to climatic, technological, and sociopolitical concerns. Abidin Kusno's study[10] goes well beyond formal perspectives to examine the way architecture has served as a political tool in postcolonial Indonesia, and as an important instrument for princely patrons engaged in the process of the nation's identity formation. Seeing the mosque as a tool of power, Kusno suggests that Indonesian mosques have been in a battle between regionalism and internationalism.

There are very few sources discussing women's prayer space in detail in Islamic architectural history. The earliest account is written by G.F. Pijper,[11] who visited several Javanese cities in the 1930s. He writes that the women's prayer room, called the *pawestren*, is an essential element of a Javanese mosque and has existed for centuries. It is usually attached to the southern side of the mosque with a separate entrance from the men's, although numerous community and sultanate mosques placed the women's prayer area to either the south or north of the men's prayer area. However, as Pijper reports, mosques that were built in the 1930s did not provide a separate space for women, requiring women to pray behind or next to the men, separated from them by curtain.

Recent studies have begun to investigate women's presence and the issue of gender-equal access to the mosque, in addition to discussing of the architectural forms. Wiryomartono, for example, writes,

> The mosque is well designed for the tropics, with an open plan and cross-ventilation. The main hall accommodates men and women: male and female groups stand side by side (men on the right, women on the left), separated by a space, not a wall. This mixing of the sexes is unusual for those familiar with the Middle Eastern mosque. Indeed, the Javanese tradition does not see male and female as equal, but different in nature and their role in society, and women are accorded the same level of respect as men.[12]

Renata Holod and Hasan-Uddin Khan[13] in their book on the world's modern mosques and their architects' and patrons' considerations, further discuss the segregation of the sexes as a persistent practice found in mosques all over the world. These authors further identify the unequal provision of space for women and that for men.

Elsewhere, I have identified the variety of the *pawestren* in Yogyakarta and Central Java provinces of Indonesia. The *pawestren* is positioned in the back, left, right, or located on the mezzanine behind the main prayer hall, which is occupied by the male congregation.[14] My study also shows that the women's prayer space is considered an annex to the main prayer hall and, thus, is often marginalised. Moreover, the *pawestren* promises both good and bad potentials to gender equality. The segregation brings about gender differences in the access to and control of the mosque's resources. Being labelled as a women's space, it is a way to reserve a space for women in the mosque, which has been generally perceived as a male space. However, such a label also limits women's access to other spaces and the activities conducted in them. The use of a temporary space as a women's prayer space may give wider access to women but may also threaten their presence in the mosque because of the absence of space that officially belongs to them.[15]

More research on the *pawestren* has been conducted by Thanti Felisiani. Researching the *pawestren* of several sultanate mosques in Central Java, Felisiani agrees with my earlier study that argues that the spatial arrangement reflects the binary opposition of men and women, as comprehended in Javanese ethics. Traditional ethics arrange a Javanese house into male space at the right and female space at the left.[16] In several cases, the *pawestren* is positioned in accordance with the Islamic interpretation that a mosque follows.

I argued that the spatial dichotomy in the mosque reflects the male-female dichotomy, and therefore also centre-periphery and dominant-subordinate dichotomies. However, my recent study has found that the issue of gender equality goes beyond merely a simple dichotomy. In the two women's mosques that I researched, gender equality is in fact achieved through the spatial segregation, although in some cases, women tend to submit to the patriarchal system and position themselves on the secondary layer.[17]

Women's Prayer Spaces and Their Significance in Islamic Architectural History

The existing Islamic architectural history fails to identify that the provision of a women's prayer space, either outside or inside the palace, is significant to the improvement of women's status in Javanese society in the twentieth century. At that time, women's education was considered secondary in society, and a Javanese woman's access to education depended on her social class. Girls from aristocratic families usually went to elementary schools and afterward stayed home until they were married.[18] Girls from clerics' and religious families learned

Islam from their older male relatives, and girls from poor families received no education at all.[19] Given the tradition of subordination and domesticity, providing a facility that promotes women's education and participation in public space was obviously a breakthrough.

Inside the palace, Masjid Keputren was built, most possibly by Sultan Hamengkubuwono V (r.1823–1826 and 1828–1855), in the nineteenth century to facilitate female royal family members and their female attendants to worship and to study Islam. The sultan sent two royal religious servants to the mosque to lead the women's prayer and to teach Islam to the sultan's daughters. Prior to the congregational prayers, one of the servants would recite the secondary call to prayer, and the other would lead the prayer. Although women were still positioned as a passive congregation in this mosque, the provision of a particular place to allow them to learn about religion was considered a significant improvement of women's status in society. Despite the fact that the mosque no longer provides Islamic teaching because the *keputren* is vacant today, Masjid Keputren is an important artefact where women's education, albeit in a limited scope, was initiated.

Outside the sultanate palace, the Sultan of Yogyakarta also constructed a women's prayer room in 1839 at Masjid Gedhe Kauman (Figure 9.2), the sultanate state mosque, which was built in 1773. The construction of the *pawestren* most possibly occurred during the same period when Masjid Keputren was established in the palace area, but it still leaves the important question of why it was built at that time, considering society's perspective on women's appearance in public space. There is no record of the use of the *pawestren* by women in the nineteenth century, but several old mosque attendees whom I interviewed told me that from the 1930s to the 1950s, women rarely prayed in Masjid Gedhe Kauman. They

Figure 9.2: Masjid Gedhe Kauman, built in 1773. Source: Muhlis and the author, 2010.

were reluctant to do so because the mosque had been well known as *masjid kakung* (male mosque), which was mainly attended by men. They preferred to attend the prayers at other smaller community mosques in the village instead.[20]

Women's first daily attendance at Masjid Gedhe Kauman was possibly encouraged by the 37th Muhammadiyah National Congress in 1967 when the members of the organisation and its wings, including the 'Aisyiyah organisation, were invited to the lectures by male Islamic scholars held at the mosque. During the nationwide congress, women prayed behind men inside the main prayer hall, instead of in the *pawestren*. The fatwa (edict) of the Muhammadiyah – whose recommendations have informed the Islamic law interpretation at Masjid Gedhe Kauman – on the spatial arrangement of a mixed congregational prayer of women and men recommends that in such prayer, women should position themselves behind the men's lines. The *pawestren* itself is now only used for women's prayer during the Friday prayer because, since the 1967 congress, women have begun to pray behind the men's lines inside the main prayer hall. Despite the abandonment of the women's prayer room, the *pawestren* has served as a symbol of women's acceptance to pray on equal footing with men in Masjid Gedhe Kauman, which was previously well known as a male mosque. The trend to equality can be seen in the large number of the female congregation who attend the prayers and the Islamic teachings in the mosque. Moreover, more and more women are involved in mosque management.

In addition to the *pawestren* at Masjid Gedhe Kauman, there are two women's mosques in Kauman Village; they are Musalla 'Aisyiyah and Musalla Ar-Rosyad. Long before the construction of Musalla 'Aisyiyah, Ahmad Dahlan and his wife, Siti Walidah, the founders of the *musalla*, had persistently urged their neighbours in Kauman Village to send their daughters to school, as a corrective to the perceived backwardness of the Muslim community at the time. They founded an Islamic afternoon school for girls, named Sapa Tresna. Countering the traditional Javanese views and practices that placed woman subordinate to man and regarded her as a secondary spiritual agent, Dahlan and Walidah promoted the return to what they believed to be the Islamic guidance that respected women as partners to men in achieving the ideal Islamic society. Thus the construction of the women's mosque was an innovation to counter the traditional Javanese view on both the (un)importance of women's education and women's participation in public space in the early twentieth century.[21] There are few documents pertaining to Musalla 'Aisyiyah in the archives, but its opening is reported in *Soeara Moehammadijah*,[22] a magazine published by the Muhammadiyah organisation. The reason for the construction, as mentioned by the 1923 Chair of the Muhammadiyah, was to provide women with a restricted house of worship to let them do their prayers more solemnly. "Women cannot do their prayers in Masjid Gedhe Kauman because [of the need for the avoidance] of their meeting with men which may happen at night as well," the 1923 Muhammadiyah Chair explained to the audience in the opening ceremony. Located in the same village as Masjid Gedhe Kauman, the women's mosque was a facility for women, who had previously been marginalised in the major mosque.

For almost a century since its establishment, Musalla 'Aisyiyah has been a centre of women's social and religious activities. Being reserved for women, this mosque makes women's religious leadership possible because in Islamic tradition, a woman may not lead a congregational prayer attended by men. Women also organise community programmes and improve their religious and social capability, as well as promote education for women and children.

Following the construction of Musalla 'Aisyiyah as the first Indonesian women's mosque outside the palace, Nyai Zaenab Humam (1900–1985) established Musalla Ar-Rosyad in 1951 in the northern part of Kauman Village. More than a hundred years ago, the site where the mosque is situated belonged to Kyai Noer, one of the sultanate officials and Nyai Zaenab's grandfather. He founded an Islamic study group, named Jam'iyah Nuriyah, for people from inside and outside of Kauman. Some of these people stayed at the boarding house provided by Kyai Noer to learn Islam more thoroughly, while others came only occasionally for the lectures. Kyai Humam, who was Kyai Noer's son and Nyai Zaenab's father, inherited the study group and in 1939 it developed into a large group of around 150 male and female attendees. Upon Kyai Humam's passing, Jam'iyah Nuriyah was handed to Nyai Zaenab Humam, who transformed it into a women-only Islamic study group, named Ar-Rosyad in 1941.[23] Nyai Zaenab built the women's mosque in 1951 and made plans for a women's Islamic school and boarding house in the mosque complex.

Women's (In)Visibility in Islamic Public Space and Architectural History

The absence of women and their spaces in architectural history can be due to either their absence in the public space or their invisibility to the public eye. While women's mosques and prayer spaces like Musalla 'Aisyiyah, Musalla Ar-Rosyad, Masjid Keputren, and the *pawestren* of Masjid Gedhe Kauman exist, their absence in the history is due to their invisibility to the public eye.

In Islamic tradition, the vision toward others is cautiously regulated. The Quranic verses clearly command male and female believers to "lower their gaze" and "guard their modesty" respectively.[24] The Islamic law, which consists of the Quran, Hadith, and Islamic scholars' conventions, carefully controls what men and women have to cover in public and in the presence of other people, who are categorised according to their familial relation to the person being seen. Men and women's sexuality in Islam is defined as different. Women were traditionally recommended to stay in their home and cover almost their whole body when they went outside. Even in the early establishment of Islam when women's public appearance and participation were permissible, as demonstrated by Nabia Abbott,[25] women were commanded to conceal themselves with cloaks when they went outside so they could be recognised as free Muslim women (Quran 33:59).

The recommendation for men to "lower the gaze" and not look openly at women has been widely translated into spatial arrangements that conceal women's appearance despite their presence in the public space. There are two mosques in the palace complex: Masjid Panepen, the sultan's shrine, which is located in the sultan's complex, and Masjid Keputren, a mosque located inside the harem quarters (*keputren*) that is reserved for the use of female royal family members and their female servants. However, not many people are aware of the presence of Masjid Keputren. In the palace, the existence of the *keputren* is well known, but as shown in my interviews with several palace visitors, few people knew where it was and some of them were even entirely unaware of its presence. The palace guests and tourists did reach the *kedhaton* courtyard in their visit to the palace, but they rarely came to the *keputren*'s outer entrance. Tourists usually stopped at the major buildings surrounding the courtyard, visited the sultan's museum and even the *kasatriyan* area at the east side but skipped over the corner where the *keputren*'s outer entrance is located. Tourist guides are trained to deliver information about the other buildings, which are considered important to the palace and sultanate history, but the fact that they say nothing about the *keputren* has prevented the women's quarters from being part of the tourists' knowledge.

First, the lack of interest in exposing and discussing the *keputren* may have been due to its physical aspect, which is hidden and not as attractive as other major areas. We have seen that some scholars and visitors who gained access to the *keputren* complex in the past described their impressions. The anonymous Englishman journal writer who visited the *keputren* with the British resident in 1828 wrote his impression of the harem, which he had previously only imagined from reading books and traveller's notes:[26] "Their apartments were reverse of splendid, exhibiting nothing of that oriental magnificence one reads of in Eastern tales; they were out of repair and dirty, the painting worn off, the furniture (such as it was) out of order, and the marks of negligence and poverty everywhere apparent."

L. Adam's[27] study on the architecture of the palace even intentionally left out the discussion of the buildings inside the harem. In a paragraph where he described the *keputren*'s Mannikhantojo Gate, Adam wrote dismissively, "The remainder buildings in the *keputren*, except for the latter called mosque [Masjid Keputren], have no special significance." He did not explain the insignificance of the *keputren*, but his explanation of the meanings and symbolism of the palace's

Figure 9.3: Masjid Keputren, built in the nineteenth century. Source: the author, 2011.

buildings and their ornaments imply the impression that such meaningful contents were absent in the plain *keputren* buildings. It is disappointing that despite his note of the significance of the *keputren*'s mosque, he provided no description of it.

Second, the limited writings and photos of the *keputren* may have been due to the fact that the visitors could not enter the women's area because of their sex or social status. Today, searching online, I cannot find any images of the quarters or even the outer gate, despite the enormous number of photos of the other palace buildings in the courtyard. Spatial restriction results in visual limitation.[28]

In terms of architectural quality, Masjid Keputren (Figure 9.3) is less designed than Masjid Panepen (Figure 9.4). Unlike Masjid Panepen, which is sophisticatedly ornamented with inscriptions and carved wooden columns, windows and door frames, Masjid Keputren is a strikingly plain space with very little ornamentation. Its front part is a semi-open porch, tiled with white terrazzo and covered by a gabled roof seated on the mosque's front wall and the four black wooden columns. The main door opens directly on to the prayer hall, which is rectangular in plan and covered by a double-tier pyramidal roof. Unlike in typical traditional Javanese mosques, the roof of the prayer room is not supported by four main pillars (*saka guru*). The mosque is humble and in contrast to Masjid Panepen, which is enclosed by a fenced compound firmly isolating it from its context, Masjid Keputren's territory is vague and the building blends with the open spaces at the harem that are formed by the fenced apartment compounds, as if the mosque is part of the *keputren* courtyard and pathways.

On the other hand, Masjid Panepen is designed to be an important part of history. As the sultan's private shrine, it has a raised platform, where the sultan prays. Its history is also inscribed on the wall mentioning the renovation of the mosque in 1909 CE, under the reign of Sultan Hamengkubuwono VII (r.1877–1921). Moreover, the inscription also declares that the mosque belonged to the

Figure 9.4: Masjid Panepen. Source: the author, 2011.

sultan and was for his private use. There is no record of when it was constructed but the chief of the palace religious corps, Raden Riyo Ridwan, assumed that the mosque was built after the initial construction of the palace complex in 1756 because of the sultan's need for contemplation.[29] In contrast to Masjid Panepen, Masjid Keputren does not reveal to whom it belonged. The absence of an inscription, which is an essential element in almost all sultanate mosque architecture, implies that Masjid Keputren is considered less important than other sultanate mosques and this may contribute to the reasons why historians have overlooked its presence.

At Masjid Gedhe Kauman, the women's prayer space is also absent from the public eye due to its spatial arrangement and quality, in addition to the prescription of women's movement in space. A plan that seems to have been produced in the first half of the twentieth century does not even include Masjid Gedhe Kauman's *pawestren*. The older layout of the women's area confined women's movement, vision and appearance to the sequestered prayer room (Figure 9.5). The old entrance gate was located at the south compound wall of the mosque. The door, which can be accessed from the small village alley, is unseen to mosque visitors who mostly come from the main entrance to the east of the mosque complex. This door, behind which are the women's washing pool, restrooms and ablution area, lead female visitors directly to the *pawestren* through its side door.[30] Because the side entrance gate, through which they entered the mosque, and the interior of the *pawestren* were hidden from the male worshippers,

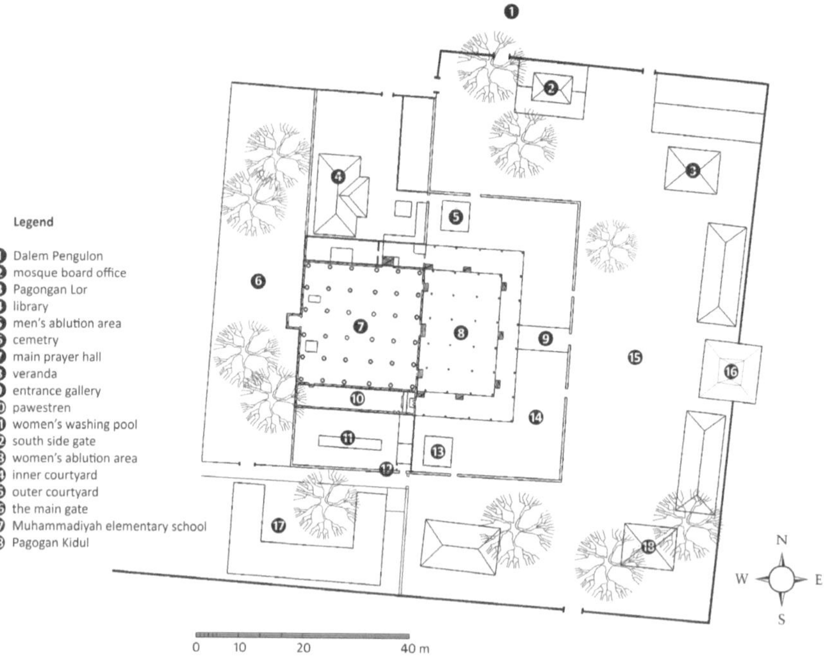

Figure 9.5: The floor plan of Masjid Gedhe Kauman. Source: Muhlis and the author, 2011.

Figure 9.6: The *pawestren* of Masjid Gedhe Kauman. 1. The door to the main prayer hall; 2. the *pawestren* door; 3. the upper verandah; 4. the lower verandah. Source: Muhlis and the author, 2010.

Figure 9.7: Musalla 'Aisyiyah, built in 1922. Source: the author, 2011.

women's arrival and presence at the mosque go unnoticed by men. This gives an impression of women's absence from the mosque and the Islamic public space in general and therefore suggests that such space is men's territory. Today as the *pawestren* of Masjid Gedhe Kauman is only used by women during Friday prayers, and remains empty during daily prayers because women pray behind men inside the main prayer hall, the impression of the absence of the *pawestren* is stronger. The use of the rear space of the main prayer hall by women suggests to spectators that women do not have their own space – the *pawestren* – and instead share the main prayer hall with men.

The impression of the absence of the women's prayer room is also contributed to by the appearance of its front façade. Its front door is located at the end of the south lower verandah, which is one metre below the main verandah (Figure 9.6). Different from the brown-and-gold-painted doors to the main prayer hall, the *pawestren* door is simply light yellow, plain, and not as tall as the door to the main prayer hall. It is always closed, except during the Friday prayer so that it can be used by the female congregation. The *pawestren* door at Masjid Gedhe Kauman is less attractive, due to the lack of ornamentation, than the glowing verandah and the doors to the main prayer hall. Thus, visitors' eyes are immediately attracted to the main prayer hall and diverted from the *pawestren* door.

Compared with the majestic Masjid Gedhe Kauman, which can be visually enjoyed by visitors from the large courtyard in front of it, Musalla 'Aisyiyah and Musalla Ar-Rosyad are nestled among houses, which does not give the impression of the monumentality possessed by Masjid Gedhe Kauman. Musalla 'Aisyiyah (Figure 9.7) is situated in the western quarter of Kampung Kauman, about 116 metres west of Masjid Gedhe Kauman, the centre of interest in the village. Standing on a site of 266 square metres at the junction of two Kauman alleys, the *musalla* is easily distinguished, particularly with its semi-modern style and

Figure 9.8: Musalla Ar-Rosyad, built in 1951. Source: the author, 2011.

tall appearance, which is unlike that of the humble wooden houses along the alleys. The architecture of the *musalla* reveals the Dutch colonial influence in the modillion at the porch, the Dutch gable roof, the molded brick columns, and the high ceiling.[31] The building sits on a 30-centimetre-high platform and is surrounded by short metal fences, allowing passersby to gaze upon its clean and simple façade.

Musalla 'Aisyiyah has been a centre for girls and women's religious education in the area. As it is exclusively reserved for women, it is only women who can pray, lead the prayer, and deliver Islamic teachings there. In support of this, the *musalla* holds programmes to educate and train women to teach Islam and lead prayers among other women. It also conducted a Quranic class to let the imams (prayer leaders) improve their Quranic fluency and preserve their memorisation. Some of these imams regularly delivered lectures at the women's Islamic groups in Kauman and nearby villages.

Musalla Ar-Rosyad (Figure 9.8) is humbler than Musalla 'Aisyiyah in appearance. It is hidden in the dense fabric of houses along the Kauman Village alleys, is L-shape in plan, and is topped by a cross-hipped roof. Without a mihrab on its west side, the mosque simply looks like an ordinary house, but the metal dome rising above the eastern part of the hipped roof signifies the building's function as a mosque. Its façade is plain, and so is its interior. The only ornamention is the red and green vine carving on the columns and the arches.

The mosque's east façade, through which most attendees enter, is entirely open to the courtyard, while the south side has windows and doors and the west (*qibla*) side has only windows. Some of these doors are usually open during the prayer times to enable access for those who come from the west of the mosque. Like other mosques in Kauman, Musalla Ar-Rosyad's building orients straight to the west to fit the existing site. In order to follow the correct *qibla* direction, the prayer lines shown by the carpet pieces are skewed toward the northwest. This mosque is typologically unusual for not having a mihrab, yet responds well to the practice of female congregational prayer in which the imam stands side by side with her congregation instead of in front.

Similar to Musalla 'Aisyiyah, Musalla Ar-Rosyad is used for the five daily prayers as well as worship and teaching during Ramadan. In addition, it regularly hosts a weekly Islamic study group on Saturday afternoon that is attended by women from within and beyond Kauman. However, unlike Musalla 'Aisyiyah where only women serve as leaders and teachers, Musalla Ar-Rosyad also invites male Islamic scholars to deliver sermons, and therefore sometimes to lead the prayers that take place immediately before or after the sermons, in front of female attendees.

Both *musallas* have been more than women's religious education and social centres. More importantly, they have served as women's representation in the community. In the 2010 Masjid Gedhe Kauman board member election, the committee invited all Kauman Muslim groups and the worshippers of the neighbourhood mosques to suggest nominees. Among community groups that were invited to participate, eight of them were women's groups, three were men's groups, and four were neighbourhood boards that could involve both women and men. This new system was definitely advantageous to women because it enabled women's voices to be better heard.

The fact that the outer gate of the *keputren*, the door of Masjid Gedhe Kauman's *pawestren*, and the women's *musallas* at Kauman village are literally visible to spectators and yet are not present in their awareness demonstrates that our preference of looking is driven by our "schemata", established by the prevailing discourse of what is worth looking at and what constitutes beauty.[32] Our eyes tend to see beautiful objects that we have learned fulfill the definition of "beauty", and exclude those that do not meet the criteria. And this "looking" also shapes the way historians select and construct history.[33] As a result, the history of the palace architecture centres on the so-classified "palace architecture", represented by the beautifully ornamented traditional buildings along the *kedhaton* courtyard and other palace spaces that researchers and visitors may access, while the women's quarters are relegated to the margins or ignored altogether. As I have argued elsewhere, the architectural arrangement of the *keputren* reflects gender hierarchies and is set to make women invisible to people, especially men, other than the sultan himself.[34] Unfortunately, this also results in women's invisibility in history.

Similarly, architectural history prefers beautifully ornamented mosques and focuses on aspects that are considered worth examining. Neither Musalla 'Aisyiyah nor Musalla Ar-Rosyad have unique architectural attributes that most historians seek to explore in their accounts. Compared with Masjid Gedhe Kauman, which features a typical traditional Javanese mosque, elaborate verandah, mihrab, minbar, and *maqsura*, both *musallas* are ordinary. In addition to their position on the periphery of the village, the plain appearance has contributed to their invisibility to the public and architectural historians' eyes. If historians do not probe the social aspects of mosques, these mosques will never be found in history.

The tendency to overlook women's presence also seems to be an effect of men's attempt to lower their gaze so as not to look directly at women and their representation. Male Muslim photographers often leave women out of the picture. In a Masjid Gedhe Kauman board meeting attended by both female and male board members (Figure 9.9), a man who took photographs did not show the women in his snapshots in spite of their presence (Figure 9.10). His photos were instead focused on the male participants and positioning the sultanate minister of the religious affair (Kanjeng Kyai Pengulu, in a black felt cap in Figure 9.10) at the centre. This provides an example of how history is in the beholder's eyes and in this case, the eyes of privileged male attendees and (male) authority. The fact that women are literally excluded from the picture proves to us that historical archives may not have provided a complete depiction of what occurs in the field and, thus, should be examined critically when a historian takes them into account.

The absence of women and their prayer space from architectural narratives can be due to the privilege of looking at the object, which is considered worth examining while setting aside the "others". As Foucault and Debord argue, the gaze is tied to human desire, which comes from deep psychic drives. In this model, the gaze is a desire for the realm of the other and is predicated on a primary division between self and other.[35] History is a constructed knowledge produced by the gaze, which is never unbiased because it is always entangled in the interests of its producers.

Architectural history often overlooks marginalised groups, including women, as actors of history. It has not regarded vernacular art and architecture, produced by common people, as worthy of study. It instead still focuses on artefacts created by princely patronage. Privileging one group over others, architectural history aggregates major events by selecting a small number of facts and listening to selected informants while ignoring the majority in it attempt to document human conditions.[36] To reveal better versions of the human story, history has to look at completeness and acknowledge diversity.

Figures 9.9 & 9.10: The Masjid Gedhe Kauman board meeting on 3 February 2011 at the Pengulon building as photographed by the author (*top*) and Pak Madi (pseudonym) (*bottom*). The sultanate minister of the religious affair (Kanjeng Kyai Pengulu) is seated in the front row with a black felt cap in both photos.

Including women's voices in constructing history, gender as one of the articulations of power relations in society can be developed as a "category of analysis" to comprehend the significance of gender groups (i.e. women and men) in the historical past by taking women's perception and experience into account. The point is to challenge the existing patriarchal historical accounts. Involving gender as a category of analysis will help scholars reveal the stories of the oppressed and examine how power inequality has been organised through the writing of history. Because gender is a primary site where power is articulated, gender analysis allows historians to investigate the ways in which the concept of gender legitimises and constructs social relationships.[37]

To Islamic architectural historians, gender analysis in investigating the Islamic architectural historiography is useful with regard to women's representation in Islamic architecture. Not only does it facilitate the examination of women's presence, but also helps us discover how they were represented through Islamic architecture in the past as an articulation of gender relations in Muslim society. Thus the question of women's existence in Islamic architecture deals with both women's presence in Muslim society and the Islamic architectural space, and their representations in Islamic architecture.[38]

Conclusion

Women's absence from mosque architectural history comprises both the absence of their appearance in the Islamic public space – either due to their physical absence or their invisibility from the public eye as in the case of the *pawestren* of Masjid Gedhe Kauman, Masjid Keputren of the Yogyakarta Sultanate palace, Musalla 'Aisyiyah, and Musalla Ar-Rosyad – and the absence of narratives of women in the mosque and their prayer spaces. As in the case of Masjid Keputren and the *pawestren* at Masjid Gedhe Kauman, women's prayer space and women's stories remained hidden and unheard in part because of the limited access, either visual or physical, that most people and historians have had to them. One outcome of the fact that, until very recently, much of history was written by men, is that men did not report on what they could not see. At the same time, there is another parallel exclusionary practice in which the *keputren* occupants do not have access to public discourse and thus cannot write about themselves. The result of both counts is the exclusion of the secluded space from public vision and even from history. However, the problem of its visibility to historians, including female historians, is more than simple visual accessibility. It is also a matter of the social preferences and way of looking at behaviour that emerges from the historian's own cultural formation. The absence of women and their space in history, therefore, reflects both their visual absence from the public realm and their absence from historians' consciousness. To see them, therefore one must begin with the premise that they *matter*.

The history of mosque architecture in Indonesia as displayed by previous scholars emphasises the authoritative power holders, such as sultans and presidents, or patrons, who are all male. The written history very rarely mentions vernacular mosque architecture built by common people, or the women's prayer space as part of a mosque, or woman's mosques as part of Indonesia's mosque architecture. One of the reasons for this could be the historians' privileging of great or monumental buildings with unique style over everyday architecture, which reveals sociocultural factors that take place within society. Another reason for not taking woman's space into account could be women's invisibility in the public space, stemming from the submission of Muslim women to the religious recommendation to stay at home.

Notes

1. Hugh O'Neill, "South-East Asia," in *The Mosque: History, Architectural Development and Regional Diversity*, ed. Martin Frishman and Hasan-Uddin Khan (London: Thames and Hudson Ltd., 1994), 225–239; Bambang Setia Budi, "A Study on the History and Development of the Javanese Mosque Part 1: A Review of Theories on the Origin of the Javanese Mosque," *Journal of Asian Architecture and Building Engineering* 3 (2004): 189–195; Bagoes Wiryomartono, *Seni Bangunan Dan Seni Binakota Di Indonesia* [*The Art of Building and Urban Design in Indonesia*] (Jakarta: Gramedia, 1995).
2. Abidin Kusno, *Behind the Postcolonial: Architecture, Urban Space and Political Cultures* (New York: Routledge, 2000), 57–67; "'The Reality of One-Which-Is-Two', Mosque Battles, and Other Stories: Architecture, Religion and Politics in the Javanese World," *Journal of Architectural Education* 57 (2003).
3. Tutin Aryanti, "Shame and Borders: The 'Aisyiyah's Struggle for Muslim Women's Education in Indonesia" in *Gender, Religion and Education in a Chaotic Postmodern World*, ed. Zehavit Gross, Lynn Davies, and Khansaa Diab (Dordrecht: Springer, 2013), 83–92.
4. G.F. Pijper, *Fragmenta Islamica: Studien over Het Islamisme in Nederlandsch-Indie* [*Fragmenta Islamica: Some Studies on Islam in the Colonial Indonesia*] (Leiden: E.J. Brill, 1934), 38–44.
5. Ismudiyanto and Parmono Atmadi, "Demak, Kudus, and Jepara Mosques: A Study of Architectural Syncretism," (Yogyakarta: Department of Architecture, Gadjah Mada University, 1987).
6. G.F. Pijper, "The Minaret in Java," in *India Antiqua: A Volume of Oriental Studies Presented by His Friends and Pupils to Jean Philippe Vogel (Ö)*, ed. F.D.K. Bosch et. al. (Leiden: Brill, Kern Institute, 1947), 274–283.
7. O'Neill, "South-East Asia," 225–239; Bambang Setia Budi, "A Study on the History and Development of the Javanese Mosque Part 3: Typology of the Plan and Structure of the Javanese Mosque and Its Distribution," *Journal of Asian Architecture and Building Engineering* 5 (2006): 229–236.
8. Wiryomartono, *Seni Bangunan Dan Seni Binakota Di Indonesia* [*The Art of Building and Urban Design in Indonesia*].
9. Mohamad Tajuddin Mohamad Rasdi, "Mosque Architecture in Malaysia: Classification of Styles and Possible Influence," *Jurnal Alam Bina* 9, no. 3 (2007): 1–37.
10. Kusno, "'The Reality of One-Which-Is-Two', Mosque Battles, and Other Stories: Architecture, Religion and Politics in the Javanese World," 57–67.
11. G.F. Pijper, *Fragmenta Islamica: Studien over Het Islamisme in Nederlandsch-Indie* [*Fragmenta Islamica: Some Studies on Islam in the Colonial Indonesia*] (Leiden: E.J. Brill, 1934), 38–44.

12. Bagoes Wiryomartono, "Postcard from the Field: A Historical View of Mosque Architecture in Indonesia," *The Asia Pacific Journal of Anthropology* 10, no. 1 (2009): 37.
13. Renata Holod and Hasan-Uddin Khan, *The Mosque and the Modern World: Architects, Patrons and Designs since the 1950s* (London: Thames and Hudson Ltd., 1997), 2.
14. Tutin Aryanti, "Segregasi Ruang Masjid Menurut Jender: Fenomena Pawestren Pada Masjid-Masjid Di Jawa Tengah" [Gender and Spatial Segregation: The Phenomenon of the Pawestren in the Mosques of Central Java] (Master's thesis, Institut Teknologi Bandung, 2000).
15. "The Center vs. The Periphery in Central-Javanese Mosque Architecture," *Dimensi Teknik Arsitektur* 34, no. 2 (2006): 73–80.
16. Ibid; Thanti Felisiani, "*Pawestren* Pada Masjid-Masjid Agung Kuna Di Jawa: Pemaknaan Ruang Perempuan" [The *Pawestren* in the Old Grand Mosques in Java: The Meaning of Women's Space] (Bachelor, Universitas Indonesia, 2009).
17. Tutin Aryanti, "The Claim to Space: Debating Female Religious Leadership in a Muhammadiyah Mosque in Indonesia," *The Muslim World* 103, no. 3 (2013): 375–388.
18. Kumari Jayawerdana, *Feminism and Nationalism in the Third World* (London Zed Books Ltd, 1986), 136–154; R.A. Kartini, *Habis Gelap Terbitlah Terang* [*Out of Dark Comes Light*], trans. Armijn Pane (Jakarta: Balai Pustaka, 1963).
19. Jayawerdana, *Feminism and Nationalism in the Third World*; Ahmad Adaby Darban, *Sejarah Kauman: Menguak Identitas Kampung Muhammadiyah* [*The History of Kauman: Revealing the Identity of a Muhammadiyah Village*] (Yogyakarta: Tarawang, 2000); Junus Salam, *K.H. Ahmad Dahlan: Amal Dan Perjuangannya* [*K.H. Ahmad Dahlan: His Acts and Struggles*] (Tangerang: Al-Wasat Publishing House, 2009; repr., Yogyakarta: Depot Pengajaran Muhammadiyah, 1962).
20. Tutin Aryanti, "Branding the Islamic Village: Modesty and Identity in Yogyakarta Kauman Village," *Procedia-Social and Behavioral Sciences* 184 (2015): 126–134.
21. "Shame and Borders: The 'Aisyiyah's Struggle for Muslim Women's Education in Indonesia" in *Gender, Religion and Education in a Chaotic Postmodern World*, ed. Zehavit Gross, Lynn Davies, and Khansaa Diab (Dordrecht: Springer, 2013), 83–92.
22. "Keterangan Pemboekaan Langgar Perempoean" [The Notes on the Opening of the Women's Mosque], *Soeara Moehammadijah* 4 (1923): 208–210.
23. Darban, *Sejarah Kauman: Menguak Identitas Kampung Muhammadiyah* [*The History of Kauman: Revealing the Identity of a Muhammadiyah Village*], 52–58.
24. Quran 24:30–31
25. Nabia Abbott, "Women and the State on the Eve of Islam," *The American Journal of Semitic Languages* 58, no. 3 (1941): 259–284; "Women and the State in Early Islam," *The Journal of Near Eastern Studies* 1(1942): 106–126.
26. "Journal of an Excursion to the Native Provinces on Java in the Year 1828, During the War with Dipo Negoro," in *The Journal of the Indian Archipelago and Eastern Asia*, ed. J.R. Logan (Singapore: Kraus Reprint, 1853), 241.

27. L. Adam, "De Pleinen, Poorten En Gebouwen Van De Kraton Van Jogjakarta" [The Squares, Gates and Buildings of the Yogyakarta Palace], *Djawa* 20, no. 3 (1940): 195.
28. Tutin Aryanti, "Vision and Gendered Space: Making Women Invisible in Yogyakarta Sultanate Palace," *Space and Culture,* 22 June 2016: DOI: 10.1177/1206331216647353.
29. Interview with Raden Riyo Ridwan, 12 April 2011.
30. Tutin Aryanti, "Women's Prayer Space: Body and Boundary," *The International Journal of the Constructed Environment* 2, no. 3 (2012): 177–190.
31. Helen Jessup, "Dutch Architectural Visions of the Indonesian Tradition," *Muqarnas* 3 (1985): 138–153.
32. E.H. Gombrich, *Art and Illusion: A Study in the Psychology of Pictorial Representation*, 11th ed. (Princeton: Princeton University Press 2000).
33. Henry Glassie, "History," in *Material Culture* (Bloomington and Indianapolis: Indiana University Press, 1999), 5–39.
34. Aryanti, "Vision and Gendered Space: Making Women Invisible in Yogyakarta Sultanate Palace," DOI: 10.1177/1206331216647353.
35. Martin Jay, *Downcast Eyes: The Denigration of Vision in Twentieth-Century French Thought* (Berkeley, Los Angeles, London: University of California Press, 1994).
36. Glassie, "History," 5-39; Dell Upton, "The Vaf at 25: What Now?," *Perspectives in Vernacular Architecture* 13, no. 2 (2006–2007): 7–13.
37. Joan W. Scott, "Gender as a Category of Historical Analysis," in *Gender and the Politics of History* (New York: Columbia University Press, 1988), 28–50.
38. D. Fairchild Ruggles, "Vision and Power: An Introduction," in *Women, Patronage, and Self-Representation in Islamic Societies*, ed. D. Fairchild Ruggles (New York: State University of New York Press, 2000), 1–15.

EPILOGUE

A Fluvial Regionality?

MARK CRINSON

The essays in *Southeast Asia's Modern Architecture* demonstrate not just a wide range of architectural topics and an equivalent range of ways of thinking about them, but also a sense of urgency and possibility. The material is often deeply marked by the big world-historical events: global war and its continuation in hot and cold varieties, the departure of European empires, the coming of mass forms of tourism as well as mass migrant labour, the first tiger economies, new forms of fundamentalism, the growing influence of India and China. And as they approach the present, the essays become more suggestive, as if for analysis to make sense of this inherently mutable field it must find a hypothetical and explorative tone; its frameworks had better stay provisional. The sense of contingency and open-endedness reminds us that this is the regional intellectual home of "imagined communities", and that what we have here might suggest ways of imagining not architectural regionalism (yet again!) but architectural regionality, a communality of history and practice across space that is irreducible and implicitly critical, that is neither of the nation state nor of the world, that sets aside old continents as much as old empires. And the sense of urgency and possibility lies, perhaps, in this in-between state of temporality as much as the in-between state of territoriality, which is the region.

Like any region, at least in modern usage of the term, Southeast Asia is an area recognised as having a logic, even a character, different from other geographical designations. The editors of this book also use terms like "taxonomic device" and "geographic device" but their predominant means of designating Southeast Asia is as a region. And as a region there is both a revealing etymology and a substantial genealogy.

Region comes ultimately from the French and Latin terms *regio* and *regione* meaning king or leader but also an area drawn out or divided from others. Accordingly, the region in medieval sources meant a realm or kingdom as well as an area of the earth with something about it that made it distinct from other areas (this distinction could be on cultural grounds as much as natural).[1] So region was an inherently flexible term and one seemingly without associated theoretical extrapolation, and much of this continued up to the present. But at some time in the late nineteenth century (the Oxford English Dictionary [OED] dates first usage to 1871), the term "regionalism" emerged and clearly its emergence was related both to the triumph of the nation state at this moment (the militant assertion of German nationhood after the Franco-Prussian war) and to the brief flickering of anarchist opposition to the governance of the nation state. Relatedly, this was also when the academic study of geography in France was energised by these displaced passions. French usage was crucial here – *régionalisme* meant both the character of the region and the development of regions as political-cultural entities. Regionalism, then, emerged so as to specify a territory controlled by a government claiming to rule in the name of the people of that bounded area. It was a policy or a form of recognition of geographical entities subsidiary to the nation state and its centralising impetus. And soon it was also brandished in the form of an anti-national local patriotism, in the cases for instance of Provence in France or Catalonia in Spain, both of which were seen as sites of greater authenticity, a regionalism whose novels, paintings and architecture extolled the landscape as the soil in which regional character was rooted, like an accent that had developed local expressions and sounds or even an entirely different language that had preserved a pre-modern consciousness.

What the OED does not record is the important appropriation and redirection of regionalism at this very same moment by Elisée Reclus and Patrick Geddes. For these geographer-anarchists, the region was not just a counterweight to the nation state but also to such rising tendencies as ethnic-nationalism and identitarianism. In this way of thinking, regionalism was linked to a benevolent idea of internationalism. Reclus, for instance, wanted to build a "Great Globe" at the Paris Universal Exposition of 1900, to encourage knowledge of the world as a counter to reactionary nationalism.[2] Visitors would study how the earth was a system ruled by laws that needed uncovering, and that nation state and other political boundaries were artificial constraints on the links and amities produced by more natural boundaries and systems. In Geddes' most famous concept, the "Valley Section", the region was a geographical area defined by following through the rise of a river at its source to its arrival at the sea, passing through a great city and "central world market" on its way. Understood like this, the region was highly specific and localised but also large scale, globally networked and generic. Geddes emphasised what he called the "rhythms of the land masses of the earth" which encompassed "the individuality, the uniqueness, of each of the towns and cities of men".[3] In their alternative idea of regionalism, Geddes and Reclus de-emphasised the passing political entities attached to artificially bordered spaces, and did not exalt the provincial or the local for reasons to do with indigeneity but as part of a flow, differentiated and specific but linked to larger planetary entities: the fluvial course led one outwards from an understanding of local particularities to the world networked city.[4] The way that the laddered scale of a Geddesian Valley Section related small to large without sentimental recourse to "spirit of place" or atavistic notions of provincial character, became of some interest to later modernist architects who turned away from CIAM's (International Congress of Modern Architecture) claims of modernist universalism. How might the modern find its way back instead to the ways that different settlements had been formed by their topography, climate and traditions of inhabitation?[5] One might say that this is exactly the conundrum that a critical regionality will continue to embrace.

But in the meantime something happened to the concept of region, something that threw out of joint this critical regionality. This was the emergence sometime in the mid twentieth century of a new all-enveloping conception of the region as a supra-national configuration with little or no regard for landscape or other natural features. These are geopolitical entities now, geographic blocks that have often broken free of imperial designations, becoming useful instead in Cold War power games and development policies. To take the measure of this upscaling matters here; it matters as globalisation and its neoliberal global bodies take over the normalising role of empire or nation state, and it matters because upscaling requires flexibility. The "new regional relationships" that Anoma Pieris has pointed to are a later resonance of the same historical developments which are an inevitable presence behind much of what is covered in this book. And this too goes back to the urgency and possibility noted earlier. If Reclus and Geddes' regionalism, and we might attach Rabindranath Tagore's pan-Asianism to this too, was premised as much on opposition to the violent parochialism of the nation state as it was to the nation state's inadequacy as a unit of analysis, then today a reclamation of the region can serve in opposition to the forms of power that are called globalisation.

If architecture can be regionally defined, whether that region is province-size or along the scale of Southeast Asia, subnational or extra-national, it must as we have already seen raise the issue of its relation to geography, even its geographic determinism. There is a cautionary history here too. In early twentieth-century art history, which in its classic German form included architectural history, this was given the name *Kunstgeographie* and it was practiced almost as a branch of national identity-spotting, an accompaniment to Wilhelmine and later fascist *Lebensraum*, by such art historians as Paul Schultze-Naumberg, Wilhelm Pinder, and even Nikolaus Pevsner.[6] In such accounts, climate, landscape, and a geographically bound ethnicity were given prominence in the description and understanding of art and architecture. The primary point of comparison was thus location – an object like a building, it was assumed, would have more in common with other buildings in that location than it would with buildings under any other rationale for comparison (typology, say, political regime, patronage network, and so on). So, for instance, a form of architectural mapping was proposed whereby house styles were traced cartographically, the geographic distribution of styles and forms thus demonstrating the literal place, the rootedness, of style.[7] But curiously, while the idea of the imported, the transcultural, the international, or the global are given a lesser interpretive status or even become the cause of devaluation in the cultural status of the work according to *Kunstgeographie*, the method's internal logic would always direct the interpretation of the object away from its own nature and instead onto its context; it must signal something geographical or it could not attain recognition within the method. The geography such art historians were concerned with was that bounded by the nation rather than the region, though occasionally as with Pevsner's *Outline of European Architecture* this was extended to a region understood as a consortium of nations.

Such reversions haunt many regional projects. The editors of this book are right to have established some form of governance over the diversity of their subject through their trio of bridging concepts – "translation", "epistemology", and "power". Beyond the rich veins of thinking the concepts have behind them, it's their obliqueness in relation to architecture that I find most useful; they energise our way of thinking about it and that may be partly because they are neither commensurate with it nor with each other. Think, for instance, of epistemology's rarefied usage (I mean who uses the term and where), as against the everyday coinages involving power; and think also of both the technical and analogical deployments of the term translation. And what does it tell us about these concepts that they are so rarely used with definite articles, as happens with nouns when no distinction is necessary? (And the same could be said of architecture – with the others it has a fall-back existence as abstract and generalisable that must always raise our critical hackles.) And of course, as intended, the choice of concepts proliferates questions. Why translation and not the more spatial "transplantation", or the less resonant "transfer" and "transmission"? Not knowledge, but – pushing Foucault's double-headed spectre behind the screen – epistemology?[8] The overloaded power, not the now underpowered politics? (And indeed politics is here but should we take it as a second order concept, outmuscled by the more pervasive sense of power?) And the questions are posed as much by each concept about the others (the epistemology of power? The power of epistemology? Translation as power, as epistemology?) as of them together as a coherent threesome. Just as important too, especially given some of the material in the book (female mosques, Democracy Temple, People's Park, Bali Style), and some of the arguments concerning resistant practices or at least reframings, is that the master concepts are made equally unstable, so that we could be encouraged to speak of epistemological fantasies and delusions of power as much as literary theorists talk of the impossibility of translation.[9]

If there is a Venn diagram of overlaps between the conceptual trio then one of the things most surely caught in their triangular overlap is identity, pondered in passing by many of the contributors even while they tend to be suspicious of that most identity-minded of recent academic mills, postcolonial theory. It might be useful to think of the trio as colouring or infecting each other so that their area of overlap belongs to none of them exclusively. One useful effect of this, and I find it in several of the essays, is to prevent power from becoming the master term, so that it too can be activated in new ways by the other two concepts. But where is history? Obviously, it is generally here in the invocation of historiography and particularly here in the form of heritage debates or discourses on memory, or in the invocation of the modern and the vernacular, which appear in many places in the essays, but does its absence as a conceptualised theme mean, as sometimes happens with such absences, an all-pervasiveness greater than the three master tropes, a reassertion of the role and identity of the historian?

And then I'm wondering, again surely intended by the editors, if I really have grasped what each of the framing concepts could mean. We tend, for instance, to think of translation as an act of remaking one thing so that it works in another context, but any translator knows how approximate that act is, indeed how creative their translation needs to be if the new work is to be understood in an equivalent way in its different language context. Translation is, therefore, both necessary if cross-cultural understanding is to exist and always at the same time inadequate because, as Walter Benjamin observed, it can only render the original in reduced, informational terms; content and form are prised apart.[10] That is not to say that the translation cannot be equally expressive; just that the expressiveness is a new one, added by the translator. It's a form of kinship, then, rather than likeness that results from translation, according to Benjamin. We can accept all that but still wonder if translation really can be an adequate way of thinking about the cross-cultural in architecture. How far are translation's inherently provisional character and its textuality really comparable to architecture's manifold material and social realities? And when architecture manifests cross-cultural misunderstanding, at best, or coercion at worst, is that not to do usually with the idea that the equivalent of translation is not required?

And as for epistemology, well, as Nietzsche suggested, knowledge is more a matter of commonplaces than it is of the cutting edge, and even the cutting edge is a tracing back of the unfamiliar to the familiar, to that understanding of the world that makes us feel at home in it: "our need for knowledge [is] … the will to uncover among everything strange, unusual, and doubtful something which no longer unsettles us".[11] So epistemology is the name given to the world we feel at home in. Which, needless to say, is powerfully resonant with much of what we expect from architecture.

Modern architecture, of course, is really what is at stake here and by placing the triangular grid or overlap of translation, epistemology and power across it we end up with some important insights. All three are clearly at work when we consider colonial modernity as surveillance regime, as biopolitics, in American-controlled Manila, and perhaps almost as much in the modern domes of Bangkok or that simulacrum of the city, the People's Park in Singapore. But there are useful problems too with the overlap. To take translation again, its invocation might seem a little like a way of dealing with that old saw about modern architecture being "disseminated" – instead of this, it helps to be reminded that translation is just as much in the hands of the translators (I was particularly reminded of this by Lawrence Chua's chapter). So translation is often an absorption or appropriation rather than an imposition from the culture of the original. One can conquer by translating.[12]

Modernists knew that their architecture would involve transfers of ideas, transplantations of forms, and translations of actual texts (from manifestos to building manuals). They wanted to reinvent architectural knowledge by asking new questions of what architecture should do, finding new methods, and ending with new answers. And they came to accept that modernism must respond to region. While there was undoubtedly pragmatism, political influence and profit at stake – power, for want of a better word – there was also the idealism of the "new man", the "new world" (power, again). Language and language analogies were bound up in this. Was modernism an architectural language that everyone could easily understand, a return to a pre-Babelian state of world community, a universal recognition of the logic of form and function? I'm sure this is what was happening when CIAM filtered its new national group members, checking out the kind of architecture they were designing: to be properly modernist was not to need translation. In terms of actual languages there was righteous anger at suggestions that English should be the language of communications for CIAM, and serious consideration of adopting Esperanto as an apparently neutral language in which to conduct CIAM's business (as there was in the League of Nations, and later in UNESCO). Of course, this is a very limited idea of modernism in architecture, not to speak of modern architecture in general. But it reminds us of how power, epistemology and translation (literal and phenomenal), are already inherent in theories of modern architecture.

Regions are mutable realms. Some disappear, become part of the past; their natural boundaries become borders, they change into some other entity. Others emerge with new formations and recognitions. They need no constitution, no rules, no proper size or temporality to be a region; even the sense they make is provisional. And their metaphorical allusiveness increases when we think of them, as the editors encourage us to do, as "fluid, open and relational … imaginaries". Architecture, and even the three master concepts, take unexpected forms. The diagram transmutes.

Notes

1. My source here is the online Oxford English Dictionary, https://en.oxforddictionaries.com/.
2. Mark Crinson, *Rebuilding Babel: Modern Architecture and Internationalism* (London: I.B. Tauris, 2017), 45–48.
3. Patrick Geddes, lecture given at the New School of Social Research, New York, in 1923, as published in Patrick Geddes, *Cities in Evolution*, revised edition (London: Williams & Norgate, 1949), xviii, xxvi.
4. Whether many actual river-based regions could be understood in Geddes' terms was pointed out by Geddes' contemporaries: Crinson, *Rebuilding Babel*, 254 n. 70.
5. Peter Smithson, "Valley Section. Doorn Manifesto (1954)", republished in Alison and Peter Smithson, *The Charged Void: Urbanism* (New York: Monacelli Press, 2005), 31.
6. See Thomas DaCosta Kaufman, "The Geography of Art: Historiography, Issues, and Perspectives", in *World Art Studies: Exploring Concepts and Approaches*, ed. KittyZijlmans and Wilfried van Damme, (Amsterdam: Valiz, 2008), 167–182.
7. Ibid, 173.
8. Foucault explicitly preferred "discursive formations" to the Archimedean idea of epistemology, even coining a verb ("epistemologise") and a process ("epistemologisation") as if to designate these as always specifically historical activities subsidiary to their discursive formations: Michel Foucault, *The Archaeology of Knowledge* (1969), trans. A. M. Sheridan Smith (New York: Pantheon Books, 1972), 38, 186–192.
9. Emily Apter, *Against World Literature: On the Politics of Untranslatability* (London and New York: Verso, 2013).
10. Walter Benjamin, "The Task of the Translator", in *Illuminations*, trans. Harry Zohn (London: Fontana, 1973), 69–82.
11. Friedrich Nietzsche, *The Gay Science* (1882), trans. Josefine Nauckhoff (Cambridge: Cambridge University Press, 2001), 214.
12. Ibid, 82–83.

About the Contributors

Tutin Aryanti is Associate Professor of Architecture at Universitas Pendidikan Indonesia (Indonesia University of Education). Her research revolves around gender issues in architecture, Islamic architecture, spatial justice and ethnography. She has received numerous awards, including a Fulbright PhD Scholarship, the American Association of University Women International Fellowship, the Illinois Program for Research in the Humanities Fellowship, and the International Convention of Asia Scholars Best Dissertation in Social Sciences 2015.

Jiat-Hwee Chang is Associate Professor at the Department of Architecture, National University of Singapore. He is the author of *A Genealogy of Tropical Architecture* (2016), which was awarded an International Planning History Society Book Prize in 2018 and was shortlisted for the European Association for Southeast Asian Studies Humanities Book Prize in 2017. He is also the co-editor of *Non West Modernist Past* (2011).

Lawrence Chua is Assistant Professor at the School of Architecture at Syracuse University. He has been a Marie S. Curie research fellow at the Freiburg Institute of Advanced Studies at the Albert-Ludwigs-Universität and a research fellow at the International Institute of Asian Studies at the Universiteit Leiden. His articles and reviews have appeared in the *Journal of the Society of Architectural Historians, Journal of Urban History, Fabrications, TDSR* and *Senses and Society.*

Mark Crinson is Professor of Architectural History at Birkbeck (University of London) and he is also President of the European Architectural History Network. His recent books include *Rebuilding Babel: Modern Architecture and Internationalism* (2017), *Alison and Peter Smithson* (2018), and *The Architecture of Art History: A Historiography* with Richard J. Williams (2018).

H. Hazel Hahn is Professor of History at Seattle University. She is the author of *Scenes of Parisian Modernity: Culture and Consumption in the Nineteenth Century* (2009) and co-editor of *Architecturalized Asia: Mapping a Continent through History* (2013).

She works on cross-cultural exchange in Southeast Asia and Europe, travel imaginaries, and urban and architectural history of French Indochina.

Imran bin Tajudeen is Assistant Professor at the Department of Architecture, National University of Singapore. His work on the historiographical questions in Southeast Asia's architectural categories and their epistemologies have appeared in *TDSR*, *ABE Journal*, *Colonial Frames, Nationalist Histories* (2012), *Architecturalized Asia* (2014), and *Spirits and Ships: Cultural Transfers in Monsoon Asia* (2017).

Gerard Lico is Professor at the College of Architecture, University of the Philippines Diliman and practices architecture as a conservation professional and designer of institutional buildings. He is a prolific author of publications on Filipino architecture and cultural studies, curator of architectural exhibitions, and director of documentaries on Philippine architecture.

Koompong Noobanjong is Professor of Architecture at King Mongkut's Institute of Technology, Ladkrabang. He has published several studies on the politics of representations in architecture and urban space, and critical studies of the built environment. His seminal work, *The Aesthetics of Power: Architecture, Modernity, and Identity from Siam to Thailand*, was published in 2013.

Anoma Pieris is Associate Professor at the Faculty of Architecture Building and Planning, University of Melbourne. Her publications include *Architecture and Nationalism in Sri Lanka: The Trouser Under the Cloth* (2012), *Hidden Hands and Divided Landscapes: A Penal History of Singapore's Plural Society* (2009) and *Sovereignty, Space and Civil War in Sri Lanka* (2018).

Peter Scriver is Associate Professor and Director (South and Southeast Asia) at the Centre for Asian and Middle Eastern Architecture (CAMEA), University of Adelaide. He has authored and edited a number of path-breaking books including *Colonial Modernities* (2007) with Vikramaditya Prakash, and *India: Modern Architectures in History* (2015),with Amit Srivastava.

Eunice Seng is Associate Professor and Chair of the Departmental Research Postgraduate Committee in Architecture at the University of Hong Kong; and Principal of SKEW Collaborative Shanghai-Hong Kong. Her work as an architect and architectural historian explores the disciplinary intersections and questions of agency in architecture and housing. She is founding member of Docomomo Hong Kong, and co-editor of *Housing Asia 2020* (2017) and *Dwelling Asia – Journal of Architecture* 22, 6 (2017).

Amit Srivastava is Director (India) at the Centre of Asian and Middle Eastern Architecture (CAMEA), University of Adelaide. His current research focuses on the transnational exchange of materials and processes between Australia and Asia, and its impact on the professionalisation of architectural practice in Asia. His latest publications include *India: Modern Architectures in History* (2015) and *The Elements of Modern Architecture* (2014).

Tim Winter is Professor of Critical Heritage Studies, University of Western Australia. He is the former President of the Association of Critical Heritage Studies and holds an ARC Future Fellowship on the Silk Roads of the 21st century. His recent books include *The Routledge Handbook of Heritage in Asia* and Shanghai Expo. He is currently working on books on heritage diplomacy in relation to the Belt and Road Initiative and urban sustainability in Southeast Asia and the Middle East.

Index

Note: Page locators in italics represent figures.